When Church Became Theatre

When Church Became Theatre

*The Transformation of Evangelical Architecture and
Worship in Nineteenth-Century America*

JEANNE HALGREN KILDE

UNIVERSITY PRESS

2002

OXFORD

UNIVERSITY PRESS

Oxford   New York

Auckland   Bangkok   Buenos Aires   Cape Town   Chennai
Dar es Salaam   Delhi   Hong Kong   Istanbul   Karachi   Kolkata
Kuala Lumpur   Madrid   Melbourne   Mexico City   Mumbai   Nairobi
São Paulo   Shanghai   Singapore   Taipei   Tokyo   Toronto

and an associated company in Berlin

Published by Oxford University Press, Inc.
198 Madison Avenue, New York, New York 10016

www.oup.com

Oxford is a registered trademark of Oxford University Press.

Library of Congress Cataloging-in-Publication Data
Kilde, Jeanne Halgren, 1957–
When church became theatre : the transformation of evangelical architecture and worship in
nineteenth-century America / Jeanne Halgren Kilde.
p. cm.
Includes bibliographical references (p.) and index.
ISBN 0-19-514341-8
1. Protestant church buildings—United States.   2. Architecture—United States—19th
century.   3. Evangelicalism—United States—History—19th century.   I. Title.
NA5210 .K55 2002
726.5'0973'09034—dc21   2001036140

1 3 5 7 9 8 6 4 2

Printed in the United States of America
on acid-free paper

For my parents,
William E. Halgren and Patricia Mae Halgren

Acknowledgments

It is my pleasure to acknowledge some of the many institutions and individuals that have assisted me along the way in this project. In particular, the Graham Foundation for Advanced Studies in the Fine Arts provided generous support for the production of the many illustrations. The Religious Studies Department of Macalester College provided generous financial support as well as a collegial home, intellectual stimulation, and moral support at a crucial time. My sincere thanks go to all department members and particularly to Calvin Roetzel. I also appreciate the support of the University of Minnesota, which awarded me a dissertation travel grant to initiate the project, as well as that of the University of Notre Dame's Institute for Scholarship in the Liberal Arts and Cleveland State University, both of which awarded me summer research grants.

The list of individuals who helped advance my research along the way is far too lengthy to present here, but I do want to offer my sincere thanks to a few people. Roland Delattre advised my early dissertation on this topic with a light touch, encouraging me to think creatively and across disciplines and allowing me to explore the most unlikely connections. To him I offer my heartiest thanks. John Archer, George Lipsitz, and Gayle Graham Yates read my dissertation and offered valuable suggestions in the areas of architecture, cultural studies, and feminism. As I moved beyond the dissertation, reworking and expanding my research, I received insightful comments and valuable criticism from (in chronological order) David Schuyler, Paul Groth, James F. White, Richard Butsch, Michael Driscoll, James B. Stewart, David Bains, David Morgan, Jeanne Barker-Nunn, Richard Kieckhefer, Marilyn Chiat, and Ed Blum. Their comments pushed me to develop and deepen many of the arguments, and I am most grateful to them. I also want to extend a special thanks to Peter W. Williams, who has offered not only valuable comments on my work but also support and encouragement for my investigations of religious architecture. It is largely through Professor Williams's stewardship that the study of U.S. religious architecture now claims a position of respectability within the field of U.S. religious studies, and I have benefited enormously from his wisdom over the last several years.

I want to thank the many church administrators and archivists who responded to my inquiries over the years. More than sixty churches answered an initial survey I conducted in 1987, and many of their representatives responded graciously to my numerous letters, phone calls, and requests for information. In particular, Ron Solokofsky at Trinity Church in Denver, Ann Hage at First Congregational Church in Minneapolis, Layton Brueske at First Baptist Church in Minneapolis, the Reverend Laurie Hafner at Pilgrim Church in Cleveland, the Reverend Dennis Alexander at Wesley United Methodist in Minneapolis, the Reverend Deborah Tinsley at First Congregational Church in Pueblo, Colorado, Dolores Shaw at Lovely Lane Church in Baltimore, Harmon Ruliffson at the Scottish Rite Temple (formerly Fowler M.E.) in Minneapolis, and Roland Baumann at the Oberlin College Archives were most generous in sharing their time and their extensive knowledge with me. I also want to thank William P. Halgren, who developed several of the contemporary photographs, and Brian Longley at Macalester College, who did much of the photographing of period materials. Special thanks also go to Sarah Turner at Macalester, who assisted with countless tasks during the production phase.

I am especially grateful to my husband, Paul R. Kilde, who during the course of this study played many roles, including photographer, developmental reader, copyeditor, cheerleader, and counselor. Lastly, I am pleased to express my gratitude to my parents, William E. and Patricia Mae Halgren, by dedicating this book to them. It is not the great American novel they thought I would write, but nonetheless it is largely through their lessons in persistence and independent thinking that this work has come to fruition.

Portions of chapter 2 previously appeared in Jeanne Halgren Kilde, "Architecture and Urban Revivalism in Nineteenth-Century America," in *Perspectives on American Religion and Culture*, edited by Peter W. Williams (Malden, Mass.: Blackwell, 1999): 174–86.

Contents

Illustrations

When Church Became Theatre

1

Transformation of Protestant Architecture

Late in the fall of 1814, the congregation of the First Church of Christ, New Haven, Connecticut, prepared to move into its new meetinghouse. The building project had been initiated two years earlier, and, though construction had been slowed somewhat by the intervening war with Britain, the nearly finished church was an estimable example of the prevailing trend in religious architecture. These Congregationalists had purchased plans from Boston architect Asher Benjamin, whose several architectural pattern books had already established his reputation throughout New England. Benjamin's plans had been modified by architect Ithiel Town, who had also directed the construction. The two-story brick building blended stylistic innovations with familiar spatial elements that had served Protestant architecture for nearly two centuries (fig. 1.1).

Though displaying a greater flamboyance than was typical, the exterior of First Church incorporated main trends among Congregationalist, Presbyterian, and Baptist meetinghouses in the early decades of the nineteenth century. The classical Greek and Roman elements of the exterior were borrowed from the work of earlier generations of British architects, particularly that of Christopher Wren, who rebuilt many of London's churches after the Great Fire of 1666, and his pupil Nicholas Hawksmoor. These designers had transformed London's religious landscape with their Georgian-style churches throughout the eighteenth century, and by the final decade of the century, as the new American nation was struggling to be born, Benjamin, Town, and other architects were doing the same in the United States.[1] First Church was a rectangular building oriented on an east-west axis. At its east entry, the church presented a formal facade to the public square on which it stood. While many Federalist meetinghouses featured a pedimented entry bay, Town projected the bay out several feet from the body of the building to form a porch supported by Doric columns in front and pilasters behind. Classical semicircular heads defined the second-story windows, while their lower counterparts exhibited segmental-arch heads. Beneath the pediment and entablature of the porch, three round-head doors pierced the front facade, each flanked by rusticated Doric pilasters supporting entablatures. Above the doors but set back from the porch, a five-stage steeple rose to a height of some 210 feet and alluded to James Gibbs's famous St. Martin-in-the-Fields Church in London.[2]

Fig. 1.1. First Church of Christ, New Haven, Conn. 1814. Ithiel Town, arch., after Asher Benjamin. Photograph by Jeanne Halgren Kilde.

The interior space of the meetinghouse was similarly representative of U.S. Protestant churches of the period, though again somewhat more elaborate. Though no plan or photograph of the original interior exists, Asher Benjamin's generic plan for a meetinghouse would have closely resembled First Church's interior arrangement. Unlike earlier colonial meetinghouses, which were often oriented horizontally toward a pulpit centered on a long wall (fig. 1.2), this new, more churchly style oriented the rectangular space on the longitudinal axis, centering the main door on the short east wall and the pulpit opposite it on the west (fig. 1.3). The pulpit dominated the room. Described in congregational sources as "a lofty structure . . . supported by graceful columns," it was elevated several feet above the main floor, and the minister reached it each Sunday morning by ascending one of the curving staircases that flanked it on each side. The large west window behind the pulpit provided the minister with sufficient light to read his scriptural text and sermon. The ceiling was almost completely covered by a shallow oval dome in the center of which was an ornamental, circular, plaster relief surrounding an open grille, and it is likely that a chandelier hung from the center. The double

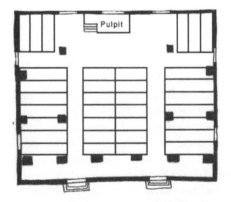

Fig. 1.2. Generic meetinghouse plan, cross-axial orientation. Drawing by Mark Carlier.

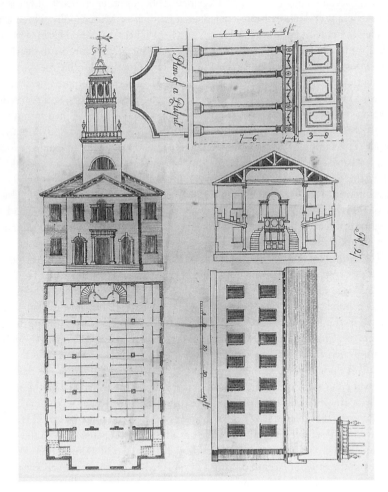

Fig. 1.3. Meetinghouse plan and views. Asher Benjamin, *A Country Builder's Assistant*, 1798. Courtesy American Antiquarian Society.

sets of double-hung windows, five on each side, let in air and unfiltered light. Box pews filled the main floor and galleries, supported by Ionic columns that ran the length of the room on both sides.[3]

Despite its updated facade and interior orientation, this church and dozens like it replicated the spatial characteristics that had satisfactorily fulfilled the requirements of Protestant worship for centuries: a large, rectangular seating area for congregants filled with box pews, which not only kept out drafts but also relegated individuals to assigned places and kept them there for the duration of the service, and a large and elaborate backlit pulpit from whose height the minister could survey and preach to his entire flock. The formality or "churchliness" of the Federalist exterior and interior decor, so different from the earlier unadorned meetinghouses of the Congregationalists' Puritan ancestors, pointed to the processes of evolution that would continue to shape and re-shape Protestant church architecture.

Just over seventy years later, on 19 December 1886, another church highly representative of its era was dedicated—the First Baptist Church of Minneapolis. Three generations after the construction of the First Church of Christ in New Haven, few of the features of that church or the bellwethers of Protestant architecture in the early nineteenth century could be seen in this new midwestern building. Unlike the symmetrical classicism of the Federalist church, the exterior of First Baptist, designed by Minneapolis architect Fred Kees, featured a complex assortment of bays, towers, and pointed- and round-arched windows (fig. 1.4). The architectural vocabulary had shifted from the classical pastiche of Greek and Roman to a medieval one with Gothic and Romanesque elements. The building, rendered in rough-faced yellow sandstone, exuded an air of solidity and massiveness that, had the two churches stood side by side, would have rendered the elegant brick of First Church quite delicate, if not insubstantial.

The interior of the new building exhibited even more profound changes. The rectangle of the Federalist church with its easily read longitudinal orientation had been replaced by a square room oriented diagonally toward a corner that housed not a pulpit hung high upon the wall but an elaborate stage elevated some three feet above the main floor. The term *stage* was truly an appropriate one, for the room was arranged more like a theatre or opera house than a church of previous generations (fig. 1.5). The lavishly articulated stage functioned as the focal point of the room. A portable lectern, which served as a pulpit, claimed the center but was dwarfed by the features located behind and above it—the baptistery and choir, partially obscured by a short curtain, the grand organ console, and the stenciled organ pipes that soared to the ceiling. An elaborate proscenium arch framed the entire stage area.

The main floor continued the theatre motif. The floor sloped from the back of the room toward the stage at the front, and arcs of curved pews radiated up it from the stage. A balcony encircled most of the room, dropping slowly down to the stage level in a series of steps that distinctly resembled opera boxes.[4] True to its theatrical roots, this audience room resembled nothing so much as the inverted spatial cone of the classical Greek and Roman amphitheatre. Thus, although the classical architectural vocabulary so favored in the early nineteenth century had vanished, that ancient influence was readily visible within the spatial arrangement of the audience room itself. This space was a far cry, however, from the rectangular formalism of the Federalist church.

Fig. 1.4. First Baptist Church, Minneapolis, Minn. 1886. Frederick Kees, arch. Courtesy First Baptist Church Archives, Minneapolis, Minn.

Perhaps even more startling was the transformation in the atmospherics of the worship room. Whereas ornamentation and furnishings in Federalist churches like New Haven's were generally limited to carving on the pulpit, dado, and gallery faces and perhaps a set of pulpit curtains to cut the glare of the west window, in First Baptist a new aesthetic of abundant ornamentation and materiality reigned. Wainscoting lined the walls, which were further adorned by a dado and frieze of intricate, frescoed designs. An inscription of biblical verse, generously highlighted with gilt, ornamented one wall adjacent to the stage. The ceiling vaults displayed further frescoing in deep blue, gold, and yellow, and a large gas chandelier with crystal pendant reflectors hung from the center of the ceiling dome supported by the vaulting. The rich colors were repeated in the three large stained-glass windows, which cast warm, amber light throughout the room on sunny days. A neutral-toned Brussels carpeting covered the floor, and horse-hair cushions made the pews inviting.

Representative of dominant trends in Protestant architecture at the time of their respective construction, New Haven's First Church of Christ and Minneapolis's First

Fig. 1.5. First Baptist Church, Minneapolis, Minn. 1886. Frederick Kees, arch. Courtesy First Baptist Church Archives, Minneapolis, Minn.

Baptist Church provide graphic illustration of a distinctive revisioning of Protestant worship space that occurred among evangelical Protestant groups over the course of the nineteenth century. This revisioning consisted of radical transformations in architectural style, space and spatial arrangement, and furnishing and ornamentation. While these physical changes are significant in and of themselves, they are also indicative of profound alterations that went far beyond the material, for they were intimately connected to religious, social, and cultural transformations, which reshaped evangelical Protestantism itself.

If we could witness the services presented within each of these churches in their respective heydays, we would see important differences in the way the two congregations worshiped. In the early part of the nineteenth century, the Congregationalists of the First Church of Christ would have gathered on Sunday morning to listen to the minister offer prayer, read Scripture, and deliver a lengthy sermon explicating Scripture. The congregation might recite, or "line out," a psalm or hymn with the help of a precentor, and occasionally a tune might have been presented by a violinist. Departing the church for a brief meal, the congregation would have returned in the afternoon to hear another sermon and more prayers. By the 1880s, however, the services of evangelical Protestants had changed significantly, and although our example is a Baptist congregation, changes in the service were evident among all evangelical denominations—particularly among Congregationalists, Presbyterians, Baptists, and Methodists. The sermon, which for the New Haven Congregationalists in the Federalist period could continue for two hours, had shrunk by the close of the century to a mere half hour, and it often addressed social topics quite afield from Scripture. Prayers, usually extended and extemporaneous in the early part of the century, were by the end of the century often read from a book. The congregation now engaged in recitative exchanges with the minister, voicing either a psalm or a prayer of petition or praise. Music had become a more prominent part of the service. No longer did the congregation require a precentor to line out psalms and hymns, for worshipers now held in their hands individual hymnals with complete lyrics and musical notations for four-part harmony. Congregationalists and Presbyterians worshiping in buildings quite similar to First Baptist would raise their voices to the Gloria Patri and the doxology when prompted by the program they received from an usher upon entering the sanctuary. And most evangelical congregations not only listened to stirring organ solos and their own voluntary choir but also heard performances by professional quartets hired for the service.

These transformations in worship practice were closely linked to broader changes within evangelical Protestantism, which were themselves spurred by social and cultural changes throughout the nineteenth century. As U.S. Protestants modified their religious beliefs and practices to better address their changing lives, they also altered their church buildings. By focusing on what inspired or instigated this transformation in the material setting of evangelical worship, this book draws attention to the complex role that worship space has played within Protestantism. While churches have provided a physical setting for worship practices, they have also inspired, fostered, and sustained significant changes in both belief and practice. By examining these buildings and the discussions that surrounded their construction, this study probes the religious and social motivations of the people who built them. By attending to the evolution from the early nineteenth-century Federalist church to the late nineteenth-century evangelical auditorium and to the forces and influences that brought it about, this investigation explores the complex relationships between space and worship, architecture and meaning, religion and society.

Meaning in Religious Buildings:
A Cultural Approach to Religious Architecture

Religious buildings have always been imbued with important meanings. Anyone who has lapsed into a hushed whisper upon entering a sanctuary, gazed in speechless awe at soaring fan vaults in a cathedral, or felt the weight of ages while exploring a musty undercroft has experienced the profound impact the messages carry, be they mystical, spiritual, historical, or social. By conveying such meanings, churches form a connection between abstract idea and physical expression, functioning as what Victor Turner has called a ritual process, linking the abstraction of the divine to the physicality of human existence. In other words, churches connect the divine with the human, values with social forms, and aspiration with present reality. At once messengers and agents, mirrors and actors, they enable people to think through their ideas about religiosity and convey them to the rest of the world while, in turn, influencing those ideas and shaping religion and society.

Within church spaces, God, clergy, and laity meet and negotiate their respective relationships. Consequently, the meanings associated with church architecture are often about power and authority. Three categories of power are apparent within these religious spaces: supernatural power, or power associated with the divine; social power, or human influence and authority within specific sociopolitical contexts; and personal power, or the spiritual empowerment of the individual.

Churches are most readily associated with the first of these, the power of the divine. Though power is negotiated in many types of spaces, including domestic and civic spaces, within religious spaces the process has a distinctive character because believers perceive the presence of the supernatural within the buildings. Some historians and scholars of religion, most notably Mircea Eliade, have looked to these understandings of the supernatural to explain the dynamics of power within religious space, investigating the meaning of religious space in terms of the special power that suffuses it through divine or supernatural presence. In this view, a church is a sacred and power-full place because God, the All-Powerful, exists within it. While this view is highly compelling to believers, it is less useful to the historian of religious architecture; while such a presence can readily be verified as a belief, it cannot be verified as a historical reality. Consequently, this study of the processes through which power is invested in religious space focuses on the second of these types of power, social power. Assuming that religious or sacred space is space that has been imbued with specific religious meanings by society, this study explores the social processes that create those sacred meanings and attach them to specific buildings. This study reads the process backward, starting with the final products, the churches, and exploring the meanings and values associated with them. Of particular import is the fundamentally hierarchical nature of the sacralization processes surrounding church buildings. While sacralization differentiates space of heightened significance from other, less-significant space, it also, as Jonathan Z. Smith points out, serves to place one's self or one's group in proximity to (and preferably closer to) perceived power sources, be they human or divine, secular or supernatural. This study looks to the social contexts that define relationships to power not only within the church space but among clergy, laity, and the wider community.[5]

In Christian churches, displays and tensions over specific types of social power—the authority of the clergy, the relative influence of benefactors, the role of the laity—are strikingly evident. Since their earliest gatherings, Christians have come together in spaces designed both to accommodate their physical presence and to designate distinctions among those gathered—for instance, the holiest people nearest the altar in the chancel, lay worshipers farther away in the nave; women on the left, men on the right; whites on the main floor, blacks in the balcony. The exteriors of Christian churches also have broadcast the social significance of the buildings, the congregations, and Christianity itself throughout the broader landscape. A modest storefront church sends a far different message than does a massive cathedral sited prominently upon a hill. Inside and out, Christian buildings designate rank and position in social hierarchies. In their capacity as social designators, then, church buildings and spaces are political places, places in which social power and authority are asserted, tested, and negotiated.

Importantly, however, this is not exclusively a top-down imposing of power by social elites, whether clergy or benefactors, for the third type of power, personal power, also plays a crucial role in the meaning of churches. What has kept Christianity vital throughout the last two millennia is its amenability to adaptation and interpretation, which has allowed individuals to find all types of meaning within its broad outlines. Religiosity is at once ecclesiastic and spiritual, social and personal. In religious buildings, individual believers experience spiritual, emotional, and psychological power or well-being from both proximity to divinity and interaction with other believers. Salvation, absolution, *communitas*, and succor are all found by individuals within church buildings. These are powerful motivators, which can spur worshipers to exert enormous influence within churches and to lay claim to the interpretation of the meanings of religious buildings. Thus, supernatural, social, and personal power are intricately intertwined, drawing upon one other for their very existence and, at the same time, often communicating competing meanings within a given religious site.

Given the capacity of architecture both to embody and to broadcast ideas and meanings, to impose and to maintain them, the church buildings of evangelical Protestants provide evidence of their beliefs, missions, rituals, challenges, and fears during the turbulent period of the nineteenth century. What follows is as much a study of evangelicalism and evangelicals as of architecture, the latter serving as a text created by the former through which we gain access to the thoughts of these creators.[6]

Historical Development of Protestant Church Architecture

To comprehend the significance of the changes wrought in evangelical architecture throughout the nineteenth century, a brief history of Protestant architecture is in order. Protestants have been engaged since the earliest years of the Reformation in a quest for appropriate worship space. The sixteenth-century Christian reform movement that quickly escalated into the Protestant Reformation minimized the essentially visual nature of centuries of Christian worship, which had been dominated by the celebration of the Eucharist, and emphasized a new linguistic, particularly aural, experience. Martin Luther and other Reformed theologians, influenced by the development of the printing press and growing literacy, argued that written and spoken language were the exclusive representations of divine power and therefore the purpose of worship should be to strive to understand God's Word. As a result, the sermon, a reasoned discourse explicating a piece of Scripture, emerged as the centerpiece of Protestant worship, linking otherwise disparate Reformation movements and replacing the Mass, a predominantly visual and sensual ritual. The substitution of linguistic forms of worship for visual and sensual ones erupted in iconoclasm as some Protestants attacked the rich material culture of medieval Christianity, destroying stained glass, sculpture, and paintings.[7]

Not surprisingly, this shift in the focus of Christian worship brought radical changes in the spatial arrangements of churches. Protestant services, unlike the Roman Catholic Mass, required the fixed attention and participation of audiences. Listening became the primary worship practice, and, in a remarkable shift in Christian design priorities, facilitating listening emerged as an important principle in Protestant worship space.[8] The existing Christian (i.e., Roman Catholic) churches of the Reformation period, however, had not been designed to facilitate listening. Catholic churches generally followed the basilica form, an oblong building with an axial or longitudinal orientation on an altar located in a culminating apse at one end. The voices of clergy positioned at the altar carried only a few dozen feet down the nave, and in vaulted basilicas and domed centralized spaces, sound traveled up to the recesses above and became trapped there. Further, the stone walls and slate floors of many churches bounced sound from here to there, often making the rooms amazingly "live." Hearing a single preaching voice within such spaces was frequently impossible, and Protestant reformers immediately recognized the need to modify traditional worship space to aid worshipers' reception of the sermon.

Initially reformers focused on the furniture, replacing the central altar with a pulpit as the locus of significance. The Protestant pulpits of the sixteenth and seventeenth centuries—huge, intricately carved, and looming high above the main floor of the church—improved hearing and served as visual statements of top-down clerical authority. In Luther's time, these elaborate desks often incorporated three levels—the highest space for preaching and the lower two for the reading of the Gospels and the work of the precentor—and were elevated several feet above the heads of the congregation. A massive soundboard loomed above, projecting the minister's voice out over the audience rather than upward into the rafters. In converting older basilica churches for Protestant services, congregations placed the new pulpits to one side midway down the length of the nave. Seats were then turned sideways in the nave to face the pulpit. As Protestant church building began, reformers generally favored rectangular plans that were less narrow than the earlier basilicas, and they placed the pulpits on a longitudinal axis with the door. In both the converted and new churches, the large elevated pulpits not only aided the projection of the minister's voice but also provided visual interest and a focal point for the service, which was nevertheless primarily an aural event.

Thus, the desire to enhance the audience's ability to absorb the sermon took Christian architecture in an entirely new direction. It also radically transformed traditional power relationships between clergy and laity. Whereas the basilica form had evolved from the imperial building of the Roman Empire and had functioned effectively to establish and maintain the authority and power of those granted access to the chancel area (i.e., the priests), the new buildings expressed and naturalized a new, dialogic relationship between clergy and audience. Clearly, elevated pulpits physically expressed and naturalized the elevated position, the high authority, of the minister. With the power to explicate and interpret the Word of God itself, the minister literally as well as figuratively transcended his audience.[9] At the same time, however, the new spatial situation accorded religious audiences a new and more significant role in the service and thus marked a significant change in the nature of the religious power wielded by the clergy.

Like traditional basilicas, the axial plans of the Reformation churches physically articulated clerical power; they did so, however, in a way that illustrated a crucial shift in the source of that power. Roman Catholic priests had derived their religious authority from a direct connection to the divine through the historic episcopate, a lineage of power that descended from Jesus and his apostles through the succeeding generations of bishops. The sanctity, exclusivity, and secrecy of the chancel articulated this source as did the ritual alternation between the concealing and revealing of God in the Eucharist service.[10] Reformed, Lutheran, and Calvinist ministers, rejecting the doctrine of apostolic succession, theologically and visually severed the connections between divine power and their own authority. Instead, the sheer power of their language and erudition as interpreters of Scripture became sources of authority for Protestant ministers. This type of authority, however, must be granted by audiences; worshipers must agree that an individual's talents warrant his claim to the pulpit. Given this new dialogic relationship, the elevated pulpits lent great support to ministers' claims to leadership by physically expressing their superiority. Their lofty position aided clergy in dominating the space visually, as Catholic priests had always done, but, more importantly, aurally.[11]

Yet the elaborate pulpits suggest that Protestants were not completely willing to eradicate all visual elements from their services. Because watching as well as listening to the minister was important, the elevation of the pulpit ensured that he could be seen from all points in the house, from both the floor and the galleries. Protestants, therefore, maintained an equivocal relationship with the visual elements that had previously defined Christian worship. Lutheran and Anglican groups generally retained such visually important elements as clerical vestments, altar cloths and crosses, richly ornamented Communion cups and plates, and well-adorned baptismal fonts. In contrast to these High Church tastes, many Reformed groups, including the Calvinists and Puritans who influenced the American religious scene, eschewed vestments in favor of simple black robes or academic gowns, replaced altars with unadorned Communion tables, and used more utilitarian Communion plates and cups; similarly, a pewter bowl on a stand might suffice for a baptismal font. Nevertheless, some ornament was almost always evident even within Low Church groups. Even the sparest New England Puritan pulpits of the seventeenth century were often graced by an hourglass, which was used to keep track of the passage of time during a sermon (one or two turns of the glass was normal for a sermon).[12] Though Protestants eliminated the visual focus on the performance of the eucharistic ritual, the strategies they retained and created were employed to aid listening and to suggest the centrality and religious authority of the minister.

The Protestant project tempered this highly visual clerical power by also fostering a new type of power among congregants. Protestant services required both the presence and the participation of a congregation. Whereas the sacrifice of the Mass proceeded with or without an audience of worshipers, Protestant services required not just an audience, but an attentive one. Thus, Protestant audiences gained a power over services that, while more subtle than that of the clergy, was no less significant. The gathered worshipers themselves constituted the Christian community, giving them the power to acknowledge, and thus grant, ministers' authority. That some congregations refused to do so through the post-Reformation period was evident in conflicts between ministers and congregations, which regularly resulted in the replacement of ministers.[13] In these ways, congregations gained new types of religious social power that most had never before experienced. While the wealthy had always wielded some influence over clergy, in the new Protestant situation the needs of the congregation became central to a church's success and lent power to all gathered.

The building of Reformed and Protestant churches in the sixteenth and seventeenth centuries, however, was made sporadic by the suppression of Protestant activities by various monarchies. Rarely did Protestants have an opportunity to consider anything other than the most utilitarian of spaces when building churches. Puritan emigrants to Massachusetts in the 1630s, for instance, drew upon the model of the market halls or guildhalls with which they were familiar from their homeland in order to satisfy their frontier communities' needs for multipurpose meeting spaces. As architectural historian Marian Card Donnelly has noted, these public building models squared the traditionally rectangular space of churches somewhat and centered the pulpit on the long side, placing the door opposite (as was seen in fig. 1.2).[14] Other groups, however, notably the Dutch Reformed, Lutherans, Presbyterians, and Anglicans, followed the medieval parish model of an axially oriented rectangular room with a modified chancel at the front containing pulpit and Communion table or altar, a building type that was essentially a variation on the basilica. This is the basic design that Wren would sheath with classical architectural features in the late seventeenth century and that would eventually evolve into the Federalist church so popular in America at the end of the eighteenth century.

Yet during the sixteenth century there did exist two distinctive, if short-lived, attempts to create an entirely new Protestant worship space, and within these attempts lie the roots of the nineteenth-century architectural transformation that constitutes the focus of this book. From the earliest days of the Reformation, reformers had been aware of the desirability of Protestant worship spaces emanating from a single, central point—centrally planned spaces shaped as circles, squares, or octagons. Because these spaces allowed a large number of observers to be placed near a pulpit mounted on one wall, Martin Luther praised them as particularly amenable to sermon-centered services, much more so than the longitudinally oriented basilica plans.[15] Following his directive to use such centralized spaces, some Protestants experimented with oval, circular, and polygonal spatial forms. Donnelly has traced the earliest of these experiments to sixteenth-century French Huguenot temples built during sporadic and brief periods of religious tolerance. While most of the buildings were demolished after the Edict of Nantes was revoked in 1685, and while information on the few temples that were actually constructed is sketchy, an extant drawing of one, the Temple Paradis in Lyon (1566), depicts an oval or circular building in which benches ring the edges of a main space interrupted only by a large elevated pulpit, which dominates the room (fig. 1.6). A narrow gallery circles the entire room, and straight rows of backless benches face the pulpit while side rows face in toward the center bank of benches, giving the room a somewhat divided focus. Despite its lack of a strong central focus, the arrangement allowed all worshipers to see and hear the preacher above them.[16]

Although this building broke with the traditional rectangular spaces, it stopped well short of the radial-plan amphitheatre, which would become prominent in the auditorium churches at the end of the nineteenth century. In addition to the divided focus, the main floor was level, although the benches may have been inclined slightly at the sides of the room. Though existing sketches are somewhat ambiguous, they do depict the figures closest to the walls as larger than those in the center and farther from the viewer, thereby suggesting that the audience members nearer the walls sat at a higher elevation. Another example of an amphitheatre spatial arrangement appears in Philibert

Fig. 1.6. Temple Paradis, Lyon, France. 1566. Courtesy Bibliothèque Publique et Universitaire, Genève.

de l'Orme's design for the Huguenot Temple at La Rochelle, a building that Donnelly describes as "an octagon, of unequal sides, with three principal doors in the Corinthian Order, an open roof as at Lyon, and benches arranged 'en amphithéâtre.'"[17] Here again, it is likely that the main floor itself was level but that the benches were higher at the perimeter of the room.

Another brief resurgence of this modified amphitheatre plan occurred about 150 years later, when Protestant Baroque came into its own in eighteenth-century Germany. Although the rectangular preaching hall remained the most popular type of space for Protestant churches during this period, some Reformed and Lutheran churches, as well as a number of Catholic churches, sported round, oval, and other centralized spaces. The most renowned of the Baroque churches was architect George Bähr's Die Frauenkirche in Dresden (1726). Featuring a square plan with an apse projecting from one side, the church created a dynamic seating arrangement in the centralized space by placing the raked seating of the amphitheatre around the edges of the circular audience room (fig. 1.7). Unlike the earlier Huguenot temples, however, the level seating in the interior of the Frauenkirche consisted of curvilinear pews partially encircling the elaborate pulpit and divided by both a center and an axial aisle. As in the Huguenot buildings, several rows of similarly curved pews rose along the edge of this main seating area. Double galleries, each with raked seating, completed the vertical thrust of the seating and enhanced the amphitheatre effect. Thus, while Bähr's design perhaps moved toward the amphitheatre more than any previous church had, it nevertheless retained a mostly level floor and thus stopped short of a fully articulated amphitheatre plan.[18]

The physical spaces of the Baroque amphitheatre-like churches went somewhat further than other Protestant church buildings in emphasizing the dialogical interplay of clerical and audience power. For instance, features designed to improve the audience's

Fig. 1.7. Die Frauenkirche, Dresden, Germany. 1726. Reconstructed plan. Drawing by Mark Carlier.

reception of the service tended to enhance both audience and clerical power, in that the raked parts of the buildings not only produced better movement of sound but also enhanced the audience's view by eliminating the obstruction of heads between each worshiper and the minister. Further, in the eighteenth-century examples, the curvilinear seats placed the individuals in each row equidistant from the pulpit and directed their visual focus toward the pulpit. These features allowed ministers to see directly into the eyes of each worshiper—and eye contact is a powerful tool in maintaining audience attention and asserting one's authority. Like its spatial cousin, the panopticon, an amphitheatre allows a single speaker poised at the focal point—the pulpit, in this case— to assess the entire audience at a glance.[19] In these ways, the integration of amphitheatre elements in these Baroque churches physically enhanced ministers' power over their audiences' attention. Yet this enhanced clerical power functioned in dialogue with and was mitigated by an equally important spatial enhancement of audience power. As any teacher can testify, having bank upon bank of faces gazing intently down upon one on a lecture stage can be intimidating. Audiences in an amphitheatre tend to take on a corporate presence quite unlike those that remain relatively individualized in a longitudinally oriented preaching-hall church. As later chapters will demonstrate, it is precisely this new spatial power dynamic that came to be fully articulated and exploited in nineteenth-century America.

The adoption of the actual amphitheatre as worship space came slowly to Christianity for a variety of social and cultural reasons; principally, its association with outdoor preaching and its placement of the minister below the worshipers seemed unnatural and counterintuitive. The use of the amphitheatre space for Protestant services appeared first in the context of the rise of evangelicalism and revival preaching in the mid-eighteenth century. As revivalists like John Wesley and George Whitefield sought to convert the working people of rural England, they took to outdoor preaching in direct violation of ancient Christian prohibitions on outdoor worship. Although vilified by many for doing this, these new evangelists persisted, holding mass revivals in whatever cleared field might be available. In 1750, Whitefield preached in Gwennap Pit, a large, irregularly shaped pit in Cornwall formed by mine subsidence. While little information about Whitefield's appearance exists, the site was also visited by John Wesley, who first preached there in the fall of 1766 and described it as a "natural amphitheatre," which was the "finest" he knew of in the country. "It is a round, green hollow, gently shelving down, about fifty feet deep, but I suppose it is two hundred across one way, and near three hundred the other." Most impressive to Wesley was the number of listeners the space could accommodate; he estimated his first crowd there at a "full twenty thousand people."[20]

Despite Wesley's enthusiasm for Gwennap Pit, the amphitheatre form was not widely embraced. The "tabernacles," or preaching buildings, that he, Whitefield, and other ministers of dissenting congregations built incorporated the raked amphitheatre seating only on the gallery levels, maintaining the traditional level main floor and the elevated pulpit. Although some of these buildings featured centrally planned main floors, those floors remained level and the seats faced the pulpit in banks bisected by aisles.[21] Even in outdoor preaching, the amphitheatre form was rarely adopted. Instead, revival ministers stood upon cartons, wagons, or other makeshift preaching stands to deliver their messages. Camp-meeting manuals generally recommended that organizers select level ground for meeting sites, primarily to ease the staking of the tents in which participants would live for the duration of the meeting and which would ring the preaching area in an analogy of heaven. Preaching space could be any area cleared adequately to allow for the erection of a preaching stand and the placement of a few rows of benches in front of it. Given the holiness agenda of camp meetings—the desire to invite the Holy Spirit to descend upon and infuse the individual or even the entire crowd—this spatial dynamic proved effective. It provided a safe space in which the physical manifestations of holiness—writhing, jerking, and fainting—could be welcomed; steep hillsides undoubtedly rendered such behavior hazardous.[22] Further, the elevation of the preacher also served as an indication of his spiritual elevation.

Religious and secular authority had been marked by this physical elevation for centuries. Emperors and monarchs sited their palaces atop hills and their thrones atop bema; priests elevated chancels above the main floors of churches; revival ministers climbed up on wagons or boxes when elevated pulpits were not handy. The amphitheatre, in contrast, inverts this arrangement, lowering the authority figure and placing the audience in an expanding circle above that individual. But while it remains natural for individuals to elevate themselves above the crowd to make an announcement or otherwise gain attention, sound naturally carries upward. Thus, it is far more effective to speak to a crowd of people from below rather than from above because many more individuals can hear the voice. Although projecting a single voice down upon a large gathering is often a futile exercise, the conceptual relationship between religious authority and elevation is so deep-seated that when Wesley preached at Gwennap Pit, he did so not from the base but, as he wrote in his journal, "I stood on one side of this amphitheatre toward the top, with the people beneath and on all sides."[23]

Yet a few exceptions did exist. Some preachers placed themselves at the base of hills beneath their listeners and thus used the natural slope of the landscape to carry their voices upward and to give their viewers clear sightlines down upon them. An undated English engraving, ostensibly depicting a revival preacher in Cornwall, places the minister on a covered preaching platform or stand located at the base rather than at the top of a steep hill (fig. 1.8).[24] Two huge cliffs rise dramatically on either side of a more gradually sloping hill occupied by a large flock of people in the foreground, mesmerized by the preacher. Yet here, too, the counterintuitive nature of the arrangement is evident, for had visual realism been maintained in this image, the preaching stand at the bottom of the hill, though occupying the middle ground of the picture, would have been depicted as quite small in comparison to the crowd. The artist, however, in a likely attempt to indicate the significance of the preacher's presence and authority, has painted the preaching stand, with its barely discernible occupant, as hugely overscaled and has placed it in the center of the picture, thus heightening the contrast between its dark shape and the lighter distance and repeating its vertical lines in the cliffs themselves. In an odd spatial twist, the two-dimensional perspective places the bottom of the hill on which the audience stands higher in the picture plane than the top of the hill, which appears in the foreground of the picture. Just as the amphitheatre shape directs the audience's attention to the bottom, the picture directs the viewer's attention to the center vortex, which is dominated by the oversized preaching stand. For this artist, the power of the revival preacher's presence demanded that he be writ large even against an imposing foreground of listeners, not placed below his audience at the bottom of the hill.

Fig. 1.8. Revivalist in Cornwall. Anonymous English engraving, c. 1800.

While the English engraving depicts what may or may not have been a historical event, an amphitheatre arrangement was actually used in a camp meeting held just outside of Washington, D.C., in 1809 attended by the architect Benjamin Latrobe, who sketched the placement of the speaker's platform at the bottom of a hill across which spread the audience.[25] Whether his sketch was motivated by the extraordinary nature of the arrangement is not known, but it is clear that relatively few camp meetings adopted it. Exceptions include the Sharon, Connecticut, and Rhinebeck, New York, revivals, each of which did use the natural slopes of hills to accommodate audiences, and an 1843 Millerite meeting near Long Branch, New Jersey, which also took advantage of a gently sloping hill, but the scarcity of such examples proves the rule.[26] In the early nineteenth century, physical elevation expressed religious authority. What might be done occasionally or out of necessity outdoors would remain anathema indoors. To eliminate the elevated pulpit and place a minister beneath or at least on the same plane as an encircling crowd of listeners would require profound shifts in religious thought, social relationships, and cultural circumstances.

Transformation of Architecture and Worship

Given this reluctance and centuries of familiarity with the traditional basilica form in Protestant worship, the widespread adoption of amphitheatre-derived auditoriums for Protestant worship in the late nineteenth century is truly remarkable. By the 1880s, the radial-plan amphitheatre dominated evangelical building nationwide. Enclosed in monu-

mental stone facades featuring an eclectic mix of medieval vocabularies, these new sanctuaries housed Congregationalist, Presbyterian, Methodist, and Baptist congregations
coast to coast.[27] The overwhelming popularity of the building type was such that these
churches are still familiar to many North Americans in cities and small towns alike. We
pass them on Woodward Avenue in Detroit, on Euclid in Cleveland, on Peachtree in
Atlanta, on Bloor in Toronto, on Fourth Street in Manistee, Michigan, and on Lincoln
Way in Mishawaka, Indiana—indeed, on main streets all across North America.

The story of the transformation of Protestant churches from the axial-plan Federalist
church to the neomedieval auditorium church begins with the urban revivals of the
Second Great Awakening. It was during these revivals, specifically those of Charles
Grandison Finney in New York City, that religious space became significantly influenced by theatre space, perhaps for the first time in history. Chapter 2 examines the
evangelical use of theatre forms in churches and locates the cultural significance of these
experiments not only within the sphere of religious creed and cultus but also within the
context of public democratic discourse. Indeed, these buildings, available to a broad
urban population, served as arenas for the emerging public debate. This chapter probes
the social, political, religious, and cultural contexts that informed what were quite radical experiments in religious space.

This turned out to be a fleeting period of experimentation, however, quickly derailed
by a return to traditional, indeed ancient, church architectural forms, that were also
born of debates within the public arena. The profoundly influential Gothic Revival,
which replaced the earliest auditorium churches, is examined in chapter 3. This stylistic
revival, which for Low Church evangelical congregations was not a revival at all but an
extraordinary move toward High Church Roman Catholic architectural forms, offered
a formalism that many evangelical denominations found attractive. During a period of
increasing social upheaval that seemed to herald the destruction of denominations, the
Gothic aesthetic offered an effective means of maintaining Protestant cohesion. The con-
comitant turn toward liturgy within the evangelical cultus sprang from the same sources
and concerns.

In the post–Civil War years, the emergence of the American middle class as an identifiable group led to the readoption of the amphitheatre in the form of the neomedieval
auditorium church—an icon of bourgeois evangelical religion and, many felt, a symbol of
respectable middle-class religious participation within a democratic society. Chapter 4
delineates the social and economic contexts that gave rise to this building type, focusing
on the political considerations in which congregations engaged as they chose sites for their
new buildings. The process of negotiating location required many congregations to reex-
amine and rearticulate their missions, and this chapter examines the armory-like exteriors
of the new churches in relation to those new missions. Chapter 5 moves indoors to offer
a close examination of the spatial politics of the new auditorium sanctuaries. Changes in
evangelical creed, cultus, and code all influenced the adoption of the amphitheatre form
and were in turn themselves affected by that form. Though some have argued that the
auditorium space is uniquely suited to liberal religion, this chapter demonstrates that the
meanings attached to amphitheatre sanctuaries crossed theological boundaries and served
to unite liberal and orthodox evangelicals rather than divide them.

Chapter 6 delves further into the relationship of physical church design and decor
to the evangelical conception of the Christian family. The rhetoric and function of these

new "church homes" transcended theological differences and thus offered another link among evangelicals. Extending the concept of the church home into the religious education of children, these churches fulfilled Horace Bushnell's idea of Christian nurture within an institutional setting. Yet this achievement also served to point up tensions between the two predominant evangelical missions: family ministry and spreading the gospel. Focusing on the Sunday school and institutional facilities frequently associated with these churches, chapter 7 unmasks the internal struggle between the public church and the private church that continues to characterize evangelical religion. Finally, chapter 8 discusses the rapid decline in the popularity of the neomedieval auditorium church after the turn of the century, tracing the impact of liturgical movements on liberal Protestants, which resulted in "purer" ritual forms and a reinvigoration of Gothic building principles. One group, revivalist evangelicals, nonetheless continued to erect these buildings. Attempting to attract as many people as possible with frequently theatrical and highly emotional meetings, revivalists like Aimee Semple McPherson used the buildings much as their predecessors had. Thus, the spatial dynamic that had united evangelicals in the nineteenth century became the stronghold of conservatives (and the bane of liberals) in the twentieth. Not surprisingly, as evangelical congregations grew in the 1970s and 1980s, the amphitheatre space enjoyed a significant revival as well. The neomedieval auditorium church of the late nineteenth century has evolved into the megachurch of today. Within this "new" building type, however, the heritage of the evangelical amphitheatre is clearly visible.

For this study, then, church buildings offer a means of accessing cultural changes that might otherwise go overlooked. They are valuable cultural texts that embody the values and meanings important to middle-class evangelical Americans at precisely the period of their greatest influence. It is important, however, to point out that the fruits of this inquiry do not demonstrate an inviolate cause-and-effect relationship between human intention and architectural product. Cultural production and use is hardly a linear process. Instead, this study of church buildings and the congregations that built them reveals instances of both intentional and serendipitous correspondence and situations of both widespread agreement and intense contestation, all of which attest to the diverse motives, the varied strategies, and the mixed reactions of American Protestants as they strove to make sense of a rapidly changing world at a particular time. Ultimately, the significance of these buildings is as examples of this process of making sense.

2

Redefining Clerical and Audience Authority in the Architecture of Urban Revivals

At the heart of any fundamental alteration in ritual space lies iconoclasm. Though the term conjures images of violent destruction—shattered stained glass, defaced statuary—the physical elimination of the old and its replacement with the new accomplished by less-violent means is certainly no less momentous. Born of transformations in religious creed and cultus, iconoclasm instantiates conceptual theological changes in the physical world. In the case of the development of the auditorium church, this process began with a series of radical revisions in ritual practices made by evangelical preachers during the height of the revivals known as the Second Great Awakening, which swept the northern and central United States during the 1820s and 1830s. To engage ever-larger audiences in the spiritual message of salvation and to encourage their participation in revival meetings, revivalists like Charles Grandison Finney initially adopted spellbinding oratory and dramatic delivery techniques. Soon these revivalists broadened their strategies to transform Protestant services through ritual practices called "New Measures." These included the public confession of faith, the altar call, and the individual struggle with the soul, which proceeded publicly upon an "anxious bench" facing the congregation. A similar experimentation with ritual space—that is, with the Protestant church building itself—was a natural outgrowth of the desire to increase audience participation and to extend the revival as widely as possible, yet it led to consequences that the revivalists could not have anticipated.

Religious revivalism does not usually inspire architecture. Revivals are spontaneous and transitory, architecture is deliberate and permanent. The revival is launched with the arrival of a preacher, conversions are witnessed and souls saved, and the preacher then moves on to the next location. The architectural icon of the revival is the tabernacle. Its heritage stretching back to the biblical "tent of meeting" erected by Moses, the tabernacle is temporary, portable, and inexpensive. It is designed to be erected quickly and broken down and transported to the next site with equal rapidity. For Protestant revivalists, a tabernacle might consist of nothing more than a large canvas tent or a hastily constructed wooden shelter covering crude benches. In early nineteenth-century America, many revivalists did not bother to erect a tabernacle at all, opting instead to stage their performances on a cleared field or commons or in an existing building rented for the occasion.

Nevertheless, one might assume that the revivalism of the Second Great Awakening influenced religious space and building precisely because it so profoundly altered religious creeds and the relationship between preacher and audience. Salvation lay in repenting one's sins, accepting the gift of saving grace, and striving to live a virtuous life. Consequently, the revival preacher, unlike orthodox ministers whose role was to educate the faithful on theological points, served, along with the revival audience itself, as prosecutor, confessor, and forgiver, guiding the convert through each step. Revivalism required and fostered an extraordinary intimacy among all of its participants. Yet the spaces of most churches, with their elevated pulpits and cell-like box pews, kept preacher and audience widely separated, consigned to their designated spaces. Although it would seem natural that the revised roles of the preacher and audience would have been articulated in a new physical arrangement within churches, for the most part, this did not happen. Traveling or itinerating across the country, saving souls as they went, revival preachers simply did not stop long enough to construct buildings; instead, they made do with whatever space they could find available.

Yet, as we shall see, a handful of novel revival buildings were in fact constructed in the 1830s, radically transforming, if only for a brief time, the physical relationship among participants. Revivalists in New York City borrowed from theatre architectural strategies to free both preacher and audience from their assigned places. Unexpectedly yet concomitantly, one of these revival buildings was also transformed into a site for religiopolitical performance. Expanding participation in the religious performance taking place within the new ritual setting encouraged audiences to claim the space for agendas other than personal redemption, particularly for the political ones that erupted within the volatile context of the Jacksonian democratic revolution. This chapter will show that as Finney and other revivalists sought to increase the public's participation in services, they produced spaces that transformed the role of audiences in both religious and political contexts. In the process, evangelical religion carved out a new role for itself within the new political economy.

Bringing the Revival to New York: The Free Church Enterprise

The initial American use of the religious amphitheatre began with the architectural iconoclasm of evangelicals favoring utilitarianism over convention in a quest to carve out a new role for religion in the tumult of 1830s New York City. Geographic, population, and economic expansion in the United States followed the 1814 cessation of conflict with England, particularly in seaport towns, and by the late 1820s, New York was expanding rapidly. Native-born citizens of the eastern seaboard as well as immigrants from the British Isles and Western Europe moved into the city, doubling its population between 1810 and 1830 to a total of some 202,000 people.[1] The growing ethnic and economic diversity brought political volatility to the city as a myriad of interest groups, eager to participate in defining the agendas of the nation, coalesced and declared that in a republic, with a government formed by the people, all voices had the right to be heard. Democrats, long thwarted by Federalist interests, gained the presidency in 1828 with the election of Andrew Jackson, legitimating a new constituency defined less by its educated engagement in the public arena (Jürgen Habermas's classic notion of a bourgeois public[2]) and more by its social, intellectual, and ideological diversity. New publics formed and dispersed as their members' shared identities (as Americans, as African Americans, as whites, as laborers, and so on) or issues (nullification, anti-Freemasonry, abolition) waxed and waned. The spaces of these publics included the pages of the new penny press, theatres, merchant and mechanics halls, museums, hotels, and even the streets themselves, the latter readily accommodating both planned and spontaneous assemblies.

At a time when the control of public space and public debate, which traditionally lay with educated social elites, was being energetically tested, the role of religion also came under scrutiny. Denominations that leaned toward ecclesiastical and liturgical formalism and held more highly hierarchical views of social organization found themselves in sympathy with Federalist and Whig political ideologies. Presbyterians, for instance, generally favored strong ecclesiastical structures that guided denominational activities and placed great power in the hands of a fully vetted clergy carefully trained within seminaries. Christian morality, they argued, was a cornerstone of the republic and must be actively expanded and monitored throughout society. Less formalist groups, such as Methodists and Baptists, who encouraged lay leadership and affective worship, agreed that the republic required a firm foundation in Christian morality, but they believed that this would be achieved on a person-by-person basis, not through ecclesiastical institutions imposing moral constraints. These groups, stressing the freedom of the individual, leaned toward the anti-elitist limited government ideology held by the Democratic party. From these general positions arose a spectrum of opinions on the correct role of religion in government, from those of Ultraist activists, who felt government should energetically pursue and enforce Christian agendas, to those of antiformalists, who felt that government had little business pursuing most social agendas, much less religious ones.[3]

In terms of religious practice, or cultus, the formalist and antiformalist styles appealed to strikingly different audiences. Methodists and Baptists seemed to embrace the plebeian as well as the more educated public, using enthusiastic preaching, often in the streets, to attract people to their modest churches and Sunday schools. Presbyterians, on the other hand, having cultivated a more elite status, attracted a more educated, established population. The exclusivity of Calvinist theology, erudite sermonizing, and costly pew rentals determined the worshipers at most Presbyterian churches.

Nevertheless, amid the social and political tumult of New York City, interest in antiformalist evangelism began to develop among even the stodgiest of New York Presbyterian congregations. In the mid-1820s, as revival religion swept through much of rural New York state and the eastern seaboard, a small group of New York City Presbyterian businessmen, sometimes called the Association of Gentlemen, vowed to launch a Presbyterian revival among the laboring classes of New York. Spurred on by what they perceived as a lack of moral grounding among the new population, their mission was at once local and national, individual and social. By converting the poor to Christianity, they believed, the entire population would rise spiritually; by converting the city, the nation would improve. Thus, they reasoned, evangelical religion would improve the social order itself. Their views were articulated in an anonymous article entitled "To Wealthy Presbyterians in the City of New York" in the *New York Evangelist* of 31 July 1830:

Our Savior preached to the poor, and thus fulfilled the predictions of the prophets. In scriptural meaning the poor are the great body of working men. The reason of his direct-ing his efforts to this class is obvious to an intelligent observer. They are the foundation of society; all classes rest upon them. It is so in every age, and every nation; especially in this. The moral tendency is upwards. Enlightening the common people is making the whole mass wise. The poor rise and spread, and pervade, and direct, and govern all. Incidents act upon this state of things. And Christians would act philosophically as well as scripturally, if they imitated their example. (70)

To accomplish this, they turned to antiformalist techniques, offering their own version of enthusiastic religion by inviting avant-garde revivalist preachers to address their congregants. Most important, their new services were free, without pew rentals, and thus available to the entire urban population.[4]

This "free church" scheme, so-named because of the elimination of pew rentals, chal-lenged Presbyterian orthodoxy on three fronts.[5] First, there were economic and political distinctions that discouraged congregations from opening their churches to the urban masses. Most churches depended financially upon pew rentals, and the high fees and resulting elite membership of the major churches precluded the participation of all but the most devout poor, who were relegated to free seats in the galleries.[6] This exclusion of much of the urban population was, in fact, intended. Wealthy congregations, deeply sus-picious of democratizing forces within the country, attempted to insulate themselves within their traditional religious and social institutions. Gardiner Spring, the influential pastor of the elite Brick Presbyterian Church in New York City, lamented the consequences of what he termed "the absurd doctrine of liberty and equality," asserting in an 1843 ser-mon that "the bonds of authority hang loosely around the rising generation" and con-tribute to "the bold assumption of the power of the law by an infuriated mob."[7] Thus, the intended network of Presbyterian churches in which every seat would be free challenged the social vision as well as the cultural authority of established Presbyterian leaders.

The second challenge the devotees of evangelism posed for orthodox leaders was theological. Free-church Presbyterians felt that the best way to attract urban audiences to their worship services was to turn to a method of saving souls that had already proven successful in several rural areas: the revival. Orthodox Presbyterians, however, believed that the Spirit of God directed the spiritual regeneration of individuals, and therefore only the Spirit could instigate a widespread revival. For their part, moderates like Spring and Congregationalist Lyman Beecher viewed revivals as important events, but depen-dent upon God's agency and not legitimately subject to human initiation. Popular re-vivalists and free churchers took a different view, declaring that individuals must exer-cise free will by turning toward God and renouncing sin, thus in effect initiating their own conversion. Moving increasingly toward the Arminian view that individuals could effect their own salvation by pursuing conversion, revivalists gave scant mention to God's agency, relegating it a lesser role than human self-determination and choice. In this view, the duty of clergy was to exhort nonbelievers to change themselves in order to avoid eternal punishment, and revivals, or mass attempts to move human hearts toward God, were seen as an important means by which the process of conversion could be initiated on a large scale.[8] In regard to the growing urban population, traditional Calvinist Pres-byterians saw little purpose in human efforts to improve the spiritual situation of the poor or of even the "respectable" working classes, while the free churchers saw such efforts as absolutely necessary to ushering in the millennium.

Third, revivalist preachers embraced a style of religious expression wholly counter to that of their more orthodox coreligionists. The formalist Presbyterians favored the traditional model of worship based upon edification, the centerpiece of which was a carefully crafted explication, analysis, and application of Scripture. Revivalism, however, was located squarely within antiformalism. Services were participatory exercises in developing the spiritual passions. Sermons were aimed at arousing the affections as a conduit through which the individual could connect with the holiness of God. Audience engagement, strongly encouraged by preachers, ranged from enthusiastic singing to exhorting and giving testimony from the floor to the physical jerking and fainting of camp-meeting fame. Given these challenges to tradition and orthodoxy, free-church revivalism stood poised to rock the very foundations of American Presbyterianism.

Among the new revival preachers, perhaps the most widely hailed was Charles Grandison Finney, whose reputation for saving souls burgeoned with a series of revivals he conducted throughout central New York state from 1825 to 1829. Borrowing both style and substance from the antiformalist Methodists, he preached stirringly in everyday language, attracting thousands in Rome, Utica, Auburn, Troy, and Rochester, as well as in Providence, Philadelphia, and Boston. Hundreds were inspired to convert—to review their lives, repent their sins, and be reborn into a new evangelical Christian lifestyle. In 1828, the Presbyterian Association of Gentlemen brought the revival to New York, inviting Finney to address Spring's Brick Presbyterian Church and Samuel Cox's Laight Street Presbyterian Church. Although these services (or meetings, in revivalist parlance) were well attended, rumors flew soon afterward that Cox had not approved of Finney's speaking from his pulpit. Finney's theology, many charged, was essentially Arminian, denying God's ultimate authority over the salvation of the individual. His sermon "Sinners Bound to Change Their Own Hearts" laid the work of salvation at the feet of humankind. He employed his New Measures to encourage people to take their salvation into their own hands—to repent and to convert. This was strong evidence that he had subordinated divine power to human free will.

To such charges, Finney responded that although God graciously offered humankind salvation through Jesus Christ, human nature was inclined to spurn that offer. The struggle to accept and become a believer, a Christian, involved a soul-wrenching transformation, which individuals must commence for themselves. The role of the revivalist was to initiate this struggle and aid those who grappled with their souls, and his New Measures were designed to do just this. Finney preached in the plain language of his audiences, using his legal training and dramatic abilities to present solid arguments in ways that touched the heart and emotions, including fear, love, guilt, remorse, grief, and longing. He called those who wrestled with their souls to do so publicly on what was called the anxious bench, located very visibly beneath the pulpit, and he exhorted those in the regular seats to pray for those on the bench. He solicited testimony from the floor. He demanded that those who identified themselves as Christians stand at their seats or in the aisles to be counted openly. He allowed women to speak freely and to pray publicly during meetings. He sent confederates among his audiences to search for individuals who seemed to be affected by his sermons, and he led protracted meetings that went on late into the night and resumed the next day, pushing audiences' endurance and participation to extraordinary levels. Each technique was calculated to facilitate the reception of the revival message by the greatest number of people.[9]

Not surprisingly, anti-Finney feeling coalesced among several prominent ministers, even in the face of strong support by the very businessmen whose financial contributions were crucial to their established congregations. As the Association of Gentlemen continued to lobby to bring Finney to New York on a more permanent basis, conservative ministers stalled. Given the vocal opposition, Finney himself was reluctant to attempt an extended revival in New York, but in the fall of 1829, pressed by the association, particularly Anson Phelps, a wealthy importer and manufacturer who vowed to find him his own church, Finney agreed to come.[10]

Given the social and political position of this group of Presbyterians within New York, the selection of Finney was an interesting one. Most of the Association of Gentlemen, having forsaken their native New England for the commercial opportunities of New York, had adopted Presbyterianism on the basis of its shared Calvinist heritage with their native Congregationalism. Though their New Divinity understanding of Calvinism accorded with that of the Presbyterians and provided the foundation upon which they united with that church, many felt constrained by the organizational apparatus of the synod and the Presbytery of Elders, a formalist hierarchy quite different from the independent Congregationalist communities of their heritage. Finney fell midway between these poles. Having been raised in a relatively latitudinarian household, he had attended as a youth a variety of churches, including Presbyterian, Baptist, and Methodist. Although ordained in the Presbyterian church, he too sometimes found himself at odds not only with Presbyterian polity but with doctrinal points as well. Yet there were differences between Finney and the association, too. While the association strongly pursued Christian conversion as a means of improving society by achieving widespread moral reform, Finney's focus was on the salvation of the individual. While Lewis Tappan, who would emerge as a leader within the association, spent the late 1820s distributing literally thousands of moral tracts throughout the city in an effort to eradicate everything from alcohol consumption to sabbath breaking, Finney, as historian Charles Hambrick-Stowe has argued, embraced an evangelicalism that was "relatively ambivalent toward American society."[11] Thus, although the agendas of the association and Finney aligned on the need for conversions, their understandings of the ultimate need for them diverged widely.[12]

Converting the Chatham Theatre

Bringing the revival to New York and establishing Finney in a church on a permanent basis reversed the familiar revival model of preachers going out to the people for one in which the people came to the preacher. The movable tabernacle would be replaced with a permanent, or at least semipermanent, building. In this task, U.S. revivalists were breaking new ground. What would a permanent revival building look like?[13]

To house Finney's earliest New York revivals, Phelps leased a small church, in which he and the association organized the Union Presbyterian Church. The success of revivals was generally measured in conversions, and thus the *New York Evangelist*, published by free-church supporter Joshua Leavitt, reported, "From the fruits of this revival 103 persons have joined this church by profession and 42 by letter—in the whole, 145 souls. . . . Many who have expressed hopes, have united with other churches. . . . More than 200 have been hopefully renewed by the power of the Holy Ghost."[14] But success also brought complications. As they expanded their efforts, forming more free-church congregations throughout lower Manhattan and installing more preachers, space became a critical issue. Rapidly growing congregations needed large rooms, but adequate, affordable, and appropriate meeting space became increasingly difficult to procure.[15]

Renting municipal lecture halls, available churches, and commercial spaces, the free-church association selected buildings on the basis of their audience capacity and their location. They wanted to accommodate large crowds within the commercial districts of the city, but buildings in such places were associated with a wide variety of activities and meanings, and the free-church organizers quickly realized that they needed to consider at least some of those meanings in selecting their sites.[16] For instance, at one point during this period, the association purchased four connecting buildings, intending to unite their second-floor rooms into one large meeting hall. The sale of liquor by grocers leasing the ground floors of the buildings, however, seemed to taint the space for religious services, which ultimately led the church organizers to demand that their renters pledge not to sell alcohol. With the former connection between the space and the illicit sales sufficiently severed, the second-floor space became the home of a new congregation.[17]

While it might be risky to locate a worship space above a former gin joint, the free churchers soon took what would be seen as an even more daring step: moving into a theatre. In the spring of 1832, Lewis Tappan and William Green obtained a ten-year lease on the Chatham Theatre, a playhouse that catered to working-class audiences on Chatham Street just off Pearl Street in lower Manhattan.[18] Here they planned to install Finney permanently and, they hoped, attract even larger audiences. This move, however, plunged the enterprise into the center of the heterogeneous public, resulting in consequences that significantly challenged the role of religious space within the context of U.S. democracy. As we shall see, two intertwined contexts—theatre and popular politics—would shape the free-church enterprise in novel and unexpected ways.

From the start, the free-church organizers recognized the challenge posed by the theatre context. By moving into a theatre, the group had undertaken to establish worship services in a space that had previously held activities widely perceived as immoral.[19] Theatrical performances had been long condemned by devout Protestants for both the deceit upon which acting is based (actors purposely misrepresenting themselves) and the theatre's association with illicit behavior, including rowdiness, drunkenness, and prostitution.[20] In addition to performance space, most theatres of the period contained one or more saloons, a cheaper third tier of seating above patrons' boxes frequented by African Americans and women who were widely perceived as prostitutes, and various private rooms often used by patrons for immoral purposes.[21] The free churchers were well aware that the Chatham Theatre shared the worst of these connotations. Built in 1824, the Chatham had enjoyed a brief period of respectability, offering well-known actors at moderate prices, but a series of disappointing seasons had reduced its ability to attract respectable patrons, and by 1831 the Chatham's reputation had suffered irreparable damage. Its third tier reputedly housed prostitutes, its gallery accommodated a saloon, its fare of equestrian and circus shows was less popular with wealthier theatre patrons, and its admission prices had dropped to levels that marked the establishment as distinctly low on the social scale.[22]

Finney was clearly reluctant to conduct worship in a former den of iniquity, sensitive perhaps to the kind of criticism that might be leveled at him by established preachers in the city. He wondered whether "the location [was] too filthy, etc. for decent people to go there" and whether the "place [could be] made decent inside & out for the worship of God."[23] Writing to allay his fears, Tappan cleverly reinterpreted the negative associations of theatres as he urged Finney to preach in the new chapel:

> The *sensation* that will be produced by converting the place, with slight alterations, into a church will be very great; and curiosity will be excited. . . . By taking this theatre & appropriating it for a church the whole city will talk of it, wonder and inquire [illegible]. We then have secured the attention of a vast multitude, and the measures subsequently taken will be made known to them. Strangers will be desirous of visiting this place, will talk about it when they go home; & they will be stimulated to similar efforts. It will have the effect [that] storming a redoubt, or taking cannon & turning them upon the enemy, has in an army. The time seems to have come to take bold & decided measures. (emphasis in original)[24]

Recasting this potential drawback as a fundamental strength, Tappan reveled in the singularity of bringing Christianity into this bastion of Satan. For him, taking on the evil enemy where he lived would attract attention to the enterprise, generating publicity and thus assuring its success as curious visitors, potential converts all, entered the doors.

Tappan's militaristic language emphasized the extent to which meaning and authority were at stake in moving into the theatre. If Christianity could transform a theatre, surely it had the power to transform any degenerate soul. The free churchers immediately launched a campaign to "convert" or alter the meanings associated with the Chatham Theatre. Stories of the spiritual conversion of the place were circulated, countering the immoral connotations of the theatre and redefining the building as powerfully Christian. Tappan testified that during lease negotiations, he and Green had convinced the representative of the Chatham's owners, one Reverend Dr. Janeway, of the sinfulness of his involvement in a theatrical enterprise. Similarly, theatre lessee William Blanchard, a circus manager, was so overcome by Tappan and Green's suasion that he wept and agreed to assist in converting the building to religious use.[25] The Reverend Joseph Thompson, writing about the chapel a generation later and familiar with the oral traditions within the free-church movement, maintained that the very first prayers offered in one saloon-cum-prayer room were made by a reformed former actor who had once appeared on the Chatham stage. Moreover, Thompson claimed, within three months of the conversion of the theatre into a chapel, "not one of the thirty grog shops that once flourished around the building" remained.[26] Apocryphal though they may be, these stories illustrate the process of negotiating meaning, as they placed into public discourse the contention that the theatre that had once been a sinful place had been fully converted into a spiritually powerful site, the Chatham Street Chapel.[27]

While the immoral nature of the theatre was a readily visible challenge to the free churchers, the second context, democratic politics, was perhaps not so easy to discern, for it grew from a secondary set of theatre associations common to the period. By locating in the Chatham, the free churchers unwittingly positioned themselves in the center of populist politics. Theatre in New York was mixed-class entertainment that brought working-class actors and audiences together with wealthy patrons. Nob and mechanic alike socialized, watched each other, openly judged performances, and interrupted the action by loudly interjecting comments, throwing refuse, shouting unpopular performers off the stage, or demanding numerous encores from popular ones. Actors were viewed as somewhat akin to servants, duty bound to entertain those who could ante up the price of a ticket. Thus audiences held great power over stage performers and theatre managers. What audiences demanded, the nascent entertainment industry tried to provide. The situation accorded well with democratic politics. Given the theatrical focus on popular desires, it is not surprising that the theatres in which elites and laborers met provided a literal stage for political outbursts. Demonstrations against elite privilege and calls for broader participatory democracy united with denunciations of pro-British actors and productions, rendering the theatre a critical site for public discourse. Further, theatre managers' choices of which stories to represent and who to perform them were inherently political. In the volatile context of contemporary struggles over alternative visions of the United States, many managers, including those at the Chatham, realized that politics sold tickets, and so they decorated their buildings with patriotic signs and symbols of U.S. democratic politics. The stage of the Chatham, for instance, proudly displayed busts of Washington, Jefferson, Franklin, and Jackson, and a bas-relief above the proscenium depicted two huge figures supporting an eagle, replicating the national coat of arms (fig. 2.1).[28] Democratic leaders encouraged the creation and performance of American plays while Whig patrons tended to favor British and European plays and actors. Disruption of the performances of British actors suspected of insulting U.S. causes was common, and during the 1830s and 1840s, as the sociopolitical stakes that grounded

Fig. 2.1. Chatham Theatre, New York City. 1825. Lithograph after Alexander Jackson Davis. Courtesy of the Emmet Collection, Miriam and Ira D. Wallach Division of Art, Prints, and Photographs, New York Public Library, Astor, Lenox and Tilden Foundation.

these demonstrations multiplied, struggles over the stage increasingly disgorged into the streets. Theatres like the Park, the Bowery, and the Chatham served as sites for demonstrations of working-class dissatisfaction, Jacksonian critiques of privilege, and embattled republicanism.[29]

Within this context, the occupation of the Chatham Theatre by Presbyterians, who were usually thought of as Whiggish, elite, and formalist, might easily have been construed as an ecclesiastical gambit in an escalating sociopolitical power struggle. Indeed, given the efforts of such free church men as Lewis Tappan to impose civil sanctions in support of Sabbatarianism, a position opposed by many working people—laborers, artisans, and entrepreneurs alike—strong disapproval must have been expected from Chatham Theatre regulars. Initially this did not materialize, however, as the free-church movement—with its significantly modified Calvinist theology and antiformalist style—was also something of a populist enterprise, despite its Presbyterian label and its leaders from within the commercial elite. The free-church services and vernacular preaching allowed wide participation, and the antiformalist nature of the free church's separation from established Presbyterian churches reflected democratic ideology in a religious context. Furthermore, the revival audience mirrored much of the social and economic heterogeneity of the street, with the exclusion only of the dissolute, the criminal, and the violent. Describing their intended audience, Tappan argued that the location would be a signal factor in attracting a diverse crowd: "Chatham St. is the greatest thoroughfare in the city next to Broadway, and the middling class of society, be they inhabitants or strangers pass & repass [herein?] this street. By middling I do not mean the vagabond classes, but the substantial working interests." For Tappan, the free-church movement was formed to remedy "the almost total exclusion of the poor from the Presbyterian and Dutch churches," and "principle [sic] efforts are made to bring in the neglected, the poor, the emigrant, and those who in the arrangements in the old churches, have been almost entirely overlooked." Though the end being sought was to impose a specific moral agenda upon the masses, the free churchers opened up the Christian big tent to all who might wander in.[30]

The Chatham Street Chapel succeeded in attracting a spectrum of working people from among the middle and lower classes. Businesspeople and property owners came, but so did other generally upwardly mobile groups, including clerks, mechanics, and artisans, both white and black. As in most Protestant churches of the period, women were predominant in the pews. This socially disparate group of people shared not only their search for salvation but also their belief in and aspirations to respectability. As reflected in their insistence upon the elimination of pew fees, the free-church organizers did not view the categories of *poor* and *respectable* as mutually exclusive.[31] Itself a broadly populist aspiration, the notion of respectability encompassed new sets of behaviors rather than explicit class or political identities. The desire for respectability marked both urban mechanic and rural farmer, both Whig and Democrat. For those seeking such respectability through church membership, the religious landscape offered a number of alternatives. The Methodists, very successful in evangelizing among the poor, were upstarts in the city, making inroads into the religious landscape from the grassroots level and relying heavily on emotional religious expression. Yet their origins and antiformalist methods afforded them only the most tenuous claim to respectability. The Baptists, longer established in the city than the Methodists yet similarly successful among the poor, were working hard to solidify their own respectability, but this would require shedding a number of their traditional practices, such as love feasts and foot washing, which carried "low other" connotations.[32]

Finney's revivals, then, negotiated a middle ground between the less-than-fully-respectable Methodists and Baptists and the excessively refined (and therefore equally suspect) formalist Presbyterians. Finney's experiential brand of religion allowed, indeed required, expressions of emotion and audience participation, antiformalist practices that were precisely what the Presbyterian orthodoxy objected to in his meetings. Nevertheless, by remaining under the aegis of the Presbyterians, the meetings maintained their respectability, for the denomination itself was inherently respectable. At the same time, Finney's middle-ground, pietistic religion condemned the complacence and materialism that often accompanied "refinement." While the elite members of Brick Presbyterian Church might show off their finery at Sunday services, for instance, Finney railed against luxury of all kinds, denouncing extravagances in clothing or residence as obstacles to true religion. Moreover, his theology softened the Calvinist belief in a predestined elect by implying a self-determination within a religious context similar to that emerging in a political context. Finney's middle-ground religious respectability thus echoed democratic egalitarianism, whether or not he announced the point from the pulpit.[33]

Even the name, Chatham Street Chapel, was born of the desire to claim this negotiated middle ground. When deciding upon a name, Finney had suggested the term *tabernacle*, harking back to the revival tabernacles of Wesley and Whitefield in England. The common associations of the term with Methodism and with impermanence, however, may have been off-putting to the free-church organizers (who were stable Prebyterians, after all). In any case, Tappan abruptly announced that the group did not favor it. The free churchers, influenced by the New York Sacred Music Society, which had contributed to the renovation of the building, considered naming it Chatham Hall or Chatham Chapel, but they ultimately selected Chatham Street Chapel. While little explanation of the reasoning behind these negotiations over the name exists, it is clear that the Sacred Music Society preferred the secular title of *hall* and the free churchers did not want the building to be called a *church*, perhaps due to its formalist, ecclesiastical overtones. In the end, the revivalists, eschewing the High Church *church* and the Low Church *tabernacle*, ideologically located the new establishment in a middle territory with the title *chapel*, a term sufficiently religious to announce a pious intent and permanence while not so ecclesiastical as to suggest elaborate refinement.[34]

The Chatham Street Chapel, thus wrest from the clutches of the entertainment business and repositioned in the context of revivalism and respectability, would serve as a new religious middle ground. Because pious respectability held a strong attraction for wealthy and poor alike, the Chatham Street Chapel quickly became a popular site of evangelical revivalism.

Clerical and Audience Power in the Chatham Street Chapel

While this conversion of the meanings associated with the Chatham as theatre was accompanied by some remodeling of the physical space itself, the physical alterations disrupted the original theatre arrangement only minimally. By maintaining many of the theatre's original features, the free churchers unwittingly launched an experiment that would eventually transform Protestant architecture. While Protestant churches to this point had favored the elevated placement of the minister in a raised pulpit indicating his authority and proximity to God relative to the assembled audience, the theatre-cum-chapel retained the prominent features of the relationship between the actor and the paying audience in which the performer had use of a large stage to attract the attention of the spectator and the audience's needs were paramount. This arrangement, as we shall see, generated something new in the relationship between preacher and congregation by creating a space that significantly altered traditional expressions of religious authority.

Built in 1824, the Chatham Street building articulated the social hierarchy of the New York theatregoing public in spatial terms. The original auditorium, described as "a semi-circle of forty-five feet span, from one side of the stage to the other, and thirty-one feet deep, from the centre box to the stage," could hold about 2,000 spectators squeezed in closely.[35] As in all theatres of the period, the social positions of audience members within the room were transparent because the seating recapitulated social rank. Three tiers of boxes lined the auditorium, the first and second of which accommodated those who could afford their significantly higher ticket price. These patrons could peer down upon theatregoers seated in the pit, as the main floor was called, who paid far less. While the boxes had individual chairs and easy access to private rooms and the saloon, the pit offered only crude backless benches, which extended the width of the room with no central aisle. Comfort and elevation were markers of wealth, while inconvenience and a backache were the conditions of the less well-off.

Yet things had begun to change even before the theatre's conversion to its use as a church. An 1826 remodeling had aimed at moderating the social dichotomy in order to attract more respectable female patrons. An advertisement proudly announced, "The former unpleasant arrangement of obliging ladies to walk across the seats, has been remedied—the benches are now hung with hinges, which can be raised so as to form an avenue to the front row."[36] Subsequent renovations attempted to increase audience comfort. Enhanced ornamentation, ventilation, and the creation of a private garden for patrons' use were all aimed at attracting a more "middling" or respectable audience. The renovations failed in their purpose, however, and, as has been noted, the Chatham's reputation continued to decline.[37] When the free churchers took over the space, they also inherited a legacy of transparent social status within the house.

In addition to the inscription of social rank within the audience room, the Chatham, like all theatres, created a distinctive spatial relationship between the audience members and the actor on the stage. In the theatre, pleasing the audience members was paramount; their desires had to be met. Plays were selected for their topical and patriotic appeal, and actors, similarly, had to satisfy the demands of politically engaged audiences. Multiple amenities were provided. The house lamps, though dim, burned throughout performances so that audiences members became both viewers and performers in a spectacle, which might rival that on the stage. In this setting, audiences held great influence, listening to or ignoring actors on the stage as they wished, voting with their feet or even shouting down a performance if they were displeased.

Yet actors could influence their audiences through their performances. A talented actor could mesmerize the audience, and American audiences lionized those performers who could.[38] Yet this type of authority or power rested not only on the skills of the performer but on the goodwill of the audience, which had to choose to watch and listen. Aiding the actor in attracting and maintaining the audience's attention were architectural features like the stage, the ornamentation, and the proscenium arch. The proscenium arch, developed along with perspective stages in the seventeenth century, acted like a frame around a picture, directing the audience's gaze into its confines and marking the boundaries between the framed (imaginary) space of the stage and the exterior (real) space of the hall. A powerful tool in directing audience attention, it also clarified the relative importance of the spaces within the room. Within the boundaries of the proscenium, only the world of performance existed.[39]

Although the free-church organizers inherited this complex set of relations among the various groups as they signed the lease on the Chatham Theatre, they decided not to gut the building but to "preserve the *form* be [sic] of a theatre as much as possible," in Tappan's words (emphasis in original).[40] Most significantly, the free churchers retained the stage. The Chatham founders, cognizant that they would need to rent the space to other groups in order to replace the funds lost through the elimination of pew rentals, arranged to do so with a variety of organizations, foremost among them the Sacred Music Society. This large vocal group would require a sizable stage, and thus from its outset the chapel was intended as a performance hall as well as a revival space.

This decision resulted in a significant alteration of relationships between minister and congregation within this building. For services, a portable lectern most likely was placed in the middle of the stage for preaching purposes, and Finney's trademark anxious bench was set below the stage. The result, of course, was that perhaps for the first time in U.S. religious architecture, the preacher was fully released from the cage of the elevated pulpit and given the physical performance space that a secular orator commanded. Although the visual link to a higher authority was severed, the preacher now had access to the performative authority of the actor.

The free churchers did renovate the audience area somewhat, but builder Joseph Ditto, a member of the new congregation, built upon and enhanced, rather than destroyed, the theatrical features of the space to create a room that effectively facilitated the audience's reception of the service. The main floor of the original theatre had been constructed at a higher elevation than most of the period to provide better views for its occupants, and Ditto improved upon this by inclining the floor from just below the stage to what had been the first tier of boxes. The sloped floor created an amphitheatre effect, which allowed people to see over the heads of those seated in front of them. Pew slips, rather than boxes, were installed on the main floor, where the bulk of the audience sat, and aisles traversed the rows of pews, allowing easy movement through the room, particularly from the seats to the anxious bench.[41] In addition to its unobstructed sightlines, the small auditorium also had good acoustics. As one writer from the *New York Evangelist* observed during the opening services, "The speaker's voice was distinctly heard in all parts of the house."[42] Being seated quite near the pulpit and being able to easily see and hear the full proceedings, audiences experienced a very intimate service. Just as in the theatre, the chapel's architecture focused its audience's attention on the stage, now the framed world of spiritual regeneracy. The design of the space announced that the audience's needs—to see, to hear, to participate—were of the highest priority. In the theatre, of course, paying patrons had always expected spaces that catered to their desires and enhanced their interaction with the performances. In the church, however, such audience sovereignty was new and consistent with both antiformalist revivalism and populist democracy.[43]

In preserving the theatre form, then, the free-church Presbyterians also preserved much of the spatial power dynamics of the original theatre. At the same time, the preacher who occupied the chapel stage had to be guaranteed the attention of and control over the audience, although given the self-selected audience of revival meetings, maintaining clerical control was not likely to be a problem. In addition, the new renovations, particularly the inclined floor and the pew backs, somewhat worked against the prerogatives of the theatre patrons by heightening the congregation's focus on the stage and encouraging them to remain comfortably seated and facing forward for the duration. They also gave the preacher an unobstructed view of each individual in the audience, a definite advantage for New Measures preachers like Finney, who often addressed audience members individually and by name. He could maintain eye contact with individuals and convey approval or censure as necessary through his facial expressions. Only those seated in the upper tiers would have been able to hide from his gaze, and Finney placed assistants throughout the tiers to monitor behavior and encourage those who seemed to be affected by the preaching.[44]

Within the Chatham Street Chapel, audience and preacher in effect shared power in remarkable ways. The stage itself was a powerful tool in the hands of a skilled preacher, allowing him much greater freedom in using his entire body to convey messages than did the traditional elevated pulpit. Released from the confines of a pulpit, a preacher could pace the width of the room and use expressive physical gestures to communicate with the audience, thus creating a far more dramatic presentation than was possible in a traditional church. At least as significant to the performer's ability to connect with the audience, however, was the proscenium arch that framed the stage. The eighteenth century had seen the wide popularization of the proscenium theatre throughout Europe, a phenomenon that architectural historian Michael Schwarzer has linked to the growth of a new, self-aware bourgeois social class, which sought not simply entertainment but moral lessons in the theatre. "The new public theatre," he writes, "placed critical value on the spectator's private contemplation of the enormity of human life as depicted on the stage."[45] This function well served the revivalists' agenda, for achieving a similar private contemplation of the salvation of one's soul was their very goal. The elaborate proscenium that framed the Chatham stage drew the audience's attention into its confines, visually indicating the importance of the performance taking place within its expanse.[46] Within the frame, the revival preacher's intention was to engage audiences in the worship spectacle. Finney's New Measures, born of the belief that regeneration occurred unexpectedly (on the spot, as it were) in the fierce struggle of conversion, were designed precisely to instigate and facilitate that battle. The whole purpose of revival meetings was to initiate the conversion process, to convince sinners of the need to repent, to encourage them to publicly acknowledge their situation, and to aid their journey to conversion. The Chatham architecture, with its theatre auditorium, stage, and proscenium, assisted the preacher in communicating his message to those gathered, helped to underscore the profundity of the event, and encouraged the audience's active participation. In comparison to traditional church buildings, which isolated the minister from the audience and showed little regard for the worshipers' needs, the audience-oriented chapel effectively sustained Finney's New Measures. Thus, this new space itself may have functioned as an unacknowledged new measure.

The unusual worship space of this former theatre, therefore, redefined clerical authority in terms of personality and charisma. While Finney addressed his audience wrapped in the cloak of his prestige as a renowned preacher, the stage setting designed to privilege the authority of the stage performer also worked to establish and maintain the power of Finney's intense personality and message. And Finney was nothing if not intense; like an actor, and in an actor's setting, Finney manipulated his performance and his audience with finesse. Gesturing with arms and body, he whispered some words and shouted others ("hell" being a favorite); dragging his piercing gaze from face to face, he scanned the crowd for sinners, addressed individual sinners by name, and excoriated them publicly.[47] The Reverend Henry Ward of Boston condemned a performance of Finney's at Utica in 1826, writing, "He has talents, unquestionable talents, but no heart. He feels no more than a mill-stone . . . acting a cold, calculating part. . . . His tones of voice, his violent, coarse, unfeeling utterance, his abject groanings, his writhing of his body as if in agony, all testify that he is a hypocrite, and yet I try not to be uncharitable."[48] But theatricality, whether sincere or fabricated, was critical to the success of revival preachers, who stood before diverse and untested audiences and could not draw upon traditional sources of clerical authority. For revivalists, as for actors, authority on stage derived not from erudition nor from connections to elite society or respected institutions but from charisma—from their popularity as speakers, from their ability to personally connect with audiences, from their authenticity and sincerity, and from the skill of their performances. Finney was a master of performance.[49]

Such charismatic power differs from traditional clerical authority in that it requires the consent of the audience. Audiences bestow charisma through their acknowledgment of it. In the theatre of the early nineteenth century, if audience members liked a stage performance, they could force the actor to repeat it several times; if not, they similarly could shout for changes in the performance or hound the individual off the stage. Further, they could vote with their pocketbooks, choosing to pay to see their favorites while ignoring others. Revivalists too needed the consent of audiences, for without it—without the crowds, without the mass conversions—they simply could not be revivalists. Moreover, revival preachers like Finney preached a message geared toward convincing those assembled of their own responsibility for their eternal souls, a message that at its heart bred antinomianism and necessarily brought traditional clerical authority into question. Indeed, evangelical preachers relinquished the cloak of traditional authority as they postulated conversion based upon personal struggle with one's own conscience guided by God. Similarly, they gave up the cloak of intellectual authority as they rebuked the educated ministry and exhorted extemporaneously in the vernacular. Instead, they derived their authority from the audience's fascination with their personal magnetism or ability to inspire. While Finney would have been the last to claim that such attributes were of divine origin in the traditional sense of *cháris*, or grace, what his followers may have thought is another matter. Some did indeed feel he was "more blessed with the Spirit of God than any of us."[50] In any event, Finney's popularity was clearly linked to his personal magnetism and dramatic performance. His passion in the pulpit convinced people of his conviction and dedication to a holy agenda, while his stern, unyielding persona attested to his moral rigor. The space of the Chatham Street Chapel served to enhance Finney's power by intensifying his performance and authoritarian strategies—by underscoring and enhancing his charisma. Commanding this type of social and religious power, Finney had no fear that his potentially antinomian message would result in challenges to himself as the messenger.

At the same time, his message of the equality of all who admitted their sinfulness and became true Christians located his charismatic power squarely within the increasingly popular democratic political ideology. It also appealed to the emerging philosophy of rugged individualism, as charismatic power rested upon individual effort, not social position or hereditary privilege. Thus, using the power of personality to deliver an antinomian message to audiences gathered in a space that privileged no one but accommodated all, Finney and the free churchers created in the Chatham Street Chapel a religious space that effectively merged popular culture, political ideology, religious belief, and worship practice.[51] In this novel arena, dramatic performance and charisma were the preacher's strongest tools, not an authority based on hierarchical sources, and audience consent and satisfaction were the measures of his success. Endorsing audience sovereignty while at the same time facilitating preaching performance and charismatic power, this new religious space articulated a model of shared religious authority that was highly attractive to Americans struggling with the construction of authority within the public sphere. This was religious space designed for a new, democratic society.

Chatham Theatre and Chapel as Contested Ground

The membership of the Chatham Street Chapel rose steadily during the months of Finney's residency, reaching in 1834 a total of 426 members, including 302 who were admitted on their own profession of faith and 106 who were baptized at the chapel.[52] Under Finney's direction, the chapel attracted people who shared aspirations of respectability and a strongly evangelical outlook and who were attracted by his demanding message: acknowledge sin, repent, and live a Christian life defined by moral rigor. Perfectionism infused much of Finney's preaching at the chapel. Admonitions against elaborate dress, strong drink, and stimulants like coffee and tea, along with moral tales about breaking the sabbath, filled his talks to an audience that was concerned with becoming and being "respectable."

Finney aimed his messages of repentance, conversion, and perfectionism at the individual; his calls were for personal rectification within the sphere of private life.[53] Insofar as the revival meetings taking place within the chapel maintained their focus on the individual, the chapel itself could be construed as a newly privatized site. However, just as a public identity developed for the middle-class private household as a result of its growing interaction with public economic structures,[54] the publicity of this religious site increased as it became intertwined with various political economies. As we shall see, within two years of the Chatham Street Chapel's founding, disparate ideologies would result in a bloody struggle over the space. This struggle grew in part from the novelty of the chapel itself as well as from its ever-growing public character and its markedly heterogeneous usership.

From its opening, the chapel's users were characterized by racial and political diversity. The chapel supported itself through collections and rental income from the several groups booking its relatively large assembly hall.[55] The all-white Sacred Music Society; the General Trades Union of the City of New York, another all-white and ideologically democratic organization; and the Phoenix Society, an organization of blacks and whites offering educational services to African Americans, all held lectures in the building. At least one black Methodist congregation also held services and meetings in the chapel. In addition, this house of antiformalist preaching soon became identified with several reform associations that used the building. The American Anti-Slavery Society organized within the chapel, as did the New York Female Moral Reform Society. In the first week of May 1834, twelve societies held anniversary meetings in the chapel, including the American Tract Society.[56] Though the purposes of these societies conformed well with Tappan and the association's goal of Christianizing society, some of their activities contrasted with Finney's general dislike for religious involvement in public issues. Nevertheless, the chapel's tenants—blacks, whites, laborers, musicians, reformers—constituted a significantly diverse public, and the chapel took its place as an important site for public assembly within the political landscape of New York.

Offering this new type of public space also entailed certain risks, as was discovered in 1834, when the chapel gained political notoriety as a result of its association with the explosive topic of colonization. Colonization, an attempt to solve the social and racial issues surrounding slavery by establishing colonies for black Americans in Liberia, held a strong attraction for many white Protestants, including many clergy to whom it represented a far less disruptive means of social change than abolition.[57] In the late 1820s, even many abolitionists, including William Lloyd Garrison, placed their faith in this solution. By the early 1830s, however, opposition to colonization had coalesced among African Americans, who presented an array of economic, social, and political arguments exposing its faults that convinced some whites of the limitations of this "solution"; Garrison, for instance, abandoned the position by 1832. The chapel had been identified with the antislavery cause since 1832, through the influence of Arthur Tappan, Lewis's brother and one of the founders of the American Anti-Slavery Society, but in 1834 their sponsorship of public discussions of colonization within the chapel significantly raised the political stakes.[58] Bringing together a new heterogeneous public, the anticolonization meetings of the summer of 1834 proved highly controversial within the tumultuous political landscape of New York City and ultimately served as the catalyst that ignited a simple disagreement over which group had reserved the chapel for a particular evening into a full-blown conflagration over who had legitimate claim to the chapel itself.

On 9 and 10 May of that year, the Anti-Slavery Society hosted a public examination (a formal question-and-answer session) of Thomas C. Brown, a free African-American carpenter from Charleston, South Carolina, who had recently returned to New York after living in Liberia for fourteen months. His reports of depreciating land prices, rising debt, corruption among Colonization Society agents, and high levels of sickness and death exposed realities that neither colonizationists nor pro-South whites wanted to hear. Hecklers in the audience booed and hissed, attempting to shout down the speaker.[59] Shortly after this meeting, charges arose that the Anti-Slavery Society had been given special preference by the chapel association by being allowed to hold the meeting even though it meant supplanting a meeting on the state of religion in France, which had been previously scheduled. This prompted the *New York Evangelist* to publish a special supplement denying the charge and making public a transcript of the proceedings. Resentment was clearly brewing with respect to the Chatham Street Chapel's involvement in the slavery question.

Two months later, on 4 July, hecklers crying "treason" and accusing the organization of desiring to overthrow the Union broke into the chapel to disrupt an address by David Paul Brown, who was also speaking against colonization to the American Anti-Slavery Society. Three days later, members of the Sacred Music Society, apparently unaware that their regular meeting had been moved to a different location, arrived at the chapel to find it occupied by a meeting of African-American Methodists. A fight broke out, resulting in the overturning of pews and the beating of several male and female congregants. Two evenings later, a crowd gathered at the chapel, bent upon breaking up another rumored antislavery meeting. Finding the gates closed and the building empty, they headed to the Bowery Theatre, where they harassed an English actor who had been rumored to have used "some disrespectful expression towards Americans." They then moved on to Lewis Tappan's home, which they ransacked and looted. Thus began four days of intense race rioting in the city, which left many African Americans dead, scores of blacks and whites wounded, and an enormous amount of property damaged.[60]

In what was in part a turf battle, the chapel served as a lightning rod for white fears about race, economic conditions, mobility, job competition, democracy, and control over the destiny of the city and the nation. This battle was fought in the physical public spaces of the city—in the chapel, in the streets, in other churches, and in homes and workplaces—as well as in the discursive public arena of the penny press. The *Journal of Commerce*, the *Commercial Advertiser*, and the *Courier and Enquirer* deplored the use of the chapel for anticolonization and mixed-race meetings, which allowed blacks and whites to mingle together. These practices, they charged, encouraged abolition and thus threatened the Union, amounting to treason. The *Journal of Commerce* concluded its report on the first disruption:

> The lease of the Chatham Chapel was purchased, and the house changed from a theatre to a place of worship, and dedicated to the service of Almighty God, by the contributions of Christians, many of whom are friends of Colonization. The money was paid to procure the house, for purposes well known and specified. These abolition contests and black assemblies were not part of the design, but are in derogation of it, and result at least in the desecration of the place. The blacks have other places of worship, and there is no reason for their assembling in Chatham Chapel, unless it be to brow-beat public opinion, and exasperate the community.[61]

According to the *Journal*, the chapel's religious character had been compromised not just by its use for anticolonization purposes but by its use by African Americans. In the paper's opinion, a pollution of holy ground had taken place. Chapel leaders, including both Tappan and Finney, would have agreed that a desecration had taken place, but for them it was the violence itself that constituted the desecration. The abolitionist paper *The Emancipator* quickly countered that anticolonizationists and African-American groups had also contributed to the chapel and thus had as much of a claim on it as anyone, and the *New York Evangelist* carried lengthy commentaries supporting the black chapel users.[62]

Thus the debate broke out over who had legitimate right to the chapel: the abolition-ist chapel leaders or those who opposed abolitionism or supported colonization (this latter group comprised some Presbyterian congregations, much of the Whig commer-cial population, and many Jacksonian Democrats). The very public nature of the Chatham Street space—its former secular purpose as a theatre, its miraculous conversion, and its open-door rental policy—made it vulnerable to such convergences of public discussion. The chapel had purposely invited public use and provided a forum for the expression of disparate views. Because the chapel had previously been a public theatre attended by audiences asserting their influence within its walls, it was drawn more easily into the sociopolitical fray than it probably would have been had it simply been a traditional church building. Moreover, the earlier Chatham Theatre, with its statue of the new president on its stage and the national coat of arms above its proscenium, had embraced the cause of Jacksonian democracy. For working-class whites to have this space appro-priated not just by religious revivalists but by free blacks, whom they perceived as both socially inferior and in competition for their jobs and livelihoods, was like touching flame to gasoline. But it was not only these "outsiders" to the evangelical agenda who felt justified in claiming the chapel for their own purposes. As the violent response of the Sacred Music Society members to the black users demonstrated, those who rented the new chapel did not necessarily agree on political issues, particularly race. Despite the re-ligious purpose of the meeting site, the heterogeneous public associated with the Chatham Street Chapel was potentially as volatile as any street corner assembly.

More precisely, the chapel's notoriety within the political environment of New York City stemmed from its radical reconfiguration of civil society. The revival agenda's need for the financial benefits of building rental fees had invited the highly varied and ra-cially mixed clientele of the chapel and resulted in a newly constructed public unimag-inable a generation earlier. The public of the Chatham Street Chapel, which was brought together by a fundamental belief in public assembly and participation in civic issues, merged with what Jürgen Habermas has called the bourgeois public and the plebeian public.[63] Or at least it attempted to do so. The free churchers, implying or perhaps simply assuming that the building itself was neutral ground available to anyone who could pay the rent, had offered up the potential for the reconfiguration of radical partici-patory democracy. In their mind, widespread political participation could be regulated by evangelical self-control and moral discipline. Civil authority, the theatre-cum-chapel space suggested, could be shared among leaders (on the stage) and a right-thinking, disciplined public (in the seats). The chapel leadership demonstrated what historian James Stewart has argued is a strikingly modern sensibility by placing black and white users on an equal footing, and this is precisely why it became a target in the turbulent racial politics of the period. It not only was an "amalgamation" church, the bane of white racists, but it was a color-blind church, which treated, or attempted to treat, all users alike under the aegis of revival religion.[64]

The innovative church architecture of the Chatham Street Chapel played a signifi-cant role in this social, political, and religious dynamic. While elevated pulpits and box pews announced a rigid top-down type of authority, the chapel's arrangement implied something new. A black man speaking from the stage carried the same type of authority as a white man, that is, authority linked to merit and ability rather than to traditional social hierarchies. Racial politics, however, are complex and motivations vary. While some antislavery whites welcomed a shift in authority in order to challenge the discriminatory racial policies in the country, those who opposed abolitionism were often eager to effect such a shift in authorities to strengthen their own political power but not to change traditional racial hierarchies. Since religious authority remained a stronghold for traditional, hierarchical power, the importance of Chatham Street Chapel's novel and authority-challenging space lay in the fact that it was religious space. While a number of lecture halls might similarly serve the function of housing public assemblies (and they did), the possibility that religious activism in a new egalitarian religious space could overturn traditional racial hierarchies raised the political stakes significantly. At the same time, however, it also narrowed the public nature of demonstrations like those of July 1834. Those rioters, perhaps aware that focusing their actions exclusively on the chapel would not effectively demonstrate the encompassing nature of their discontent, quickly left the chapel for other venues: the homes of abolitionists and African Americans and several black churches and businesses within the city.

The move into the former theatre, done more out of pragmatism and the need for space than by design, serendipitously exposed revivalists to the many advantages of theatre space. These advantages—a large meeting room, good sightlines and acoustics, a strong visual focus, more physical freedom for preachers, and greater intimacy between preacher and audience—coincided with and helped advance the practices of revival worship, the religious agenda of individual moral responsibility, and the charismatic power of preachers. Highly democratizing, these same features, along with the need to share the space with other civic and religious organizations, served to construct the chapel as a new type of institution within the urban landscape, one that lent a privatized, religious, ideological support to essentially public activities. By opening its stage to the sweep of public debate on political and social issues, the chapel carved out a new role for religion within the public sphere. Quoting historian David Zaret's observations on seventeenth-century popular religion's role in "cultivating . . . the critical, rational habits" that characterize the bourgeois public sphere, the chapel also "legitimated the reasonableness of public opinion as a forum and arbiter for criticism and debate."[65] Revival religion's association with politics suggested a "public sphere of religion"; its "participants saw it in terms of 'critical reflections of a public competent to form its own judgments.'"[66] In essence, the practice of revival preaching, the physical form of the building, and the site intimated that "conscience and opinion were both associated with public reason" and were "accessible to the common lay person."[67] The legitimacy of the endeavors of the various heterogeneous publics that used the chapel was confirmed by the religious character of the space, which in turn became identified with their particular agendas. For the chapel organizers, the energy of the space itself could be seen as advancing their own religiopolitical agenda, for under the aegis of evangelical religion and individual conversion, they believed, social class, race, and political and economic loyalties would dissolve into a single public devoted to the Kingdom.

This utopian vision was not to be achieved, however. The riots of the summer of 1834 represented the limits at which the revival could sustain itself within the politically dynamic space of the Chatham Street Chapel. When agendas and claims on the space conflicted, violence erupted. Thinking, perhaps, that the chapel's respectability and its founders' hopes for revival religion as a political force had been jeopardized by the association with civil disorder, the congregation took steps within the year to construct a new building.

Corporate Identity in the Broadway Tabernacle

Within three years of moving into the chapel, free-church leaders George Cragin, William Green, Isaac M. Dimond, and S. W. Benedict laid plans to found a new free church "especially for Mr. Finney."[68] This new building, which would be called the Broadway Tabernacle and which Finney himself would help to design, would be specifically created for revival meetings. Finney explained, "I had observed the defects of churches in regard to sound; and was sure that I could give the plan of a church in which I could easily speak to a much larger congregation than any house would hold that I had ever seen."[69] This building, then, would be the architectural culmination of his years of experience as a revivalist. But by the time the building was complete, the revival was, for all practical purposes, over. The Broadway Tabernacle, however, would serve other purposes: as the congregational home for the new Sixth Free Church and as a site for gatherings of the many moral reform societies that had been renting the Chatham Street Chapel. This new revival space, leaving behind the goal to convert the masses, would acquire a fresh mission: formulating a new religious code out of the vision of the Kingdom that had energized the public engagement of the Chatham Street Chapel.

A renegotiation of mission was evident in a number of ways. First, the desire to claim a solid respectability informed the discussion of where to locate the new Broadway Tabernacle. Broadway Avenue, the popular thoroughfare that attracted the city's most prestigious businesses and institutions, would be the new location and would give the site its name. Unlike the 1832 decision to locate Finney's first revival church in the heart of the commercial district in order to attract the unconverted, the decision to move to Broadway broadcast entirely new messages about the congregation. Attending a church "on the avenue" indicated respectability and refinement and would thus solidify the new community identity as far different from that associated with the Chatham location. Whereas the appeal of the Chatham location near the busy Chatham and Pearl streets intersection lay in attracting the curious passerby, the Broadway locale offered no such welcome to the city throng.[70] For a poor laborer, attending a public meeting at a former theatre on Chatham Street would not have caused much social self-consciousness, but attending a meeting at a shining new Broadway church would be another matter entirely. Free or not, a church on Broadway would have been intimidating to many. Yet the organizers were so determined to have a Broadway location that although the building actually fronted Anthony Street, they fashioned a passage from the west side of the auditorium that passed between two existing buildings and exited onto Broadway.[71] The tabernacle had not quite "arrived," but clearly it was working at it, and the publics that would come together within it would strive to accomplish this change for themselves.

A revival space without a revival mission, the new Broadway Tabernacle congregation retained much of the moral tone of the Chatham Street Chapel. The question the members faced was not how to best save souls but how the congregation should interact with the public world. As they had at the chapel, many of the converted put their energies into extending Christian morality and discipline into public discourse. To strive only to personally lead a Christian life, they had come to believe, ignored the social responsibilities of Christianity. In many converts' eyes, to work toward the establishment of the Kingdom was a duty that required their involvement in social and political issues. Thus, organized moral reform emerged as the mission of the Broadway Tabernacle despite the fact that little in the rhetoric of the First and Second Free Churches, the two congregations that merged to create the Sixth Free church at the tabernacle, indicated an outreach agenda. The community soon united in purpose, however, and took an initial step toward claiming a new and self-created public identity by throwing off its Presbyterian heritage and declaring itself Congregationalist from the outset.[72]

This new evangelical community was housed in a startlingly innovative building whose design strongly indicated the authority of the gathered congregation. The Broadway Tabernacle surpassed the chapel in facilitating performance and audience reception by drawing upon the prototype of all theatrical spaces, the classical amphitheatre. As church architecture, the building was the first of its kind on the U.S. religious landscape.[73] Given the plan's unorthodox character, it is not surprising that when Finney turned to Joseph Ditto to erect the building, the builder initially proved singularly reluctant. Finney noted that Ditto "objected to it that it would not appear well, and feared that it would injure his reputation to build a church with such an interior as that."[74]

Completed in 1836, the tabernacle was more strongly audience-oriented than even the Chatham Street Chapel had been. The large auditorium could regularly seat some 2,500 people with space for another 500 if necessary.[75] The main floor of the auditorium was given over almost entirely to the audience. Only the projecting stage and background wall, which was reserved for the musical elements of the service, intruded upon the audience space (fig. 2.2). The room itself was a square with dimensions of about 100 feet per side. Within that space, a circular arrangement of curvilinear pews was inscribed with a radial orientation toward the stage. The circular motif was repeated in a shallow ceiling dome and an encircling gallery interrupted only by the organ case. Clearly alluding to the classical amphitheatre as a prototype, the tabernacle gallery, with its eight ranks of pews rising one above the other, created a marked vertical slope in the upper regions of the room. The rising ranks of choir stalls behind the pulpit also mimicked the spatial cone of the classical amphitheatre. The main floor of the tabernacle, however, like German Baroque churches, appears to have been level, with only the section under the gallery ranked. If so, the design fell short of reproducing the amphitheatre prototype in full.[76]

Architecturally, the Broadway Tabernacle was similar to eighteenth-century German and French developments in theatre design. Departing from the then-predominant court theatre, with its dual focus on stage and royal box, to create a theatre space appropriate to the growing bourgeoisie, these theatres incorporated inclined or bowled seating, which focused attention on the stage alone and leveled the hierarchy among audience members by giving each person a good view and a comfortable seat. Historians of space have argued that this design physically articulated the social equality of bourgeois audiences by merging audience members into a "corporate body" of undifferentiated social equals sharing a mutual agenda, a phenomenon that Rudolf Arnheim suggests derives from the audience's ability to view and thus perceive itself as a mass of equals willing to cooperate in a shared enterprise. In U.S. civic spaces, Charles Goodsell has argued, this corporate identity promoted "popular sovereignty and democratic rule, . . . viewing the people as individuals rather than an undifferentiated mass, and . . . establishing the moral equality of the rulers and the ruled."[77] In such a space, inequalities in vision or distance to the speaker's podium caused by square corners were eliminated; every mem-

Fig. 2.2. Broadway Tabernacle, New York City. 1836. Lithograph, 1845. Courtesy Eno Collection, Miriam and Ira D. Wallach Division of Art, Prints, and Photographs, New York Public Library, Astor, Lenox and Tilden Foundation.

ber of the council had a clear view of the center desk, and each ranking member shared a position equidistant from the center, creating an audience in which each member shared an equal position.

In the Broadway Tabernacle, arcs of curvilinear pews on the main floor, almost encircling the thrust stage, similarly ensured that every seat in the house provided an equally good view of the pulpit. Perhaps more significantly, though, the curvilinear seating allowed audience members to view one another from across the room, an effect that underscored the audience members' awareness of their participation in a shared enterprise of equals. This sense of belonging to a corporate body both paralleled and reinforced the evangelical theme of the equality of the regenerate as well as the democratic political ideology that placed all citizens on an equal civic footing. In this socially, religiously, and politically independent congregation, these identity-facilitating features composed a constant reminder of shared purpose and shared commitment. To gaze around the room at one's fellow soldiers in the struggle for a Christian nation solidified conviction. Indeed, a signal element of the corporate body phenomenon is surveillance. Similarly, the social and religious agendas of this group, particularly the achievement of respectability and moral reform, encouraged watchfulness. One learned to be respectable not simply by listening to sermons, but by watching and comparing one's self to others and making qualitative judgments. Moral laxity was to be identified through careful vigilance. Here, again, the physical arrangement of the auditorium advanced the agendas of the corporate body. The spatial arrangement strongly alluded to the sovereignty of the audience through its seating arrangement and its roots in the popular culture of entertainment. Yet this was not a sovereignty of individuals, as had been the case in theatres and the Chatham Theatre-cum-Chapel. This was the sovereignty of the group as an entity, of a self-identified corpus.

This is not to say that the tabernacle diminished clerical power in a kind of zero-sum equation. As had the chapel, the tabernacle also enhanced the performance of the stage speaker and the ability of talented preachers to establish and maintain charismatic power over the audience. Rather than framing the performance with a proscenium as had the chapel, the tabernacle intensified the visual and aural elements of the service—the spectacle—and thus made the stage a more compelling place to look. While the chapel organizers placed the choir on the stage behind the pulpit, a strategy unprecedented in ecclesiastical settings, the tabernacle placed the organ pipes on the back wall behind the pulpit, creating a highly dramatic visual background for the speaker. Organ pipes towered above the stage, rising behind five rows of choir desks at the rear of the stage. The thrust stage itself jutted out almost midway into the room, and on it stood an assemblage of chairs accommodating various individuals. And, of course, the preacher himself, whether standing above the stage on the pulpit dais or walking on the lower apron, provided the most interesting spectacle of all. Not only could the preacher use his whole body to convey his message, the space demanded that he do so, for the thrust stage and encircling seating required speakers to turn often to avoid having their backs to part of the audience for any length of time.

On the other hand, the drama and spectacle of the room—the towering organ pipes, the many visible faces in the audience and the choir, the hovering dome, and the massive Corinthian columns supporting it—also risked dwarfing the platform speakers, as sketches of the tabernacle suggest. To command authority in such a space, the speaker would need to present not only a powerful oratorical performance, but a visually interesting spectacle to compete with the complexity of the stage. Because the amphitheatre also served to level the authority differential between audience and speaker—the feature that created an effective space for democratic forums—dominating the stage of such a place required the performative charisma that Finney had been developing for years.

The potential for audience sovereignty in such a space seems to have caused Finney little concern; he was clearly pleased with the space, declaring it "altogether the most spacious, commodious, and comfortable place to speak in that I have ever seen of its size."[78] Although many preachers undoubtedly would have heightened their theatricality in order to transfix the large corporate audience, Finney seems to have reduced the dramatic elements of his performance from his earlier years. Several commentators on his later preaching style noted that he now depended more upon reason and logic to move his audiences than his earlier "soul-stirring appeals to the heart and conscience."[79] Why the change in style? As one of his friends suggested, the "peculiar circumstances in which [he has been] placed have lead [sic] . . . to a discussion of abstract theological subjects."[80] Although these "peculiar circumstances" probably included his acceptance of a professorship at Oberlin College, they may also have included the reality of preaching to more homogeneous audiences at the tabernacle. In the tabernacle, Finney preached to the converted rather than to random gatherings of urban sinners, and the converted did not have the same need to have their attentions seized and their souls wrested from distractions. It would take something other than antiformalist revival strategies to keep his flock together. Finney's message and his style changed to suit his audience, much as theatre producers and actors changed their performances to suit specific audiences.[81]

Unlike revival meetings devoted to the immediate saving of souls, the Broadway Tabernacle services, like Finney's sermons, had a more contemplative flavor as the earlier conversion dramas gave way to new practices. For instance, musical performances became an important means of orchestrating audience attention. Finney began each meeting with congregational singing, and music director Thomas Hastings, who had come to the tabernacle at Finney's insistence, would intersperse choral and organ performances throughout the service. But the physical participation of individual audience members during services generally declined as revivalism waned. This was in part affected by the space itself, for curved pews traversed by few aisles would have significantly hindered members' ability to move to the front to respond to calls to publicly declare themselves. As a more staid form of worship accorded well with the tabernacle congregation's aspirations for respectability, little regret was expressed about the changes.[82]

Strong internal cohesion marked the congregation as a bulwark of social reform activity, and under the direction of Lewis and Arthur Tappan, it was the congregation's moral reform and abolitionist agendas that defined the church in the city's political milieu.[83] Less socially diverse than the Chatham Street Chapel, the tabernacle congregation succeeded in translating populist political activism into a respectable enterprise, but their labors nevertheless carried a commitment similar to that of those who contested the chapel. They too sought to define the new republican nation. The patriotism that sparked riots against English actors at the Bowery Theatre could also fuel efforts to uplift the moral character of the nation. Thus, though the tabernacle's activities were not as broadly popular as those of the Chatham Street Chapel, they do indicate that the distance between the "laboring" and the "respectable" was not as far as one might surmise. In fact, the building itself suggested a certain congruity between the two groups. While the theatre space of the Chatham maintained an architectural foot in the popular camp that indicated its populist agendas, the tabernacle's prestigious location and innovative space broadcast the increased exclusivity of the congregation and the societies that met there. In the tabernacle, popular political activity became respectable.

In the religious arena, however, the iconoclasm of the Broadway Tabernacle was clear. In comparison to the conventional elevated pulpit and preaching box arrangement, the tabernacle's more egalitarian physical relationship between platform speaker and audience symbolized the democratic intentions of the moral reform projects of the congregation. In this, the tabernacle broke new ground, and, as the new congregational polity indicated, the congregation and Finney himself would continue to challenge established ecclesiastical authority.[84]

Thus the significance of the establishment of the Chatham Street Chapel and the subsequent Broadway Tabernacle follows from their innovations not only as spaces for evangelical worship, but also as spaces that negotiated new relationships between clergy and audience and that participated in the construction of new publics within a rapidly changing urban context. As U.S. religion scholar Peter Williams has pointed out, the revival processes of the Second Great Awakening encompassed new approaches not only to religion but also to authority and community.[85] Through their antinomian theology, the revivals of the early republic reinforced democratic belief in the sovereignty of the individual and participated in the redefinition of cultural and political authority and of the role of the citizen. Earlier beliefs in a natural aristocracy, hierarchical society, and deference to one's betters were besieged by populist democratic egalitarianism, which Finneyite revivalism implicitly endorsed. The same cultural forces that pitted Federalists against Democratic-Republicans in the political arena pitted formalist ecclesiasticists against antiformalist revivalists in the religious one, particularly as the latter challenged conventional ideas of clerical authority. The political and the religious paralleled and cross-pollinated one another. In the words of historian Charles Sellers, "Direct access to divine grace and revelation, subordinating clerical learning to every person's reborn heart, vindicated the lowly reborn soul against hierarchy and authority, magistrates and clergy."[86] Cultural power of all types—political, religious, social—was becoming increasingly subject to negotiation.

In the social sphere, revivals brought together disparate individuals by means of a common goal—the salvation of the soul—thereby creating a community of self-identified Christians. Identification with this community had behavioral corollaries, among them compliance with genteel behaviors and lifestyles made possible by the growing market economy. This move toward respectability, like salvation itself, usurped the power to define individual and group identity from traditional elites. Moreover, revivalism's moral reform agendas offered new outlets for patriotic activism and political participation, which in turn solidified community identity and challenged traditional authorities. Engagement in abolitionist, benevolence, or temperance movements provided a tool for improving the nation for believers convinced of the role of free will in striving toward individual, urban, and ultimately national purity.

With these cultural processes of creating identity and meaning, Finney's revivalism negotiated varying views of religious and social authority by deploying what historian Nathan Hatch has termed "the indigenous methods of popular culture" in order to introduce "democratic modifications into respectable institutions."[87] Finney, while acknowledging individuals' power to seek out salvation and its social corollary, the validity of the ideas and opinions of common people, nevertheless strove to maintain the stature and authority of clerical office. His strongly participatory, audience-centered meetings displayed his democratizing tendencies even as his much-heralded stern demeanor and roots in Presbyterian polity suggested his authoritarianism. In Finney's hands, audience influence and clerical authority did not have to exist in a zero-sum equation. Instead, community flourished under charismatic authority. The church buildings that sheltered his New York City revivals furthered these ideals. Overturning decades, even centuries, of architectural precedent, the Chatham Street Chapel and the Broadway Tabernacle brought popular and charismatic authority into dialogue with one another.

Finney's Final Experiment in Spatial Authority

Although the Broadway Tabernacle would be Finney's most successful architectural accomplishment, he served as its primary minister only briefly. In the spring of 1836, just before the tabernacle was completed, he accepted the position of professor of theology at Oberlin College and preached at the tabernacle only through the following winter. Oberlin, founded as a Christian colony and school in 1833 by Finney admirer John Jay Shipherd, was linked with several progressive agendas, including abolitionism, temperance, women's rights, and peace. Most important to Finney, however, was the opportunity that Oberlin afforded him to develop his ideas of perfectionism and to pursue his growing interest in ministerial education. The latter seems to have fueled his final design effort. In 1841, Finney became involved in the design of a new Congregational meetinghouse to replace Oberlin's University Chapel, which had grown too small for the expanding student and faculty population.[88] The original architectural plans for the new building depict yet another extraordinary religious space, one that would draw upon the amphitheatre form but this time to produce a space that would strongly privilege the authority of the speaker.

The process by which the meetinghouse plan developed is somewhat obscure. In March 1841, the Oberlin Society, the official governing body of the institution, elected a committee to draft a plan for a new meetinghouse. In August the society decided to consult with architect Willard Sears of Boston "to build a house of brick—70 feet wide & 110 feet long."[89] Although the minutes of the Oberlin Society make no specific mention of any communication between Finney and the building committee during this period, despite the fact that he was in residence on the campus during much of it, he was previously acquainted with Sears, and the suggestion that the building accommodate lecture and recitation rooms appears to reflect Finney's affinity for small prayer meeting rooms.[90] Plans from Sears arrived in Oberlin in November, and two building committee members were instructed to continue their communications with Sears and with Finney.[91] Then, a second set of plans arrived from Boston in early 1842, these produced by one R. Bond, presumably Richard Fifield Bond, an up-and-coming young architect to whom Sears had assigned the job for $50.[92] During these several months, it was Finney who served as a liaison between the architects and the Oberlin building committee, traveling to Boston and keeping the committee apprised of the status of the plan.

Bond, presumably acting upon Finney's instructions, created a church plan with an amphitheatre more suggestive of a lecture hall than a theatre. The plan of the main floor presents the most significant innovations, showing a tight circle of pews radiating from a central pulpit at ground level located at the center of two semicircles (fig. 2.3). Eight rows form full circles around the pulpit, and the remainder of the space is filled with nine nearly semicircular pew arcs following the curve of the inner circle. The arcs are bisected by two primary aisles running longitudinally to the pulpit and five secondary aisles radiating from the pulpit circle. Notes written on the plan specify a sloped floor.[93] The elevated gallery sweeps around the entire room, as it did in the Broadway Tabernacle, although it is not interrupted by an organ. Its pews are placed on stepped ranks, affording people in the back a clear view of the speaker.

The configuration of the gallery appears to have been the subject of some discussion between architect and client, for a drawing that may be in Finney's hand appears on the back of Bond's plan (fig. 2.4). In it a male figure stands at a pulpit looking up at an audience in a gallery opposite him, and lines connect the eyes of this preacher figure to the figures of the tiny audience members. Interestingly, the sketch is the exact spatial inversion of one published by John Scott Russell in the *Edinburgh New Philosophical*

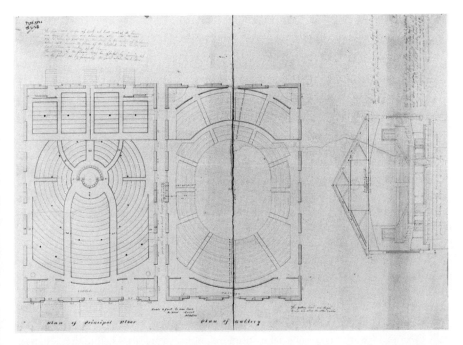

Fig. 2.3. Proposed plan for Oberlin meetinghouse. 1841. Richard Bond, arch. Courtesy Oberlin College Archives, Oberlin, Ohio.

Fig. 2.4. Sketch on reverse of Oberlin meetinghouse plan by Richard Bond. 1841. Courtesy Oberlin College Archives, Oberlin, Ohio.

Journal in 1839, in which a minister seemingly located in a more conventional elevated pulpit peers down on his listeners and lines connect his mouth and their chests (fig. 2.5).[94] The Oberlin sketch, whether produced by Bond, Sears, or Finney himself, demonstrates that while its artist was willing to forgo the convention of the elevated pulpit, he was not insensitive to other means of manipulating the relationship between speaker and audience. Finney, of course, had experienced the benefits of placing the speaker lower than the audience in both the Chatham Street Chapel and the Broadway Tabernacle. In relation to conventional church architecture of the period, then, the Oberlin plan, like the tabernacle's, was exceptional. The inclined main floor of the Oberlin plan was extraordinary, perhaps having only the two New York free churches as precedent. And although galleries with stepped ranks were quite common in churches of all denominations by this time, the gracefully curving gallery of the plan, sweeping around the entire room and requiring curved pews, was similarly precedented in church architecture only in the tabernacle.[95]

Appropriately, the model for Bond's circular pulpit and ring of seating resembled amphitheatre lecture halls that had developed from sixteenth-century medical dissection theatres in which raked galleries encircled an examination table where the instructor would demonstrate medical techniques upon a corpse. As oratory performances in which educators lectured to large groups of students became common educational practice in universities, the lecture room, usually containing a semicircle of raked seats, increasingly became a fixture in educational institutions. Some thirty years before the design of the Oberlin space, however, the panopticon plan of encircling seating had been developed by educational designers to aid in the monitoring of students (or, sometimes, prisoners or asylum inmates). Geared toward both curricula and the social progress of students, designs like Jeremy Bentham's twelve-sided "Chrestomathic" monitorial school, which seated 900 boys in the "middling and higher ranks of life," allowed a small number of teachers located in the center to watch many students at once (fig. 2.6). The appeal of such designs, of course, was that they allowed for greater control over youngsters than did a level seating arrangement. English Sunday schools, in particular, adopted

Fig. 2.5. Acoustical projection drawing. John Scott Russell, *Edinburgh New Philosophical Journal* 27 (Apr.–Oct. 1839): 133. Courtesy Special Collections and Rare Books, University of Minnesota Libraries, Twin Cities.

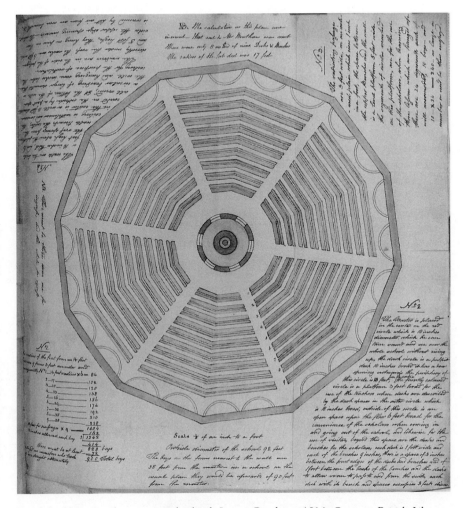

Fig. 2.6. Chrestomathic monitorial school. Jeremy Bentham. 1814. Courtesy British Library, Place Collection (60), Set 60, Section C, no. 8.

the panopticon form.[96] Just how this panopticon form became integrated into the Oberlin meetinghouse plan is not quite clear. Finney, of course, had previously experimented with the amphitheatre in the Broadway Tabernacle. Bond had recently completed the plan for Gore Hall on the Harvard University campus, a building that may have contained a lecture hall as well as the library. Sears, a good friend of Finney, had been designing churches for several years, and it is likely that the sketch of the man in the pulpit (assuming Finney did draw it) was intended for him.[97]

Finney, staying in Boston during the late fall of 1841, could well have consulted with Bond on the design, and it does seem to reflect the wishes of the artist of the sketch. The view from the pulpit would give the preacher access to the eyes of every individual in the audience. No congregants could escape his gaze, and he could maintain strong visual control over the room. Maintaining order, certainly discipline, may well have been of concern when those lines were drawn from the minister's eyes to those of the individuals in the gallery, for in the Oberlin meetinghouse, as in the college chapel, its predecessor, the students occupied the galleries while the faculty took the main floor.[98] Though it is unlikely that Oberlin students were particularly unruly, given the rigid perfectionist discipline of the school, maintaining eye contact has always been an effective way for teachers to feel in control of their students. Thus it seems that upon taking up the academic robe, Finney abandoned at least part of the critique of traditional authority implicit in his earlier buildings, as the meetinghouse was designed to afford the speaker much greater authority. No longer would authority emerge from the charisma of the speaker and through the consent of an acquiescent corporate audience, but now would come from the speaker's expertise and erudition, the authority of the professorate. Yet a panopticon-like circular space would not have served Finney's needs effectively, for it would have required the orator to turn constantly in circles to address the entire audience. More likely, the seats "behind" the center pulpit would be reserved for a choir; as part of the performance, the singers could be favored with the preacher's back.[99]

Apparently the Oberlin committee did not feel particularly obligated to follow the Bond plan, for the completed building demonstrates the limited extent to which revival strategies were incorporated into church architecture at large during the period (fig. 2.7). Most significantly, the committee abandoned the innovative lecture room design of the

Fig. 2.7. Oberlin meetinghouse, Oberlin, Ohio. 1844. Photograph, c. 1859. Courtesy Oberlin College Archives, Oberlin, Ohio.

ground floor. In the finished building, no spatial cone of pews encircled the pulpit stage. Instead, the room combined the rising organ pipes and choir seating of the tabernacle stage, features that became commonplace in churches during the 1840s, with a fairly restrictive pulpit and the box pews of the conventional meetinghouse arrangement (fig. 2.8). The floor, intended to incline slightly, did not. The effect of these alterations was to create a more traditional church, an outcome that may have been informed by the committee's oft-repeated desire to build a "plain" church or by the desperate financial situation of the Oberlin Society during the early 1840s (fig. 2.9). One important feature of the original plan, however, was implemented: the ceiling was slightly domed, curving down to meet the top of the wall to eliminate dead corners. By retaining this crucial feature, the committee did demonstrate some commitment to creating a space that would enhance oratory.[100]

The finished building featured a large room in which the pulpit platform, complete with background organ pipes and choir ranks, clearly dominated the space. The audience, seated on the main floor, looked up at the stage, the faces of their fellow congregants out of their sight, thus impeding the development of an identity as a corporate body. Students in the galleries, though able to view their counterparts across the room, were also under constant surveillance by the speaker. In a period in which any student authority was unthinkable, the spatial arrangement well articulated the top-down author-

Fig. 2.8. Oberlin meetinghouse, Oberlin, Ohio. 1844. Photograph, c. 1944. Courtesy Oberlin College Archives, Oberlin, Ohio.

Fig. 2.9. Oberlin meetinghouse, Oberlin, Ohio. 1844. Photograph, c. 1859. Courtesy Oberlin College Archives, Oberlin, Ohio.

ity of the professoriate and the clergy. Yet the presence of the choir and organ at the front of the room did provide an extraordinary visual spectacle, and performance played an important role in the spatial matrix. Though lacking a stage, the performers—preacher, choir, and organist—nonetheless executed their arts together, just as performers had done in the tabernacle.

Thus, although the school was theologically radical, in terms of architecture it remained relatively conservative, at least in comparison to the theological and architectural radicalism of New York's free-church Presbyterians/Congregationalists. While Finney's Oberlin pulpit platform gave him a bit more room on which to maneuver than did a traditional elevated pulpit, it remained elevated above the audience, which was located in a relative position of powerlessness beneath him. In this, the Oberlin society mirrored a hesitancy on the part of evangelicals at large to abandon traditional forms of religious authority. As explored in the next chapter, midcentury evangelicals increasingly adopted architectural forms that enhanced formalism and even embraced liturgicalism in their struggle for denominational and social legitimacy.

Although the midcentury saw an embracing of traditional church architecture forms, earlier in the century U.S. religious architecture had moved toward innovation that went hand in hand with the volatile political environment. The evangelical revivalism of the Second Great Awakening constituted a religious expression of the broader struggle for democracy that energized the country. At the same time that U.S. citizens—white men, that is—were gaining equal political rights, religious revivals attracted thousands by emphasizing an individual's personal relationship with God. To be "reborn" in Christ was to enter a community of Christians in which all, at least in theory, were equal. The architecture of the urban revivals would effectively, if only temporarily, reify audience equality in the worship space of the amphitheatre and significantly minimize the auto-cratic power of the minister with the pulpit stage. Creating a religious space that had the potential to elevate audience power significantly above clerical power proved to be of only fleeting interest, however, and ultimately this generation would not see wide-spread adaptation of the amphitheatre form. Nevertheless, in their architectural experi-mentation during the 1830s, evangelical revivalists inverted the spatial relationship that favored.clergy at the expense of audience needs and in the process became iconoclasts in the evolution of American religious architecture.

3

Formalism and the Gothic Revival among Evangelical Protestants

In 1858, as New York property values skyrocketed, the Broadway Tabernacle congregation sold the theatre-inspired tabernacle building, which they had occupied since 1836, and made plans to relocate some three miles uptown. Opened for worship in April 1859, their new building, a large Gothic Revival church designed for them by up-and-coming architect Leopold Eidlitz, abandoned the Low Church, revivalist architectural roots of the congregation (fig. 3.1). Enveloped in the latest trend in English Gothic facades, boasting a cruciform plan with a nave 90 feet long and 70 feet high, with apse, transepts, galleries, and vaulted ceiling, the new church was a veritable cathedral of Congregationalism. This was a building designed for liturgical services and hierarchical social relationships, not the affective worship and egalitarianism that had characterized the congregation's revivalist foundations. Underscoring the ecclesiastical nature of the architecture, the congregation named the building the Broadway Tabernacle Church.

In selecting the Gothic Revival style, the Broadway Tabernacle congregation emulated hundreds of others across the nation. The theatrelike innovations of the Chatham Street Chapel and the Broadway Tabernacle, inspired by revival religion, had been largely ignored. Most congregations had remained loyal to their modest Classical Revival and Federal style churches throughout the revival period. With the cessation of the revivals, evangelicals turned toward more ecclesiastical worship practices and worship spaces, embracing the High Church architecture of the Gothic Revival, a style derived from medieval Christian sources. The Gothic had appeared occasionally during the eighteenth century, particularly in domestic architecture and as an expression of the European Romantic movement. In the nineteenth century, however, English Anglicans and Anglo-Catholics celebrated medieval Gothic architecture as the epitome of Christian church form. By midcentury, U.S. congregations, both High and Low Church alike, agreed, and the Gothic replaced classicism as the preferred architectural vocabulary of the period.

The widely popular Gothic Revival stands as a generation-long lacuna between Finney's initial but isolated experiments in bringing theatre architecture into the church in the 1830s and evangelicals' widespread enthusiasm for theatrelike religious spaces in the final quarter of the century. Yet the extensive adoption of Gothic Revival architecture for nonliturgical Protestant churches constitutes a puzzle. The hegemony of the Gothic

Fig. 3.1. Broadway Tabernacle
Church, New York City. 1859.
Leopold Eidlitz, arch. *Congregational
Quarterly* 22 (Jan. 1860): 65.
Courtesy Special Collections and
Rare Books, University of Minnesota
Libraries, Twin Cities.

as *the* generic Christian style was overwhelming at midcentury despite the fact that it seemed to contradict evangelical history and ideology in several ways. An adaptation of the early Roman basilica, the cruciform Gothic church plan, with its nave, chancel, choir, and transepts, was ideal for establishing and maintaining the mystery of the Mass and the power of the clergy in the eucharistic sacrament. It was inimical, however, to Protestant worship that focused on the sermon, because it widely separated the congregation from the minister. In addition, the sculptural vocabulary of pointed arches and vaults, lancet windows, buttresses, and finials created ornate facades, which significantly countered the sparer classical aesthetic previously associated with Protestantism. In the context of the nineteenth-century United States, the richness of Gothic ornament harked back to a European feudal past, which the American political experiment deplored.[1] Moreover, Protestant embracing of the Gothic occurred precisely at a moment in history in which Catholicism was most suspect and disparaged by the Protestant majority in the United States due to Catholics' growing numbers and increasingly visible public presence. Yet throughout this period, Congregationalists, Presbyterians, Methodists, Baptists, and other Low Church, nonliturgical groups that traced their architectural heritage to colonial meetinghouses enthusiastically built Gothic churches, even cathedral-like buildings such as the Broadway Tabernacle Church.

Viewing this paradoxical adoption as an essentially aesthetic phenomenon, architectural and social historians have generally explained Low Church congregations' interest in High Church buildings by locating it within the growing desire for refinement, education, and taste. As congregations increasingly competed for members, a fashionable building demonstrating the latest trend would, many apparently believed, give the congregation it housed an edge on the competition. As historian Richard Bushman asserts, "good taste" and "beauty" monopolized church-building criteria in such denominationally approved pattern books as *A Book of Plans for Churches and Parsonages*, published by the General Congregational Assembly in 1853. Architectural historian Phoebe Stanton's classic study of the Gothic Revival demonstrates its influence as the hegemonic standard of aesthetic taste at midcentury.[2]

While this aesthetic interpretation of the powerful attraction of the Gothic Revival carries a great deal of merit, particularly in its emphasis on the connections between denominational competition and social mobility, it underreports the influence of other crucial political and economic factors. Using the Broadway Tabernacle congregation as a case study, this chapter traces part of the Gothic's appeal to roots in the volatile political sphere dominated by the issue of slavery and the changing economic realm, which increasingly separated activities and institutions into public and private spheres. Within these evolving contexts, evangelicals like those at the Broadway Tabernacle renegotiated the history of Christianity and reconceived the meaning of evangelicalism itself. Their new Gothic Revival churches publicly announced their new creed as well as the new cultus that accompanied it.

As an architectural arrangement, the Gothic Revival championed clergy over laity and liturgy over sermon, instantiating a top-down version of clerical authority that seemed to contradict the Jacksonian struggles for democratic participation which had informed the evangelicalism of the previous generation. The Broadway Tabernacle Church of 1859, for instance, seemed to renounce all that the congregation had been founded upon: congregational polity, the individual's relationship with Christ, and open-door inclusiveness. Yet such conclusions mask the complex social, religious, and architectural transformations that occurred nationwide in the 1840s and 1850s. In fact, the new building aptly demonstrated the challenges midcentury evangelical Protestantism faced as it struggled to claim both public and private roles within the rapidly changing sociopolitical context. As the situation at the Broadway Tabernacle congregation illustrates, the desire to keep congregations and denominations unified created a situation amenable to the widespread embracing of a new generic architectural style that claimed to be neither Congregational nor Presbyterian, neither Methodist nor Baptist, but simply Christian.

Ultraist Challenge to Congregational Polity

Even though the original Broadway Tabernacle's location, interior space, and shared reform agenda suggested a cohesive congregation, rifts became apparent shortly after the congregation moved into the building in 1836. When Finney departed New York in May of that year for Oberlin, he left the Reverend George Duffield in the tabernacle pulpit. Duffield had earned his New School stripes, having been brought up on disciplinary charges and tried for heresy by the Presbytery of Carlisle, Pennsylvania, in 1832.[3] In addition he had served as senior minister at the Chatham Street Chapel in Finney's absence. Yet he enjoyed little success at the tabernacle, for the times themselves seemed to weigh against him. During the early months of 1837, an intense financial panic swept through the U.S. economy, wiping out hundreds of businesses, including every bank in New York City, and placing the continuation of the congregation in jeopardy. Arthur and Lewis Tappan, Isaac Dimond, and other free-church and tabernacle supporters were ruined. The loss of their support was devastating to the tabernacle. In 1838, mortgages totaling $50,500 of the original $66,500 building cost remained, and ground rent ran about $1,000 per year. On top of this, maintenance costs, heat and lighting, the minister's salary, and the sexton's wages all depleted resources. Sometime in 1838, pew rentals were instituted, an official abandonment of the free-church plan. Many feared the congregation would have to disband altogether.[4]

In February 1838, representatives of the Broadway Tabernacle met with counterparts from the similarly financially pressed Dey Street Presbyterian Church (formerly the First Free Church) to discuss a possible merger of the two congregations. The plan was to join the tabernacle congregation (technically, the Sixth Free Church) with the Dey Street congregation under the jurisdiction of the Third Presbytery. Though the Broadway Tabernacle had declared itself Congregationalist two years earlier, given the financial crisis and the 1801 Plan of Union between the Presbyterians and the Congregationalists, a merger seemed appropriate. Agreeing to unite, the two congregations met together in the tabernacle on 13 April 1838, with Duffield and Presbyterian minister Jacob Helffenstein elected as copastors.[5] The situation, however, proved untenable almost from the start, probably due more to the financial burden of supporting two ministers than to ideological differences. Helffenstein soon left for a pastorate in Philadelphia, and rumors flew that Duffield would be willing to resign if another minister, specifically Joel Parker, could be induced to return and take the pulpit. Parker, one of the first New Measures revivalists to preach in New York and former pastor of the Dey Street Church, had moved to New Orleans a few years earlier.[6] Though certain polity issues were raised regarding Duffield's resignation, by October 1838, Duffield and Helffenstein were gone, and the tabernacle had called Parker to take over all ministerial duties.[7]

Whether Parker proved to be a lightning rod in the increasingly volatile political climate within the tabernacle or whether certain individuals decided to use his installation as a litmus test for the tabernacle's sympathies is difficult to ascertain. In any event, controversy over the issue of slavery soon engulfed the congregation. With reform and benevolence societies beefing up their platforms and activities, the relationship between these organizations and the Broadway Tabernacle came under scrutiny, particularly as the slavery issue crystallized opinion. Like the Chatham Street Chapel, the Broadway Tabernacle was closely associated with antislavery activity and sympathies. During its construction, rumors that it would be an "amalgamation" church were rampant, establishing its reputation even before the congregation existed.[8] The official Principles of the Church specifically refused membership to slaveholders: "This church is established on Temperance and Anti-Slavery principles. No one is admitted who will not promise never to buy, sell, or hold slaves."[9] Both black and white attendees and members constituted the congregation.

Yet despite this population and the antislavery statement, not all who used the building affirmed all types of antislavery activism. Anticolonization, for instance, the position that had ignited the riots associated with the Chatham Street Chapel in 1834, continued to draw fire from those who hoped that the cure for racial tension lay in colonization.[10] When tabernacle member and donor Lewis Tappan and others began to promulgate an Ultraist stance on religion and antislavery activism, diversity of opinion within the tabernacle created tension. The Ultraists believed that Christian duty required all Christians and, thus, all Christian churches to work actively and aggressively toward the elimination of sin and evil in the world. The tabernacle, they felt, must remain a symbol for antislavery and a beehive of abolitionist activity. Lewis Tappan took this agenda a step further and argued not only for immediate emancipation but also for "amalgamation," or the full integration of society. While detractors scornfully labeled the tabernacle an amalgamation church, Tappan embraced the concept and argued that the tabernacle should serve as an example of Christian brotherhood in its acceptance of black Christians as equals in the congregation. Others feared the consequences of such aggressive reform activity.[11]

Parker's installation laid bare the diversity of sentiments. Like most of the Presbyterian (and Protestant) clergy of the period, he supported colonization as a means of gradual emancipation.[12] He and Tappan were soon at loggerheads. Parker's position, however, was apparently attractive to many of the leaders of the Broadway Tabernacle/Dey congregation. In any case, Tappan's antislavery Ultraism and Parker's colonization stance brought them into conflict on several occasions. For instance, Tappan's repeated requests that Parker read aloud notices regarding the situation in Liberia during congregation meetings were not well received. When Tappan announced in mid-December that some thirty members of the congregation intended "to form an antislavery society in the Tabernacle Church and Congregation," Parker and the Session, the group of men who led the Congregational wing of the union church, countered with a statement of disapproval. Tappan's group, having swelled to about eighty, then attempted to gather in the tabernacle but found the lecture room locked. Upon gaining admittance and convening the meeting, they were interrupted and asked to leave the premises. These efforts to organize a tabernacle-sponsored association seem to have been the last straw for the Session, most of whose members supported Parker, the colonizationist. Within days, it formally charged Tappan with "disorderly and unchristian conduct." The disciplinary trial lasted two weeks, resulting in the conviction of Tappan for contumacy (rebellion against the Session) on a vote of fourteen to eleven. The Session excommunicated him. Tappan appealed the charges and the decision to, first, the Third Presbytery, which upheld the Session's work, and then to the Presbyterian General Assembly, which in May 1839 sustained his appeal.[13]

Such internal division was by no means exclusive to this single congregation in New York City. Congregations of all kinds throughout the new nation struggled with how to retain members despite deeply held differences of opinion on social and political issues. At least one witness deemed the Tappan-Parker dispute a conflict between "Whigs and Van Buren men," all of whom were strongly dedicated to the tabernacle enterprise.

Congregations struggled with the question of what the role of the church ought to be vis-à-vis the public political arena. Though the tabernacle's Principles of the Church included a strong antislavery statement, the question was to what extent the church should be involved with publicly countering slavery. Tappan's group, which favored aggressive political activism, was not without influence. As a friend observed to Finney, "Parker is at the Tabernacle, but they will have no quietness there until they all [agree?] to Lewis Tappan's views of human rights."[14] Parker, on the other hand, clearly disapproved of the Ultraist platform, and his opinion was apparently shared by much of the church leadership. Ultraism they declared, would not be tolerated.[15]

One anti-Ultraist who came out in support of Tappan offered a compromise solution. David Hale, editor of the *Journal of Commerce*, a Christian weekly founded by Tappan in 1828 to cover commercial, political, and general interest topics for Christian readers, was Tappan's employee. Yet there seems to have been little affection between the two. Hale's defense of Tappan rested on a critique of the trial procedures, not on any sympathy for the defendant or for his antislavery mission. Alarmed by the apparent destruction of feelings of Christian brotherhood indicated by the savagery of dissent among Whigs and Democrats over this issue, Hale feared that such internal strife within a free church, within a Congregational church, spelled its demise if left unchecked. In Hale's analysis, the proceedings against Tappan were treacherous shoals, toward which Protestantism itself was hurtling as the tumult of politics breached sanctuary walls.[16]

Yet, in Hale's estimation, Congregationalism stood in an advantageous, indeed superior, position to respond to this threat. The Congregationalist model of independent church polity, he argued, founded on the idea of democracy and self-determination, not only brought constitutional rights into the sanctuary (indeed, he argued, it preceded the idea of political democracy), but could and should be employed to ensure justice and due process in church discipline cases. Championing the "democratic" nature of Congregationalism, Hale faulted the Session for the antidemocratic procedures of its inquiry against Tappan. In an impassioned address to the entire membership of the church, he charged that the Presbyterian model of polity in which elders make decisions on behalf of the congregation was necessarily antidemocratic and was, in fact, corrupting the Congregationalist Session. Elders could not and did not represent the views of the congregation. Certain men on the committee, he charged, had made up their minds before the trial had even begun. Further, democratic procedures and due process had been violated several times in the course of the trial.[17] Using the analogy of a civil trial, Hale argued that the autocratic nature of the Presbyterian order was what allowed such injustice to go forward. The only remedy, he countered, was a fully Congregational polity in which major decisions were voted on by the entire membership, not just a representative Session.[18]

Lacking overseeing bodies, Congregationalism was held together by a series of social compacts among members and thus had a great deal at stake when issues threatened congregational cohesion. If Finney, along with other revivalists, looked to a relationship with Christ to claim some measure of equality among all Christians, he nevertheless favored a blend of strong clerical and lay authority leading congregations. Hale, on the other hand, looking to political equality as a model for church polity, favored full lay-membership decisions over representative bodies of lay members. Although Hale claimed Puritan precedent for his conception of radical church democracy, this was a polity never imagined by the likes of John Winthrop or Cotton Mather. Based more on John Locke than Jonathan Edwards, Hale's model of church polity merged the concept of congregational independence with that of full participatory democracy.[19]

The main problem the tabernacle faced was that, in an increasingly complex society, the social compacts that had previously held church members together were coming under fire with increasing frequency. Not only did the slavery issue rend congregations, but other issues did as well. The consequences of democracy itself loomed like specters on the political landscape, and religious organizations were loath to address them. Between the elections of 1824 and 1840, political participation rose to unprecedented levels, with voting reaching 80 percent in the 1840 presidential election. Propelled into activism by anxiety over the changing economic order, this was a democratic society that burst with frightening frequency into street demonstrations and riots—over slavery, race, the politics of actors, Catholicism, Freemasonry, labor issues, and so on. If such disorder were the fruit of democracy, Whig ministers like Gardiner Spring announced from the pulpit, surely democracy was not a godly thing. Finney questioned the efficacy of liberalism as well. As historian Mark Hanley points out: "For Finney, liberalism foundered on the principle that man necessarily acted from complex motives and that rational self-interest could produce individual and communal harmony. Christianity was no moral code designed to 'control' self-interest, he regularly insisted. True faith removed self-interest as a motive through the supernatural intervention of the Holy Spirit. Individual regeneration and personal piety . . . were the indispensable agents of a Christian community."[20] Democracy could work only among a fully Christian group.

Diversity of opinion within Protestant religious organizations was not a particularly new phenomenon. Since the early eighteenth century, laity had been gaining increasing power to voice opinions and pursue agendas. However, whereas local or regional disciplinary measures or congregational-level schisms had previously smoothed troubled denominational waters, such measures were proving less and less effective in the face of national crises on which almost everyone held an opinion. The Presbyterian Schism of 1837, particularly, caught many unprepared, as New School and Old School theological conflicts rent the national denomination. Given the southern dominance over Old School Presbyterianism, however, the schism cannot be considered an exclusively theological controversy. As historian C. C. Goen argues, the slavery question, if not precipitating the occasion for the split, certainly exacerbated the ongoing separations that followed the initial New School–Old School split.[21] If this type of political dissent tore apart Christians, what future was there for the nation? Where could society look for order, for guidance?

Hale's solution to the tabernacle crisis in 1839 took the explicit aim of averting further schism. At all costs, he felt, Christians must stay united, and if religious ideology or creed severed Christians, they still shared one thing—cultus, or worship practice:

> Our peace was first interrupted by the commencement of an anti-slavery society, to be formed in the Broadway Tabernacle Church. . . . I think it was an error to introduce the subject in this form, and an error exceedingly dangerous to our peace. This is the Broadway Tabernacle Church of Jesus Christ, not of Anti-Slavery; and it must always be dangerous for a church as such to depart from the single design of its formation. We are associated as a church, only for the worship of God, and an attendance on the ordinances he has established. There may be in our number some of all the various parties which divide our country. We have Whigs and Van Buren men, tariff and free trade men, abolitionists, and colonizationists. We differ about all these things and many more, yet there is one thing about which we all agree, and on this we unite. This is the corner-stone of our fabric, and while we adhere to it alone, we shall be likely to remain harmonious. In maintaining this unity of purpose, we sacrifice nothing of our opinions or our rights with regard to other topics. We are pledged to each other as a band of *Christians*, and whoever introduces any thing else into our association, however good or honorable it may be, *perverts the ends of the association.* (emphasis in original)[22]

If the political order threatened unity, the solution, Hale reasoned, was to remove the church from the political order, and he proposed to emend the tabernacle's Principles to accomplish this and to guarantee that discipline cases be brought before the full membership. His proposals, however, were voted down, no doubt disliked both by the Ultraists, who wanted even more political involvement, and by the Session and trustees, who were unwilling to give up representative polity.

Another financial crisis, however, gave Hale the opportunity he needed to transform the tabernacle polity. In the spring of 1840, William Green, a long-time free-church supporter who had been hard-hit by the 1837 panic, called in his mortgage on the Broadway Tabernacle and set the congregation spinning toward crisis.[23] The Presbytery was unwilling to underwrite the mortgage, despite the presence of the Dey Street Church in the building, and as the closing date advanced, little hope remained that the building would not be sold to the highest bidder by the chancery court. In an eleventh-hour move, David Hale gathered a small group of friends with whose help he put up $34,000 to purchase the building in his name.[24] He then reorganized the Broadway Tabernacle with an explicitly Congregational polity, the first sentence of whose Permanent Rules stated: "The design of a Christian Church we understand to be the enjoyment of Christian ordinances and the maintenance of the worship of God."[25] With these words, the rules made it clear that the new tabernacle would separate church activity from the political order.

Hale's biographer and second minister of the new Broadway Tabernacle, Joseph P. Thompson, cheered this stance in his 1850 book, *Memoir of David Hale*:

> Such a declaration was of great importance at a time when there was a strong tendency to transform churches into societies for particular reforms, and even for political action. The working of this principle in the Broadway Tabernacle Church has been most happy. Though some of the prominent members of the church are zealous for particular measures of reform, the church itself has never been agitated by these subjects, for since every brother is left at liberty to advocate any reform, and to join or to organize any reform society, all are satisfied with this unrestricted personal influence without demanding church action in their favorite cause. Prayer and remarks, with reference to such subjects, are unrestrained; personal action is free; but legislation in the church upon subjects so foreign to the design of a church is not desired by any.[26]

This policy represented less a profound shift in the conception of the mission of the church than a rift that had been in the free-church movement since its origins. Finney's belief that to purify the nation each individual in it must be purified undergirded New Measures revivalism. As free churchers became more and more involved in reform issues, however, Ultraist leanings eclipsed this grassroots concept. The elimination of sin, particularly egregious sins like slavery, must take place in a sweeping, universal fashion, which could only be accomplished through widespread political action. Hale's new church discipline coincided with the revivalist-individualist camp sans the reform rhetoric. As Thompson pointed out, the rules specified:

> Each member of the church is responsible to his brethren for his general walk and conversation, but may appropriate his efforts to any department of benevolent labor to which, in his own judgment, he is called by the Master, to whom he is directly responsible for the use of all the talents which have been committed to his hands. At the same time any member of the church, in voting upon the reception of a candidate into church fellowship, may make the opinions and practice of the person with regard to the use and sale

of intoxicating drinks, slaveholding, dancing, and any other act of questionable morality, a test of piety, and the whole church may have a common moral sentiment upon such subjects which shall express itself as occasions arise, while they avoid the dangerous expedient of legislating on specific moral questions in the abstract.[27]

In Hale's scheme, individuals pursued their own courses and were to be judged upon their individual beliefs. Hale's and Finney's individualism, however, sprang from differing sources. While Finney's revivalism grew from the desire to save and purify individual souls, Hale's individualism sprang from a political ideal as a strategy for maintaining harmony within the congregation and unity among Christians.[28] This is not to say that Hale acknowledged the political origins of his ideas about religious individualism, liberty, and polity. In fact, he clothed his conception of religious individualism in the legitimacy of history, tracing the idea to the Puritan founders of Congregationalism. "The question between us and the session," he argued, "is precisely the same with that between Luther and the Pope; the Puritans and the Hierarchy, the revolutionary patriots of '76 and Lord North. It is the question whether sovereignty is in the people or in the rulers. . . . The doctrine that the people are the sovereigns, and have the right to manage their own affairs, is the doctrine of the Gospel. . . . It was the doctrine of the men who landed at Plymouth, and will be maintained by their descendants."[29] While Finney's sounder theological background led him to reject the oppressive theology of his Calvinist ancestors (including its concept of predestination) in favor of the individual sanction of a moderate Arminianism, Hale, in a historicizing sleight of hand, traced his belief in the ideals of liberty and individualism back to these same Puritan sources. The legitimacy provided by this reinvented past reconciled the religious with the political, arguing that the former sprang from the latter. Unity could be accomplished by "returning" to the Congregationalist founders' (i.e., the Puritans') model of individual sovereignty.[30] If maintaining congregational order and harmony meant sacrificing organizational political activism, so be it.

By the time the new Gothic Revival Broadway Tabernacle Church was completed in 1859, then-pastor Joseph Thompson had not only eulogized Hale as the inspiration behind the congregation, but had also emphatically asserted the "conservative" nature of the congregation. That is, the congregation's role was to provide an anchor in the tumult of the contemporary landscape, by exhibiting and extending fellowship to all "true believers."[31] Hale had successfully transformed the mission of the church from revivalism and reform to worship. Adopting worship practice, ritual, as its raison d'être, this congregation, like many others, set the stage for radical change. In the tabernacle's case, what had previously been a nonformalist New Measures free church soon made the transition to liturgical and architectural formalism.

The tabernacle congregation's struggle with Ultraism and Hale's solution of unity through worship serves as a case study of the challenges facing evangelical Protestants throughout the country in the 1840s and 1850s, as they struggled to refashion a role for organized religion within a society more interested in material gain, outspoken politics, and civil disruptions than eternal salvation. The context of political dissent, and particularly the slavery issue, induced several groups to echo Hale's call for a separation between religion, which should minister to individual souls, and politics. As Goen demonstrates, many churches decided that, in regard to slaveholding, silence was the best response. The Baptist General Convention, for instance, attempting to avert schism in 1844, similarly used political neutrality to maintain unity within the denomination: "We disclaim all sanction, either expressed or implied, whether of slavery or antislavery; but as individuals we are perfectly free both to express and to promote our own views on these subjects elsewhere, in a Christian manner and spirit."[32] Likewise, in a last-ditch effort by the one remaining national Presbyterian body, the Old School Assembly argued in 1845 that "the church of Christ is a spiritual body, whose jurisdiction extends only to the religious faith, and moral conduct of her members."[33]

Like Hale, these organizations hoped that a new religious mission devoted to worship and ministry to the individual would sustain Christianity despite the context of political turmoil. But their agenda went further. If Christians could remain united in what was rapidly escalating into a national crisis, then the country, too, would remain united. An author writing in the Richmond, Virginia, *Religious Herald* expressed the sentiment in 1844: "If the Baptists, unmindful of their duty to Christ and their country, shall bite and devour one another, and array themselves into two great parties, the Northern and the Southern, what conservative principles, what salt of the earth will be left to restrain and modulate the madness of political strife and ambition and save from ruin our Republic?"[34] As James Henley Thornwell put it in 1851: "We are solemn and earnest, not only because we deplore a schism in the body of Christ, but because we deplore a schism among the confederated States of this Union."[35] For many, Christian unity was coded language for internal denominational cohesion, yet for others the agenda went further. Christianity could be the solution to the national crisis, but only if Christians themselves put aside sectarian and political differences. Formalist evangelicals—among them Presbyterians, Congregationalists, Baptists, and Episcopalians—urged not only denominational cohesion but also cooperation among all Protestants and, most important, coherence in Protestant worship. The rhetoric of "Christian spirit" and "unity of the spirit" asserted that harmony among Christians was not only possible but was necessary if true Christianity were to exist and if the U.S. political experiment were to succeed.[36]

But was the new mission emphasizing ministry to individuals strong enough to hold Christian groups together? The answer was in doubt, for not only were political issues tearing apart denominations, but Protestant worship itself was far from uniform among evangelicals. In 1846 a Presbyterian writer argued in the *Princeton Review* that while the spirit of God might reasonably express itself in a variety of forms among different nations, "when people of the same nation and of the same social usages, dissent from one another in their forms of religious devotion, and make their respective peculiarities matters of grave and conscientious scruple, their dissent 'cometh of evil.'"[37] General principles should guide all Christian worship, this writer argued, a position that assumed that an alignment of religious practice would be a necessary consequence of a shared Christian belief. Congregationalist minister J. C. Webster, writing in the July 1862 *Congregational Quarterly*, urged congruence among the worship practices of all Christians.[38] A number of religious leaders envisioned templates for generic evangelical services heavy on congregational prayer and hymn singing. Others, however, opposed such calls, either implicitly or explicitly. For example, an 1855 review of Charles W. Baird's *Eutaxia; or, The Presbyterian Liturgies: Historical Sketches* (1855) implicitly countered such calls for unity in worship by hailing the need for Calvinist liturgical forms. Though arguing that the whole concept of liturgy smacked of "Romish" control, the Old School author did support the compilation of a book of Presbyterian (Calvinist) prayers and forms upon which ministers could draw at their discretion to fulfill the specific needs of their congregations.[39]

Ironically, the discussion of Christian unity grew just as Congregationalists were reevaluating their union agreement with Presbyterians and, like the tabernacle group, moving toward severing those ties. By the 1850s, the Congregationalists—formerly a relatively loose association of autonomous individual churches—were ready to move toward centralization and the development of a national denominational organization.[40] At the Albany Conference of 1852, some 463 ministers and lay delegates terminated the 1801 Plan of Union, which had formed an alliance between the Congregationalists and the Presbyterians. Despite the severing of ties, from the Congregationalist perspective the decision was not meant as a sectarian move. As historian John Von Rohr demonstrates, Congregationalists' stated intention was to promote evangelicalism unfettered, to promote "in the freest and most efficient manner the world's salvation in Jesus Christ."[41] The trick was to separate from the Presbyterians and consolidate the denomination without sacrificing Christian unity. Indeed, sectarian isolation was more a specter than a goal in the minds of Congregationalists as they trod the treacherous path of creating new associations of independent Congregational churches. While they desired a clear denominational identity and release from the sometimes overwhelming influence of the Presbyterians, they did not want to generally distance themselves from other Christian groups, particularly when they, like other evangelicals, placed store in the concept of Christian unity to define and legitimize the church's role in a society rife with political dissent. Having begun the effort to distance the church from the tumult of secular politics, evangelicals could not afford to be charged with rampant sectarianism and division among themselves.[42] New means of articulating unity, within the context of denominational distinction, would be necessary.

Christian Unity and Church Architecture

Demonstrations of Christian unity emerged in various forms. The restoration movement of the time, seeking to recreate the primitive Christianity of the Early Church period, lobbied for the elimination of denominations and the unification of all churches. Such idealism, however, was limited to fairly small groups like Alexander Campbell's Disciples of Christ and Barton Stone's Christian Church. Their dream of total unity among Christians, however, was short-lived, crushed under the reality of denominational diversity produced by U.S. religious voluntarism. More realistic attempts at unity emerged in the form of cross-denominational cooperation, including widespread participation in evangelical organizations such as local and national antislavery societies, the American Sunday School Union, and the American Tract Society. Unity for these groups existed in shared public activism. Inside churches, new approaches to worship brought some uniformity to services. For instance, the proliferation of hymns and hymnbooks across denominational lines reduced some distinctions. *The Southern Harmony* (1835) reputedly sold some 600,000 copies by the 1860s, and *The Sacred Harp* (1844) went through multiple printings to satisfy the national demand. In addition, calls for greater cross-denominational uniformity in liturgical elements were heard.

The most visible and likely the most influential of the demonstrations of unity or coherence among Protestant Christians at midcentury, however, was the domination of the religious landscape by Gothic Revival churches. Many felt that if the potential for a unified Protestant Christianity were to come to fruition, surely it would be made clear by uniformity in the houses Christians dedicated to God. By the mid-1850s, U.S. Protestants had achieved this goal, overwhelmingly embracing a single architectural style—the Gothic—as appropriate for Christian worship. Just as the Broadway Tabernacle congregation illustrated the turmoil over political issues and the search for Christian unity through worship, the new church the members completed in 1858 provides a useful stepping-off point for a consideration of efforts to use architecture to create at least an image of Protestant harmony if not actual unity among congregations. This congregation serves, once again, as an example, but in this case of the Protestant embrace of Gothic vocabularies and design.

Abandoning the increasingly valuable location in the commercial district to move uptown in 1858, the congregation selected a site in a residential neighborhood near the intersection of Broadway, Sixth Avenue, and Thirty-fourth Street.[43] The new church, designed by architect Leopold Eidlitz, one of the major apologists for Gothic Revival in the city, boasted the acme of Gothic design. The exterior roofline indicated a cruciform plan formed by a nave intersected by trancepts. A four-stage tower adjacent to the "west end" of this nave anchored the building to the corner site. The Broadway side presented a highly ornamented face to the public. Tripartite pointed-arch doors with tympanums were topped by gables and tracery-filled pointed windows above. The tripartite theme, symbolizing the Trinity, was also reflected in the three lancet windows in the tower. Fully buttressed, this imposing feature was topped with a belfry that boasted pointed-arch vents and opposing gables topped with pinnacles. The buttresses also culminated in pinnacles, making the belfry one of the most highly ornamented features of the exterior. Inside, the church featured a basilica plan (not a cruciform one as the exterior suggested) with a 90-by-34-foot nave. Columns divided the space into side aisles and soared to a vaulted ceiling nearly 70 feet above the congregation. Clerestory windows and stained glass along with the tripartite transept windows let abundant light into the building.[44]

Despite these High Church features, the building indicated a desire to bring the Gothic into the Protestant fold. The apse had been modified to house not a chancel with altar but a pulpit stage with a choir gallery elevated some 20 feet above the main floor and surmounted by the pipes of a large organ. This arrangement of the front-space feature was one of the few legacies of the Broadway Tabernacle and indeed of Finney's extraordinary experiments in religious architecture. Through the 1840s and into the 1850s, larger pulpit desks elevated on a broad stage and backgrounded by choir and organ slowly gained in popularity. Its integration into the Gothic churches by evangelical Protestants indicated that there were in fact limits on the extent to which such denominations were willing to embrace the medieval style. Further, although the exterior of the building indicated a cruciform plan, the interior was essentially basilical, a plan that accorded to some extent with the preaching box of traditional Protestant churches. Given the theoretical significance that High Church Gothic Revivalists invested in the principle of maintaining congruity between the exterior form and interior spaces, its contradiction also indicates some unwillingness by this group of evangelical Protestants to fully accept the Gothic.

Despite such syncretism, much of the language used by the Broadway Tabernacle Church's minister, the Reverend Joseph Thompson, in describing the building would have been quite alien to previous generations of Congregationalists. Praising the "interior effect" as "rich and imposing," he pointed out that "through the rich oak-hued case of the organ, there are glimpses of the groined ceiling before described, and the mellow tints of the clere-story windows above the chapel."[45] A touch of equivocation can also be detected, however, particularly in his observation that "the style of the building is perpendicular Gothic, carried out with a chaste and almost severe simplicity." Like the reorganized apse, this seemed to suggest a desire to integrate the pseudomedieval features into a sparer Protestant aesthetic economy. Although he concluded his point by stating that the simplicity "imparts an air of grandeur and beauty to the whole structure," a word choice suggesting a somewhat more grandiose aesthetic, such equivocal language suggests a certain permeability or exchange between the Protestant tradition and this medieval style.[46]

Nevertheless, the cruciform roofline, nave, apse, vaulting, columns, aisles, galleries, clerestory, and stained glass of the Broadway Tabernacle Church illustrate not only a new type of Protestant church but also the new language of evangelical Protestant church architecture. The foundation upon which this new language evolved was Christian unity. Postulated as an ideal by religionists but taken as an accomplished fact by architects, Christian unity permitted the Protestant embracing of the Gothic Revival style. As the Broadway Tabernacle Church, along with many similar contemporaneous buildings, demonstrated, Gothic Revival architecture, perceived as generically Christian, bridged the ideological chasm between its liturgical Roman Catholic origins and nonliturgical evangelicalism. In their search for Christian coherence, evangelical Protestants separated the architecture from its liturgical function and imagined a generic Christian origin. Retaining its claim to ancient roots, this generic Christianity not only coincided with, it also defined and advanced the unified Christianity that evangelicals sought amid the political turbulence of the United States.[47]

The historicization of the Gothic as a generic Christian building style had arisen in England in the late 1830s and early 1840s among Anglicans and Anglo-Catholics interested in the historical study of church architecture and liturgy. Organizing the Cambridge Camden Society and spawning what became known as the Ecclesiology movement, academicians and clergy members searched for meaning in the hundreds of medieval churches, many of which were little more than ruins, that dotted the English countryside. The remarkable accomplishment of the movement was its claiming of medieval (specifically, Gothic) architectural forms not only as appropriate for Anglican use but also as fully expressive of a nationalist Anglican religious ideology.[48] Reformation quibbles over the role of the clergy, the sacraments, and worship practices evaporated as Gothic design and, more precisely, English Gothic design (often called "pointed architecture") was hailed as the only truly Christian building style precisely because it embodied Christian (i.e., generic Christian) principles. Ecclesiologists argued that medieval builders' piety and reverence so infused their work that their buildings, and particularly their churches, were uniquely Christian. Gothic proportions, structural honesty, and transparent relationship between interior and exterior could only have been achieved by true Christians.[49] That these were pre-Reformation Christians did not greatly trouble the Anglican Ecclesiologists. When A. W. N. Pugin argued for the ongoing significance of their Roman Catholic contexts, he was denounced by the Oxford Ecclesiologists, who claimed Gothic features as purely Christian and therefore intimately linked with Anglicanism. As historian James White points out, the Anglican Ecclesiologists argued further that because the Catholic church had abandoned the Gothic style in the Renaissance for the pagan forms of classical architecture, it had relinquished its claim to Gothic construction, form, and design.[50]

Ecclesiology, or the study of church architecture and liturgy, quickly migrated across the Atlantic. American architects Richard Upjohn and James Renwick, leading designers of Episcopal churches, were drawing upon the English scholarship in the late 1830s. By 1841 a well-read author in the *New York Review* argued that the Gothic style was eminently appropriate for ecclesiastical architecture, initiating what would eventually become a widely public discussion of the style. By 1848 the architectural community had grown so interested in the topic that a group formed the New York Ecclesiology Society as a professional forum in which to discuss the relative merits of Gothic design.[51]

Ecclesiologists' work lent a powerfully expressive architectural component to discussions of Christian unity, particularly among architects interested not only in design but also in professionalizing their growing field of expertise. The Gothic Revival served the newly organized profession of architecture well by providing a context within which specialized design knowledge became invested with heightened respect and authority. Not only did the American Institute of Architects (AIA) build its reputation on this new foundation of specialized expertise, but many an architect established his professional credentials in the same way.

In the United States, these professionals were particularly interested in the question of the appropriateness of Gothic for ecclesiastical buildings and often used language connecting the style to a kind of generic Christianity. Further, these discussions were not isolated within the architectural community; they often reached a relatively broad public audience. For instance, in an article that appeared in the *North American Review* in 1836, architect Henry Russell Cleveland lamented the state of religious architecture in the United States and effused that "the sublime, the glorious Gothic . . . was the architecture of Christianity."[52] His sentiment was echoed eight years later in the same periodical when Arthur Gilman proclaimed Gothic "*the Christian Style.*"[53]

Although these first U.S. apologists, like the British Ecclesiologists, were speaking primarily about Episcopal or Anglican church buildings, the sentiment rapidly claimed a more sweeping territory. For instance, Eidlitz, designer of the new Broadway Tabernacle Church and cofounder of the AIA,[54] suggested a Platonic model by which the Gothic expressed Christian sentiments. In two papers presented to the AIA in 1858, he argued that the best architecture is that which physically expresses the idea that instigated building in the first place—*idea* being both function, or purpose, as well as the ideologies associated with that function. For instance, Greek temples articulated the idea of "the material presence of the Deity." As "structures erected for the purpose of representing the mysterious abode of that Deity," he wrote, they "were intended to be impenetrable to the profane eye of the people, . . . destined to remain outside." Temple design, Eidlitz argued, embodied this idea admirably in "the well defined and excluding squareness in the form of the main temple, the absence of openings for light and air, the magnitude of its colonnades, the majesty of its elevation above the surrounding grounds, the gigantic proportions."[55] Clearly, he surmised, these ideas embodied within

Greek architecture made that style inappropriate for Christian buildings, a sentiment that handily dismissed the majority of the existing Protestant churches, which had been built on Federalist and classical models. Gothic architecture, in contrast, embodied the idea of the transcendent Christian God and the necessity of communal worship:

> The God in Christianity is comprehensible only to the inner man, and only to be rendered in the monuments of Christianity by loftiness of structure, the termination of which in every direction, is to be comparatively removed from the eye. The tendency of the structure must be continually upwards . . . leading the mind to the infinite *above*, which conveys the idea of the presence of God, not only beyond the limits of the building, but beyond the limits of space appreciable to the physical sense. . . . Its interior must, in its architectural expression, elevate the mind above all earthly thoughts; its forms must be filled with a spirit which in its development leads the mind toward the high undefinable ideas of that All-seeing and unseen God, whose presence there and everywhere, every member of that congregation has come to acknowledge and worship.[56]

For Eidlitz, as for his English counterparts, the medieval style achieved the most effective embodiment of the Christian idea, reaching "perfection" in the spaces of the cruciform plan with its nave, chancel, and transepts; in the supporting system of piers, shafts, moldings, ribs, and arches; and in the atmosphere of light and color. This idea was, then, neither Roman Catholic nor Protestant—it was Christian.[57]

A less circumspect if more enthusiastic convert to the Gothic, J. Coleman Hart, crowed that "Christianity 'abode upon the world' and invented Gothic architecture."[58] Adopting the title "Unity in Architecture" for a paper presented to the AIA in 1859, Hart used the idea of Christian unity to argue for the efficacy of the Gothic. Echoing the earlier view of the inappropriateness of classical architecture for Christian building, Hart went further and condemned Roman churches as illustrating a "struggle that Christianity endured in order to rid herself of the material forms indigenous to a pagan religion." The round arches of Hagia Sophia and San Vitalis were "worn out . . . grown old in the service of the heathen, whose form lent no aid to the Christian worshiper, suggesting no holy thoughts." He even went so far as to condemn St. Paul's of London (among others) as a "huge architectural humor and gigantic excrescence."[59] More important, however, Hart linked the Gothic to a fairly explicit, if naive, understanding of Christianity as an increasingly unified religious outlook and argued that unification was precisely what made the revival of the Gothic both necessary and fitting: "Now that the Church is growing in 'all might, majesty, and power,' supported by the tendency of Christians to unity in belief, so is there an inclination to restore her ancient ally to its former power and greatness." Christian unity requires its quintessential architectural expression: "No two styles were invented by the same religion. Our religion has its style. We may hesitate, but there must be *unity; unity in religion, unity in architecture, and the union of both*" (emphasis in original).[60]

This position was not so quickly accepted. Questioning the premise of Christian unity, architect Richard Morris Hunt responded that, taken to its logical end, Hart's argument "substantially proved that Gothic architecture should give way to another style (in Protestant countries at least)." Because the Reformation in effect created a new religion, he asserted, "*a new style of architecture* was necessary to express the *change in religion*" (emphasis in original).[61] For Hunt, raised in a Unitarian church and schooled by Quakers, the Roman Catholicism that gave rise to Gothic ecclesiastical architecture differed substantially from Protestantism, and if one accepted the premise that each religion gave rise to a single architectural style, then Protestantism had no business appropriating the style of Catholicism.

Hunt's line of reasoning echoed sentiments expressed in the Presbyterian press four years earlier. An 1855 article by Albert and William Dod in the Old School *Biblical Repertory and Princeton Review* lamented that Protestant Christendom had contributed no art to the world. Taking the well-known Ecclesiological line, the authors condemned the use of Renaissance classicism in such buildings as St. Paul's in London. The argument was based not, however, on the grounds that the style derived from pagan origins (Ecclesiologists' reasoning) but on the grounds that it incorporated the "Jesuitical elements of Italian art."[62] Christianity, for these authors, was clearly divided—Catholic (disparagingly called "Romish") and Protestant—and only in the modern period was Protestantism prepared to advance a wholly new architecture. Just what that architecture should be, however, remained problematic for the writers. Full adoption of the Gothic style was out of the question, for both the feeling and the spaces of the "Romish" Gothic church interfered with Protestant worship.

In particular, these authors declared the medieval spaces suspect and were careful to make a clear distinction between the "elements of Gothic style" (i.e., an ornamental vocabulary that suggests a generic Christianity) and Gothic form. In this latter category, they argued that the vaulted spaces of the cathedral not only catered to liturgical worship but also posited a mysterious, transcendental God approachable only through ecclesiastical hierarchies. Assuming a kind of spatial determinism, the Dods warned against the Protestant adoption of this form:

> We may continue to use the elements of Gothic style as convenient and beautiful forms of church ornament, but the mechanical application of the forms of an elder style is a far different thing from the cordial appropriation of them. Indeed we very much question whether the Protestant faith is even yet sufficiently strong and intelligent to be with safety put to the temptation. We may imagine that our faith, in its higher spirituality, is above all visible symbolism except what we have in church and sacraments—we may fancy that we are capable of using indifferently all, any or no art, and that we are far and for ever beyond the poetic period in these respects—but, notwithstanding all this, when we consider the native tendencies of our minds to form and [sic] idol, and the insidious sway which every religious symbolism has acquired over the hearts of its subjects, we cannot but tremble at the idea of the Protestant world generally making experiment of genuine cathedral art. With all its beauty, and what stage of the true religion has ever been without it? A Gothic nave is a fearful place, and cathedral art has a power that would, in its own time and way, sooner or later, compel cathedral worshipers to a cathedral service. The only adequate cathedral service is the mass. The very idea is preposterous—turn any Protestant congregation into a Gothic cathedral, and where are they, and what have they for the place?[63]

In contrast, the adapting of certain stylistic elements, while not ideal because it bastardized the style, was, nevertheless, the Dods concluded, acceptable for Protestant churches.[64] Stained glass, pointed arches, and clustered columns had their place in Protestant architecture, assuming they were not used in excess and that they helped to create a "feeling of worship" characterized as "a true Sunday impression, the elements of which are sacred rest, freedom, and joy; the correlatives in style would be quiet, extent and simplicity, in a word the power and tranquillity of aerial expanse . . . a feeling excited by the contemplation of nature at rest," an "atmosphere . . . [that] should be perfectly genial."[65] For the Dods, then, while full adoption of Gothic architecture by Protestants was out of the question, integration of the pointed vocabulary was acceptable.

As architects framed the question, the only alternative to pointed style was the pagan classical style—and this was no alternative at all. In 1858, the new Classical Revival church built by Gardiner Spring's Brick Presbyterian congregation in New York was excoriated by an AIA writer for being unidentifiable as a Christian building: "Why is it modeled after a Roman temple, if it be a Presbyterian church? Or if it be a temple, why has it a spire? A temple was, with the heathens who originated it, the abode of a deity—to be looked on from a distance, not entered: therefore the nakedness within, and the boldness and simplicity of the features without." The author went on to ask, "Is this building a fair embodiment of Presbyterianism?" Resorting to not-so-goodnatured humor, he answered resoundingly in the negative: "The only features which we can discover that have any reference to Presbyterian doctrine, are the flowers festooned in frames like picture-frames, over the windows on each side of the tower—their very presence in such a place is strongly emblematic of the total depravity of man. And the anteas in the corners formed by the front of the building and the tower, where they break at right angles, will readily be acknowledged as original sin."[66] Ultimately, however, the author blames this catastrophe not on the architect, but on the congregation itself, whose building committee "sadly hampered" the otherwise well-respected designer.[67]

Despite reservations about its non-Protestant origins, it is clear that if a congregation—Episcopalian, Presbyterian, or otherwise—was to have a new church designed by an architect with professional credentials, the building would likely be Gothic. In this context, the concept of unified Christianity could be assigned a historical dimension through architectural expression alone. For many less-technical religious writers, the goal was to create a church that "looked like a church." Gothic verticality, delicate spires, and pointed windows served as iconic signs of otherworldliness and ecclesiasticism. As congregations of many denominations—Baptist, Congregationalist, Presbyterian, Methodist, Unitarian, Lutheran, Episcopalian, Catholic—built Gothic Revival churches throughout the United States, Christian unity became a visual feature of the American landscape itself.[68]

As critical as the Gothic style was to advancing the concept of Christian unity (along with the professionalization of architects), its rapid hegemony on the religious landscape must also be understood within the context of denominationalism, for strengthened denominationalism played a key role in the construction of these buildings. Again, Congregationalism serves as a useful example. Among the steps taken at the 1852 Albany Conference to form a national Congregationalism was the organization of the American Congregational Union, a committee charged with encouraging "church expansion"—the organizing of new Congregational churches in frontier areas—that authorized $50,000 to be disbursed through loans or grants to new congregations needing church buildings.[69] The conference encouraged all Congregational churches to solicit "simultaneous contributions" on the first Sunday in January 1853 to be dedicated to the new Congregational Union for building purposes. Some $60,000 was collected and ultimately disbursed, "showing the wisdom of assisting young and feeble churches to erect houses of worship."[70] From its 1859 inception on, the *Congregational Yearbook* carried a report of the union's activities, the amount of income into the funds, the loans made, and pleas for established congregations to give generously to the fund in order to advance Congregationalism throughout the West. As a result of the union, hundreds of newly formed congregations as far afield as Wisconsin, Minnesota, Iowa, Kansas, Nebraska, New Mexico, Colorado, and the Dakota Territory received grants or loans to be put toward construction costs.

Disbursing these funds, Congregationalists expanded ("extended" in the parlance of the period) the denomination on a national scale previously unimagined. Other denominations followed suit. The Presbyterian General Assembly, which had created its own Board of Church Extension in 1844 (most likely providing the model for the Congregational Union), reevaluated the board's organization, role, and funding in the 1850s, voting in 1853 to appropriate $100,000 for church expansion.[71] Chicago Methodists founded the Northwestern Church Extension Society in 1855 to raise money in the East for western church building, and the General Conference followed suit in 1864, forming the Committee on Church Extension (later the Board of Church Extension).[72]

Given their increasing involvement in building funding, it is not surprising that national denominational bodies soon became involved in providing plans and suggestions for appropriate architectural style. Between 1851 and 1853, the New School *Presbyterian Magazine* published a total of eleven exterior illustrations of Presbyterian churches, seven of which were Gothic.[73] Following the Presbyterians by a few years, the *Congregational Quarterly* began with its third issue, July 1859, to regularly publish drawings of new Congregational churches and their plans. With few exceptions, the buildings featured were Gothic.[74] The April 1860 issue, for instance, presented an article on the Gothic Revival Clinton Avenue Congregational Church in Brooklyn, hailing its 90- and 110-foot towers, as well as its "audience-room 104 feet long by 68 wide, entirely free from obstructions, and over-hung by the triple arches of a groined ceiling, with large pendants and corbels, from which spring the many principal and cross ribs, all richly ornamented" (fig. 3.2). The pointed-arch windows, "filled with stained glass of the richest patterns," and the lush woodwork of the gallery fronts and pew ends added to the effect, producing, in the eyes of the author, a "house of worship [that] is conspicuous and beautiful."[75] In this description, as in Thompson's of the Broadway Tabernacle Church, the blending of High and Low Church concerns is again evident. Published accounts like these rendered Gothic buildings appropriate for evangelical services while the buildings served as models for other congregations to follow. Thus advanced a Gothic stylistic hegemony that would be well established by the 1860s.

Denominational publications often favored the work of particular architects. The *Congregational Quarterly*, for instance, presented the work of individual architects and advice from architecturally experienced clergy to its readers. The July 1859 issue included a full-page advertisement for architect J. D. Towle, which included the names of two clergymen prominent in the church-building movement as references. The same issue published the Reverend I. P. Langworthy's article "Ventilation of Churches," and the Reverend H. M. Dexter's "Meeting-Houses: Considered Historically and Suggestively" had appeared in the previous issue.[76] This denominational publication and others like it, which aimed at providing local congregations with up-to-date information on building, lent a national denominational imprimatur to Gothic church architecture.

Denominations also sanctioned architectural pattern books. For instance, in 1858 the Boston Conference of Methodist Ministers praised the Reverend George Bowler's book, *Chapel and Church Architecture*, stating that "the plans and sketches of church

Fig. 3.2. Clinton Avenue Congregational Church, New York City. 1855. *Congregational Quarterly* 2 (Apr. 1860): 213. Courtesy Special Collections and Rare Books, University of Minnesota Libraries, Twin Cities.

architecture, designed and drawn by our brother, Rev. George Bowler, evince, in a high degree, correctness of taste and skill in execution, combining in themselves, to an extent seldom equaled, beauty, economy, and convenience; and we feel confident that the publication of the work would be of essential service to the churches in this country."[77] Though Bowler's examples presented an array of stylistically eclectic buildings, the frontispiece of the book depicted a Gothic Revival church and a Gothic Revival parsonage as icons of evangelical Protestantism, although they remain framed by classical columns and entablature (fig. 3.3). Moreover, though the book depicted buildings whose estimated costs ranged from $1,200 to $30,000, the upper price ranges consisted exclusively of Gothic buildings.[78] Thus, while ideas about Christian unity may well have moved both architects and building committees toward the Gothic, desire for denominational extension, spurred in no small part by the perception of competition from other denominations and the desire to erect the most fashionable church possible, accomplished the widespread dissemination of the style. The most up-to-date and progressive congregations would worship in Gothic Revival churches.

In this complex architectural and religious context, the role of the church building on the urban and rural landscape shifted somewhat. With the Gothic Revival, evangeli-

Fig. 3.3. George Bowler, frontispiece, *Chapel and Church Architecture* (Boston: Jewett, 1856). Courtesy Art Institute of Chicago.

cal churches looked to a newly reconstructed past for their legitimacy, which a historicized Christian architectural style, the Gothic, provided. The Gothicized Christian landscape in the United States carried a new ideological self-consciousness. While Classical Revival architecture of the eighteenth and early nineteenth centuries had claimed a relationship between Christianity and the humanistic ideals of the Roman Empire (including, but not limited to republicanism), it had not been used to legitimize religion itself. Christian or, specifically, Protestant legitimacy and authority preceded the adoption of the classical architectural style. With the Gothic Revival, however, the architectural style legitimized modern Christianity, particularly Protestantism, by historicizing it, by visually underscoring the connection between an idealized medieval Christian piety and modern congregations, modern worship.

In the social context of upheaval in which factionalism and schism characterized many congregations, Protestants groped for some firm ground upon which to stand. Christianity needed legitimizing in ways never before required, and art, specifically architecture, could accomplish this in a highly visible way. The historicizing of nineteenth-century Protestantism's medieval Christian roots occurred simultaneously with the historicizing of other evangelical forms as Puritan. For instance, the strategy David Hale used of invoking the Pilgrim and Puritan fathers' imprimatur upon democratic decision making and due process was quite common at midcentury, when claiming Puritan origins legitimized a wide variety of Protestant actions and ideas.[79] Thus, when in 1839 the Broadway Tabernacle congregation, embroiled in the slavery controversy, asked, "What is the role of religion?" the answer, "to worship God," was articulated by the tabernacle church's Rules, which bespoke Puritan sources. This same answer was reiterated two decades later by their new Gothic building, which bespoke the medieval triumph of Christianity.[80] Both strategies set the church apart from the fray; its distinctive ancient character indicated its purity in a troubled world. Nevertheless, religious organizations also used the Gothic Revival aesthetic to publicly assert a vision of universal Christianity; while not necessarily representative of the current situation, it did project an ideal of unity that might someday be achieved. In so doing, evangelical groups laid claim to a continuing role within both the public landscape and the public arena. The church would be an institution *in* public, but not necessarily *of* the public. A church must not only look like a church, an institution distinct from and somewhat apart from the world, but it must also *act* like a church in distinctive and otherworldly ways.

Audience and Clergy within Evangelical Gothic Churches

Struggle for unity, then, animated the realm of church architecture at midcentury. One final context for the negotiation of power remains to be examined: the worship service itself. Within these buildings with their ecclesiastically oriented spaces and awe-inspiring trappings, ministers and laity necessarily continued to negotiate their roles and relative influence vis-à-vis one another. If the mission of the new church was to emphasize worship, just what form would that worship take? Would it be clergy-centered as the new Gothic settings suggested or would it be audience-centered? Retaining the evangelical tenor of the earlier revival period—and flying in the face of the history of High Church Gothic forms—responses came back in favor of the latter, and discussions typically centered on one question: How could the clergy get the people in the pews more involved in worship services? Increasing audience participation emerged as a signal goal as changes in worship were discussed.

The evolution of worship practice was, of course, not a new phenomenon, as the earlier discussion of revivalism has shown. Congregational services, for example, had undergone significant changes in the eighteenth century. While seventeenth-century services often included an interpolated reading of Scripture (often a full chapter or more, complete with annotation and discussion), clerical and lay prophesying, and a period devoted to questioning the preacher on points raised in the sermon, the gradual elimination of these parts of the service in the eighteenth century not only significantly reduced audience participation, but also excluded those gathered from the interpretive portion of the service, thereby concentrating this important power in the hands of the clergy.[81] Perhaps to mitigate this result, the role of music was expanded and stressed during the eighteenth century to enhance the expression of praise and devotion. Lining out psalms (i.e., having the congregation repeat each line after it was sung by a precentor) proved awkward and was slowly displaced by the singing of religious songs, or hymns. Congregationalist Isaac Watt brought forth his hymnal at midcentury, which gave an enormous boost to that denomination's music. This growing emphasis on praise introduced inevitable performance issues—some congregation members could sing, others could not. By the 1760s some congregations placed good singers together to lead the audience. Congregationalists in Hollis, New Hampshire, for instance, urged "that those persons that have taken pains to instruct themselves in singing may have the two fore seats below on the men's side" in order that they might lead the rest of the congregation.[82] Such grouping of the better singers led naturally to the formation of voluntary choirs and later to the hiring of professional singers. As musical performance was increasingly valued, instruments were added to services. The bass viol is noted in services as early as the mid-1700s, and the clarinet, violin, flute, bassoon, and cello all appear from time to time in congregation records.[83] The first organs made their appearance in American Congregational churches in the 1770s and 1780s. Integrated initially as an aide to congregational singing, instruments and choirs quickly moved to anthem performances sans congregation. By 1800 the usual Congregational order of service included the opening blessing, followed by a psalm or hymn, a Scripture reading, a prayer and an anthem, the sermon, another prayer, another psalm or hymn, and the closing blessing.[84] Congregational participation consisted mainly of psalm and hymn singing.

Generally speaking, changes in the spatial settings of worship accompanied these changes in the services. The eighteenth-century minimizing of the interaction between minister and audience helped to usher in the shift in Congregational meetinghouses from their original width-wise orientation to a longitudinal orientation. This arrangement placed congregants much farther from the minister but had the advantage of accommodating more people within the space. The growing use of organs also led to a shift in spatial arrangements. When first introduced, organs and other instruments were located within the gallery opposite the pulpit, and congregants stood and faced the back of the room during musical pieces. Early nineteenth-century revivalism, however, relocated the organ and choir to the preaching platform and eliminated the earlier awkward practice.

The spatial arrangements made for the celebration of the Lord's Supper in Low Church services, including those of Congregationalists, also varied throughout the eighteenth and early nineteenth centuries. Observing the sacrament once a month (this too varied; some took Communion four times a year), congregants partaking in the supper would generally advance to the table placed just under the preaching platform to be served the bread and wine by the minister. Some congregations, however, placed tables within the main aisle and served communicants there. Experimentation is apparent during the early nineteenth century. One nineteenth-century writer described a church in which hinges partway up on the sides of the high-walled box pews allowed them to be "turn[ed] down and serve as part of the table."[85] Lewis Tappan commented on taking Communion in the Unitarian Stone Church near Boston by kneeling at an altar rail. In his opinion, however, the method was not satisfactory, as serving each individual communicant was a long process, which extended the service to nearly double its normal length. Other congregations, adopting a more expedient strategy, began to serve communicants within the pews.[86]

Congregational and Presbyterian worship were profoundly affected by the revivals of the 1820s and 1830s. Focused on the goal of converting sinners by confronting the unchurched with the reality and profundity of damnation and the saving grace of the Lord, a distinctive revivalist order of service, sometimes termed the "frontier tradition," emerged. This tripartite service began with prayer and praise (preliminaries), moved on to the sermon (the centerpiece of the service), and then concluded with the "harvest" of souls in which potential converts were called to the anxious bench and exhorters spoke from the floor.[87] Pleased with the success of such services during the eastern revivals of the 1830s, both Congregationalists and New School Presbyterians advanced this basic order as they extended their denominations into the newly opening western lands.

As revivalism waned, however, various individuals pointed out that on any given Sunday the majority of those gathered at church were already converted Christians. While revivalism had in some churches meant the adoption of New Measures techniques, which shifted the emphasis from the corporate body of the church to the affective response of the individual, the cessation of revivalist evangelizing left clergy scrambling for new strategies. What remained from the revival era, however, was a concern for "results," for goal-oriented services. At midcentury, worship goals were twofold, encompassing "adoration and praise" and "edification of members in divine love." The evangelizing goal had evolved, and ministers' new task was to use gospel preaching, music, and prayer to elevate, improve, and refine—not save—those Christians gathered on Sunday morning.[88]

Two main interior innovations appeared in the Gothic Revival churches, both derived from the urban revivalist churches of Finney and both designed to enhance the fundamental heuristic nature that the old evangelizing and the new edifying services shared. The first of these was the universal replacement of the elevated pulpit with a preaching platform that housed a pulpit and, in some cases, a lectern. Behind the pulpit, choir seating rose in ranked pews and above them rose the pipes of an organ. As it had during the revivals, this arrangement provided much greater freedom of movement for the preacher and helped to maintain the visual attention of the congregants. The second innovation was the general replacement of box pews with the benchlike "slip pews" that remain common today. Arranged in parallel rows angled toward the preaching platform (fig. 3.4), these created more direct sightlines to the pulpit platform than had their predecessors. The slanted arrangement of rectilinear pews, a rather modest adaptation of Finney's more radical arcs of pews in the original Broadway Tabernacle,

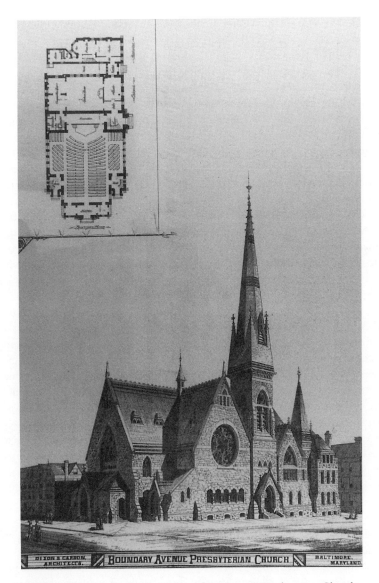

Fig. 3.4. Drawings for proposed Boundary Avenue Presbyterian Church, Baltimore, Md. Dixon and Carson, archs. *American Architect and Building News*, 10 May 1879, plate follows 148. Courtesy Special Collections and Rare Books, University of Minnesota Libraries, Twin Cities.

achieved widespread popularity within architectural literature, indicating the extent to which designers were addressing the didactic requirements of the service. As William and Albert Dod pointed out in 1855, "The three attributes of worship, teaching, and government, are the scriptural attributes of the Christian congregation," and each must be provided for within the church building. In regard to the audience room and its function of serving worship and teaching, they called for rooms "constructed in reference to facility of sound, and the convenient position of the congregation." In regard to government, they called for the placement of seats for the presbyters at the front of the audience room.[89]

Significantly, these worship forms placed most of the responsibility for success or failure squarely in the hands of the minister. Just as in the Finney revivals, the minister held great power over the situation. Yet, as the previous chapter indicates, revival audiences also could and did assert their influence, particularly in response to an ineffective preacher. As edification and praise superseded evangelizing, audiences retained the power of influence, but the context had shifted markedly with the intended goal or product. While the revival preacher's performance was calculated to produce an affective response and thus benefited greatly from the stage techniques of the actor, congregations desirous of respectable gentility renounced the emotionalism of revivals, taking religious response out of the realm of the affective. The preacher, aiming to edify his audience rather than touch their emotions, needed to emulate the teacher and be the authority figure rather than the actor. Once again, clerical authority shifted toward education, a shift illustrated in Finney's move to Oberlin College. Furthermore, as long as evangelizing preachers offered salvation, they offered something very dear indeed and thus retained a strong power over their audiences. When ministers offered opportunities for praising God, they offered little that many worshipers could not do in the privacy of their own homes, and, in fact, this period saw significant growth in home devotionals.[90] When ministers offered edification, they similarly offered something that many middle-class congregants may have deemed of relatively little value, for new literature, journals, lyceums, and concerts gave people wide means for self-improvement. Thus, the stakes of Sunday services lost their immediacy. Whereas in earlier periods audiences had discussed the sermon and scriptural interpretation during services, by the mid-nineteenth century, they were no longer involved in the theological foundations of worship. They had lost their stake in defining and articulating their beliefs. In effect, they had fewer reasons to engage with the proceedings.

A lack of congregational interest particularly concerned Presbyterians, who focused much of their lively debate over worship practice on the question of audience participation in praise and devotional services. This Presbyterian discussion of participation emerged precisely at the disjunction between affective New School evangelizing and Old School fortification of the faithful through scripturally precedented methods. New Schoolers particularly found themselves at a loss with the ebbing of revivalism, for if evangelizing techniques were discarded, along with them would go much of the congregation's participation in the service. John Hall articulated the fears of many when he wrote:

> I am sure of the sympathy of hundreds of ministers in saying, that there is scarcely a
> more depressing influence on preaching-energy and on the devotional sentiment, than
> the indifference of a congregation to the act of praise. How melancholy, after reading
> such a psalm as "firm on a rock He made me stand / And taught my cheerful tongue /

To praise the wonders of his hand, / In a new thankful song" . . . to look over the congregation, and see even those "saints," whose very hearts should exult in such suggestions, sitting as listlessly as if deaf and dumb; not a voice, nor a tear, nor a look implying emotion, nor even attention; the psalm-book, if held at all, held away from the eyes.[91]

Many others similarly lamented the indifference they read in the faces in the pews, in the singing, in the general lack of attention, in the whispering, spitting, and even sleeping during services.[92] Both New and Old School Presbyterians felt that the solution lay with the congregational community itself, gathered on Sunday morning for the explicit purpose of praising God in the most edifying manner possible. But while both groups acknowledged that this was a worthy goal, parishioners, by and large, were not entering into it with the enthusiasm of earlier revival converts.

New Schoolers particularly feared that disengaged Presbyterians were seeking the Romanticism of Anglican and Roman liturgicism to fulfill their spiritual needs. Hall noted a veritable exodus of Presbyterians to Episcopal churches whose appeal, he lamented, "lies not in conviction, nor altogether in the spirit of fashion; but very much in the increased interest given to the public worship by the new spectacles exhibited; the increased attention to architecture, chanting, postures, and superstitious formulas."[93] Liturgicism was the draw, and Hall echoed the Dods and others when he warned that worship within Gothic buildings necessarily moved toward the rote forms of the Anglican and Roman Catholic churches:

> We are making great strides in architectural decorations, and in choral elegancies; we build dark Gothic churches, and spend thousands for an organ, and hundreds for the wages of singers; but all these innovations on our primitive simplicity have the effect of exciting a liturgical taste, whilst at the same time they take from our worship those very qualities of popular interest which belong to our peculiar forms when rightly observed, and which are supplied by the greater variety and display of modern liturgies. The very scenery of a grand church excites the expectation of corresponding services.[94]

This result was not inevitable, however. In Hall's estimation it could be countered by congregational participation in one specific activity—singing—which he described as "the only part of worship in which the people are expected to unite audibly." He entreated his audience to "let the voices of the whole congregation cause the groined ceilings and the pillared roofs to echo with the Psalms to the good old tunes which our fathers taught us; let the organ, in its highest swell, and the choir, in their strongest voice, be heard only as the guides and supports of the voices of the people—the men, women, and children, each with Psalm-book in hand." Then, he concluded, "there will be a conformity of the place and the service."[95] Vocal expression of piety, singing, was the cure for the problem of disaffection. The extent to which true religious feeling was absent, he insinuated, jeopardized Christianity itself, and only through a return to the "gospel simplicity" of "our ancient customs" would the church achieve "through the divine favour, a general revival of our piety."[96]

Such methods of enhancing audience participation were embraced by the New School *Presbyterian Magazine,* which regularly reported on such efforts throughout the country. For instance, in 1855 it carried a notice that congregational singing in the Fifth Avenue Church had been enhanced through the dismissal of the choir and the relocating of the organ to the front of the audience room. The instrument was "used merely to give the

pitch and keep time" while the audience was led in the singing of "the old tunes, familiar to us an age ago" by a precentor standing near but below the minister.[97] The New
School solution, then, was a return to, if not the same enthusiasm of the revival days,
certainly a similar individual piety expressed in prayer and song.[98]

William Dod had similarly warned of the influence of Gothic spaces toward Romanism
with its incumbent liturgicism, yet he and other Old Schoolers did not necessarily fear
the latter. Instead, using a historicizing strategy similar to that which claimed the Gothic
as universal Christian expression, they fixed their gaze on the past to demonstrate that
in its earliest form Reformed religion and liturgies did indeed correspond. Charles Baird's
1855 book, *Eutaxia; or, The Presbyterian Liturgies: Historical Sketches*, reconstructed the
early Protestant liturgies of John Calvin, John Knox, the German Reformed church,
and the Dutch Reformed church. Reviewing *Eutaxia* in the *Biblical Repertory*, Princeton's
well-known Old School apologist Charles Hodge commended it and urged the compilation of a collection of prayers and liturgical forms for special occasions from the works
of these early Protestants. Treading carefully to appeal to American sensibilities, still
suspicious of ecclesiastical power, Hodge argued that because Reformed liturgies remained
optional, not universally imposed by ecclesiastical hierarchies, they remained consistent
with "Christian liberty," a concept that Hodge advanced to conflate egalitarian political
philosophy with Reformed Protestantism. Having such material available to ministers would both improve the prayers of ministers and maintain congruity in the celebration of the sacraments and other important events like marriages and funerals.
Baird published just such a collection of prayers two years later, and thus with Hodge's
imprimatur, many previously Low Church Presbyterians moved distinctly toward
liturgical formalism.[99]

Clearly, this shift occurred simultaneously with the adoption of Gothic vocabularies,
yet the relationship between the two phenomena is not easily discernible. Historian
Julius Melton notes that while both shared roots in the Romanticism of the period, the
discussion of liturgy was rarely specifically connected to the increasing use of the Gothic
in churches. Presbyterians, he argues, were not wont to "philosophize or theologize"
their reasons for adopting the style.[100] While it is true that discussions of the Gothic
published in Presbyterian and Congregationalist journals do not go much beyond hailing
the style as most "harmonious" or "churchly," the ideological discussion does appear in
the architectural trade literature. As church-building committees addressed the issues of
style, their understanding of its appropriateness rested, in all likelihood, on the skill of
the architect in articulating the concept of a historicized, universalized Christian style. The
historicization of the Gothic in this fashion made it a legitimate choice. In a similar way,
the historicization of liturgical prayers and forms as descended directly from the founders
of the Reformed church legitimated them. The solution to the problems of worshiper
disinterest and clerical incompetence lay in the recovery of an ancient past.

Thus, the adoption of the Gothic and the interest in liturgy shared a similar method:
the appropriation and reinterpretation of the past for the purpose of reshaping and
reformulating the Protestant church to respond to contemporary situations. Fear of disruptive politics and the need for and idealization of Christian unity led to increasing
formalism, both in architecture and liturgies. At a time in which worship practice was
seen as a remedy for the disastrous effects that political quarrels wrought within congregations, the medieval architectural vocabularies and spaces—the Gothic Revival—helped

to instantiate and maintain the legitimacy of the new formalistic approaches to evangelical worship, which separated church mission and cultus from the volatile public sphere. Born of an unwillingness to sacrifice congregational unity in the face of individual political convictions, the more formalized worship transformed services into internalized individual encounters with supernatural power, with God. Outward expressions of emotion, either political or pietistic, could be avoided. New understandings of Christian and Puritan heritage located congregants within a proud history. Such strategies kept the church relevant, if not fully involved in the social and political turbulence raging throughout the nation. However, the formalism that evangelicals achieved in both worship and worship setting would be soon modified, and later strategies would render this period in evangelical Protestantism an interlude between the iconoclastic revivals of the 1830s and the new evangelical strategies of the closing decades of the nineteenth century.

4

Spiritual Armories on the New Suburban Landscape

As the Union victory and the end of slavery resolved many of the social and political concerns that had prompted midcentury calls for Christian unity, evangelicals found themselves in a new era, which brought with it new demands. The postwar transformation of the U.S. economy into full-blown industrial capitalism during the closing decades of the nineteenth century brought an abundance of new ethical and social challenges, particularly to cities, which attracted thousands of rural Americans and new immigrants seeking work. Pittsburgh, Cincinnati, Cleveland, Detroit, and Chicago, all well established before the war, doubled and even tripled in population during the closing decades of the century. The most stunning urban growth, however, took place in western cities like St. Paul, Minneapolis, St. Louis, Denver, Seattle, and San Francisco, which, aided by the growing network of railroads, grew from frontier settlements before the war into full cities by the 1880s.

The changing urban demographics and geographies caused by rapid industrialization and population growth would significantly alter the lifestyles, values, and social class definitions of city residents and have a profound effect on evangelical religion in the postwar period. Separation between social classes grew to chasmlike proportions as working-class laborers and their families, demonstrating both the opportunities and the degradations of modern industrial life, subsisted on minimal wages and crowded together in often substandard housing while at the same time a new middle class coalesced, identifiable by its shared values of individualism, respectability, and materialism, and fueled by new access to consumer items and luxuries. Experiencing the same process that had ensued within established eastern cities such as New York earlier in the century, middle-class congregations in the Midwest found their social constituencies changing in the postwar years as old neighborhoods succumbed to commercial and industrial pressures. As businesses, industries, and workers moved into the city, established residents chose to move to new residential areas being developed at some distance from the city center. Such shifts challenged churches to reevaluate their positions. They needed to decide whether to remain in their original locations, and by so doing reshape their ministries to serve the new urban population, or to follow their congregations, rebuild in new neighborhoods, and retain their previous ministry, just as the

Broadway Tabernacle had done before the war. Congregations' consideration of these alternatives was further influenced by the escalating cost of maintaining church buildings and ministries, and many congregations found themselves competing with other churches for attendees who had the financial resources needed to support a religious congregation. Although evangelicals had long competed with other religious groups for members, by the late nineteenth century they energetically sought out the new middle-class families that were becoming the bellwethers of American society. In so doing, they significantly departed from the impulse to convert the working classes that had informed the earlier revivalism of Charles Grandison Finney's day.

The congregations under consideration in this chapter all chose to relocate with their members and to build new, monumental churches. As in earlier periods, these decisions raised important political and moral issues. Again, as we shall see, location and building type served as indicators of congregations' desires and religious missions within the problematic social contexts that characterized the post–Civil War period. Although the debates over these complex questions—where to build, what type of building to erect, and how the new church would convey the values of the congregation—rarely found their way into congregational documents, they are manifest in the actual decisions those congregations made and in the meanings embedded in the church buildings they erected. Each of the buildings erected by these congregations was a state-of-the-art, neomedieval auditorium church, a church type that was adopted by hundreds of evangelical congregations throughout the country, thus creating a veritable revolution in Protestant architecture in the closing decades of the nineteenth century.

That this enormously influential style developed within the historical contexts mentioned above is of particular relevance to this study. Highly expressive and complex cultural artifacts, these churches brought together widely shared meanings associated with social and economic change as well as domestic life. These meanings, embedded within these churches, will be the subject of the rest of this book. The current chapter launches that investigation, focusing on the social contexts that influenced four evangelical congregations in different cities as they each faced the questions of whether and where to build their new church and in what style. Together, these examples demonstrate how congregations used location and architectural style to address issues raised by the postwar economic and social situations and, in the process, redefined the role of evangelical religion within the new urban communities.

Politics of Church Location

The process of selecting a location for a church has always had political ramifications. For instance, within the early Puritan colonies, according to historian Marian Card Donnelly, the stipulation of "convenience" as a criterion for the location of churches in several charters reflects its importance in a society in which church attendance was a legal requirement.[1] As towns increased in size during the colonial period and families moved farther away from their churches, disputes over mandatory attendance and tax rules sometimes resulted in conflicts that could lead to schism. The growth of the outer precincts of Salem, Massachusetts, for instance, and the desire for church autonomy, as historians Paul Boyer and Stephen Nissenbaum have shown, were significant factors in the social and cultural disruption that underlay the notorious witch trials.[2] Contention over church location also arose in Anglican parishes in Virginia. As architectural historian Dell Upton has shown, while the general rule was to locate a church as near the center of a parish as possible (presumably to make it relatively convenient to all within the parish), the variety of groups involved in negotiating a location decision—from vestry committees to parishioners to the House of Burgesses to even the governor—could render the process highly contentious.[3] In the eighteenth century, the New England model of locating the church on the common green at the center of town gave way over time to the erection of competing denominational churches, resulting in skylines dotted with spires attesting not only to the presence of a Christian community but to the reality of Christian diversity and competition. As we have seen, during the revival era of the early nineteenth century, when religious groups targeted new audiences for conversion, the decision by free-church pioneers Lewis Tappan and Charles Finney to establish their church near the busy intersection of Pearl and Chatham streets was based on the recognition that attracting the unchurched city residents, who might find the regular Presbyterian churches intimidating, depended upon a highly visible location.

At midcentury, however, as congregations adopted the rhetoric of worship as the primary purpose of services, denominational literature produced by church extension boards advised that new churches should be located not on busy urban streets but on less prominent sites. In a widely distributed book on church architecture, for instance, church designer George Bowler suggested sardonically that a church should be located on a busy street only if the congregation desired "a temple of Mammon, to be filled with the tables of the money-changers," for, in his estimation, the influence of such surroundings "is calculated to press the mind into this one idea of gathering gold and heaping wealth together."[4] Likewise, he took previous generations to task for building upon the "highest summit with the intent to 'catch the eye of the traveller,'" as such thinking indicated a lack of "regard to the convenience of any man," particularly of the aged who "can repair [there] only with extreme difficulty."[5] Instead, Bowler argued, a church intended "solely for purposes of solemn heart-worship" should be located in "a spot congenial to the humble spirit of a true worshiper of the living God; not far away from the homes of the people, but amid the cheerful and hallowed associations of the dearest earthly joys, and yet away from the noise and bustle and confusion of the busiest streets of trade."[6]

Bowler's analysis illustrates that by the 1850s, casting the question of church location in terms of church mission and constituency had come to rest on a dichotomized view of public and domestic worlds. Like many denominations' spokespersons, Bowler felt the church should cast its lot with those true worshipers whose homes were defined in opposition to the life of the city. The domestic sphere with its "hallowed associations" was perceived to be in opposition, both physically and morally, to the public life of the city.[7] Locating new churches within a residential milieu, therefore, was a material articulation of the rhetoric of church leaders like David Hale, who had urged the church toward worship and away from involvement in public issues.

Yet others had not been so sure. Given the growing social complexities within cities, many had asked whether the church should function like a private institution, for the benefit of its own homogeneous family, or as a public institution serving a diverse urban population. As we have seen, in the 1830s, the free-church Presbyterians, along with other groups like the Methodists and Baptists, had purposely located their missions in the realm of the democratic project, choosing to serve the diverse urban and rural public and to be involved in pressing social and political issues of the day. Although at midcentury, domestic piety had been posited as an alternative to public involvement in the issue of slavery and had helped to reformulate the church's mission as worship rather than as outreach or social activism, by the final decades of the century, a new constellation of public issues—from poor relief to labor justice to women's rights—pressed upon congregations, and many church members, if not always the churches themselves, were becoming involved in public concerns.

Now, within the changing urban contexts of the late nineteenth century, the politics of evangelical church location was again being substantially transformed as commercial businesses, industries, and working-class residents filled the city centers and middle-class residents fled the congestion, pollution, and noise for the newly developing suburban setting on the outskirts of the midcentury city boundaries.[8] With an increasing number of church members leaving the city, congregants faced the question of whether to travel back to their home churches for services on Sunday morning or to build new churches closer to their new homes. Although many long-term members felt that the primary purpose of their churches was to serve their own spiritual needs—and thus the church should follow them into the suburbs—others argued that it was the duty of the church to remain in the city to evangelize among the growing tide of working people. These people felt that the church should not retreat from the needs of the evolving urban populations and spaces.

A significant factor in these decisions was the changing nature of evangelical worship and its rising costs from the midcentury on. To attract converts to worship, services increasingly were led by better-trained clergy, who demanded higher salaries, incorporated more music performed by paid professionals, and featured a host of elaborate accoutrements, including vestments and Communion articles, unknown to earlier generations. The growth of voluntary associations within churches—for women, for youths, for men—also increased the activities and raised the expenses of churches. But it was congregational competition that most significantly raised costs. To recruit new members from the "cultured" middle classes who could contribute to the financial well-being and social status of the church, congregations were willing to pay large sums for the best ministers and most artistic musicians and to build and furnish the most beautiful church buildings. Given the shrinking base of affluent citizens living in the heart of cities, it is not surprising that many congregations chose to build new churches near the new homes of old and potential new members. Yet within the more socially homogeneous new residential areas, they often found themselves locked in intense competition with other denominations and congregations for the same members.[9]

Defining Mission by Choosing a New Church Location

Whether in established eastern or newer midwestern cities, no reason for church construction was more powerful than the desire to continue serving members moving to new residential areas. As middle- and upper-class families sought neighborhoods safer, cleaner, and more fashionable than their former ones, urban congregations faced the loss of precisely those members who were most likely to participate in the life of the church community and to contribute substantially to its financial support. Consequently, in cities across the United States, church after church threw its lot in with the residential life of its members and followed its affluent constituents to new subdivisions. Yet the process was rarely simple for, by the 1880s, most congregations were quite aware that location was a strategic decision that not only could determine the continued existence of the congregation but also could influence, even redefine, the very mission of the church. Not surprisingly, differences of opinion among members occasionally arose. The following three examples of Methodist Episcopal congregations demonstrate a range of responses to this relocation issue.[10]

First Methodist Episcopal Church in Baltimore

The First Methodist Episcopal Church of Baltimore, which descended directly from the very first Methodist congregation established in the United States, stood in the heart of the old city at the corner of Charles and Fayette streets, only three blocks from the harbor.[11] Since the 1840s, the congregation had been influential, serving as a "mother church" that had spun off several other congregations, among them the Mount Vernon Place congregation that in 1872 had erected a large Gothic church costing more than $300,000.[12] By the early 1880s, however, times had changed. When a new pastor was installed in 1883, the congregation was $40,000 in debt, and it ranked only fifteenth among the twenty-nine M.E. churches in the Baltimore Conference in donations to conference programs that year.[13] What had previously been a strength—its ability to spawn new congregations—had become a liability, for the membership of First M.E. had been dispersing and declining throughout the 1870s. As early as 1866 congregation members had realized that their downtown location was no longer conducive to attracting attendees. As a history of the denomination's work in Maryland written that year pointed out, "The encroachments of business upon the center of the city have left but few families residing near the church. The erection of other prosperous churches have properly drawn away many who had strong ties to the Mother church [First M.E.]; these causes have diminished the congregation."[14] By 1882, the church's membership stood at only 300, and in May of that year the official board of the church suspended its Sunday school due to declining attendance.[15] A year later the new pastor, John Franklin Goucher, lamented that while Sunday school teachers were available, "The parents live so far from the Church and so scattered that I have been unable to get more than three children together at one place."[16]

Another threat to First M.E. was the strong competition from other Methodist churches in the downtown area. Mapping the location and drawing area of the Methodist churches in the area, the members of First Church determined that their territory was encroached upon by those of several other churches, a situation that probably contributed to their declining membership at least as much as did the removal of their members to the fringes of the city and to new congregations.[17]

The need to take action on these problems took on a greater urgency in the fall of 1879 when the city of Baltimore announced plans to widen Fayette Street and notified the congregation that its church would have to be removed to allow for the new thoroughfare.[18] Though they apparently had several years to do it, the congregation had to face the question of where to move, and this quickly became a matter of contention.

The main dispute was whether the church should find a new site, merge with another church in the downtown area, or relocate to some newer residential area. Several trustees argued in favor of relocating and building a large new church to attract new and more affluent members in order to solve both the membership and debt problems. Trustee Durus Carter and several supporters, however, argued that the church should remain downtown because a majority of the current members still lived there. Echoing the early colonial criteria for church location, Carter's group argued that a site on the fringes of the city would be "too inconvenient to secure the attendance of the large body of the members" and that "the poor members [would] be alienated from the benefits now enjoyed . . . especially the aged and infirm." They condemned the proposal to build a large church as "ruinous in the extreme."[19]

In a handbill intended to counteract the authorization of First Methodist's board of trustees to sell the property at Charles and Fayette streets, Carter proposed that only part of the property be sold to the city for street improvements and the rest be retained for the erection of a new church constructed out of the materials of the old church. This plan, he estimated, would result in a surplus of some $7,000, which would allow the congregation to "pay off all current expenses and more, without any collections from the members, and enable us to employ a man to hunt up the poor, and build up our members, save souls, and honor the Lord."[20] His position, however, amounted to a crusade against the forces of change. Church historian David Gilmore Wright argues that Carter's arguments were marked by the fierceness and rigidity of one who felt himself morally sanctioned, and his rhetoric was sprinkled with derogatory remarks about his opponents. Clearly, his vision of the church was grounded in a sense of place embodied in the history of the congregation. In Carter's view the church, after a century in the heart of Baltimore, should maintain its mission of converting and ministering to the people in that area, even, as he declared, if those people—now an increasingly diverse group of working-class and immigrant residents—had to be recruited by a paid visitor or social worker, a strategy that had long been used by urban missionaries. In Carter's view, the needs of those members who remained in the city, most likely the elderly and families of more modest income, took precedence over the needs of members who were relocating to the outskirts of town.[21]

Although the handbill initially persuaded several board members, Carter's support gradually eroded until he stood alone in opposing the suburban move. The relocation discussion continued throughout 1882 and 1883, briefly interrupted by the calling of the new minister, John Goucher, who imposed a moratorium on the increasingly contentious discussion of the issue for a three-month period following his arrival. Upon the conclusion of the moratorium, Goucher, who had presided over two previous Methodist congregations that had raised new church buildings, quickly moved to implement a strategic response to the relocation question, drafting a charter that defined the board of trustees as the representative body for the governing male members of the church (composed of all male members in good standing over the age of twenty-one). This document cleared the way for the board to act, granting it legal authority to sell the current church property, to obtain new land, and to act as agent in the process of building a new church, while at the same time voiding all previous relocation and building plans discussed by the male members and specifying that the board should find a new lot "located as far as practicable in the judgement of a majority of the trustees to accommodate the present membership and congregation of the First Methodist Episcopal Church."[22] Though charged with addressing the needs of the current members, the board, with congregational power now consolidated within it, clearly had the final say, and it followed the wishes of the new minister.[23]

Even as Goucher drafted the new charter, he had a location under consideration, a site two miles distant from the original church and quite outside any area that could conceivably "accommodate the present membership."[24] The area, called the Belt, was a tract of open land that was just beginning to be developed at the time but within five years would be a thriving residential community. The lots for which Goucher negotiated were owned by two church members, William W. Spence and Henry Shirk, along with a third partner, John Gill. Spence and Shirk, who had supported the relocation project since Goucher's charter resolutions, offered the lots to the church at a "low price." The final land-purchase agreement was drawn up on 23 August 1883, less than two months after Goucher first took action.[25]

This final decision to move the church to the suburbs prompted a lengthy article in the *Pioneer*, a Methodist-affiliated newspaper printed in Baltimore, attacking the trustees for subverting their corporate responsibilities as defined in the 1810 charter that governed the Methodist Episcopal church in the city and precincts of Baltimore. The anonymous author (possibly Carter himself) argued that while the 1810 charter allowed for groups within a congregation to *separate* from that congregation and erect their own church (an occurrence fairly common in the history of First M.E.), it did not allow such a group "*to claim all the church property and sacred charity funds*, under the pretense that they are the church, and that those who do not choose to separate therefrom are deprived of all interest in the church property and other assets" (emphasis in original).[26] In question was who, in fact, owned the church. Under the corporate model established by Goucher's charter, the general membership, male members included, would have to accept the actions of the trustees. Durus Carter and his colleagues were not only disenfranchised, they lost their whole church.

The relocation dispute illustrates a fundamental difference in the vision of the church mission. Carter's pleas for the church to remain in the downtown area may have stemmed more from his fiscal conservatism than anything else, but they also suggested that a city church had broader responsibilities to consider than simply membership numbers. His rhetoric made clear that moving the church meant abandoning certain constituents, both long-term members and new city residents, and, whether his supporters recognized it or not, constituents in these two areas would have strikingly different needs. The church's decision to build in a barely developed subdivision intended for affluent families shows equally clearly its resolve to cast its net for middle-class and affluent members. In this, the trustees' desires meshed well with those of developers Spence and Shirk, whose motivation for selling the land to the church at a low price probably reflected their hope to develop the area into an upper-middle-class neighborhood. An established congregation housed in a handsome new building, they likely surmised, would serve as a strong attraction for potential residents. Thus, this church did not follow families to the suburb—it preceded them. First M.E.'s hope was to be the first church to offer services in the area and thus to get a jump on the competition. Their new building, a $240,000 neomedieval auditorium church designed by architect Stanford White, proudly broadcast these aspirations of the congregation (fig. 4.1).[27]

Fig. 4.1. First M.E. (Lovely Lane) Church, Baltimore, Md. 1884. Stanford White, arch. *American Architect and Building News*, 26 Mar. 1887. Frontispiece. Courtesy Special Collections and Rare Books, University of Minnesota Libraries, Twin Cities.

In relocating to the precincts, First Methodist of Baltimore was not alone, for a similar pattern can be seen in other parts of the country: the Centenary Methodist congregation of Minneapolis, for instance, was similarly accused of "going way out in the woods to build their church" when they left their downtown location in 1888.[28] Yet Baltimore's First M.E. Church did not completely abandon the city. Reflecting the tension between domestic and public ministry, the congregation separated the two, establishing the new church in the residential subdivision and developing a new missionary program downtown. By November 1887, the new church listed three mission churches to its credit: the Royer Hill Church, the Guilford Avenue Sunday School and Chapel, and the Oxford Church and Sunday School. Thus, the physical distance between the middle-class members of the congregation and the urban working classes allowed a two-pronged mission to arise: a family ministerial and worship mission focused on the pastoral needs of the suburban members and an outreach mission focused on the perceived religious, moral, and social deficiencies of the urban population.

Trinity Methodist Episcopal Church of Denver

A similar outcome from somewhat differing circumstances occurred in the situation of Denver's Lawrence Street Methodist Church.[29] By all accounts, Lawrence Street was a successful congregation, for a number of years the preeminent Methodist congregation in the heart of Denver. Growing from a mission church in the early 1860s, it had incorporated in 1863 as First M.E. Church and within two years had erected a large brick Gothic church seating 450–500 congregants.[30] From its first services in the new building in February 1865, the church boasted an elite congregation, which included several highly visible political and social leaders of the city. As Bishop Earl Cranston later recalled, "I found myself pastor of Lawrence Street in the year 1878. That is to say, a church constituency that could have run the state government creditably in case of emergency. In my official board I had two Ex-Governors [Evans and Elbert], a Supreme Court Judge [Elbert], the Attorney General [A. J. Sampson], the State Superintendent of Public Schools [Joseph Shattuck], several county officers, a leading lawyer, ditto doctor, ditto druggist, mining magnates of all degrees, a noted author, and business men in almost every line of trade."[31] The church experienced fairly steady growth during the 1870s, its membership increasing from 120 in 1870 to 452 by 1880.[32]

But circumstances changed as the city prospered. Between 1870 and 1880 Denver's population increased sevenfold, from 4,759 to more than 35,000.[33] While the downtown area flourished as the commercial center for this growing population, wealthy and prominent citizens relocated their residences to the fringes of the downtown area. Most attractive to the social elite of Denver during the late 1870s and early 1880s was the Capitol Hill area about ten blocks east of the central city. The Denver *Rocky Mountain Daily News* stated that with the construction of a house in the area by a wealthy banker, a "mad rush for the hill began."[34] Several churches followed their congregations to this desirable location, initiating a veritable race among church groups to build bigger and more impressive churches. Between 1878 and 1892 the Presbyterians, Episcopalians, Congregationalists, and Baptists all moved from downtown locations, building large expensive churches to serve their prosperous members.[35]

Directly affected by this rush to the hill, Lawrence Street Church saw the departure of many wealthy members between 1880 and 1886, among them former governor and prominent businessman John Evans, Judge William B. Mills, and real estate magnate H. B. Chamberlin. As historian Linda Kirby points out, those who relocated and subsequently left the church constituted "almost the entire leadership group of the church, and though individual giving records do not exist, assuredly those whose wealth had supported the church."[36] Those members who remained perceived the combination of the exodus of former leaders and increasingly desperate financial circumstances as a life-and-death situation. Peter Winne, an early historian of the church and a member during the period, recalled, "We found that we could persuade very few of the congregation to stay with us much longer, first because it was too far down town for a family church and . . . too far from the trend of business to be desirable for that purpose. We were 'on the horns of a dilemma'—stay and dissolve, or move and unite."[37]

Yet, as Kirby explains, Winne's recollection gives a somewhat distorted view of the situation, for the membership numbers of the Lawrence Street Church were in fact rising throughout the period. Although the financial status of these new members—residents of the downtown area—is unclear, they may well have been of less affluent means, people living in low-cost housing near their jobs in the city. Thus, the crisis that the remaining members identified probably had more to do with the loss of the financial backing of affluent members who had previously been leaders within the congregation rather than the number of members itself. The financial situation was, in fact, deteriorating. In February 1883, the church was $930.25 in debt, a figure that rose to $1,000 by that summer.[38]

Clearly, the congregation could no longer afford things to which it had grown accustomed. Throughout the 1870s Lawrence Street worship services and activities had evolved under the direction and support of the several wealthy members and, therefore, reflected their tastes and interests. The Sunday services featured hired professional musicians, including the organist, choir director, choir members, and, on occasion, orchestral musicians. The ministers, too, were well paid.[39] The church sponsored several special events and world missionaries and contributed funds to charitable institutions. As affluent members left the church, it apparently had not scaled back its programs to compensate for the withdrawal of support, which may explain the rising debt. For instance, $200 of the debt was unpaid salaries for the church's musicians.[40] Thus, those members, like Winne, who had been at the church during its earlier heyday, perceived the financial crisis as one of failing membership rather than of overspending or misplaced mission. As Winne recalls, "The wealthy members had nearly all left—a number going to other denominations—and up to June, 1886, the combined wealth of the membership with four exceptions, would not exceed $100,000 and with these four would not exceed $250,000."[41]

Yet the situation was not exclusive to the Lawrence Street congregation but part of a broader crisis within Methodism itself in cities all across the country where competition for affluent members had been stepped up in the face of the changing urban population and the relocation of residents. In Denver, the crisis also affected several other Methodist congregations. For instance, Governor John Evans, a former member of the Lawrence Street congregation, built a Methodist chapel in the Capitol Hill area in honor of his daughter, and it quickly attracted many regular worshipers, several of whom left the distant Lawrence Street Church for the relative convenience of the new building. Three other Methodist churches also drew members from overlapping geographical areas in the city, a situation that echoed that of Methodists in Baltimore.[42] In Denver, just as in Baltimore, Methodist leaders viewed the competition as a critical element in what they considered a crisis situation, for the Evans Chapel drew those affluent families that had already moved to Capitol Hill.

In response to this situation, Methodists from all over Denver gathered in October 1882 to form the Denver Methodist Episcopal Church Association. In order to minimize competition and more systematically advance Methodism in the region, this organization attempted to use business principles as a model for reorganizing and operating the denomination. The association's board of trustees, composed of seven prominent business and civic leaders (four of whom were either current or former members of the Lawrence Street congregation), defined their mission as the overseeing of a religious corporation whose goals included buying and managing real estate, including but not limited to churches, assembly rooms, schools, hospitals, camp meetings, Sunday schools, missions, and mission schools. The association was to raise money through the sale or rental of that real estate, oversee donations and bequests, invest any surplus funds in more property, and arbitrate differences of opinion among the various M.E. congregations in Denver.[43]

This consolidation of the efforts of the Methodist churches in Denver follows a nationwide pattern of increasing incorporation of economic activity, illustrating in a religious context motivations that historian Alan Trachtenberg has described in secular terms as "the desire to control competition and the wish to facilitate access to capital."[44] In the case of the Denver Methodists, both motivations were evident. First, they hoped to eliminate the threat of competition among individual congregations in choice residential locations by the association's impartial overseeing of Methodist expansion. The impartiality of the association would be assured by requirements spelled out in the charter for democratic representation of all of the Methodist churches. Second, this same group was intended to function as the trustee for major Methodist capital investment, particularly in real estate.

Yet the disproportionately strong representation of members associated with Lawrence Street's interests did threaten to stack the deck in its favor, particularly when the association took under consideration questions of church location. Plans to merge the ailing Lawrence Street and California Street congregations were discussed, but agreement on a suitable location for the new congregation could not be reached. Of great interest to the association, however, was a proposal by Lawrence Street members to erect a large office building, or "business block," on the site of the Lawrence Street Church (or an alternate site nearer the business district) and to furnish the second floor with an auditorium suitable for worship services that would serve "all Methodist societies in the city."[45] The profits from renting the other floors would be directed into missionary work and education by the M.E. Association. In addition to the business block, a new church would be built to house the Lawrence Street congregation and "all others who desire to join them in the enterprise."[46] Although this plan was adopted by a majority vote, none of the association members would agree to financially assist in erecting the office building, and the plan was abandoned.

Meanwhile, the Lawrence Street congregation and its new minister, Henry A. Buchtel, acting independently of the association, purchased lots within the new Capitol Hill district at the corner of Broadway and East Eighteenth Avenue. The fate of the original property on Lawrence Street quickly came under scrutiny by the association, which demanded the deed be turned over to it, and the Lawrence Street congregation, even with its prominent representation in the association, found itself imperiled at the outset of what promised to be an expensive building venture. To surrender the deed to an association that was not legally bound to assist them in the construction of their new building would bring certain ruin. Thus, the Lawrence Street group questioned the authority of the association. After more debate the association recanted, allowing several original congregations, Lawrence Street among them, to erect new buildings.

While incorporation produced few substantial results in the case of Denver Methodism, the attempt illustrates the extent to which the local denomination had come to view itself as a part of the economic context of the city. The association's efforts to run the denomination as a business suggest that they perceived a strong correspondence between religious and socioeconomic realms. In effect, they had come to see their religious goals as allied with the financial opportunities available in the city. Through its consideration of engagement in the economic life of the city, the Denver M.E. Association not only adopted the corporate principles of commercial capitalism but at least briefly contemplated engaging in secular capitalist enterprise for the purpose of profit. Many apparently felt that if the problems facing Methodist churches were financial, expanding the capital base of the denomination through real estate investment might solve them. In this regard, the Denver Association briefly considered constructing a downtown business block in imitation of the four-story Methodist Church Block in Chicago, which housed a congregation and provided rental office and retail space.[47]

Although such schemes might solve financial problems, they did not solve the problem of relocating members. Downtown churches were simply no longer convenient to those who had moved out of the city. In the end, the Lawrence Street leaders, like those in Baltimore, threw their lot in with their former members, favoring the residents in the new Capitol Hill subdivision over those within the city. In the fall of 1886 the congregation hired architect Robert S. Roeschlaub to design a monumental church for them. Renamed Trinity M.E., the church would become one of the most fashionable in Denver (fig. 4.2).[48]

Clearly, the decision to relocate solidified the affluent identity of the Trinity congregation. In June 1887, the congregation moved into the Tabor Opera House to await the completion of the new church (fig. 4.3). While worshiping in the opera house, the foremost institution of Denver's elite, certainly would have been uncomfortable for any but solidly middle-class and well-to-do congregants, it may well have served as a means of winnowing the congregation. The name change adopted upon moving into the Tabor—the Trinity Methodist Episcopal Church—further distinguished the "new" congregation from the earlier one. The Lawrence Street Church also remained in operation, sponsored by the Trinity congregation first as a Sunday school and then by 1890 as a mission called the Church of the Strangers. The social chasm inherent in this change in nomenclature points up the distance the Trinity congregants felt from those of the mission even though they had left the area only two short years earlier. As with Baltimore's First Methodist Church, Trinity's outreach work constituted one prong of a two-pronged code (their official congregational mission), which developed out of the physical relocation of the church to the suburbs. For the religious life of its own members, the Trinity congregation proceeded to establish programs dedicated to family ministry and to support a variety of civic and fine arts programs. But while the primary function would be ministry to the new suburban families, the church would not neglect its public duty to those less fortunate, and Trinity subsequently became a leader in charitable programs and relief work focused on the poor of Denver.

As the examples of Baltimore's First Methodist and Denver's Trinity illustrate, the process of relocating could have far-reaching effects on the perceived purposes and roles of churches. Nonetheless, it does not appear that religious groups necessarily thought seriously about their changing role in regard to society or Christianity itself in selecting new locations for their churches. Apart from the protests of Durus Carter, little evi-

Fig. 4.2. Trinity M.E. Church, Denver, Colo. 1887. Robert Roeschlaub, arch. Photograph by W. H. Jackson, 1887. Courtesy Colorado Historical Society (WHJ2062).

dence remains that these particular congregations deeply considered the consequences of their decisions to follow their migrating middle-class and wealthy members, despite the fact that moving clearly required a choice between two disparate publics. The leadership of these congregations perceived value in the progressive model of growth and expansion that drove the secular world and thus quite naturally applied that model to their religious institutions, seeking to expand church membership and wealth. To reinvent the church as a self-invested business enterprise run along corporate lines was to avert failure, and a church failure was not simply equivalent to a business failure; it carried the added component of coming up short in a godly enterprise. Not surprisingly, then, church leaders strove to preserve and maintain the goodwill of wealthy members. The results included a decisive physical separation from the less-affluent populations of the city, a redefining of church mission that redirected mission services back to that population, and among the affluent, a rapid escalation in competition as congregations attempted to attract as much life-sustaining support as possible.

Fowler Methodist Episcopal Church of Minneapolis

Numerous other urban congregations throughout the United States found the attraction of the new residential subdivisions irresistible, although the extent to which con-

Fig. 4.3. Tabor Grand Opera House, Denver, Colo. 1881. Photograph by
J. Collier. Courtesy of the Colorado Historical Society (S0025104).

gregations used the occasion of relocating to engage in self-examination varied widely.
While in Baltimore Durus Carter was a nearly solitary voice encouraging just such self-
assessment and arguing that First M.E. should remain engaged financially and physically in the city, the Trinity congregation in Denver decided with little apparent reflection on the members who would be left behind to follow their affluent members out of
downtown. In contrast, the Reverend J. Wesley Hill, a Methodist minister in Minneapolis, left a brief but clear critical evaluation of how the mission of a church related to

a particular church location decision. In his view, the creation of Fowler M.E. Church, a mission church founded in the heart of an exclusive subdivision, offered an opportunity to reconsider just what the role, or mission, of a "mission church" should be. In this instance, as we shall see, the mission of the church would be to serve the wealthy families fleeing the city center.

When streetcar magnate Thomas Lowry began developing the hilly area southeast of downtown Minneapolis following the 1890 extension of his streetcar line through it, Minnesota M.E. Conference leaders were eager to realize the potential benefits of establishing a Methodist presence in what promised to be a highly exclusive subdivision. Lowry created a protective greenbelt buffer between his residential development, soon dubbed Lowry Hill, and the industrial district to the north, and then sold the first two houses he built on the hill to department store owner William Donaldson and industrialist William S. Nott. Further improvements, selective sales, and promotion succeeded (although slowly) in creating an exclusive neighborhood in which houses "cost not less than $4,000, and from that up to $50,000 and $75,000."[49] As intended, the area attracted prosperous families well into the early twentieth century, for it was close enough to the city center for residents to do daily business there, yet it retained a decidedly exclusive suburban air. In 1892, concurrent with the development of the subdivision, the Minnesota M.E. Conference decided to organize a mission church (or, more precisely, a new church intended to gather a new congregation from among the neighborhood residents) in the new neighborhood, to be supported by the Hennepin Avenue M.E. congregation, one of the leading downtown churches.[50] Two years later, the Hennepin congregation organized the Fowler M.E. Church, purchased a lot near the corner of Franklin and Dupont avenues, and had plans drawn up to erect a church building. That same year, the Reverend J. Wesley Hill arrived from Montana to serve the embryonic congregation.[51]

A year after his arrival in Minneapolis, Hill discussed the founding and mission of the church in *Twin City Methodism*, a collection of brief vignettes on all of the Methodist churches in Minneapolis and St. Paul along with biographies of prominent Methodist men in the area. In the section on the Fowler M.E. Church, Hill discussed the changing role of religion and the ramifications of Methodism's foray into wealthy neighborhoods. The move to Lowry Hill, he indicated, was a significant move for Methodists because the new neighborhood was "the largest territory unoccupied by the Methodist Church in Minneapolis" and in it "wealth and intelligence [were] surpassed by none in the city."[52] Lowry Hill offered not simply a potentially stable membership but a wealthy one at that, and Hill, like Lowry himself, foresaw even greater development of the area.

A champion of Methodist expansion, Hill believed that the denomination was entering a new era in which the new middle classes would reshape their religious organizations to meet their specific needs, and their needs, according to Hill, centered on families. Hill viewed his job as ministry to a special group: "It will be a family section. God pays especial attention to families. He uses the family as the unit of moral power. Its sanctity is hedged about with all the power of His Divinity. The family is the fort in which He entrenches Himself in the race. From this stronghold He goes down for the rescue of the wayward and for the conquest of the world. As soon as he rescues the first He places the desolate in families and as rapidly as He conquers the latter He hallows and blesses it by the benign presence of His church. In this generation Fowler Church will be a Family Church."[53] As the upper-middle class residents of Lowry Hill organized their lives around the single-family unit, the mission of the church would be to tend to the needs of those families, a focus that represents something of a shift from earlier generations' focus on converting the individual. Families, Hill asserted, would play a crucial role in the new dispensation, for as God's "unit of moral power," they constituted a kind of "fort" from which would be launched a holy war against the "wayward," who needed "rescue" and "conquest." Thus, in Hill's vision, privileged families were transformed into a kind of sacred army charged to do battle with an opposing force. But what or who was this opposing force? Made obvious by their absence in Hill's discussion are the working-class people left behind in the city by the migrants to Lowry Hill. Apparently devoid of families, the working classes are the unnamed adversary juxtaposed against the middle-class familial ideal.

Hill's reasoning that an affluent population needs Methodism as much as does an impoverished one was hardly revolutionary. What is most astonishing about the argument is that it appeared in a book in which three-quarters of the text is composed of Horatio Alger–like biographies of leading Methodist men of the Twin Cities and vaguely disguised advertisements for their businesses. A less reflective author would have deemed the point self-evident. More remarkable, however, given Hill's apparent confidence in the sanctity of his middle-class families, is that an unstated question animates his discussion of Fowler: Do Methodists neglect their duty by serving the wealthy? Should not Methodists focus their efforts on saving the souls of the poor? Attacking the unstated question head on, Hill boldly asserts, "Methodism is called of God to care for all classes."[54] Nonetheless, he contends, individual churches cannot be all things to all classes. He writes that the Methodist church "has made a glorious record by her care for the poor. She has long felt that the church that preaches to the most poor of this generation will preach to the most rich of the next. Making her people prosperous she has no right to abandon them as soon as her lessons in virtue, in good habits, in industry, have brought forth their legitimate fruit of prosperity. She must minister to all classes. She must be present on Lowry Hill with appropriate and efficient agencies for the shepherding of that growing and important community."[55] For Hill, the attainment of worldly prosperity did not mean that salvation or continuing religious development was ensured. Thus it was the duty of the church to minister to rich and poor alike. In contrast to the situations in Denver and Baltimore, Fowler Church was not created by a congregation relocating but was the result of a conference decision to launch a religious offensive in a newly developed neighborhood. Rather than being an active participant in the separation of the classes, the conference simply addressed the reality of the situation as it found it. There was an unchurched population growing in the Lowry Hill area, and the church had a duty to minister to them.

Yet given the implied question that Hill clearly addresses, his discussion must be viewed within the larger context of ongoing discussions of the responsibility of Christians to the oppressed urban population, for not only had evangelical Protestants embraced missions to the poor for generations, but many at this same time were in the process of redefining Christianity's responsibility to the poor. The work of Washington Gladden and the growing body of thought called the Social Gospel, which asserted that it was Christianity's duty not simply to convert the poor but also to address and alleviate class divisions and the ravages of poverty, were becoming well known. In 1891, a

Wisconsin bishop had declined an invitation to dedicate the new Centenary (Wesley) M.E. Church in Minneapolis, charging that "Methodists don't spend money on build-ings; they spend money on missions. You have violated that principle and I refuse to come and dedicate that sinful structure."[56] Twin Cities Methodists—and likely Hill him-self—were by no means unaware of the hardships endured by many who resided in their cities.

Fowler M.E. Church, a monumental Richardsonian Romanesque church of pink Lake Superior sandstone designed by Minneapolis architect Harry Jones, was finally dedicated in 1907 (fig. 4.4). A state-of-the-art neomedieval auditorium church, it be-came a distinctive landmark in the community. At its dedication, Hill's juxtaposition of the wealthy against the poor once again emerged and constituted a theme of the ser-vices, at least in the printed program, which carried an anonymous poem entitled "The Gospel of Labor" on its first page. The poem paints a vignette of Jesus' redemption and focuses on "laboring men," who need Jesus the most. Upon seeking and finding Jesus and having their sins forgiven, these working class people find a transcendent fulfill-ment, which mitigates their earthly struggle: "And the[ir] cries of envy and anger will change to the songs of cheer, / For the toiling age will forget its rage when the Prince of Peace draws near."[57] For Fowler congregants, whose connection with laboring men was as their employers, this couplet constitutes a near-utopian situation. Labeling the working-class struggle for justice "envy and anger," the poem legitimizes the business practices of industrial capitalists and offers up Christ as a palliative. This message, of course, counters that of the more radical Social Gospel leaders like Walter Rauschenbusch,

Fig. 4.4. Fowler M.E. Church, Minneapolis, Minn. 1907. Harry Jones, arch. Photograph, c. 1908. Courtesy Minnesota Historical Society (33132).

who called for sympathy and fair treatment of workers, although it does correspond to the widespread belief among middle-class evangelicals that only through Christ would social accord be accomplished. Neither the poem nor the rest of the dedication program suggests that the members of Fowler held significant responsibility for achieving such a goal, however.

Although Hill did feel that the Methodist church had a duty to the poor, his juxta-posing of this duty with the Fowler task of ministering to the wealthy suggests some uneasiness on his part—or at least a perception that the two missions required reconcili-ation. For Hill, as for the congregations in Denver and Baltimore, the mission to the poor and the mission to the wealthy (and middle class) were distinctly different and separate, and Fowler simply happened to serve the latter. Its mission was clear: "The purpose of the Trustees and friends of this church is to produce a church that will glo-rify God, help forward his kingdom among men, honor the great denomination whose appliances it augments and commend itself to the judgment and taste of the people in the midst of whom it is planted."[58] The final statement is telling: the church would be subject to the intended members, rather than the other way around. But even Hill real-ized that "the judgment and taste" might not be as godly as one would hope, for he concluded his discussion of the Fowler Church with the conviction that there was work to be done in the area: "It is confidently expected that at the altars of this church mul-titudes will find pardon and from its service man will graduate into heaven."[59]

Despite Hill's justification for Methodism's mission to the affluent, within a decade and a half the point had been rendered moot. Though by 1910 Fowler had attracted more than 700 members, a year later the congregation merged with the Hennepin Avenue congregation, which had initially helped to sponsor it, and the combined con-gregations erected a large Gothic Revival church midway between their existing build-ings (fig. 4.5). Fowler M.E. was sold to the Scottish Rite and remains a temple of Freemasonry today.[60]

Ecclesiastical Adoption of the Neomedieval Architectural Style

As urban congregations across the United States wrestled with rearticulating their pri-vate and public missions within the new economic, social, and geographic contexts, they also were faced with a much broader array of stylistic choices for the architectural facades of their new churches. Unlike the midcentury adoption of Gothic architecture for evangelical Protestant churches, which had combined theological and social motives, by the 1870s materialistic motivations eclipsed concern for the character of Christianity as churches adapted more fully to the growing consumer-oriented industrial culture. While clerical analyses or interpretations of architectural style had never been abundant in denominational literature, by the latter decades of the nineteenth century they had disappeared almost entirely, and design decisions during the postwar period rested predominantly with professional architects, who viewed church architecture in the same light as public, commercial buildings that celebrated the industrial and commercial progress of the United States.

Essentially, two new approaches to evangelical church architecture were offered dur-ing this period by church extension boards that published perspective drawings and

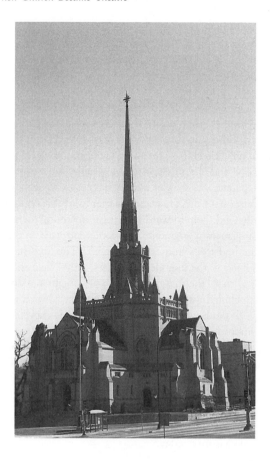

Fig. 4.5. Hennepin Avenue
United Methodist Church,
Minneapolis, Minn. 1914. Hewitt
and Brown, archs. Photograph by
Paul R. Kilde, 2000.

descriptions of church buildings, by pattern books produced and widely distributed by
architects, and by architects through consultation. The first of these were modestly priced
wooden-frame churches, ornamented in the new Stick, Shingle, and Queen Anne styles,
that dominated domestic architecture of the period. These were intended for small rural
and urban congregations. Among the many domestically inspired designs that appeared
in Congregational publications were those of New York architect Lawrence B. Valk,
whose Perrysburgh Congregational Church was featured in the 1879 *Congregational
Yearbook* (fig. 4.6). This modest church, which cost some $3,500, combined a shingled
tower, with gables sporting bargeboard and bands of stick ornament, and rectangular
windows outlined with stick moldings and filled with stained glass. Similarly, the Methodist Episcopal Church Board of Extension published drawings and plans of modest
Queen Anne churches with highly textured shingled exterior walls and prominently
decorated gables costing in the $3,000 range in their 1884 collection, *Sample Pages of
Catalogue of Architectural Plans for Churches and Parsonages*. The domestic appearance
of these picturesque eclectic churches drew attention to the individual and familial aspects of piety and worship increasingly deemed appropriate for evangelical Christians.
Looking much like family dwellings, these would become the church homes of their
modest congregations.[61]

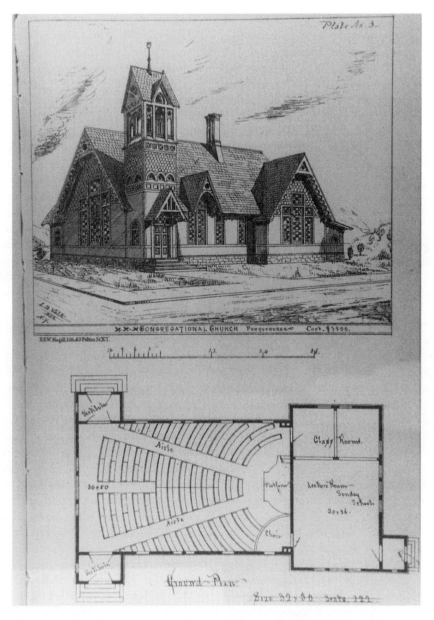

Fig. 4.6. Perrysburgh Congregational Church, Perrysburgh, Ohio. Lawrence B. Valk, arch. *Congregational Yearbook 1879* (Boston: Congregational Publishing Society, 1879), 19. Courtesy Special Collections and Rare Books, University of Minnesota Libraries, Twin Cities.

Small domestic churches, however, were of scant interest to congregations intent upon attracting middle-class or wealthy members within a competitive urban setting. As congregations sold their downtown churches and lots, some realized profits that allowed them to build elaborate buildings in their new locations.[62] For these congregations, denominations and enterprising architects published plans and perspective drawings of the second stylistic alternative: the neomedieval auditorium church, a new building type that enclosed a theatre-derived audience room within an eclectic architectural shell composed of medieval vocabularies. While chapters 5 and 6 will focus on the interiors of this dramatically new church type, comment on their exteriors is appropriate at this juncture because the architectural style adopted by the vast majority of evangelical congregations seeking to attract middle-class and affluent members was, in fact, this neomedieval auditorium-style church. Its historical connotations and striking visual presence embodied and conveyed strong messages about the congregations housed within the new buildings.

The fundamental element in the new style was stone. Sandstone, limestone, and granite blocks, quarried from sites in Indiana, the Lake Superior region, South Dakota, Texas, and Colorado, were shipped by rail or barge throughout the country to be used in churches, the new ten- and fifteen-story business buildings, municipal courthouses and jails, and the homes of the wealthy.[63] Exploring the expressive and ornamental possibilities of stone, architects of the period, most notably Henry Hobson Richardson and the hundreds who followed his lead, experimented with random ashlar walls of rough-faced stone, which were battered (sloped outward) at the base to indicate the weight of the building. Stone arches, often defined by polychromatic voisseurs resting on compressed columns, sheltered doors and main windows, and contrasting stringcourses and ornamental patterning animated the walls. Complex perspectives marked by multiple masses pierced by numerous windows filled with stained glass also characterized the style, and buttresses, lancet windows, finials, and crenellations lent a distinctively medieval aura to the buildings. Such designs dominated denominational and architectural publications and constituted a means for many local architects to gain reputations. Warren H. Hayes, for instance, educated at Cornell and practicing first in Elmira, New York, and later in Minneapolis, gained the imprimatur of the National Council of Congregational Churches during the 1890s when he was the architect most often featured in the *Congregational Yearbook*. Lawrence Valk, Robert Roeschlaub, George Kramer, and scores of other designers around the country built solid regional reputations producing these types of churches.[64]

In the case of each of the churches described above, the congregations considered the type of church to be constructed a significant factor in attracting the affluent members they desired. Trinity M.E. in Denver, First M.E. in Baltimore, and Fowler M.E. in Minneapolis were all monumental stone churches in the Richardsonian Romanesque style, and all cost more than $150,000. Unfortunately, in none of these instances have specific instructions from the congregations regarding architectural style survived among their respective papers, although surviving materials in each case do indicate a strong desire for an impressive building. For instance, the building committee of Trinity Church of Denver, whose papers are most complete, left only vague references to the exterior. Member and congregational historian Peter Winne is more explicit, however, when he writes that the trustees directed architect Robert Roeschlaub "to erect a first-class building, substantial in construction, artistic in design, and above all, to make it complete in every detail, even to the hitching posts on the street."[65] Baltimore's First M.E. congregation expressed its desire in similar terms, repeating the intention to build a "monumental" church. This congregation first considered creating such a building in 1866, stating, "The erection of other prosperous churches have properly drawn away many who had strong ties to the Mother church; these causes have diminished the congregations, but a glorious future is predicted for those who still sustain this place of worship, and who contemplate the future erection of a Monumental Methodist Episcopal Church, which may furnish ample material for the future historian."[66] In Minneapolis, the Ladies Aid Society of the Centenary M.E. congregation enthusiastically expressed its approval of the design of the forthcoming Wesley M.E. Church:

> A judicious committee have in hand the securing of plans for the new edifice, and the plans which they are now considering will give the members of this church, a structure that will be an honor to Methodism, and surpass anything within the bounds of this great state in convenience and imposing grandeur. It will not only be a source of joy and a blessing to us all in a spiritual sense, but a refining and inspiring force in the education of our children. . . . In such a representative church and congregation large numbers of strong and cultured Methodist families yet to come to our beautiful city from royal Eastern circles will find a delightful church home. And not only this but at its altars hundreds of precious souls shall find the pearl of great price, and rejoice with us, not only in time but throughout eternity.[67]

As these projects commenced in the mid-1880s, monumentality could mean only one thing in a building—a massive stone exterior marked by medieval references. In particular, it meant the eclectic blend of medieval stylistic elements that became known as Richardsonian Romanesque, after its creator Henry Hobson Richardson, which became the epitome of monumental public buildings during the period.

Each of the three congregations discussed above built large, stone churches, and two of these clearly traced their stylistic features to Richardson. In Baltimore, First M.E. minister John Goucher selected architect Stanford White to design the building, a seemingly odd choice given the fact that White's firm, McKim, Mead and White, was not known at the time for designing churches. However, White was a fortuitous choice. He had worked in Richardson's firm, and he had been exposed to European architecture during a recent tour to the Continent. The neomedieval design he created for the Baltimore Methodists was a strong statement of massiveness and monumentality (ref. fig. 4.1). (So much so that the massing or arrangement of heavy stone walls drew criticism from Montgomery Schuyler for what he considered its unrelenting plainness and excessive massiveness, which bordered on "rudeness.")[68] At the same time, the building's dark-gray granite façade is pierced with numerous windows. The streetside walls are relieved by porches defined by round-arched arcades, and the corner is anchored by the massive tower, a ten-stage landmark capped with a conical roof that matches the red tile of the rest of the roof. In this building, a feeling of monumentality is created through the interplay of size, stone, and tower. A similar combination appeared in the neomedieval façade of Wesley M.E. Church in Minneapolis (a.k.a. Centenary Methodist Church), designed by Warren H. Hayes and completed in 1892 (fig. 4.7).[69] In this building, St. Cloud pink granite, quarry-faced and laid in a random ashlar manner, was relieved by contrasting brownstone stringcourses. Here, too, a massive tower anchored the building to the corner. The building apparently fulfilled the congregation's enthusiastic hopes, while it depleted their pocketbooks of more than $150,000.

Fig. 4.7. Wesley (Centenary) M.E. Church, Minneapolis, Minn. 1892. Warren H. Hayes, arch. Photograph by Louis D. Sweet, 1905. Courtesy Minnesota Historical Society (40412).

The widespread enthusiasm for the Richardsonian Romanesque style in the closing decades of the nineteenth century sprang from several sources. In part, a historicizing sleight of hand similar to that of the Gothic Revival occurred as elite Americans read into the medieval Romanesque forms a strength and vitality that many felt was all too lacking in contemporary life. Many, like Richardson himself, who was an ardent medievalist, found in the style an aggressive masculinity that countered the disempowering effects of the increasing urbanization and feminization of U.S. society. In addition, the growing and increasingly affluent populations of midwestern and western cities, wishing their cities could compete with eastern ones, were immediately attracted to the messages of confidence, permanence, ambition, and security exuded by the massive stone facades— meanings that also echoed the desires of the growing bourgeoisie struggling to define itself as a distinctive class.[70]

Another factor in the popularity of the style had to do with its extraordinary integration of the burgeoning building trades. As historian Alan Gowans has pointed out, the popularity of Richardson as a designer stemmed in part from the modernity of his business practices; indeed, Richardson built, in Gowans's estimation, "an architectural corporation" characterized by an assembly-line-like delegation of tasks, from his staff engineers, to draftsmen, to accountants, and then out to subcontractors. Further, his buildings advanced the skilled building trades by incorporating not just elaborate stonework, which relied upon new quarrying techniques, the expansion of railroad transportation, and engineering expertise, but also steelwork, terra cotta, glass, heating and cooling systems, lighting, and furnishings. A building erected by Richardson's firm was an industrial production, a triumph of capitalist cooperation, although it might be disguised as a medieval fortress.[71] This blend of new and old engendered the lionization of Richardson's work as an abundance of new architectural trade periodicals like the *American Architect and Building News* and the *Inland Architect and Builder* carried information about his design and production techniques to builders throughout the United States.

All of these associations likely figured into the decisions of evangelical congregations contemplating building churches with facades featuring Romanesque elements, whether filtered through Richardson's aesthetic or paired in eclectic combinations with Gothic (or, in some instances, classical) elements. But this stylistic choice was also informed by a desire to convey a message about the mission of Christianity in the modern world. These churches, unlike their Gothic predecessors, trumpeted the new public role of evangelical religion. While the Gothic Revival had indicated a retreat into medieval piety and internal worship practice, the new Romanesque churches announced that their congregations envisioned their churches as participants within the public setting of the new urban or semiurban neighborhoods. For the facades of these churches did not set them apart from other public buildings but, in fact, mimicked commercial and public buildings. Richardson's famous Allegheny County Courthouse and the library and rail-road station in North Adams, Massachusetts, had convinced architects nationwide that monumental buildings offered an appropriately triumphalist indication of the significance of their civic purposes. As a result, new libraries, courthouses, and stations across the country were designed with the massive stonework and Romanesque vocabularies of the developing style. Similarly, after Richardson's Marshall Fields warehouse in Chicago, the style became widely adopted for retail purposes, its appropriateness stemming directly from its rich, material character.[72] While these commercial buildings expressed the new hegemony of industrial capitalism, the municipal buildings staked the claims of government and law throughout the country. The firm stone walls appeared unshakable—permanent and unyielding, no matter what onslaught might threaten them. During a period in which that hegemony was regularly challenged by civil unrest, labor strikes, and visible poverty, the buildings became a metonym for middle-class desires for order and stability. With their medieval references, suggestive of a feudalistic era easily romanticized as a period of class stability, these buildings pointed toward a benevolent ruling class. Bourgeois Americans held out similar hopes for U.S. society. Certainly, the power and confidence exuded by these huge stone piles affirmed a vision of society guided and stabilized by precisely this class of people.

The appeal of the style was particularly strong among the wealthy, who used it for domestic purposes as well as civic and commercial ones, and in many cases, congregations that erected monumental churches with Romanesque facades did so under the leadership of wealthy members already living in Richardsonian Romanesque homes. For instance, John S. Pillsbury, Minnesota entrepreneur and governor of the state from 1875 to 1891, lived in just such a home during the period in which he served on the building committee of the First Congregational Church in Minneapolis, a church designed by Hayes in the same style. Similarly, in the small town of Pueblo, Colorado, locally prominent architect Charles H. Stickney designed that community's First Congregational Church, of which he was a member, using the same Richardsonian Romanesque treatment that he had used on his own home.[73] In homes, the style worked well to create a large building that nonetheless settled into the natural landscape with some ease. The rough-hewn stone suggested something of a natural outcropping, and the addition of low-slung roofs with deeply shading eaves emphasized an organic character, which was readily transferred into the home by integrating natural elements into stained glass and furnishings. Romanesque homes could be strong and monumental without being grandiose, yet like their commercial and civic counterparts, they were showcases of construction and artistic skill, filled with the latest in engineering and domestic luxury—veritable shrines to the new industrial consumer ethic.

In their adoption of the style for religious purposes, congregations embraced the public nature of the style as well as the domestic. The welcoming, domestic aspects of organicism suggested a kind of church home while the monumental character made a distinctive public statement regarding social and economic hegemony. Like the homes of the wealthy, these churches attested to the modernity of their congregations as well as to their social and financial status. Architecturally rich and lavishly furnished, the new church buildings were designed to appeal to the consumer-oriented taste of the middle class. At the same time, however, the mighty towers and stone facades claimed a strong public presence as did hundreds of courthouses and warehouses throughout the nation. Thus, the ecclesiastical use of the Richardsonian Romanesque style blended elements from both the private domestic realm and the public commercial/civic realm.

Spiritual Armories and Their Mission

The blend of public activism and private retreat was perfectly symbolized by one distinctive component of this architectural style: its martial character. The crenellations, towers, lancet windows, and even sheltering arches sprang from military origins during the medieval period. Far from being deemed inappropriate to evangelical worship, such features articulated the social ambivalence many congregations deeply felt during this period precisely because they emphasized the paradoxical relationship between offense and defense. These buildings could serve either purpose. This chapter has already discussed some congregations' ambivalence toward the socially heterogeneous urban population. The writings of Fowler M.E. pastor John Wesley Hill particularly indicate the concerns that construction of monumental churches posed for evangelical congregations in regard to their perceived social duties as Christians.

The significance of the neomedieval building type in conveying the paradox of activism and retreat is well illustrated in the cornerstone-laying service for another Minneapolis church, First Congregational, erected in 1886–1888 (fig. 4.8). In the late afternoon of 28 September 1886, some 150 people gathered at a construction site on the corner of Fifth Street and Eighth Avenue in Southeast Minneapolis, an area known at the time as St. Anthony, to witness the laying of the cornerstone for the new First Congregational Church. Eight feet above the site an 18-inch sandstone cube hung from a large block and tackle. Reddish, with roughly hewn sides, it had been one of hundreds shipped to Minneapolis by rail from a quarry on Lake Superior. With the stone swaying overhead, those assembled directed their attention toward a group of distinguished-looking men seated on a temporary stage. "Praise God from Whom All Bless-

Fig. 4.8. First Congregational Church, Minneapolis, Minn. 1888. Warren H. Hayes, arch. Photograph by Jeanne Halgren Kilde, 1988.

ings Flow," the doxology, burst forth from the choir, opening the ceremony to lay the cornerstone for the new church.[74]

The oratorical elements of the ceremony that followed focused on the meaning of the construction project for the congregation and in so doing offered a new conceptualization of the role of the church building within Protestantism: this building would be both a private "home" and a public building. The first lesson, from 1 Kings 8, related the tale of Solomon dedicating the temple to the Lord; the second, from Revelation 21, described the new Jerusalem. Both invoked the presence, the in-dwelling, of God within architectural space, using the terms *house* and *dwelling* to characterize the forthcoming buildings and the relationship between the divine and the human. This was to be a church in which the divine would reside, a concept that, as we shall see, was a fairly radical one for evangelical Protestants. After the lessons, the Reverend M. M. Dana delivered the main oration, which emphasized three related themes.[75] First, alluding to the denominational support for church building that had begun in the 1850s, he championed recent improvements in Christian building and Christians' newfound concern for constructing lasting buildings to be used by generations to come as "hopeful sign[s]" for the advancement of Christian society and humankind itself. Second, he moved beyond the domestic image of the church asserted in the lessons to locate a further significance of the church building within the evangelical mission to spread the gospel publicly. "Churches," he claimed, "are spiritual recruiting agencies," and Christian activism should characterize the church. "The best church makes the best men. . . . The church is not a place for drones, for it ought to be a hive of industry. It is not a place for [stifling] and spiritual dyspepsia, but a place for distributing what is received." In a most remarkable turn of phrase, he went on to implore his audience, "You are building a spiritual armory, and it rests with you to fill it with weapons."[76] Lastly, he stressed that this "armory" was "for fellowship." The church, he concluded, "offers to men the truest fraternity, receiving all classes, without respect to dress or grammar." Together, God and congregation would negotiate the ambiguous terrain between battling against the unspecified enemy with "spiritual weapons" and extending fellowship to all. Extending a hand outward, the building would link an in-dwelling God to the future of the surrounding community. Upon the completion of this sermon, the Minneapolis crowd watched as John S. Pillsbury, a former governor of the state and a prominent figure within the First Congregational Church, "handling the trowel with the skill of a veteran," guided the swaying stone, filled with memorabilia, into place and pronounced it "located permanently."[77]

Rich with implications, this ceremony illustrates the multivalent concerns of middle-class evangelical congregations as they faced the challenges posed by the new industrial city. The church would be a home for God and congregants, a temple, but it would also be a redoubt, a spiritual armory from which to launch their forays into the dangerous world of the city. It would serve both defensive and offensive purposes. The echoing of the militaristic language that Lewis Tappan had used back in 1832 to characterize the free-church move onto Pearl Street in New York was not coincidental. Although the religious social activism of the antebellum period had waned and churches had retreated from the strains of the slavery issue into their historicized Gothic worlds, in the postwar period, evangelicals embraced a new, more activist stance. In part, this militancy was informed by the legacy of the Civil War itself. Nostalgia, respect, and obligation mingled as communities championed veterans' displays of military discipline in parades and other public demonstrations. In the 1880s and 1890s, many Christian congregations formed Boys' Brigades; led by aging veterans, these organizations, with participants as young as age eight, practiced parade ground drills and firearm use. This same militarism informed the construction of municipal armories, huge buildings in downtown areas used to train local militias as well as to establish a visible military presence in areas experiencing civil and labor unrest.[78] Comfortable with this militarism, particularly within the context of seemingly embattled relationships among socioeconomic classes, congregations used it as another tool in their competition for middle-class and affluent members. Armory-

like, the new Richardsonian Romanesque churches claimed kinship with these municipal institutions as well as with the commercial ones discussed earlier.

A second source for the interest in militarism, however, points up the complexity of
the web of meanings embedded in these fortresslike churches, for these buildings also
drew upon the developing concept of "muscular Christianity." Conceived as a means of
responding to the uneven gender ratio of Protestant churches, in which women predominated, muscular Christianity encompassed a vast array of strategies designed to
appeal to men's (supposedly) more aggressive and activist natures. The Boys' Brigade,
which not only appealed to the youngsters' aggressive natures but also helped to discipline and direct that energy in positive directions, was one of a host of programs launched
by congregations across the country. These also included the formation of Young Men's
Christian Associations and Baraca Clubs aimed at interesting young men in Christian
activities. In these instances, militancy formed the foundation of evangelicalism itself.
As Dana had declared, the new First Congregational Church would not be a place for
drones or for spiritual dyspepsia, but for activists. The people themselves would be the
weapons in the battle, a message that meshed perfectly with the goals of muscular
Christianity.

Armory-like, these churches stood for order, for institutional authority, within the
urban context. Armory-like, they also suggested a defensive nature, a protective function. For a Protestantism grappling with urban and economic turmoil, the neomedieval
buildings suggested continuity with a past ideal, a securely ordered world. Such a sanctuary readily allied with the domestic sphere, the new suburban subdivisions, and the
homes of the wealthy. But in their offensive connotations, the buildings also alluded to
activism, to the duty of Christians, and particularly male Christians, to play an active
role in responding to and improving the urban situation.

In the Protestant churches of the late nineteenth century, then, location, architecture,
and mission intertwined, influencing and altering one another, merging in the process
of meaning creation. Through selecting new sites for their churches and erecting buildings that echoed commercial, civic, and domestic architecture, evangelical Protestants
articulated and created their spiritual and social positions and their desired roles in the
rapidly changing nation. The buildings would serve to foster not only class distinction
and the separation of these affluent congregations from the heterogeneous urban throngs
but also, paradoxically, the strong public involvement of these same congregations. For
now separated in their new churches, these congregations would embrace a proactive
responsibility to improve the lives of the poor. These churches thus played a distinctive
part in the revisioning of the role of evangelical Protestantism itself within the changing
nation. As we shall see in the following chapters, however, negotiating among these
multivalent desires, missions, and meanings was far from easy, and the interiors of these
new church buildings offer evidence of several more issues of contention.

5

Church Becomes Theatre

The May 1859 issue of the *Crayon*, one of the leading arts magazines of the period, reprinted a unique appeal. The trustees of Plymouth Church in Brooklyn had invited architects to participate in a competition to design an auditorium church. In itself, such a request was not out of the ordinary, but the main requirement specified by the trustees was colossal: a worship room to accommodate 6,000 attendees. Moreover, everyone gathered in the projected room must be able to hear and to see the distinguished minister who would occupy the stage, Henry Ward Beecher. No roof-supporting columns should obstruct the audience's vision. The acoustics must be superb. Either one or two galleries might be incorporated to increase the seating capacity. The preaching stage should accommodate not only a pulpit but also some 150 choir members and a large organ. Sources for such a building, the trustees speculated, might be found in secular architecture, and architects, they piped, "are left free to their own sense of fitness, untrammelled by any supposed restrictions to *church* architecture" (emphasis in original). In this regard, they also made one further suggestion: the form of the audience room might be curvilinear.[1]

The Plymouth trustees' vision appears to have been strongly informed by the original Broadway Tabernacle, a building just across the East River, which was being razed almost simultaneously with the competition announcement. The newly conceived Plymouth Church, had it been constructed, would have clearly been the progeny of Finney's earlier vision, complete with preaching stage, choir bank, organ pipes, and amphitheatre seating. The trustees' vision, however, would not be fulfilled. The editor of the *Crayon*, John Durand, expressing the opinion of the leaders of an architectural profession still in its adolescence, voiced distinct scorn for the entire enterprise in commentary that he interspersed throughout the announcement. Most appalling to him was the competition itself, a means of soliciting work without having to pay for it. But the conceptualization of the desired church building also elicited derision. Calling it an "immense preaching balloon," Durand considered the huge auditorium scheme not simply a pipe dream but a "folly" born of a misplaced faith in science and technology. What the trustees desired, the *Crayon* insinuated, was simply not possible, and any architect who would accept such a challenge was either a fool or an egomaniac—or both.[2] To Durand's consternation, however, several architects, some well-respected professionals, did submit plans. In the end, however, the Plymouth congregation abandoned its scheme. Its desire for an auditorium sanctuary, it turned out, was about a decade ahead of its time, and it had the misfortune to be launched in the city in which the process of architectural professionalization would brook relatively little inventiveness, particularly from upstart evangelicals who did not understand what a church should look like. The situation would change rapidly, however, in the 1860s.

Interest in the auditorium sanctuary developed exactly contemporaneously with the exodus of middle-class evangelical congregations from their earlier downtown locations and the growth of the first ring of suburban developments flanking city centers. The new auditorium sanctuary, which featured a plan derived from the basic form of the classical amphitheatre and which harked back to Charles Finney's Broadway Tabernacle, made its first appearance in Chicago in the 1860s.[3] First Baptist Church on Wabash Avenue was among the first, opening its doors in 1866. This building, like the earlier Broadway Tabernacle, boasted curvilinear pews encircling a platform stage, but the audience room floor did not slope like that of an amphitheatre. That same year brought the dedication of First Congregational Church at Ann and West Washington streets also in Chicago. Designed by architect Henry Gay, this church featured the sloped floor and spatial cone that would become characteristic of evangelical churches over the next twenty years. Within two years, the new sanctuary plan could be found in new churches constructed across the United States. The year 1868 saw the construction of the Church of the Disciples, a large amphitheatre church in Boston designed by Isaac B. Samuels, and a year later Chicago got another example, Union Park Congregational by architect Gurdon P. Randall (fig. 5.1). Over the next four decades, similar churches with large amphitheatre-like auditoriums would be built by hundreds of Methodist, Congregationalist, Presbyterian, and Baptist congregations in small towns and major cities throughout North America.[4]

Amphitheatre audience rooms shared a number of characteristic features. Large and broad to bring large numbers of people within the sound of a preacher's voice, they were usually square, circular, or octagonal in plan, although oblong, wedge-shaped, Greek cross, or free-form plans were not uncommon. To minimize visual obstructions, load-bearing walls supported ceiling and roof, dispensing with the need for interior columns except the slender iron ones that supported the galleries. Direct sightlines were enhanced by inclined or bowled floors that sloped from the back of the room down to the pulpit stage, and curved pews arranged in semicircular arcs faced the preaching stage, bisected by aisles radiating from the stage like the spokes of a wheel. In many instances, a gallery encircled the audience space, embracing the sanctuary like huge arms. At the front, a preaching stage several feet in length and raised three or four feet above the main floor housed the pulpit, altar or Communion table, lectern, and chairs. Almost invariably, an elevated choir loft or alcove occupied the rear stage wall, and above it dramatically rose a large case of organ pipes.

Just as it had in Finney's time, this amphitheatre space radically transformed the spatial relationships between audience and clergy, but this time the transformation reached well beyond a single congregation to influence evangelical worship across the nation. For while Finney's generation had largely ignored this exceptional religious space, late nineteenth-century evangelicals welcomed it and reproduced it enthusiastically. What

Fig. 5.1. Union Park Congregational Church, Chicago, Ill. 1869. Gurdon P. Randall, arch. Photograph © George A. Lane, S.J., from Lane, *Chicago Churches and Synagogues* (Chicago: Loyola University Press, 1981), 31.

had occurred within evangelical religion that made the new auditorium sanctuaries quint-essential spaces for Sunday services? This chapter interrogates the new auditoriums as religious texts and asks how they shed light on the religious and social features of evangelical religion at the end of the nineteenth century. As we shall see, the buildings functioned within three distinctive but related contexts, which figuratively correspond to four fundamental elements of religious systems: code, cultus, creed, and community.[5]

Designing the Auditorium: Meeting the Needs of Worshiping Audiences

As chapter 4 demonstrated, evangelical congregations of the late nineteenth century were increasingly middle class and, as they contemplated their positions within their surrounding communities, they increasingly focused on family ministry as the role they wanted their churches to play in their own lives. But theirs was not a desire to simply or passively receive clerical ministering. Evangelical Protestants in the post–Civil War period were actively involved in their churches. In greater numbers than ever before, evangelical congregations formed church committees that engaged individual members in every facet of congregational—and even denominational—business. Unwilling to let influence over congregational affairs be concentrated in the hands of the minister or a small group of trustees, late nineteenth-century congregations took literally the idea that the church is "the people," and lay members, both men and women, eagerly shouldered the tasks of church leadership.[6] That such members would demand that their needs in the pews on Sunday morning be addressed is hardly surprising. With regard to their physical needs, these congregations simply refused to put up with the shortcomings of traditional Protestant worship spaces that had plagued earlier generations.

The situation of Pilgrim Congregational Church in the Tremont neighborhood of Cleveland provides an instructive example. Organized in 1859, the congregation worshiped in a cruciform Gothic Revival church seating about 600. The space was far from satisfactory, however. The sound of the minister's voice rose straight up to the timbered roof and stayed there, leaving congregants in the back pews straining to hear the sermon. To make matters worse, worshipers seated in the back of the church could barely see the minister, their vision hindered by distance. Thus, for those who arrived at church a bit late on Sunday morning, the service dissolved into a vexing experience of catching bits and pieces of the sermon and peering around heads and shoulders to see the front of the room. Frustrated by these problems, the congregation had struggled to develop a fair and democratic system for allotting the pews that offered a reasonably facilitative worship experience. With many fewer decently positioned pews than families able to afford them, the congregation drew lots and even eliminated pew rentals in order to give everyone a fair chance at the good seats. The attempts were to no avail. Those families and individuals who had traditionally occupied the best seats continued to do so, and those stuck in the back continued to complain. Moreover, the congregation itself was growing, and not only did latecomers to Sunday services risk getting a poor seat, on some occasions, they got no seat at all. An increasingly active congregation began to demand a new church, one that would eliminate these frustrations and accommodate each worshiper with a good seat. In 1894 they solved their problems, dedicating a new state-of-the-art auditorium church.[7]

While good acoustics and unblocked sightlines were crucial to congregations like Pilgrim, spaciousness also emerged as a fundamental requirement to satisfy congregational needs. Congregations expected to grow, and their buildings would have to accommodate their ballooning numbers. In Denver, lay member Peter Winne, writing about the design of Trinity Church, explained the congregation's wishes: "The main thought . . . was to secure a room to accommodate as much of a throng of people as the ground space would permit; to give each hearer a comfortable seat, and secure for each one every facility for seeing and hearing. It is a great audience room, with the faults too often found in churches eliminated, and some of the excellent, well studied features of the theatre and concert room utilized, and yet it is churchly in every detail."[8] Similarly, Methodist bishop Charles H. Fowler advised, "Secure, first of all, by all means an attractive auditorium. Have it large enough for all possible occasions. If a magnificent auditorium is all you can secure, get that and leave the rest to coming time. Experience has proven the wisdom of this advice. The swing of a congregation is helped wonderfully by the magnificent, large and attractive auditorium. A large audience room is ever calling for a big congregation. . . . There is no better habit than that of habitually going to an auditorium where you feel roomy and sure of securing a good seat on the main floor of the Church."[9] For Fowler, spaciousness itself drew congregants.

Congregations took their demands to accommodate their physical needs to architects, who were increasingly eager to address functional issues in architectural design. The prominent professional architectural periodical, the *American Architect and Build-*

ing News (*AA&BN*), took on the task of informing its readers of these fundamental church design criteria. Reporting on architectural discussions at the Congress of the Protestant Episcopal Church held in New York in 1877, the *AA&BN* editorialized that "only a few persons . . . have considered the adaptation of the form of the church proper first of all to hearing and seeing the minister; that is, of bringing the congregation together compactly into an unencumbered space about the chancel or pulpit, yet this is usually the first problem which a church committee nowadays lays before its architect."[10] This lament did not go unheeded; indeed, the situation was rapidly changing. For instance, two years later, the *AA&BN* carried a two-part series entitled "Modern Church Building" in which architect John A. Faxon asserted that Protestant services needed "simply a lecture or preaching room," and the ideal would be "light, cheerful, good for seeing the pastor and people and hearing the spoken words of the former." An amphitheatre-like room, he acknowledged, might be the best solution in some cases.[11] In 1880 the *AA&BN* published a favorable review of E. C. Gardner's *Common Sense in Church Building*, praising its analysis of the design problem "to afford convenient opportunity for a large number of people to listen to the voice of one man."[12] In the journal also appeared A. F. Oakley's article "Notes on Modern Church Building," which asserted that "the governing requirements of the Protestant church of to-day are much the same practically as of a lecture-room or concert-hall; viz.: seating capacity, ventilation, heating, daylight, artificial light, and acoustical properties."[13] Utilitarian concerns for accommodating audiences had gained enormous influence by the mid-1880s, when up-and-coming architect Stanford White explained the architectural problems in a letter to John Franklin Goucher, minister of Baltimore's First M.E. Church: "The congregation's attention is concentrated upon the minister and as his function is entirely that of addressing the congregation, the whole architectural treatment should concentrate and lead up to this point. It is essentially a problem in which air, lights, comfort, seeing, and hearing must not only not be interfered with, but dictate the forms and treatment."[14]

In developing means of satisfying these new worship room requirements, architects turned to the theatre and concert hall projects with which they were also engaged. Just as Finney's amphitheatre space owed much to the architecture of the theatre, so too did these churches. Just like new church construction, theatre, concert hall, and opera house construction experienced a building boom in the late nineteenth century, largely due to the growth of middle-class audiences. Given the similarity in function among buildings designed for secular entertainment and churches—providing space for a speaker/performer and an audience desirous of seeing and hearing that performance—architects' understanding of spatial form and acoustics advanced through work on both simultaneously. For instance, architect Dankmar Adler, who earned a reputation as one of the foremost auditorium designers in the country, began designing auditoriums with two church projects—Unity Church in Chicago (1873) and First Congregational, Oak Park, Illinois (1874)—both of which featured amphitheatre sanctuaries. From these early projects, Adler learned valuable lessons about auditorium design that formed the foundation of his later works.[15] Architects generally found little need to distinguish between requirements for secular and religious auditoriums, and as a result, technologies for secular and religious auditoriums overlapped considerably.

The amphitheatre form itself, the inverted spatial cone, gained popularity in the theatre and opera house at precisely the same time as it did in churches. Although the plan had been used occasionally in European and English auditoriums since the eighteenth century, early nineteenth-century Americans had generally eschewed the form, opting instead to replicate more traditional spaces, which placed wealthier patrons in boxes with good views of both stage and floor and relegated others to the inexpensive and inconvenient benches of the main floor, or pit.[16] In the 1840s and 1850s, as theatre managers focused on attracting middle-class audiences, particularly women, a few theatres replaced their rustic pit seating with inclined parquet seating, which offered unobstructed views of the stage throughout the house. The Castle Garden Theatre was among the first to attempt this in 1845, but it remained something of an anomaly for more than a decade (fig. 5.2). In the mid-1860s, Gay and Randall replicated the form in their early auditorium churches in Chicago, and only then did architects, like the just-starting-out Dankmar Adler, begin to work seriously to develop the potential of the space. Probably the most renowned amphitheatre of the period was Gottfried Semper's Festspielhaus in Beyreuth, Germany, designed in collaboration with composer Richard Wagner in 1876 (fig. 5.3). Considered highly innovative at the time, its amphitheatre plan both legitimated amphitheatre space for opera performance and strongly influenced theatre design for successive generations. By the 1880s, the inclined, curvilinear seating had become the leading theatre design, and Adler, who had already incorporated it into several buildings, adopted it for the Chicago Auditorium building, completed in 1889

FIRST APPEARANCE OF JENNY LIND IN AMERICA .
At Castle Garden Sept. 11. 1850.
Total Receipts £ 26238.

Fig. 5.2. Castle Garden Theatre, New York City. 1845. Courtesy Eno Collection, Miriam and Ira D. Wallach Division of Art, Prints, and Photographs, New York Public Library, Astor, Lenox and Tilden Foundation.

Fig. 5.3. Beyreuth Festspielhaus, Beyreuth, Germany. 1876. Gottfried Semper, arch. Courtesy Harvard Theatre Collection, Houghton Library, Harvard College Library.

(fig. 5.4). Thus, church amphitheatres did not actually follow or imitate secular auditoriums. Both religious and secular auditoriums were part of this design transformation.[17]

Perhaps because the amphitheatre plan was so new to U.S. architects, they experimented with it quite freely, producing several distinct variations, some of which became widely popular. The inclined floor and curved pews of the amphitheatre were fitted into an amazing variety of spatial plans, from oblong to wedgelike to round to polygonal. Room orientation varied widely. In Roeschlaub's Trinity M.E. in Denver, the oblong audience room was oriented on a pulpit platform centered on the long wall (fig. 5.5). In the oval First M.E. in Baltimore, designed by White, the pulpit occupied one end of the room (fig. 5.6). Diagonally oriented square sanctuaries, in which the pulpit stage occupied a corner, also enjoyed wide popularity by the late 1880s, due in large measure to the publication of several such buildings designed by Minneapolis architect William H. Hayes in the *Congregational Yearbook, Scientific American,* and the *AA&BN* (fig. 5.7).[18] His First Congregational Church in Minneapolis, for instance, featured a corner pulpit stage surmounted by choir seating and organ pipes. Radial aisles and curved seating fanned out from the stage (fig. 5.8). A variation on this plan was found in architect Sidney R. Badgley's Pilgrim Congregational in Cleveland, which featured a square plan with a domed ceiling supported by four piers arranged, in the final execution, to evoke a Greek cross plan (fig. 5.9). With the pulpit stage located in one arm and the choir seating and organ in an adja-

Fig. 5.4. Chicago Auditorium, Chicago, Ill. 1889. Adler and Sullivan, archs. Photograph by J. W. Taylor. Courtesy Architectural Photograph Collection, Art Institute of Chicago.

cent one, the curvilinear seating oriented toward the pulpit required audiences to turn slightly to the right to see the musicians.

While the amphitheatre arrangement solved audiences' problems of hearing and see-ing the events on the platform, auditorium designers also needed to address the require-ments of the stage performers, who needed space in which to perform and visual empha-ses to attract the audiences' attention. In evangelical services, the principal performers were the preacher, whose sermon constituted the centerpiece of the service, and the musicians, whose contributions were dispersed throughout the service. Mirroring Finney's strategy in the Broadway Tabernacle, designers turned again to the theatre and its vertical division of the stage to accommodate these two types of performances. For centuries, theatre stages had been divided vertically. Ancient Greek stages housed the skēnē, a two- or three-tiered construction that formed the back wall of the performance space and allowed actors to appear on either the main level or a higher one. Centuries later the Elizabethan theatre used upper lofts and galleries to expand the performance space within the limited ground plans of its circular theatres. While the eighteenth-century Reformed churches in Ger-many used bilevel pulpits, the feature appeared in only a few U.S. churches in the early nineteenth century. Finney, for instance, had created a multilevel stage in the Broadway Tabernacle and Beecher's Plymouth Church had followed the model, but it was not until the 1870s that it became predominant, indeed almost universal, in evangelical churches.

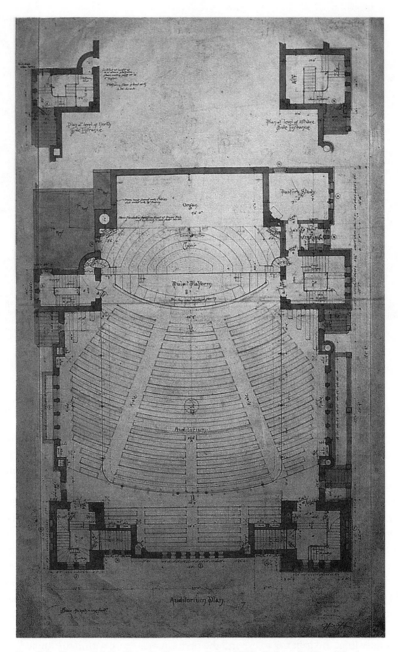

Fig. 5.5. Trinity M.E. Church, Denver, Colo. 1888. Robert S. Roeschlaub, arch. Courtesy Colorado Historical Society (92.275.144).

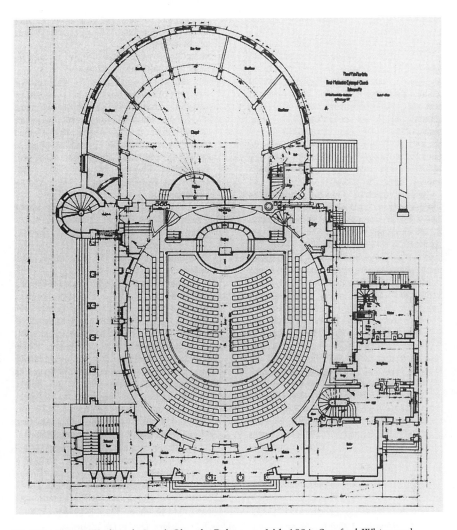

Fig. 5.6. First M.E. (Lovely Lane) Church, Baltimore, Md. 1884. Stanford White, arch. Courtesy Lovely Lane United Methodist Church.

In the pulpit stage arrangement, the lower level housed the pulpit, which could be an elaborate desk dominating the center of the stage or a modest lectern or pulpit rail. Above and behind it rose a bank of choir seating. Solving the long-standing problem of where to put the choir, these elevated choir lofts created a visual distinction between the clerical and the musical performances, providing a fine view of both, with a minimal reduction in audience seating. Communion table and font were often placed below the pulpit on the main floor, although in some cases, the lectern was shifted to the side of the stage for Communion services and the table, retrieved from a back room, was placed in the center. First Congregational Church in Manistee, Michigan, designed by William LeBaron Jenney, featured a semicircular pulpit stage with choir seating that

FIRST CONGREGATIONAL CHURCH, MINNEAPOLIS.—W. H. HAYES, ARCHITECT.

Fig. 5.7. First Congregational Church, Minneapolis, Minn. 1888. Warren H. Hayes, arch. *Scientific American: Architects and Builders Edition* (Jan. 1887): 16. Courtesy Special Collections and Rare Books, University of Minnesota, Twin Cities.

dominated the sanctuary (fig. 5.10), and Henry Ward Beecher's Plymouth Church in Brooklyn, remodeled in the 1880s, similarly featured a pulpit stage raised several feet above the main floor and an elevated choir loft on the gallery level (fig. 5.11). The choir seating in two Warren H. Hayes churches in Minneapolis, First Congregational (fig. 5.8) and Wesley Methodist (fig. 5.12), was less dominating, placed on the same level as the pulpit or just a few steps higher. Similarly, in Plymouth Congregational in Seattle, a relatively low alcove, just two or three steps above the preaching platform, housed the choir (fig. 5.13). More elaborate facilities appeared in Denver's Trinity M.E. Church, which featured a pulpit platform elevated some four feet above the auditorium floor and, above and behind this, choir seating ascending in two sweeping banks (fig. 5.14). Rich wood housings and railings further emphasized the complexity of the various spaces

Fig. 5.8. First Congregational Church, Minneapolis, Minn. 1888. Warren H. Hayes, arch. Photograph, c. 1889. Courtesy First Congregational Church Archives, Minneapolis, Minn.

for choir, minister, and organist. For instance, an elevated music loft in the First Baptist Church in Minneapolis contained space designated for an organ console and a baby grand piano as well as the choir (refer to fig. 1.5), and panels and railings carefully segregated the specific parts of the loft. In many churches, a curtain placed in front of the choir box shielded the performers' faces from the congregation during much of the service; singers would simply rise at their cue to perform and sit again after completing the songs (fig. 5.15). In some examples, however, the curtain, although present, did not block the congregation's view of the seated choir.[19]

The most prominent element accommodated by the evangelical pulpit stage, however, was the organ. Positioned against the front wall of the church, above and behind both pulpit and choir loft, the huge bank of organ pipes soared to the ceiling of auditorium sanctuaries. Congregations boasting of the "largest," "finest," "most musical" organs in the land wanted them placed in full view of visitors.[20] Intricately stenciled, elaborately encased, or arranged in a solid screen, or "pipe fence," organ pipes lent both an aural and visual richness to the worship experience. Yet variation here is also evident. Pilgrim Congregational in Cleveland, as mentioned above, shifted the pipe fence to an alcove adjacent to the pulpit stage, while Central Music Hall in Chicago featured two huge banks of pipes, one on either side of the stage. The more common front-and-center placement of the organ, however, visually indicated the central importance of the organ as the quintessential ecclesiastical instrument.[21] With pipes that might reach 16 feet high, the instrument suggested something of the awe of Gothic verticality despite cases that often featured classical detailing. Even in evangelical churches many organ

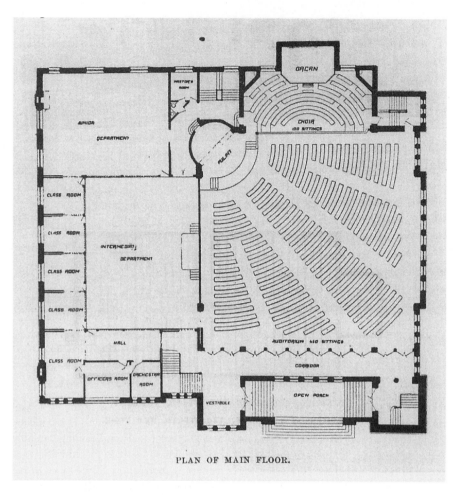

PLAN OF MAIN FLOOR.

Fig. 5.9. Pilgrim Congregational Church, Cleveland, Ohio. 1894. Sidney Badgley, arch. *Church Building Quarterly* 13 (Oct. 1895): 226.

cases also supported statuary, such as the gilded Gabriel blowing his trumpet that topped the organ in Pilgrim Congregational in Cleveland.

While this pulpit, choir, and organ arrangement generally distinguished church auditoriums from secular ones, the close relationship between the two is evident in the inclusion of the hallmark of theatre décor—the proscenium arch—in both. As chapter 3 explains, a proscenium arch effectively focuses viewer attention on the stage, and in the late nineteenth-century theatre, with the development of theatrical realism, the proscenium took on a highly significant function. Realism reconceptualized the relationship between audience and performer, erecting a metaphorical "fourth wall" between stage performers and audiences that transformed audiences into voyeurs who from a privileged, omniscient position witnessed the events. Performers on the stage, engaged in the "real" activities, are not aware (so the fictive conspiracy of realism goes) that they are watched.

Fig. 5.10. First Congregational Church, Manistee, Mich. 1887. William LeBaron Jenney, arch. Courtesy Manistee County Historical Museum, Manistee, Mich.

Fig. 5.11. Plymouth Church, Brooklyn, N.Y. 1850. Stephen M. Griswold, *Sixty Years with Plymouth Church* (New York: Revell, 1907), following p. 172.

Fig. 5.12. Wesley (Centenary) M.E. Church, Minneapolis, Minn. 1892. Warren H. Hayes, arch. Photograph by Jeanne Halgren Kilde, c. 1988.

Architecture assisted in establishing this relational fiction, as composer Wagner explained as he assessed the Beyreuth Festspielhaus: "In the proportions and arrangement of the auditorium, you will find expressed a thought which, once you have grasped it, will place you in a new relation to the drama you are about to witness, a relation quite distinct from that in which you are normally involved when visiting theatres."[22] The intended relationship was one of far greater intimacy with the problems of the players and it resulted from a more intense psychological focus on the stage. To encourage and

Fig. 5.13. Plymouth Congregational Church, Seattle, Wash. 1892. Photograph, by Nowell and Rognon, 1911. Courtesy of Plymouth Church, Seattle, Wash.

Fig. 5.14. Trinity M.E. Church, Denver, Colo. 1888. Robert S. Roeschlaub, arch. Photograph by W. H. Jackson, c. 1888. Courtesy of the Colorado Historical Society (WHJ 3447).

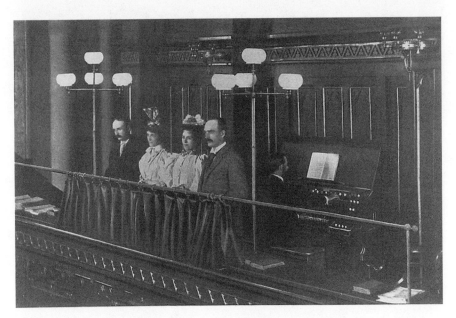

Fig. 5.15. Quartet choir. First Presbyterian Church, Chicago, Ill. Photograph, c. 1874. Philo Adams Otis, *The First Presbyterian Church, 1833–1913*. 2d rev. ed. (Chicago: Revell, 1913), plate VIII.

enhance such focus, uninterrupted sightlines and acoustical strategies were joined by a greater architectural distinction between the stage and the audience. Consequently, in the late nineteenth century, theatre and opera house prosceniums became highly elaborate. Over the stage in the Beyreuth Festspielhaus (see fig. 5.3), Semper erected a double proscenium with a dark space between the two, called the *mystiche Abgrund,* or the mystic gulf, which clearly indicated the distinction between the audience and the "real" world on the stage while it simultaneously encouraged the audience to "live," at least temporarily, wholly within that world. In the United States, Louis Sullivan's elaborate arch in Adler's Chicago Auditorium similarly emphasized the profound differences and separation between the world of the audience and the one on the stage (fig. 5.16).[23]

Designers of evangelical auditoriums followed suit. Trinity Church in Denver incorporated an elaborately ornamented proscenium arch sculpted with papier-mâché painted red, green, and gold and studded, marquis fashion, with electric lightbulbs. Designed by architect Robert Roeschlaub, the arch was executed by the Chicago-based firm of Healey and Millett, which also fabricated Sullivan's arch in the Chicago Auditorium.[24] Similarly, the proscenium in First Baptist in Minneapolis was richly ornamented. Generally, however, church prosceniums were more discreet. The prosenium in Charles S. Sedgwick's Westminster Presbyterian in Minneapolis, formed by wooden moldings, was a four-centered arch springing from Corinthian columns. Gothic arches

Fig. 5.16. Chicago Auditorium, Chicago, Ill. 1889. Adler and Sullivan, archs. Courtesy Architectural Photograph Collection, Art Institute of Chicago.

in Pilgrim Congregational in Cleveland defined the vaulted arms of the faux Greek cross space.

Marquis lighting, such as that accenting the arches in the Trinity and Pilgrim churches, was relatively common in religious buildings during the period. As early as 1876, rows of gas jets were used to ornament Dwight L. Moody's Tabernacle in Chicago, the site of his renowned revival. In that building, jets outlined the words "God Is Love" and a cross above the pulpit platform.[25] In Minneapolis's First Baptist Church, a huge chandelier of cut glass reflected light from circles formed by 200 gas jets. In Trinity, a row of electric bulbs encircled the sanctuary at the lower edge of the gallery. The ceiling dome of Stanford White's First M.E. in Baltimore was ringed with 340 gas fixtures.[26] Although such schemes now seem unmistakably theatrical, their simultaneous inclusion in both sanctuaries and theatres in the late nineteenth century suggest that in this early period of electrical development, the distinctive marquis-lighting strategy was not perceived as an exclusively secular signifier. Congregants and the press alike considered these auditoriums altogether "churchly" and hailed their use of the latest lighting technologies. These innovative lighting schemes indicate the determination of these congregations to engage with the changing world. Just as religious groups eagerly embraced the Internet in the late twentieth century, their ancestors embraced new technologies a century earlier, harnessing their power for the evangelical project. As architectural historian Francine Haber perceptively observes, the marquis lights "created a halo reinterpreted for modern times."[27]

The actual function of ecclesiastical prosceniums is less clear than that of theatrical ones, however. While house lights in theatres were extinguished during performances by the late nineteenth century to encourage visual focus on the stage and to heighten the relational fiction of voyeurism, in churches the desire for such intense focus did not abide. The performances on the stage functioned as proxy articulations of the audience itself—theoretically, no separation should exist. Worship united all in a similar enterprise. Most likely the prosceniums did, however, aid in emphasizing the performance area and encouraging the audience to maintain its attention there, just as did those in theatres. Certainly many proscenium arches provided impressive visual spectacles that not only attracted the eye but also bore witness to the status of the audience.

In addition to proscenium arches, another direct quotation from the theatre occurred within these sanctuaries: the installation of opera or proscenium boxes. First Baptist Church in Minneapolis contained descending boxlike segments at the lower ends of its gallery. Similarly, David Swing's Central Music Hall included semiprivate boxes at the stage ends of both gallery tiers, and in Denver's Trinity Church two small private boxes overlooked the stage. These remnants of European monarchy and aristocracy necessarily suggested social distinction, and in churches like First Baptist and Central Music Hall, where pews were rented, the price of these seats may have exceeded those on the main parquet floor. Some congregations, however, seem to have abjured using them to create social distinction. For instance, the Trinity congregation members called theirs "invalid boxes" and reputedly reserved them for expectant mothers.[28]

Carrying the theatre references even further, churches installed individual upholstered, flip-up opera seats in place of pews. First M.E. in Baltimore featured rows of such seats with hat racks placed handily under each. In addition, as the popularity of lantern slide shows grew in the 1890s, designers installed projection booths in the backs of their sanctuaries. Clarence H. Blackhall's rebuilding of the Tremont Temple in Boston in 1894–1896, for instance, was among the first instances of a permanent projection booth being inserted into a sanctuary. As the twentieth century progressed, accommodations for visual technologies increased.

Congregations' willingness to adopt features simultaneously with their secular auditorium counterparts was far from naive. They were not only aware of the close relationship between their new sanctuaries and secular venues like theatres, opera houses, and concert halls, but they were quite comfortable with those similarities, perhaps in part because the secular venues were seen as necessarily having to address the pragmatic requirements of audiences and performers that church design had ignored for centuries. Driven by the power of the marketplace, rather than tradition, secular auditoriums were more responsive to consumers'—that is, audiences'—needs. In addition, many Protestants had relaxed their earlier condemnation of all theatre by the latter decades of the century, having been targeted since the 1850s with moralistic plays that espoused evangelical values, particularly temperance. Protestants were similarly familiar with musical venues as social position became linked to appreciation for "high culture" entertainment like symphonic music and opera. Thus, while the move into a theatre house in Finney's day had been extraordinary and risky, by the late nineteenth century, such secular venues were relatively routine for religious services.[29] On any number of occasions, evangelical Protestants held Sunday services in opera houses. Some 3,000 attended a revivalistic Opera House Service in New York City in 1858; in 1868, Thomas Beecher, brother of Henry Ward Beecher and Harriet Beecher Stowe, held interdenominational meetings in the opera house in Elmira, New York; Dwight L. Moody preached in the Indianapolis Opera House in 1870; New York Methodists met in the Metropolitan Opera House in 1888; Denver's Trinity congregation held their services in the Tabor Opera House for several months as they awaited the construction of their new church; and David Swing's Fourth Presbyterian Church held services in McVicker's Theatre in Chicago before moving into their new church, which they called, simply, Central Music Hall.[30] All establishments that catered to the refined and still relatively elite middle class, these performance venues, secular though they were, were not perceived as inherently different from religious auditoriums nor as inappropriate for worship.

In fact, the important difference between a theatre and a church of this period, at least to one writer, lay in the former's superiority in accommodating audiences' physical needs. "Let Churches Be Made as Comfortable as Theatres," proclaimed a headline in the Sunday, 1 April 1888, issue of the Denver *Rocky Mountain News*. Paraphrasing an article from the *London Truth*, the article proposed a remedy for low attendance at Sunday services:

> Apollyon must grin and rub his hands with delight when he considers the contrast between the accommodation attainable at the "gate of—," as some of the unco'guid [*sic*] have christened the play-houses, and that afforded by the "gate of heaven." In the churches are hard, narrow benches, cushionless, except by private enterprise. In few of them is there even a place to stand a dripping umbrella. In none of them is there a cloak-room where a mackintosh or umbrella might be left till service should be over. . . . And the church is generally either overheated or insufficiently warmed. It is the best place in the world for catching cold.[31]

If the situation were so bleak in England, Americans were working quickly to remedy it, for physical comfort was a high priority in auditorium churches. Looking again toward the theatre, some architects encouraged congregations to install individual theatre seats in their audience rooms. Connected chairs with well-cushioned folding seats with tilting backs appeared on the main floor in Chicago's Central Music Hall, Baltimore's First Methodist, and Minneapolis's Fowler Methodist.[32] Several other churches, including Denver's Trinity M.E., installed folding seats in their galleries.

To further satisfy audience desires, church designers also strove to ensure a comfortable atmosphere. As architect J. C. Worthington argued, the church should be "comfortable–, for this the most unlettered modern man asks,–abounding in pure air, warm in winter and cool in summer."[33] Many architects developed ingenious (and often loudly touted) mechanisms for heating and cooling church auditoriums. Denominational and architectural journals offered numerous articles analyzing different situations and systems, and designers responded with often ingenious solutions. For Wesley Methodist Church in Minneapolis, Warren Hayes designed a forced-air system that transferred air into the sanctuary through wall grates. The air was drawn up from the basement, where it had been either heated thermally in a chamber or cooled in an ice room, depending upon the time of year. Similarly, Stanford White's system in First Methodist Church in Baltimore brought treated air from basement chambers and dispersed it into the sanctuary through small, foot-controlled vents located under alternate seats. In addition, architects creatively solved the need for light in these auditoriums. Hayes, for instance, designed unique domed stained-glass ceilings, lit from above by skylights and systems of mirrors, for several of his churches.

These comfortable worship rooms with their elaborate performance stages represented the cutting edge of auditorium design, and congregations proudly announced their technological advances. The steeple of Trinity in Denver was the tallest masonry structure west of the Mississippi; the stained-glass ceiling dome in Wesley M.E. in Minneapolis covered the largest span of its type in the country; and an automatic vacuuming system in Pilgrim Church in Cleveland, installed as a memorial to a lay leader's mother, was years ahead of its time, as were listening tubes for the hard of hearing, installed in the Fifth Avenue Presbyterian Church in New York. Whether or not such claims were true, congregations' pride in the up-to-date character of their buildings demonstrates the importance they attached to remaining engaged with the rapidly changing modern world. The church buildings speak eloquently to the fact that these congregations were not going to turn their backs on change. These buildings show that evangelicals embraced progress and strove to keep the church relevant in contemporary life.

This championing of building technology located the postmillennial evangelical code squarely within the ethos of scientific positivism that so profoundly affected U.S. society at the end of the nineteenth century. The technological expertise that could raise a stone steeple 150 feet in the air or suspend a massive glass dome over a huge sanctuary without the aid of center support was simply a chapter in the ongoing progress of Christian society toward the Kingdom of God. Science in the service of God, as rendered within church architecture, made this progress manifest, for just as church building improved, better addressing the needs of the faithful, so too would improve the church itself.[34]

Worship in the Auditorium:
Changing Nature of the Evangelical Cultus

The setting was not the only component of evangelical worship that changed in the final decades of the nineteenth century. Worship practices also underwent significant alteration, and the new spaces both accommodated those changes and propelled them. As active participants in the transformations occurring in evangelical worship practice at the turn of the century, these auditoriums provide evidence of those changes. Drawing together oratorical and musical performance into the single, prominent space of the multilevel stage, these auditorium sanctuaries visually announced not the traditional single worship component of the sermon but two critical worship components: the sermon, indicated by the still-prominent pulpit, and musical performance, indicated by the choir seating and organ pipes. In addition, the huge sweep of amphitheatre seating indicated that the audience itself would take on a larger role in worship.

When designing evangelical churches, architects tended to articulate conceptions of evangelical worship composed mainly of preaching, but clergy and congregations were well aware that fundamental changes were taking place within their Sunday morning services and that preaching was only one component of increasingly complex orders of worship. This is not to say that the importance of the sermon diminished. Late nineteenth-century clergy certainly agreed that the sermon was a critical part of the service. *Scribner's Monthly* editorialized in 1877, "An important change is now in progress in the American pulpit, is evident to even a careless observer. The preachers now coming upon the stage are studying methods and arts as they have never done within our memory."[35] Indeed, Union Theological Seminary professor William G. T. Shedd devoted two-thirds of his popular textbook, *Homiletics and Pastoral Theology*, to the subject, ensuring its centrality to seminary education during the period. Public discussion surrounding the success of Dwight L. Moody's evangelizing tours indicated that interest in preaching and preachers extended beyond the clergy members themselves. Several "princes of the pulpit"—among them Henry Ward Beecher, Phillips Brooks, Moody, and David Swing—achieved national reputations for their oratorical skills in what has been called a "golden age of preaching," and throughout the nation many ministers gained local and regional reputations as eloquent speakers.[36]

Congregants agreed that preaching was of central importance on Sunday morning. Familiar with lyceum and Chautauqua public-speaking circuits, middle-class Americans valued effective public speaking and demanded much of the individual to whom they listened weekly—their minister. In this context, competition among congregations for skilled orators grew, and in some instances, the desire to accommodate a single exceptional speaker motivated a congregation's decision to build an auditorium sanctuary.[37] A church that possessed a particularly talented speaker would naturally want to enhance the reception of his sermons by availing themselves of the best setting attainable. Further, many skilled preachers actually spearheaded building projects, providing leadership, directing fundraising, and sometimes even designing buildings. William Tell Euster, for instance, who became widely known as the "church-building preacher," guided the erection of at least six Methodist churches in the West.[38] Similarly John Franklin Goucher and Henry Augustus Buchtel crowned previously established church-building careers with two monumental auditorium churches, First (Lovely Lane) M.E. in Baltimore and Trinity M.E. in Denver, respectively.[39]

Notwithstanding the importance of preaching, reducing evangelical services to preaching performance ignored the important discussions and reformulations of services that had been occurring since midcentury.[40] While the sermon remained the signal event of a service, even formerly nonliturgical denominations like the Congregationalists, Presbyterians, and Baptists had introduced significant liturgical elements into their services by the 1870s in order to encourage audience participation. In his directives to ministerial students, Shedd argued that the minister performed the oratorical portion of the service and the audience performed the worship elements (guided by the liturgical decisions of the minister). His chapter on "Liturgical Cultivation" clarified that worship was the natural result of eloquent preaching and consisted of "the address of the audience itself to Almighty God."[41] While there was no need to emulate the complexity of a "Romish," English, or Lutheran liturgy, he suggested, evangelicals should avail themselves of some "rules and regulations" to help ministers guide audiences through worship in the form of scriptural readings, hymns, and prayer.[42]

For both ministers and congregations desiring compelling services that stirred and expressed the deepest devotional sentiments, liturgical elements offered important opportunities for audiences to participate in the program. Many divines, including Congregationalist Lyman Abbott, suggested that prayers and scriptural readings could be presented antiphonally, that is, as responsive readings between the minister or a precentor and the congregation. Psalms were particularly effective when presented in this fashion, but other texts, he suggested, could also bear "antiphonal chanting, by a choir and the congregation."[43] Further, while congregations had recited the Lord's Prayer for centuries, Abbott suggested that other prayers might similarly be used on a regular basis, among them the General Confession and the General Thanksgiving from the Book of Common Prayer, the Prayer of St. Chrysostom, and the Prayer for all Sorts and Conditions of Men.[44] Such advice indicates that scriptural readings and prayer were becoming far more formalized in churches that continued to claim a nonliturgical, Puritan heritage. In addition, liturgical music from the Roman Catholic and Anglican services, including the Gloria Patri, doxology, and Te Deum, became fixed elements in many Presbyterian, Congregationalist, Baptist, and Methodist services.[45] These changing worship practices required new worship settings, and some architects urged their colleagues to broaden their view of the spatial needs of their Protestant clients. Architect R. S. Peabody of Boston, for instance, understood the complexity of the new services. Addressing the AIA in 1877, he argued, "In our designing of Congregational churches, we are met by two opposing influences: on the one hand, utilitarianism,—the needs of the parish in the modern order of things; on the other, ritualism,—that returning to the old symbols, customs, and decorations which the Puritans threw aside in sheer opposition, but of which, now that the exigency is past, all sects see the value and pleasure."[46]

Of the various worship elements, the performance of music vied most seriously with the sermon for the honor of being the centerpiece of the evangelical service. Not surprisingly, then, music also proved to be a lightning rod for controversy. The reconceptualization of worship practice brought into tension two distinct conventions in musical production and performance: the more modest and personal singing of hymns by all present and the professional performance of music by trained musicians. The first of these, congregational singing, reached a zenith during the period. The lining of psalms had a long history among Protestant groups, and the revivals of the mid-eighteenth and early nineteenth century had expanded gospel hymnody throughout the country as congregations sought more satisfying ways to raise their voices in worship and praise. Hymns written in the eighteenth century by Methodist John Wesley and Congregationalist Isaac Watt had achieved enormous popularity in the early nineteenth century, but these were simply lyrics printed without music in tiny pocket-sized hymnals.[47] During services, a precentor would sing a line and the audience would repeat it. *Southern Harmony*, published in 1835, used a shape-note system on three clefs to set several popular hymns to music, but hymnals containing only lyrics remained predominant at midcentury. When *The Golden Lyre* appeared in 1850, offering both lyrics and music, it was soon followed by others, including William Tappan Eustis's *Book of Praise; or, Hymns and Tunes for Public and Social Worship*, published under the auspices of the General Congregational Association of Connecticut in 1868. Generally conceived as direct addresses to God, hymns conveyed a congregation's response to the sermon and to the spiritual moment, providing means for expressing emotion and publicly articulating faith.[48] By the latter part of the century, when the use of anxious benches and public confession had ceased, hymn singing constituted the critical element of congregational participation in evangelical worship, and Shedd identified it as one of the three constituent elements of worship.[49]

For upwardly mobile congregations, however, congregational hymn singing seemed a poor cousin when compared to the growing taste for the second musical form, which was rapidly increasing in popularity: complex European art-music performed by professional musicians. Interest in European composers had grown steadily among elites in the United States since the eighteenth century, and by the 1830s familiarity with the principles of polyphonic and harmonic complexity, which characterized the work of such composers as Bach, Mozart, Handel, Haydn, Beethoven, and Mendelssohn, signaled social refinement and high status. Historian Lawrence Levine has convincingly argued that elites sacralized this music, interpreting the intricate programs as so inspired and inspiring that a divine stimulus certainly undergirded them. Transcendent orchestral and operatic music, whether sacred or secular in theme, could indeed bring one closer to God, a feeling exemplified by the young Henry Theophilus Finck, who wrote in his diary, "When I think of such an orchestra . . . I feel inclined to fall on my knees and adore the Great Power, of whatever nature it may be, that could create music, the most divine of all gifts to man."[50]

Such music was not, however, the exclusive property of the opera house or concert hall. Though Levine focuses on the process of sacralization within these secular settings, it is clear that churches also played a critical role in this process. Churches eagerly had opened their doors to sacred music societies and, consequently, European art-music as early as the 1830s, frequently offering musicians access to the only pipe organs available in many localities. Moreover, they sponsored, or at least rented space to, a variety of performing groups. The New York Sacred Music Society leased the Chatham Street Chapel and later the Broadway Tabernacle, offering performances from both stages. Thomas Hastings, music director at the Broadway Tabernacle, integrated his own organ voluntaries and professional choir performances into evangelical services. Quartet choirs composed of two male and two female soloists, paid either by the performance or, more often, hired on an annual salary by a congregation, were increasingly in demand in the 1840s and by the 1850s were fixtures in middle-class churches.[51]

In the 1870s, this growing importance of music as an expression of worship resulted in heated debate between the respective supporters of the two music traditions: gospel hymnody and European art-music.[52] Hymns and congregational hymn singing, according to many, expressed the true religious feeling of the audience. Through singing, religious audiences vocalized their devotion, "performing," in Shedd's parlance, the worship portion of the service. Hymns, he counseled, should be selected by the minister to inspire religious feeling, to logically connect to the sermon, and to express praise and thanksgiving.[53] Thus, for many, hymnody constituted a fundamental point of audience participation in the service. As the popularity of art-music and quartet choirs rose, however, many feared that by hiring them congregations forfeited their primary participatory opportunity. Hired musicians, they lamented, could not express the complete worshipful feeling of audiences and, consequently, made a sham expression of praise. "Worship by proxy" was no worship at all, opined the Reverend Charles S. Robinson, who led a charge against church musicians in the *Century Illustrated Monthly Magazine* in 1884.[54] Mrs. A. B. Blake, writing in *Harper's* in 1879, asserted that congregations dependent upon professional musicians had allowed "mechanical skill" to substitute for "genuine praise-offering" and that this lamentable situation had developed precisely because "religious fervor [had] wax[ed] cool." A renewal of religious emotion was necessary, she argued, to overcome the congregational passivity that professional music engendered. This could be accomplished, she felt, by encouraging congregational singing.[55] Similarly promoting congregational singing, Episcopal clergyman Francis J. Parker declared, "Many enjoy and need the privilege of adding their own, perhaps uninstructed voices, to the general songs of praise."[56]

Champions of congregational singing lambasted multiple aspects of the sanctuary performances of European music. Some decried the fact that operatic pieces, waltzes, and songs based on secular melodies were performed during services. These pieces, they argued, simply could neither inspire nor express true religious feeling. Furthermore, many claimed that professional performers were more concerned with the aesthetic quality of their performances than with religious sentiment. Virtuosity compromised true religious feeling. As Robinson charged, "Many of those who are paid highest prices, and are filling most conspicuous places, are utterly unfit to lead in church services, because their whole vitiating principle of action is found in personal display; they introduce into the church the ideas and suggestions of the concert-room; they give us solos of artistic exhibition, instead of leading the people in worship."[57] If these criticisms were not devastating enough, critics charged that performers themselves were less-than-admirable mouthpieces for congregational feeling. Nondevout at the least, unruly and disrespectful in many cases, musicians made a mockery of their high calling. Horror stories abounded—of organists who literally took over whole services for their own elaborate displays, of choristers who slurped lemonade and socialized loudly in hallways between their performances, of power struggles between ministers and organists over the themes and content of services. Many feared that mercenary motives among professionals eclipsed pious performances. Some also charged that the inclusion of professional musicians was one of several new steps that was at odds with the heritage of the church itself. In the opinion of Blake, the new services of the Presbyterian church reduced worship to "essentially autocratic ceremonial" in which "there is nothing of a democratic nature. . . . The offices of praise, prayer, invocation, instruction, and exposition are in the hands of the few, not the many. It is the minister who carries the entire burden of the church service, the congregation taking no more part in it than if they were attending a concert or a lecture."[58] Two remedies existed: the elimination of professional musicians and a return to congregational singing (along with efforts to improve the latter through education) or closer supervision of musicians by ministers, who should not only "set the tone for the service" but also be well schooled in hymnology and able to work closely with music directors to select appropriate songs for services.[59]

The defenders of professional performance of art-music in churches, however, were not intimidated by these arguments. Josiah Holland, the influential editor of *Scribner's Monthly*, had taken up the cause during the same year in which Blake's article appeared, arguing just the opposite position: due to its lack of virtuosity, congregational singing compromised true religious feeling. In his opinion, trained musicians could express the "feelings of the soul toward the object of its worship" and "elevate the spirit and bring it into the mood of worship and the contemplation of high and holy things." Congregational singing, in contrast, produced "very little of the inspiration of music" and "is, indeed, more of a torture than a pleasure to many musical and devout people."[60] Serving well enough for "rural communities," voluntary choirs and congregational singing, he felt, were impractical in the city, where people were too busy to get together for rehearsals, and without rehearsals, the music "depreciated." Hired musicians were the answer, and he reassured skeptics by saying, "It is just as legitimate to hire a band of professional singers to lead us in our praise, as it is to hire a band of professional men to lead us in our prayers." To Holland, the ideal arrangement was "a first class quartette, made up of soloists, who take a prominent part in the public service, with a single choral in each service given to the congregation to sing."[61]

Holland's distinction between urban and rural life is telling. With its roots in revivalism and continuing popularity at camp meetings with their emphasis on personal emotion, congregational hymn singing stood in opposition to professional musicians and European art-music not only in terms of aesthetics, but also in terms of the respectability that indicated social class.[62] For most middle-class congregations, hymnody was perfectly acceptable if "cleaned up." New hymnals included three- and four-part harmonies, indicating not only that congregants were expected to read music but that they were sufficiently skilled vocally to carry distinctive parts. Historians have long noted that the success of the Fisk Jubilee Singers among middle-class white audiences rested in part on their production of sophisticated arrangements of slave songs. Stripped of any traditional African performance techniques and recreated with European musical forms, these new "spirituals" gained widespread acceptability. Thus, one aspect of the attraction of this music was its power to indicate the refinement not just of those who performed it but, even more important, of those who appreciated it. As Levine demonstrates, the sacralization of this music was a boundary-setting process, an invented tradition through which elites legitimated their use of the music as a litmus test for refinement and social class.[63]

For religious congregations competing for middle-class members, offering virtuoso performances of European music became an important strategy for claiming an advantageous position within the social hierarchy and, thereby, for increasing their audience size. By the later nineteenth century not only wealthy congregations but also those that wished to claim any sort of respectability retained professional musicians trained in

European forms and performance standards. As much an indicator of a congregation's class position or aspirations as was the presence of a renowned minister in the pulpit or the church building's location in an exclusive neighborhood, music attracted attention. As Holland pointed out in 1875, "The churches are full, as a rule, where the music is excellent. This fact may not be very flattering to preachers, but it is a fact."[64] Blake reluctantly agreed, stating, "People go to hear the music openly and avowedly. Churches with equal frankness vie with one another as to which shall produce the most telling effect and draw the largest houses. The choir and the organ in many of our fashionable churches are of more consequence than the minister, and the congregation is held together by the clearness of the celebrated soprano's high notes or the beauty of the boys' choral singing, while the sermon and the lessons are to be endured with elegant inattention or quietly walked away from."[65] Well-performed music could attract precisely the audiences that middle-class congregations needed for social and financial support. Consequently, art-music claimed a prominent role in the sanctuaries of evangelical churches at the end of the nineteenth century. If such music was divinely inspired, humankind could do no less than dedicate the finest performances of it to God. Holland foresaw dire consequences if congregations did not embrace the highest musical standards, warning that congregational singing could "make public worship very much less attractive to the great world which it is the church's duty and policy to attract and to influence." In his view a church has no right to "surrender any attraction that will give it a hold upon the attention of the world, especially if that attraction is an elevating one, and in the direct line of Christian influence."[66] Holland, then, saw art-music as another tool for evangelizing among the middle class and elites.

Focusing on this debate as it occurred in the press, historians have seen it primarily as a sociological process, a class struggle to establish the proper credentials of refinement. Historian of music Joseph Mussulman, for instance, characterizes the situation as a struggle between the middle-class desire for "culture" and religious traditionalism focused on spiritual goals. The secular nature of the former necessarily countered religious orthodoxy, and, because music played a critical role in both spheres, it served as a focusing lens for the contradiction. He explains, "Having clothed the Muse in the elegant finery of a 'higher' type for the parlor and concert hall, they proposed that she should exchange it on Sunday mornings for a dress fit for the handmaid of religion and behave like an obedient servant, not a matinee matron."[67] For Mussulman, the two perspectives were mutually exclusive: the secular desire for refinement remained at loggerheads with the religious ideal.[68]

Clearly, perceptions of the relationship between secular and religious goals are paramount in understanding this historical situation, but where Mussulman assumes division, Levine sees interpenetration and commingling—a sacralizing of the supposedly secular music, which, in turn, bestowed a certain spiritual experience upon those who appreciated it. I think a similar interpenetration is visible within the sanctuary. While the popular press presented the situation as a polemic, congregations themselves carved out a middle ground between the art-music and hymnody positions, incorporating *both* congregational hymns and professional performances into their Sunday services. Evidence of such compromises exists in Sunday service bulletins and other congregational documents. For instance, an 1888 bulletin from Denver's Trinity M.E. Church shows that the first worship service in the auditorium included an organ voluntary, a tenor and soprano duet, a tenor solo with chorus, a choral arrangement, and a male quartet as well as the congregational singing of two hymns, their responsive reading and recitation of the Apostles' Creed, Gloria, and a unison prayer. This order of service became standard in the new church.[69]

Other congregations similarly mixed congregational performances with professional music. The 1885 *Manual* of the First Congregational Church in Minneapolis included the following order of service: organ voluntary, doxology, invocation, Lord's Prayer, responsive reading of psalm, anthem, reading of the Scriptures, prayer, choir response, notices, hymn, offering, sermon, prayer, hymn, and benediction. In this service, the congregation performed the doxology, Lord's Prayer, responsive readings, and two hymns, while trained musicians (professional soloists, a quartet, or a voluntary choir) performed the anthem and a response to the prayer. Central Presbyterian Church in St. Paul followed a "form of worship" in its early years probably similar to that touted by Hodge, and on 23 February 1902, the congregation celebrated its anniversary with an order of service quite similar to that of First Congregational but with an added hymn and a professional duet: organ voluntary, doxology, invocation, responsive psalm reading, anthem, hymn, Scripture lesson, prayer, offertory, duet, hymn, sermon, prayer, hymn, benediction, and postlude. Congregational hymns also blended with professional numbers in the services of First Baptist Church of Minneapolis. Easter services at that church in 1891 included congregational participation in three hymns, the chorus of a carol performed by a soloist, the Lord's Prayer, a responsive psalm reading, and the Gloria Patri. The choir performed three numbers: one in support of a soprano trio, one with the Sunday school, and one alone. Similarly, First Baptist's 23 November 1919 order of service included an organ prelude, doxology, hymn, responsive reading of Scripture, Gloria Patri, violin solo, Scripture lesson, solo, pastoral prayer, offertory, hymn, sermon, hymn, benediction, and organ postlude. In each of these instances, professional musicians along with well-rehearsed voluntary choirs performed several numbers during the service, and the congregation participated in recitations and two or three hymns.[70]

Despite Blake's fears, congregational participation did not disappear from Sunday orders of service. Evangelicals did not lose their voices, but neither did they eschew art-music for its secular roots; indeed, they embraced it. The very buildings in which they worshiped pointed to their desire for musical performance. The elaborate and expensive organs that dominated these rooms were intended not simply to produce an impressive visual effect but also to be played by well-trained musicians. The placement of choir lofts on the stage gave pride of place to the quartet choirs and large choirs, be they salaried or voluntary. The ample room of the pulpit stage also indicated that accommodating other musicians was important to these congregations.

Moreover, many congregations chose to erect large auditorium sanctuaries precisely in order to accommodate public concerts as well as worship services. For instance, the large audience room of the Tremont Temple Baptist Church in Boston—with its broad stage, large Hook organ, and two tiers of galleries—hosted not just religious services but also concerts and public lectures.[71] Presbyterian minister David Swing's Central Music Hall in Chicago was designed with the intention that it would be let for musical performances and that the proceeds would be used to offset the congregation's costs.[72] Congregations across the nation found that their new churches were among the largest assembly halls in their areas, and they consequently leased them for a variety of events.

First Baptist in Minneapolis, for instance, was leased for the three-day appearance of Blatchford Kavanagh, "the celebrated boy soprano," in 1890. These concerts included both religious and secular numbers by such composers as Rossini, Ernst, Verdi, Schubert, Meyerbeer, and Handel.[73]

Given this embracing of art-music, many a new sanctuary was opened with a concert rather than a worship service. The first gathering in the new First Baptist Church in Minneapolis was an organ concert inaugurating the new Roosevelt organ, donated by the George Pillsbury family. Similarly, Denver's Trinity M.E. Church staged concerts on two consecutive evenings prior to its first worship service. Trinity's intention in this, similar to that of First Baptist's, was to demonstrate the capabilities of its new $30,000 Roosevelt organ, donated by music director and organist Isaac E. Blake. Blake opened the first concert with Haydn's "Achieved Is the Glorious Work" and proceeded to perform a blend of religious and secular pieces, including Gounod's "Fantaisie on Themes from Faust," Lemmens's "Storm Fantaisie," Bach's "Fugue in G Minor," Le Maistre's "Prayer," Guilmont's "Lamentation," Faure's "Garottee" from *Mignon*, and Wagner's "Verspiel" from *Lohengrin* and "Pilgrims' Chorus" from *Tannhauser*. Soprano solos included "I Will Extol Thee" by Costa and "Elsa's Dream" from *Lohengrin*. The concert closed with Haydn's "Creation."[74] A sequel to this concert was held the following evening. Featuring, as the *Daily News* put it, music that "could be appreciated by the people" due to the "pleasant melod[ies]" of the selections, this popular concert replicated precisely the highbrow-lowbrow distinction discussed by Levine. The night's entertainment included Guilmant's "Sonata in D Minor," Stephen Foster's "Variations on Old Folks at Home," Chopin's "Military Polonaise," and, again, Lemmens's "Storm Fantaisie." Hailed as hugely successful events, concerts like these reveal not simply a willingness to commingle specifically religious music with nonreligious pieces but an eagerness to do so.[75] By inaugurating their new churches with public concerts, evangelical congregations demonstrated a similar commingling of the religious and secular worlds within which they lived. Neither First Baptist nor Trinity would separate itself from its urban culture. Both would embrace the growing sophistication and "cultural" of life in their cities, though they would do so from a bit of a distance.[76]

This is, I think, one of several important lessons to be taken from these buildings. These congregations wanted to participate in their worship, but they also wanted to take advantage of the latest advances of modern culture. As a result, Sunday services, cultus, changed to integrate performances by all three groups: ministers, professional musicians, and audiences. Despite jeremiad-like warnings of declining religious feeling and minimal audience participation, church bulletins show that audiences contributed strongly to the worship elements of services or at least had the opportunity to do so.[77] Hired music did not replace congregational hymn singing; rather, it was simply added to services. Sermons, regularly sixty to ninety minutes in the antebellum period, dropped to thirty or forty-five in the closing decades of the century, allowing time for responsive readings and congregational singing.[78] Furthermore, the arrangement of the new pulpit platforms indicated the important role played by musicians. Congregations were willing to put out large sums to support the musical elements of worship as shown by the great attention lavished on the sanctuary stages, choir lofts, and organs. That they did so indicates that they were comfortable with the changes in their worship services that these architectural transformations facilitated.

Changing Creed: Auditorium Churches and the
Modernist-Orthodox Controversy

In several ways, then, the physical, theatrelike features of these auditoriums supported
and encouraged liturgical change. It should be noted, though, that these modifications
to the evangelical cultus took place during a period of growing creedal turmoil among
Protestant religious leaders. Cultural change threatened the very biblical and spiritual
foundations of evangelical religion. Thus, the ideological context shaped by the dispute
between religious liberals and conservatives is the third area that must be examined in
relation to these new sanctuaries. Although some historians have found these religious
auditoriums distinctive articulations of humanistic liberal Protestantism, the popularity
of these types of buildings among all evangelicals points to the more inclusive nature of
these church auditoriums.

The story of the ideological split between liberal and conservative evangelicals at the
turn of the nineteenth century has been told many times. As Western culture modern-
ized, the premises of orthodox Reformed religion, particularly Calvinism, came under
fire. Higher biblical criticism and scientific research challenged customary readings of
the Bible, pointing up direct contradictions within the texts, demonstrating the physical
impossibility of miracles, revealing irregularities in translations, and questioning the
concept of its divine origins. Similarly, Charles Darwin's application of scientific methods
to biology resulted in reconceptualizations of the very foundations of existence and required theologians and clergy of a positivist bent to rethink both God and Christianity.
The emergent liberal Protestantism did just that, integrating scientific ideas of continuity
and progress into a religious framework already influenced by Romantic conceptualizations
of God as suffused through nature and pietist constructions of the intimate relationship
between God and the individual. Liberal Protestants asserted a continuity between the
divine and the human individual rather than the rigid distinction that had characterized Calvinism. For them, God was a loving, benevolent deity, whose redeeming grace
was revealed through human culture and progress. Shunning creeds that attempted to
define God in human terms and language and abandoning the idea that conversion to
Christianity occurred in an emotionally traumatic event, liberals argued that Christians
should live individually moral lives and work for the advancement of society secure in
the knowledge that they thus worked toward creating the Kingdom of God. Conservatives, on the other hand, continued to emphasize a God of judgment, infinitely separate
from a human society replete with original sin. Only through a life-changing conversion and acceptance of the abiding religious creed of their Christian forebears (e.g., the
Westminster Confession for Presbyterians) could one hope for redemption. Conservatives, too, believed strongly in individual morality and the need to aid others in converting to Christianity and living moral lives, but, particularly after the turn of the century,
they did so not from an optimistic vision of improving humanity but from an acknowledgment of duty to an all-powerful God, who demanded obedience.[79]

Despite these differing religious perspectives, evangelical congregations did not split
into clear factions until the second decade of the twentieth century. Friction between
modernists and orthodox during the late nineteenth century was largely isolated among
clergy, theologians, and seminarians, whose debates only occasionally touched wider
evangelical audiences. As historian George Marsden has argued, through the early years

of the twentieth century the people in the pews probably had little concern about the high-stakes theological debates occurring among denomination leaders.[80] While the liberal preaching of a Henry Ward Beecher or a David Swing and the conservative discourses of a William Bell Riley attracted many, ministers more often found they needed to satisfy both sides of the theological spectrum, for their congregations consisted of members with a variety of theological outlooks. As Albert C. Knudson noted in 1911, "In every evangelical church, we have representatives of both the old and the new view."[81] For instance, although the Confession of Faith of the First Congregational Church in Minneapolis was fairly moderate in that it declared the Bible the "progressive revelation of God . . . composed by holy men of old, as they were moved by the Holy Ghost," it took a liberal view on inclusive atonement, stating that "God would have all men to be saved." Taking a more orthodox position, however, John S. Pillsbury, a staunch supporter of the church, never actually became a member reportedly due to his concern that he had never experienced a profound conversion. Just as orthodoxy and modernism blended within congregations, liberals, moderates, and conservatives all worshiped in the neomedieval churches with their innovative auditorium sanctuaries. The buildings satisfied the needs of everyone, even, or especially, when they worshiped in the same congregation.[82]

Moreover, congregations that can be identified as predominantly liberal or predominantly conservative both erected such churches. Architectural historian Joseph Siry has explored liberals' use of these buildings, showing that Unitarian minister Jenkin Lloyd Jones claimed the amphitheatre plan as particularly appropriate for liberal religion during the construction of his All Souls' Church in Chicago, designed by architect J. Lyman Silsbee. Liberal religion, Jones asserted, was evident in All Souls' lack of Christian symbolism and humanistic domestic façade as well as its amphitheatre seating, which suggested a more democratic congregation.[83] In a similar vein, architectural historian Daniel Bluestone asserts that the theatrelike Central Music Hall proved comfortable to David Swing and his liberal congregation precisely because of his "sanguine view that theater and religion both represented benign, cultured possibilities of city life"—both were further indications of "human achievement" and progress.[84] Drawing upon Swing's sermon criticizing "Limestone Christianity," Bluestone suggests that liberal religion espoused "modest church building."[85] Clearly, these modernist ministers found qualities consistent with their theological positions within their auditorium buildings.

Just why Jones and Swing were moved to articulate these meanings as they erected new buildings, however, is a question for speculation. Protestants as a rule did not offer theological analyses of the religious meanings of their buildings.[86] Unitarian Jones and excommunicated Presbyterian Swing, however, both existed on the margins of mainstream evangelicalism. Architecturally speaking, both had previously worked in Gothic Revival churches. In their selection of the popular neomedieval auditorium building—a type that since the 1870s had been strongly associated with evangelicals—both may well have felt that some explanation was in order. Jones adopted the style in 1885 just as numerous Congregational, Presbyterian, Baptist, and Methodist congregations were doing the same. Directly countering the appearance that these denominations had a monopoly on the style, and at the same time distinguishing between Unitarian humanism and evangelicalism, Jones's architectural apologia laid claim to the style for Unitarians. Similarly, Swing's embracing of the music hall model seems exaggerated, for it remained the architectural choice of many other evangelical congregations. In both instances, claiming theological distinctiveness in the erection of an increasingly common church type could only have proved counterproductive, for the features that Jones and Swing emphasized were not anathema to more conservative evangelicals precisely because these congregations neither eschewed democracy nor condemned rationality.

Indeed, at the same time that these modernists were espousing the benefits of these buildings, orthodox and conservative religionists were already worshiping in and continuing to construct similar buildings. In Chicago, Dwight L. Moody was drawing large crowds to his Tabernacle, which he had rebuilt after the 1871 fire. Similarly, William B. Riley, who became a leader in the conservative Bible movement and later in fundamentalism, used First Baptist Church in Minneapolis as a base to build the conservative movement. Further, the erection of many auditoriums intended to house and encourage religious revivals demonstrates that conservative groups embraced these spaces as enthusiastically as did some liberal ones. Revival tabernacles—buildings like the Union Gospel Tabernacle (later known as the Ryman Auditorium) in Nashville, erected in 1892 by steamboat captain Thomas Ryman to house the revival work of the Reverend Samuel Jones—almost always consisted of an amphitheatre auditorium enveloped by a relatively "secular" facade devoid of spire or steeple. Just as Swing hailed his Central Music Hall as embracing the urban setting, the Union Gospel Tabernacle similarly embraced the downtown life, housing not only revival meetings but also recitals, operas, political debates, and boxing matches.[87]

Thus, a reading of these spaces as distinctively indicative of liberal or orthodox religion obscures the significance of this architectural phenomenon. Secular elements were not associated exclusively with liberal religion. Both modernists and orthodox held services in opera houses and concert halls. Both constructed amphitheatre auditoriums. Both chose between "churchly" Gothic facades and more commercial exteriors.[88] Unraveling the appeal of these buildings for both religious liberals and conservatives requires a close look at what was occurring within them. These buildings harked back to a revival heritage that appealed to all evangelicals, a heritage evident in the utilitarianism, equality, and democracy that these buildings indicated.

Evangelicals of the late nineteenth century were pragmatic people. As has been demonstrated, the amphitheatre architecture of mainline evangelical denominations emphasized practicality and comfort—a good preaching venue for clergy and a good listening and worshiping venue for audiences. If a theatre or opera house satisfied these requirements, then services would be held there, free of any concerns about the religious appropriateness of the space. Modernist and orthodox alike found these secular venues accommodating for their purposes. Similarly, when it came to building for religious purposes, many congregations made relatively little distinction between religious and secular venues for worship. The music hall model served such religiously distinctive congregations as the Tremont Temple Baptist Church, whose conservative minister, George Lorimer, inspired the youthful William B. Riley, and the modernist Central Music Hall of David Swing.

What mattered to these congregations was that their building would serve as a "big tent," an inclusive umbrella under which crowds of the converted and unconverted could gather to worship and to hear the gospel. In this, their fundamental function was to support and enhance the religious community itself. No matter where one sat in these

sanctuaries, one was guaranteed a comfortable seat within sight and earshot of the pulpit. Providing such accommodations, these auditoriums tapped into some long-held ideals
that united evangelicals in a common belief system. These rooms functioned as tools in
the evangelical arsenal. Large and spacious, they could accommodate a multitude of both
the converted and unconverted, and in this they alluded to the inclusive campgrounds,
tents, and tabernacles of earlier revivals. Seatings of more than a thousand were common, and many churches boasted even more.[89] Such huge assemblies of people, when
a congregation could manage to attract a full crowd, directly linked late nineteenth-century evangelicalism with the earlier heyday of revivalism. Furthermore, both conservatives and liberals welcomed such crowds.

But, as chapter 4 indicates, the crowds they desired were generally of a particular character. The seating arrangements in the amphitheatre sanctuaries suggested a high degree
of equality among those present, an equality that further suggested the power of the evangelical audience but could also assume a certain homogeneity. Architect John A. Faxon
recognized the power of the new seating arrangement, commenting in 1879 that "one
excellent result of the Greek disposition of seats, each rising from eight to eighteen inches
above the one in front, is not only the free view of the stage, but the opportunity it gives
for every one in the hall to see almost everybody else,—the social effect, it may be termed.
There is no more valuable adjunct to noble architecture than this sea of interested and
sympathetic faces, supplemented by the bloom of color in varied costumes."[90] Well illustrated in a photograph taken in Seattle's Plymouth Congregational Church in 1911 (refer
to fig. 5.13), the curvilinear seating arrangement suggests participation in a shared enterprise, a "corporate body," in the words of Rudolf Arnheim.

This "social effect" countered the long heritage of social distinction inscribed upon
church seating through pew rentals and, in effect, ushered in the gradual demise of
rentals in evangelical churches. When Pilgrim Congregational in Cleveland completed
its new building in 1894, it proudly announced that it would retain the free-seating
policy instituted years earlier to address the unequal-seating situation. This decision
underscored the congregation's desire for an inclusive ministry that would cater to the
entire surrounding community. With generally moderate-to-liberal leanings, this congregation, like that of David Swing, viewed inclusiveness as a signal feature of their
evangelical religion. Swing, however, did charge a nominal fee, between $5 and $20 per
year, for seats.[91] Alternatively, when conservative William B. Riley proposed to eliminate pew rentals at First Baptist Church in Minneapolis shortly after his arrival in 1897,
he argued that rentals necessarily were antidemocratic and that in the church "rich and
poor should meet together, recognizing the Lord as the maker of them all."[92] In Denver, Trinity M.E.'s official board addressed the pew rental question three years after the
completion of their building because an earlier system of pledges in exchange for a reserved seat had not resulted in adequate funds. The board announced in 1891 that
assigned seating would cost a blanket fee of $12 per year, claiming, "Thus is equality
established. The only aristocracy is the aristocracy of the fidelity. Each member is to do
his best. The spirit of Trinity does not change. It is free as ever. All who will do their
best are equally welcome. There is no great and no small among such brethren. We are
one family with a common burden to carry."[93] In fact, as early as 1883, a passing reference to pew rentals called them a "burden" and implied that such an unfortunate practice should be avoided.[94]

Emphasizing the social effect, these new sanctuaries placed the communal nature of evangelical worship in full view of everyone on Sunday mornings. Homogeneity of agendas and equality of positions suggested a democratic ideology that historian Nathan Hatch has associated with evangelical congregations throughout the nineteenth century.[95] Further, the public nature of such rooms also put individuals' behavior on display, thereby encouraging the monitoring of one's peers, which was also an important part of an evangelicalism strongly concerned with moral behavior. Again, this was often democracy among social equals. When a social worker named Rachel Wild Patterson visited Trinity in Denver to raise money for a women's home, she felt the sting of her difference from the congregation. Gazing around at the well-dressed women, she immediately and self-consciously compared her attire and social position to those around her, concluding that her red hands and lack of kid gloves symbolized the distance between herself and the other women present.[96] Surveillance, of course, undergirded evangelical morality as well. During a period in which evangelicals eagerly asked themselves the question, "What would Jesus do?"—a phrase borrowed from Charles Sheldon's enormously popular novel *In His Steps* (1896)—watching and evaluating the behavior of other worshipers was natural, and the new social effect of fan seating became simply another weapon in the evangelical arsenal.[97]

Pragmatism, sizable crowds, equality, shared agendas, and supervision, then, constituted themes across evangelicalism at the end of the nineteenth century. But more tangible than these ideals, evangelicals shared worship forms. The increasingly liturgical services and discussions surrounding musical performances touched liberals and conservatives alike. Baptists, Presbyterians, Congregationalists, and Methodists all incorporated quartet choirs, vocal solos, and instrumental numbers into their services along with congregational hymns. Continued expenditures for music and music directors as well as the elaborate performance stages of evangelical churches attest to the significance of the role of music in worship.

While creed ultimately divided evangelicals by the 1920s, cultus, including worship practice and setting, had united them in a prominent community at the turn of the century. With their revolutionary interior arrangements, these sanctuaries both reflected and contributed to the fundamental changes in the conceptualization of worship. A similar conclusion has been reached by historian Ferenc Szasz, who has argued that continuity and similarity did indeed exist between evangelical liberals and conservatives of the period, particularly, in his view, in regard to work undertaken on social issues. Liberals and conservatives, he demonstrates, worked together on many social problems previously considered by historians to be the exclusive realm of liberals; indeed, the merging of the agendas of the evangelical right and left formed the foundation of the powerful Progressive movement. Only when this alliance broke down, in Szasz's view, did Progressivism lose its momentum.[98]

This perspective is illuminating when applied to the situation within evangelical churches in the late nineteenth century, for here too continuity between liberals and conservatives is apparent. Auditorium churches became so ubiquitous that evangelical Protestants could feel equally at ease within a Baptist, Methodist, Congregational, or Presbyterian auditorium. In fact, architects regularly used the same plans interchangeably for churches of these denominations. Thus, while this church type was used almost exclusively by evangelicals and did distinguish them from other Christian groups, the buildings offered few clues to distinguish among evangelicals themselves. They did attest, however, to the efficiency of evangelical hegemony in the latter decades of the nineteenth century. Ultimately, these church buildings showed a determination to make evangelical worship relevant to contemporary circumstances while at the same time maintaining strong connections to evangelicalism's earlier heritage. In this, the buildings attest to the fourth element of religion: community. By the 1890s, the many neomedieval auditorium churches on both the urban and rural landscapes attested to the strength and hegemony of evangelical consensus and community.

6

Sacralizing the Evangelical Church as a Church Home

Describing a Sunday service in a "new church in the fashionable Back Bay district of Boston" in 1888, R. Brown, Jr., expressed astonishment that before the service congregants socialized in the pews, that during the service the minister read announcements, and that at the minister's behest congregants stood to appoint a committee to transact some business for the church. Brown summarized his chagrin:

> Now the point I wish to bring out is, that the whole service was devoid of any reverential spirit. A hall would have seemed as appropriate a place in which to hold it, as a church. The sentiment voiced was, then: "The old idea of a church being sacred to the public worship of God has passed away, and we mean to let you know that, by transacting secular business or doing anything we like in it; we have no respect for old traditions." And the architecture of the building seemed something of an echo. The open-timbered roof was fussy in the extreme. A modern painter had "decorated" the interior, but there was nothing in his work, either suggestive or symbolic of any connection with Christianity, nor did it add one whit to the Churchly feeling of this house of prayer.[1]

Democratic, congregation-oriented, and filled with the products of new technologies, neomedieval auditorium churches championed human effort and progress. These churches served middle-class and wealthy congregations well as they competed for status and members within changing urban contexts, but were these auditoriums "churchly"? Brown's sentiment was clear, yet the adoption of these churches by hundreds of congregations across the country suggests that many people felt otherwise. This chapter will assert that at the same time that these buildings and spaces engaged in manipulations of social influence and power, they also participated in and fostered crucial transformations in religious meanings. In addition to their contributions to changes in ritual and mission explored in the previous chapter, these churches also helped to transform conceptions of the numinous, of God. Perceived as physical sites for the holy, the new auditorium churches made manifest new ideas about the divinity of God as well as the relationships among divinity, transcendence, humankind, and earthly existence.

Many late nineteenth-century Protestants believed that an in-dwelling sacred presence infused their new churches, and they used Scripture to justify it. The Reverend

T. K. Noble of San Francisco articulated a careful exegesis of the issue in the inaugural issue of the American Congregational Union's *Church Building Quarterly* in 1883. Using the term *sanctuary* as a metonym for the whole church, Noble argued that the Hebrew Scriptures demonstrate that God in fact creates this space: "The primitive Sanctuary, like the oracles of divine truth, came not by the will of man but by the will of God; its building was ordained of God." Further, Noble asserted, God dwells within the space. Historically, God's presence in the church is clear: "the Sanctuary is set forth in Scriptures as the habitation of God," and "it is the house of God, a dwelling place for the Most High." He continued, "Its immediate design is to bring home to human hearts the oft-forgotten truth that the High and Holy One who inhabiteth eternity, in very deed dwells among men,—is with us, about us, above us, and that in Him we live, move and have our being. The Sanctuary is ordained of God to meet and satisfy that innate longing of soul, voiced by the patriarch Job, in the pathetic cry, 'Oh that I knew where I might find Him! That I might come even to his seat!'"[2] Retreating slightly from this position later in the piece, Noble posed a more metaphorical interpretation of God's presence. As he shifted his focus from God to the human use of the church, he stated, "But so long as we tabernacle in the flesh and dwell among the dim shadows of our earthly existence, we need a visible pattern of things heavenly, and therefore our God, who knows our frame and remembers we are but dust, has made provision for a Sanctuary which may symbolize to us His invisible but immanent presence."[3] Despite its equivocating between actual and metaphorical presence, Noble's language is far from that of colonial Calvinists, who would no more have sought God's presence in the meetinghouse than in the jailhouse. The editors of the *Church Building Quarterly*, however, clearly acquiesced to Noble's view, adopting the following epigram for the journal's masthead: "And let them make me a sanctuary; that I may dwell among them" (Exod. 25:8).

Such ideas about the presence of God within religious space are not surprising for evangelicals who since the 1850s had been growing comfortable with both Gothic Revival churches and expanding liturgies. In the church, God and human society came together. As Noble asserted, "The Sanctuary . . . is also characterized as the House of Meeting . . . a divinely appointed place where God and his people were to meet . . . a place where the people might assemble and by their worship bear reverent and grateful testimony to the unwearied goodness of the Lord their God."[4] As chapter 5 demonstrates, by the late nineteenth century this "meeting" with God meant not simply coming together as Christians to hear the Word; it also meant active worship, which was composed of interactions between minister and worshipers but which focused on and was directed toward God. Hymns and anthems addressed the divine, stressing the presence of God, his witness to worship. The great distance between God and humanity conceived by the early Calvinists had been overcome.

An immanent God required a holy locale, and the meetinghouse became the "house of God," merging flawlessly with the domestic, familial ideology prominent within the growing middle class. The family had emerged as the foundation of Christian life by midcentury. The quintessential symbol for Christian piety was the nuclear family, guided by caring parents, worshiping within the home. As we have seen in chapter 4, clergy members increasingly redefined their churches' missions in terms of family ministry as they recognized the growing power of the concept of family piety. This domestic religious ideology had also transformed the middle-class home into a divinely sanctioned environment whose sacredness was incorporated into and defined as much by its material features as by the activities of the family within it. Seeking physical expression appropriate to God's house, church designers and congregations turned to the sacralized home for inspiration as they made decisions about their new church interiors, and borrowing heavily from it, they established in their churches new conceptions of sacred meaning while at the same time reiterating and confirming the domestic ideology itself. Just as evangelicals' interest in technology, progress, high culture, and democracy served to unite them in the final decades of the nineteenth century, the new conception of Christianity symbolized by the nuclear family and articulated in private homes and church homes similarly broadcast their solidarity to the public.

Family Piety and the Domestic Ideal

The redefining of the family as the center of Christian piety in the nineteenth century was an ideological step rooted in architectural space. The so-called cult of domesticity comprised an intricate network of cultural meanings that located the middle-class home at the center of virtuous Christian life. Interpretations of the motivations behind this redefining of the family and the home vary, but two distinct aspects of the process are clear. The development of the domestic ideal had strong roots within the social context of an industrializing United States, but it also stemmed in part from a redefining of Protestant spirituality. Growing steadily through the 1840s and 1850s, the domestic ideal was firmly entrenched in the lifestyles of middle-class Americans by the 1860s.

Protestant emphasis on individual piety meshed easily with the domestic ideal, a process that stemmed in part from inadequacies within the church. As historian Maxine Van De Wetering has argued, as the nineteenth century progressed, the church was less able to fulfill personal needs for "serenity, tranquility, [and] peace of mind."[5] But more specifically, the trend indicated the extent to which modernizing society was attempting to define and keep separate newly significant categories, particularly those of public and private life. As chapter 3 demonstrates, congregations floundered as they struggled to cope with pressing social issues, particularly slavery, and the response, in part, was to refocus congregational missions on worship, thereby setting the church apart from the public debate. As theological debates between traditional Calvinists and new theology advocates raged, congregations also turned to other sources of religious authority, primarily the Bible, and there they found justification for secluding themselves within their homes. Jesus had commanded that believers "enter into thy closet and shut thy door and pray to thy Father who is in secret" (Matt. 6:6). Interpreting the entire house as the private closet, evangelical Protestants deduced that God specially blessed and sheltered the Christian home and the worshipful family within.[6] In a theologically tumultuous environment, the home offered a stable focus and locale for personal devotions to God completely separate from the public world.[7]

The view of the sanctified domestic sphere designated a proper role and function for each family member who resided within the home. The roles of father, mother, and children were seen as determined by divine plan. As H. Clay Trumbull explained in his Beecher Lectures at Yale in 1888, "When God created man, God ordained the family for the good of man and for the glory of God. . . . The family was designed of God for the uprearing of children in and for the service of God."[8] The role played by the adult female was considered particularly crucial. The wife/mother was seen as the guiding moral light of the home and family. Deemed a morally and spiritually superior figure, the wife/mother's actions, methods of childrearing, relations with her husband, and means of fulfilling her household duties set an example of what was good and proper. Of highest priority was the task of childraising, sacred in that it entailed the transmission of Christian values to children. In 1861, well along in the process of the Christian privatization of the family home, Congregationalist theologian Horace Bushnell published *Christian Nurture*, a work that developed the theological justification for the home instruction of children. Growing out of a brief pamphlet he had written for the Massachusetts Sabbath School Society in 1847, Bushnell's book culminated a movement toward redefining the nature of the child in the Christian universe. The Calvinist thought of previous generations had imagined the child as sharing the sin of the human race and thus tending inevitably toward sin if left to his or her own devices. Consequently, strict supervision was needed to bring the youngster through the tribulations of childhood to the point at which he or she could be converted into a true Christian by God. Bushnell's work patently rejected this conception of childhood, contending that children were inherently innocent from birth but could be easily corrupted. From this perspective, the critical factor in raising children was the Christian environment in which they grew. In Bushnell's view, boys and girls who matured in a proper Christian home would never be aware of evil or vice and would thus not be susceptible to it. The evangelical mother's duty then was to create and maintain this idyllic atmosphere within the home, a responsibility that included the teaching of Christianity to the children by directing them in prayer, teaching them Bible lessons, and leading them in song and worship, all within the home. In effect, the mother was to be a minister to her family. If she did her task properly, the evangelical mother would contribute upright, self-disciplined Christian citizens to a country seen as threatened by immoral forces.[9] Thus, the middle-class home became a crucial site of salvation for nineteenth-century evangelicals.

American manufacturers assisted women in their sacred task of producing moral citizens by providing a raft of consumer goods and architectural innovations for the home intended to convey Christian ideology. Bible stands, wax crosses, religious paintings, parlor organs, and even prie-dieux and altars graced middle-class homes at mid-century.[10] Architects and builders contributed cruciform house plans with alcoves for pulpits or shrines and schoolroom areas for pious home builders. These features and objects contributed to the education of children and fostered the piety of family members while at the same time announcing the Christian character of the individual family within the social context of the city and neighborhood. The sacralization of the home was in itself a social strategy that conferred prestige on the family residing within by revealing their goals and expectations. As historian Colleen McDannell points out in her study of nineteenth-century Christian families, "The Victorians were not a private people concerned with constructing a hiding place in the world, they were a public people who sought to define themselves through display of their sense of 'election.' The domestic environment was not only created for the good of the family, it had to be presented to the public as evidence for the goodness of the family."[11] Indeed, families did not keep their piety private. Christian display marked the exterior of many homes, with crosses mounted on gables, pointed-arch windows, and stained glass. Such features, borrowed directly from church architecture and visible from the street, publicly announced the Christian character of the family residing within.[12]

As the home was transformed into something of a church, tension between these two sites of evangelical piety surfaced. John F. W. Ware, for instance, praised the home over the church in his 1864 book, *Home Life in America: What It Is and What It Needs*, and complained that the full day of church-centered activities expected of Christians on Sundays took them out of this holy place:

> Before the domestic duties of the day have fairly subsided, the bell proclaims that the hour of morning service has come. An early dinner hardly gives time for a prompt appearance at the Sunday-school, and the close of the afternoon service finds old and young pretty thoroughly weary, and longing for some little relaxing. If now the Sunday-school lesson for the next Sunday is to be learned, and after tea the evening meeting of some sort attended, where is the room for the home? And what has the home to do with and what does the home for hundreds and thousands of families in our land, with whom God's blessed day of peace and joy and rest is a series of public exhortations, to the excitements or instructions of which the whole Sunday duty is narrowed? . . . If the Sabbath was made for man, it was made for man in the home, just as surely as for man in the church, and he who, through devotedness to his church, leaves the home to itself, does not remember the Sabbath day to keep it holy.[13]

In Ware's view, the church must yield to the superior influence of the private home. Thinking along the same lines, novelist Edward Bellamy, presenting a utopian picture of life to come in the United States one hundred years hence, did away with the church entirely. In his popular book *Looking Backward*, his small family of characters enjoys religious services broadcast into their homes through a radio-like device.[14]

This model of familial piety within the home fostered to some extent a perceived opposition between the private and public spheres. The Christian home was a pious, moral, and nurturing island within a public sea of commerce, which was seen as hostile, amoral, and competitive. This growing separation between public and private life, however, posed a dilemma for evangelicals: Where should the church be located in this ideological dichotomy? Was the church itself a fundamentally private institution, like the family, or was it a fundamentally public institution? The struggle to respond to such questions would continue through much of the twentieth century, but for many evangelical congregations, one factor was clear: If God chose the family, so must the church. Consequently, evangelical denominations aligned themselves with the home and embraced the concept of the domestic church, the church home, God's house.[15]

Denominational and congregational discussions about architecture reveal the strong allegiance perceived between family home and church home. The Reverend George F. Magoun, a Congregationalist minister from Davenport, Iowa, emphasized the architectural parallels in an essay in the *Congregational Quarterly* in 1859. Revealing not a little anxiety about the detrimental influence of the public sphere, Magoun argued that given their strong similarities in purpose, church homes could fall prey to the same excesses that might befall familial homes. He warned that utility should be the guiding principle in both domestic and church homes—they must be "fit for [their] use," yet many are not. "The observance of this plain principle," he wrote, "would not only remove many architectural features of homes and sanctuaries which have been added at the cost of space, adaptation, and usefulness; but it would rase [*sic*] to the ground many stately but undomestic and comfortless residences, and many temples *so* built for the worship of the Most High, as to be astonishingly unfit for the purpose."[16] Too often, he lamented, utility was replaced by desire for luxury or excessive ornament—"useless expense[s]" that reveal such unchristian characteristics as "ambition, pride, luxury, extravagance, and similar unsanctified tempers." Warning that the overlarge, overexpensive, and overdecorated churches bordered on "Romanism" (a problem he felt Methodists in particular were experiencing), Magoun urged churches to find a middle ground: "*Let ornament and cost correspond with the average of these in the homes of consistent Christians*—the average, we mean, as between the poorest and the richest, bearing in mind what consistency is, and what has been advanced touching cost and ornament [in] Christian homes. . . . The Church should strike the average, not of public secular buildings, but of *Christian homes*" (emphasis in original). Weighing the relative merits (and limitations) of the public-versus-private question, Magoun, a home missionary pastor, located Christianity squarely within the domestic camp. Such sentiment resonated widely, for discussions of church buildings during this period are replete with references to their homelike nature. A description of Plymouth Church in Cleveland, for instance, also appearing in the *Congregational Quarterly*, called the church "emphatically *homelike*, democratic, and *Congregational.* . . . It is a people's home, not a fancy one; it is simple but not severe; it is attractive, but not *distractive*; unadorned, yet beautiful in the elements of a spiritual *home*" (emphasis in original).[17] As did Magoun, this author united the egalitarian rhetoric of evangelical religion with that of the Christian home.

The creation of a church home, then, emerged as a critical element of the family church mission of middle-class evangelical churches. Just as the home became a locus for consumer spending and material goods in the postwar period, the church, too, was readily outfitted with all of the comforts of home. The Reverend W. P. Fisher of Brunswick, Maine, postulated a direct analogy between church and home in his discussion of religious architecture, stating, "The size, plan and arrangements of the private house have an intimate influence upon the family life, the ease or unnecessary difficulty of the work to be done, the comfort of the inmates and its practicable conscious hospitableness; the same is true in the house of God; the workers feel this and the results will in no small degree depend on wise and suitable adaptations."[18] Magoun, too, suggested that aesthetic questions about the church could be answered by turning to the sacralized Christian home. As the *Congregational Yearbook* asserted in 1881, "The house of the Lord demands . . . everything beautiful, and in keeping with his holy work, everything that tends to elevate and refine our fellow beings, and teach them to appreciate the beautiful, as given to us and implanted in us by our Lord."[19] Indeed, creating an appropriate church home was seen as paramount for a stable congregation and was closely linked to financial success. As the Reverend L. P. Rose of Indianapolis wrote in 1886, "A home is essential to domestic happiness and prosperity," and thus, "as in the family, so in the church, the owning of a house to worship in, *a church home*, generally awakens in the membership a self-reliant and aggressive spirit." Borrowing the ornamentation (interior and exterior), spaces, and meanings of the sacralized Christian domestic home, congregations created their church homes as similarly sacred spaces.[20]

Sacralizing the Sanctuary with Domestic Ornamentation

While homes borrowed religious symbolism from church buildings, churches recipro-cated by borrowing common home furnishings and ornament. The most dramatic simi-larities in church and home decor are found in the ways they both drew upon the sa-cred themes of the natural world. Americans had located religious significance within the natural environment throughout the nineteenth century. Inspired by European Romanticism, the transcendentalism of Ralph Waldo Emerson and his New England compatriots offered an early systematic articulation of the spiritual power located within nature. Experiencing God in or through nature established a direct, individual relation-ship with the divine and taught lessons about transcendence and God's power, a theol-ogy termed "Christianized Naturalism" by historian Perry Miller.[21] This view contrib-uted to a growing interest among middle-class evangelicals in outdoor worship in the latter half of the nineteenth century, stimulating the growth of outdoor revivals and camp meetings held in forests and under the stars. Methodist bishop John Heyl Vincent summarized the connections in an enthusiastic description of the Chautauqua Lake Assembly, an institution he founded in 1873 as a school for Sunday school teachers: "What a *campus* I have! green fields and forests, streams and mountain ranges, stretch-ing out to the sunset. What a dome surmounts my college! vast space, blue background, billowy clouds, resplendent stars!"[22] To Vincent, the natural environment provided not only the architectural site for learning but the message as well: Divine and incorrupt-ible, the natural world formed a conduit to God.

An important corollary to the idea of God's presence in nature was the concept of nature as the antithesis of the corrupted and corrupting industrialized city. Nature embodied purity; it was an unspoiled moral font that offered temporary retreat and re-newal to those burdened with the work of the world. For middle-class Americans, who might draw upon the spiritual strength of the natural world by increasing their expo-sure to it, nature also served as a nationalistic metaphor of the continuing progress of the United States, its purity illuminating the citizens themselves.

These many-layered views of nature were called upon as middle-class families organized themselves around domestic life. The ideal family dwelling, one in which children would grow to be Christian citizens precisely because it provided a naturalistic retreat from the world, was viewed as an extension of the natural environment. Middle-class householders displayed their connection to nature in several ways. Porches, porte-cocheres, and balconies tempered the distinction between indoors and outdoors and provided sheltered places from which to survey the natural world. Landscaped yards with abundant flora exemplified the semimanicured image of nature that appealed to homeowners. Indoors, large windows and bay windows created easy visual access to the outdoors while providing light. Decorative potted plants became popular, and a multitude of other natural objects were brought into the home for decoration: Pine cones, sea shells, leaves, ferns, seeds, corals, and so on all graced middle-class homes. These homes also contained an abundance of naturally stained wood, and in paint and wallpaper, the primary colors preferred through the midcentury gave way to the browns, ambers, reds, and greens of the outdoors.[23] These ornamental strategies became codified in the Aesthetic movement, which not only embraced natural display but also viewed all tasteful art and decoration as morally active, a belief that under-scored, even if it did not precisely replicate, the Christian view of God in nature.

The Christian home, then, sacralized through its reflection of God and nature, offered a ready means of expressing the holiness of sanctuaries whose theatre origins might have easily rendered them inappropriate for religious use. By the late 1870s, church ornament drew increasingly upon the natural environment. Most prominent among the nature-emphasizing decorative aspects within auditorium churches was the use of natural woods. White oak, cherry, rosewood, black walnut, mahogany, and other woods were used to fashion pews, chairs, door frames, moldings, wainscoting, gallery balustrades, altar rails, pulpits, and choir lofts. Much of this wood, particularly pew ends and divider heads, newel posts, and pulpits, was carved with ferns, flowers, seeds, nuts, and tendrils, and it was always naturally stained.

Sanctuary designers also closely followed recommendations for the naturalistic treatment of domestic walls, particularly new techniques for dividing walls vertically into three distinct parts. As art historian Martha Crabill McClaugherty explains, domestic wall treatments of the period featured a dark-colored wainscoted lower wall, a subtly patterned upper wall, and an ornate crown or frieze. Hundreds of churches also featured this tripartite treatment, creating the division most frequently in frescoes (paintings on the wet plaster) or stencils.[24] First Congregational Church in Minneapolis, for instance, featured three bands of frescoing ringing the sanctuary, one just above the wainscot, one midway up the wall, and one as a frieze (see fig. 5.8). The frieze particularly emphasized the natural world, with its repeated pattern of entwined tendrils and leaves. The abundant ornamentation on the walls contributed to the close and intimate feeling that characterized these church sanctuaries, despite their large size.

This tripartite effect was only one strategy used to create harmony in a room, a quality seen as the key to gentility. Color choice played a crucial role in harmony. As McClaugherty explains, color combinations were to imitate nature by blending, as do "the browns of meadow marshes and leafless woods, the tints of flowers . . . and the harmonies of sea-colors and atmospheres."[25] Indeed, nineteenth-century writers were quick to assess the harmony of rooms, as a newspaper description of First Congregational Church in Minneapolis attests:

> Certain it is that the entire church, both within and without harmonizes perfectly, the combination of colors on the interior being excellent. This sense of harmony is nowhere so apparent as in the frescoing, which was done by Adix Bros., artists who pay particular attention to mural painting, and ecclesiastical decorating and make a specialty of all church work. The dome is decorated in shades of blue, amber, and gold, the colors lessening in intensity and gradually verging into a light tone of a warm gray color down towards the ceiling. The color of the ceiling panels is a warm gray tone with greenish cast, ornamented in light tones of amber, blue and gold. The large cove and walls are elaborately decorated in soft gray tone, the colors darkening and increasing in intensity down toward the floor.[26]

Using similar language, the *Baltimore American* pointed out that the Pompeiian red of the upholstery in First Methodist Church in that city "harmonizes perfectly with the carpet and walls," both being of complementary red tones.[27] These descriptions indicate that the decoration of the sanctuary was seen as forming a gestalt, an integrated whole that was a result of the discrete constituent parts, from the colors to the upholstery to the woodwork to the lighting. This ideal had direct ties to domestic decoration rather than to previous church decoration, which traditionally had been characterized by an assemblage of individual expressions of piety.

Attention to harmony also informed the selection of window glass, and the neomedieval auditorium church made stained glass de rigueur for evangelical Protestant churches. This widespread adoption of stained glass overturned a long history in which Protestants associated pure light with the divinity of God and, therefore, did not filter the light that entered meetinghouses and churches. As we have seen in chapter 3, however, the Gothic Revival aroused interest in medieval stained glass, and along with the spaces and vocabularies of Gothic architecture, some Protestant evangelicals also adopted stained glass.[28] Yet that adoption was relatively isolated and modest, for only as stained glass became popular in the middle-class home did it also become fully integral to the evangelical church.

In the mid-nineteenth century the influence of the Gothic Revival had begun to spill over from ecclesiastical architecture into domestic. Wealthy Americans, enamored of the romantic medievalism that was sweeping the nation, installed stained-glass windows, often depicting family heraldry, in their homes.[29] The inclusion of stained glass in homes would grow enormously after midcentury when expansion in production brought it within the reach of the growing middle class. By the 1880s stained glass was so common in homes that in 1883 an anonymous writer in the *Inland Architect and Builder* declared, "Scarcely a house of any architectural pretensions can be found that has not stained glass in door or window."[30] Stained glass was especially prominent in the entry halls of middle-class houses, where it enhanced the "warmth" of the welcome the interior offered.[31] As with other decorative elements, the treatments echoed the natural environment, and yellow, green, amber, tan, pink, and blue predominated, as did landscapes, foliage, and abstract designs loosely based on natural themes. As the *Inland Architect and Builder* writer explained, "The nearer we harmonize with nature, the nearer do we come to securing beautiful effects in color. The effect of a blue sky is heightened by a green hillside as a flower-covered plain. So in the art world, which copies nature, and in the combinations of stained glass."[32] Encouraging empathy with nature, however, was not the only benefit of residential stained glass. Capable of concealing unpleasant street views with idyllic natural scenes, stained glass helped to insulate the family from threatening exterior or public forces, and its use in urban homes was particularly recommended.[33]

Close connections to both the home and to nature effectively legitimized the use of stained glass in churches and broadened its appeal among evangelical denominations. Evangelical churches themselves suggest something of the chronological progression in glass design. By the 1870s most churches boasted some simple, colored-glass windows, often small panes outlining the edges of clear windows, although a few congregations bought full windows containing geometric or organic images. The colors almost always echoed the natural tones of the sanctuary itself with pink, green, and yellow being most prominent. By the 1880s the windows of many churches incorporated representational images based, again, on nature themes—often flowers (particularly lilies), trees, and natural landscapes. In the 1890s, however, figural representations appeared frequently, including images of biblical figures generally rendered in a naturalistic Arts and Crafts manner with subdued colors and realistic features as well as symbolic images like anchors, bibles, doves, harps, and so on.

The windows in First Congregational Church of Minneapolis illustrated each stage of this progression. As completed in 1887, the church contained several windows with stained-glass borders in pink, green, and yellow. The sanctuary housed more elaborate but still nonrepresentational windows in two parallel horizontal rows of five windows on the east wall adjacent to the corner pulpit platform. According to the local newspaper, "One of the most attractive features of the church are the stained glass windows, which are provided for outside and inside openings above the basement. The prevailing tints are olives and browns, with some light blue, all the windows being in geometrical designs. While the outlines are plain, great attention was paid to blending and harmonizing or tints, which was done by the art director of the Tiffany Glass Co., where the windows were made."[34] The large windows at the back of the sanctuary, however, were clear glass, perhaps due to the expense of stained glass. Nevertheless, by the late 1890s, a new aesthetic reminiscent of the earlier Gothic Revival was developing, and the congregation replaced the upper bank of nonrepresentational windows with memorial windows containing figural images in brilliant jeweled glass of bright red, blue, and gold hues.[35]

Denver's Trinity M.E. Church offers another typical example of the late 1880s. The north and south sides of the sanctuary housed two banks of rectangular windows filled with abstract foliage-like designs in warm colors of gold, yellow, red, and green, designed and executed by decorators Healy and Millet of Chicago. The glass used for these windows, similar to the opalescent glass developed by Louis C. Tiffany, was popularized by the Arts and Crafts movement of the period. Above each of these banks was another small bank with a large rose window above. These windows were also dominated by yellow and gold colors with flecks of red, blue, and green. At the west end of the church was a large figural painted-glass window depicting the Resurrection, which was executed by George Lamb of New York City. The figures in this window featured warm colors—browns and beiges, ivory and cream, yellows and golds—and the realistic treatment typical of the Arts and Crafts movement.[36]

The ceilings of these churches, like those of homes, were also highly articulated in order to reflect the natural world. Domestic ceilings, designers declared, were to look like the sky, not "too flat or too plain," an effect that could be achieved through the use of ribs, beams, stenciling, or decorative painting.[37] Church designers took such advice to heart as well. The ceiling of First Congregational in Minneapolis was defined by cross beams supported by brackets at the walls (see fig. 5.8). A dome was inscribed in the center of the ceiling, and each section was frescoed with intricate patterns. First Baptist in Minneapolis featured a vaulted dome supported on pendentives, each sporting a pattern of frescoed triangles surrounded by vines (see fig. 1.5). The notion of the ceiling as a "sky" was popular, and some church ceilings were painted with clouds or stars. In a particularly intriguing case, the Reverend John Goucher devised an elaborate scheme to incorporate nature into the sanctuary of the First Methodist Church in Baltimore. In this church, architect Stanford White's sanctuary dome was inscribed with a scene of the stars in heaven as they were said to have appeared on the morning of the church's dedication, specifically, at 3:30 A.M. on 6 November 1887. A journalist present at the dedication described the work: "Every star . . . visible to the naked eye . . . occupies its relative position and has its relative size. . . . The white light of the Milky Way, with its myriad stars, is distinctly seen, and though seven hundred and nineteen planets and stars are visible, there is no appearance of being crowded since the ceiling upon which they are painted contains over twenty-five thousand square feet of surface. The artists have been careful to preserve the shade of coloring peculiar to the different planets. Mars, shining with her own red light, is quickly recognized."[38] Though this example took the desire to connect the church to the natural environment further than most, it strongly attests to the significance of nature as well as to a scientific understanding of nature, which is similarly manifest in the naturalistic carvings and the frescoed vines.

Drawing thus on the material culture of the sacralized Christian home, congregations created an aura of domestic holiness and intimacy within their new theatrelike auditoriums. Subdued light filtered through stained glass bathed sanctuaries in a warm glow. Cushioned pews and carpeted floors softened the sound and the atmosphere. Warm wood furnishings and decoration lent richness to the space. Typically, it was women's groups that raised money for much of the sanctuary furnishings, from linens and serving sets for the Communion table to carpets, upholstery, and lighting sconces. Even while these features alluded to the sacred church home, they also participated in the social categories defined by the middle-class ideology. Just as an individual family announced its piety and social position through the use of the home and the display of specific items within it, so too did religious congregations. Congratulatory descriptions of churches in both the public media and in church documents indicate the significance of properly accoutered church homes. For congregations intent upon attracting respectable and even wealthy members, conversance with the latest trends in interior fashion was a must.

Domestic Exterior of Evangelical Churches

Just as church designers adopted the strategies of home interiors to bring nature into their buildings, architects drew upon exterior domestic design principles in their new evangelical churches for the same purpose. Middle-class families not only brought bits and pieces of the natural world into their homes in order to create a closer union with the natural world, they also favored house exteriors that reflected the natural world. As architectural historian Gwendolyn Wright explains, "Builders claimed that architecture could assert almost as much natural imagery as the landscape itself."[39] This desire to imitate the natural landscape transformed houses into irregular shapes to suggest a naturalistic organic complexity. New picturesque eclectic facade styles, including Carpenter Gothic, Queen Anne, and what are now called Stick and Shingle styles became popular. Such houses featured asymmetrical facades with various idiosyncratic recesses, balconies, porches, towers, turrets, gables, and windows along with the ornamental use of banding, timbering, shingles, bargeboards, and finials.

Church designers so closely followed these domestic strategies that were it not for a steeple attached at some point on the roof, many smaller churches of the period would hardly be distinguishable from private homes. A. G. Ferree's drawing of Trinity Congregational Church in Normal Park, Illinois, is a case in point (fig. 6.1). This domestic-scale church is essentially a two-story box with a gabled roof, yet it is sheathed in layers of ornament that create a highly complex but organic whole. The corner tower boasts six distinct stages of ornament, from the coffered doors with awnings to a window level

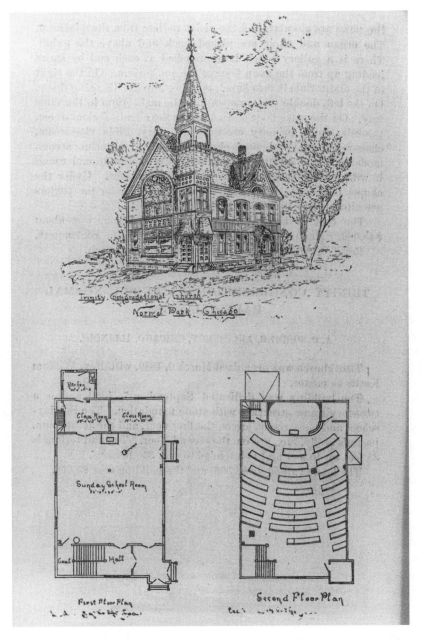

Fig. 6.1. Trinity Congregational Church, Normal Park, Ill. 1890. A. G. Ferree, arch. *Church Building Quarterly* 8 (Oct. 1890): 220.

topped with more coffers, to a shingled stage, a belfry, and a pointed cap topped with a finial. The sides of the building are similarly articulated with abundant windows—displaying a plethora of treatments from round arches to squared and semicurved lintels—a side gable, banding, a side door and porch, and a large, round-arched, stained-glass window on one end.[40] The effect is closely akin to a middle-class home, and only the broad, two-story window and the steeple indicate that this is a church rather than a home.

The materials and colors of these buildings further indicated their connections to houses of the period and the ideology of the natural environment. At this time, the exteriors of middle-class homes drew upon the same natural allusions as did the interiors. Wright explains that "rough limestone, wide clapboards, cedar shingles, green patina on slate tiles, all used for a single facade, gave the look of natural materials and venerable aging to a new house." Mineral paints and stains in natural colors were similarly popular to simulate the hues of nature, and "builders of the 1870s and 1880s favored the reds and golds of autumn leaves, the greens of ferns and lichens, the soft browns and grays of weathered woods."[41] In keeping with these domestic strategies, church builders like Ferree favored painted clapboards or stained shingles in natural colors for these modest churches.

More elaborate churches also mirrored the organic complexity and natural materials of the popular Queen Anne style. Architect Warren H. Hayes of Minneapolis, for instance, favored highly complex massing in the churches he designed. Large gabled walls punctuated by recesses or towers, usually enclosing entries or stairwells, characterize Hayes's buildings, and his rooflines are a puzzle of gables, turrets, and cupolas. These complex exterior features often mask the nature of the interior spaces, which are difficult and sometimes impossible to discern from the exterior. For example, the Fifth Street facade of First Congregational Church of Minneapolis consists of a bell tower with steeple, a recessed wall, a small turret, a large gabled wall with buttress, another recessed wall, and an anchoring tower (see fig. 4.8). Similarly, the Eighth Street facade features the bell tower, a small recessed wall, a large gabled wall with buttresses, a small apse, an anchoring tower, and a rectangular office wing. The diagonal plan of the square interior is impossible to read from this complex exterior. In fact, the deceptive roofline suggests a near-cruciform interior with a slender minaret marking the crossing. Such blatant contradicting of spatial rationality, a design principle lionized by both the Gothic Revivalists and the Beaux-Arts school, did not go unnoticed. Architect Ernest Greene complained that the diagonal plan favored by Hayes was "perhaps the most out of harmony with structural lines of any that has been devised, and for that reason it is a very difficult problem to treat it satisfactorily."[42] Nevertheless, such organic extravagances were common during the period. The facade of Trinity M.E. in Denver, for example, shows four main parts (see fig. 4.2). Reading the Eighteenth Avenue facade from the tower, the building consists of the steeple tower, a narrow recessed wall, a large gabled mass, another narrow recessed wall, a shorter anchor tower, and a small wing with an offset gable. The roof suggests a cruciform space below. Again, this facade masks the presence of the almost-square auditorium of the building.

Parallels to domestic exteriors went further than imitating the Queen Anne style and organic complexity and colors, however. The auditorium plan fit well on a standard city corner lot, and with the addition of adjacent lots, an office or Sunday school wing could be added. Thus, a neomedieval auditorium church echoed the scale of many upper-middle class homes in suburban neighborhoods. Again, the large windows and the spire announced the religious function of the building to the public; the rest of the building could easily be mistaken for the home of a wealthy family. Given this important task, the spire became a feature upon which architects lavished intense consideration. The slender stone spire of Denver's Trinity Church, for instance, soars 183 feet in the air (see fig. 4.2), and according to architectural historian Francine Haber was "one of the tallest stone towers in the United States" at the time of its completion.[43] Similarly, the steeple of Minneapolis's First Congregational rose 168 feet in the air and was decorated with small pointed gables similar to those favored by Gothic Revivalist A.W. Pugin. Stanford White's massive 186-foot tower for the First Methodist Church of Baltimore was conceived as "an adjunct" to the building rather than as "an integral part of the church" (see fig. 4.1). Drawing upon the tower of the Church of St. Maria of Pomposa in Ravenna, the tower seems to overscale the church, yet it succeeded in its intended effect, which was, if we can read between the lines of First Methodist minister John Goucher's words, to attraction attention:

> When the visitor to Baltimore, leaving the business portion of the city and traversing northwards the central residence zone, crosses North avenue, which formerly constituted the corporate limits in that direction, his eye is caught by a massive grey stone tower with a queer conical cap covered with red tiles, which send his imagination back to medieval times and lands. That tower belongs to the First Methodist Episcopal Church—the successor of the humble edifice in which the Methodist Episcopal Church of the United States was organized. . . . [The church is] one of the most distinctive architectural features of the city.[44]

The tower became a landmark, drawing all eyes to the highest architectural feature in the area. Apart from these towers and spires, however, both the scale and architectural complexity of the exterior facades of many neomedieval churches echoed domestic architecture and the incorporation of the natural environment into built environments. By so doing, these churches participated in the processes that sacralized both nature and the home and, at the same time, drew upon those sacralized sites to claim their own sanctity.

Domestic Rooms in Evangelical Churches

Evidence of the incorporation of domestic ideals into American Protestantism is nowhere so transparent as in the assimilation of domestic rooms into evangelical churches. From the early 1870s onward, the concept of the church home took on new and literal meanings in buildings that included not just a sanctuary, minister's study, and Sunday school lecture hall but also kitchens, dining rooms, lounges, toilets, nurseries, and libraries.

In the middle-class home, the specialization of rooms, which had become increasingly commonplace during the 1830s and 1840s, was essentially codified by the 1850s. The function assigned to each individual room both reflected and contributed to the formation of public-private and gender parameters. Public rooms, like the parlor and dining room, were those in which nonfamilial visitors could be entertained. Other rooms in the house, particularly bedrooms and service rooms (kitchen, servants' hall, and so on), were private and generally associated with either men or women. A library, for instance, offered private space for the affluent man to work on business matters or for quiet relaxation; sitting rooms and bedrooms were similarly used by women for both work and relaxation, and nurseries served as play space for younger children.[45] By the early 1870s these parameters for domestic room specialization, based on public-private and gender definitions, were integrated into religious architecture.

The migration of domestic rooms into the church not only corresponded to but also constituted a critical factor in the burgeoning of women's participation in evangelical congregations. To discuss the domestic rooms of a church, therefore, is to discuss the changing role of the women members and the changing power dynamics within congregations. As has been well noted by historians, during this period women constituted the majority of church members, and the nature of evangelicalism itself encouraged them to participate in the work of the church to evangelize the nation. While a few women took this mandate to the level of preaching, many more fulfilled their responsibilities through participation in church life and in church-sponsored organizations. Women's organizing activity in churches grew rapidly from the 1820s, spurred by revivals and concern for social issues like abolitionism, prostitution, and temperance. By the late nineteenth century, congregational societies included not only branches of such national organizations as the Foreign and Home Missionary societies and the Society for Christian Endeavor but also local and congregational groups, including temperance and benevolence societies and social coteries. Depending upon the size of the congregation, an evangelical church might have anywhere from a half dozen to more than twenty organizations, the majority of which were women's groups.[46]

All of these groups required meeting space. Prior to the development of the domestic church with its lounges and classrooms, meetings were held in members' private homes, yet gathering in parlors not designed for large groups proved inconvenient for many. Meeting in public spaces, on the other hand, was out of the question for middle-class women's groups because doing so blatantly violated proscriptions on women's activities and presence in public. Churches offered a middle ground between these two poles. Extending domestic space into the church did not violate popular views of women's distinct nature and suitability for domestic activity; it extended the boundaries of the cloister, so to speak, but not so far as to violate public taboos. The church home offered a suitable location for women's activities, simply shifting the site of their sacred domestic tasks.[47] Furthermore, with these buildings, congregations acknowledged and legitimated the religious work of women by committing the valuable resource of space to it.

Architectural plans indicate that maintaining the gender designation of rooms was a priority for most congregations. Women's meeting spaces were invariably labeled "ladies' lounges" or "parlors," terms that specified the function of the room and the gender of those using it. Much less common was the designation of "men's parlor," although "trustee room" was not uncommon.[48] These gender designations indicate the importance that these congregations attached to the idea of men's and women's separate natures and duties. As in the home, separate spaces were needed to accommodate these two different groups.

The parlor was a room of particular importance within homes and, we can assume, within churches as well. As the site of middle-class domestic social activity, the parlor was strongly identified not simply with women but with their responsibilities within the evangelical domestic ideology as the "angels of the hearth." As historian Karen Halttunen explains, "With the cult of domesticity, the parlor provided the woman of the house with a 'cultural podium' from which she was to exert her moral influence over American society."[49] The domestic parlor, in addition to providing a space for formal socialization, also provided a display area for consumer items and thus contributed to the link between middle-class domestic life and commercial enterprise. Indeed, the parlor was considered such a critical factor in the domestic lifestyle that in their attempts to "Americanize" immigrant and working-class residents, middle-class reformers urged them to reserve parlor space in their homes.[50] As church designers looked for means of accommodating women's congregational work within the church's walls, they naturally looked to the domestic parlor for inspiration, ultimately adopting it part and parcel from the home to the church.

Replicating the domestic model, ladies' parlors offered a stage upon which an evangelical woman could play the new role of public servant while not compromising her reputation. In effect, these spaces, safely contained within the walls of the church, legitimized women's religious work in the community while at the same time demonstrating that such work did not exceed the boundaries of proper gender behavior. Ladies' parlors offered commodious meeting spaces for the many women's organizations but also offered a measure of privacy.[51] In effect, these spaces—and the domestic church itself—helped to expand the conceptualization of just what constituted women's "proper" behavior. Although the vast majority of these church members had no intention of striking a blow for women's rights or their fuller participation in society, they could feel perfectly comfortable meeting in the ladies' parlor to organize fundraising efforts for, say, the expansion of their denomination throughout the western territories or for benevolence work in Appalachia. From their secure parlors, evangelical women participated in everything from global missionizing to national temperance work to local benevolence. As historian Betty DeBerg has argued, women created an "evangelical feminism" that, though conservative in nature, significantly pressed the boundaries of gender ideology. That they were able to do so rested in part upon the church homes that provided secure and proper spaces for their activities. Moreover, the rapidity with which parlors became commonplace in churches indicates the extent to which congregations themselves accepted women's organizational activity as not simply an appropriate feature of congregational life but an essential one. Thus, the domestic sacralization of these church buildings must be viewed as a consequence of their connection not only to the pious Christian home but also to the evangelical labor performed by women.

Although women's participation in church-sponsored organizations reached back to the early decades of the nineteenth century, by the closing decades, women's role within the church had also expanded in a new, domestic direction as they transferred their domestic labor from the home into the church. This is strongly evident in the incorporation into churches of the most obviously domestic room: the private female space of the kitchen. Church kitchens appeared in a few isolated incidents as early as the 1850s. A description of Winnisimmet Congregational Church in Chelsea, Massachusetts, for instance, published in 1859, reported that the building housed "a small kitchen, which [had] pump, sink, boiler and closet for the convenience of the Ladies' Benevolent Circle."[52] Cooking facilities along with pantries, china closets, dumbwaiters, serving rooms, and dining halls appeared relatively frequently in published church plans from the 1870s onward. Of forty-one interior plans shown for auditorium churches in the *American Architect and Building News* between 1879 and 1908, nine of them, or roughly 22 percent, included a room designated as the kitchen. The actual number of kitchens in these buildings, however, was most likely much larger because many published plans did not include the crucial basement level. Plans published in *Church Building Quarterly* increasingly showed dining facilities through the 1880s, another indication of the presence of kitchens.

Just how these new church kitchens were used, however, is not always clear from architectural or congregational sources. Rarely do church descriptions indicate what facilities these kitchens included. Tables, cupboards, and sinks were likely, and a few building descriptions mention the availability of cold water. The presence of ranges, however, is more difficult to ascertain. I have found no mention of stoves in descriptive literature, and it is likely that this essential kitchen item posed some challenges to congregations. Because most church kitchens occupied the basement, ventilation for a kitchen range would have been required, and this, along with the need to carry wood downstairs and ash upstairs for disposal, may have led some congregations to exclude stoves. Some churches may have solved these problems the same way that homeowners had done for decades: by building a kitchen lean-to onto the back of the building. Larger churches sometimes located the kitchen on the first floor of a Sunday school building adjacent but contiguous to the church and thus isolated the room from services while rendering the task of clean-up and maintenance less daunting.[53] Clearly, though, ranges were common in church kitchens by the 1880s. One can deduce their presence from the mention of china closets, for if the congregation owned dishes, it is likely that they were cleaned on the premises after use, and cleaning required hot water, hence a stove.

The presence of kitchens made possible church suppers and banquets, which became increasingly popular in the 1880s and 1890s.[54] But again, ascertaining just what portions of these meals were cooked in the church and what portions were cooked in homes and brought to the church is difficult, though some deductions are possible. For instance, the women of First Congregational Church in Minneapolis served a Washington's Birthday banquet in 1906, offering a cooked entree of roast turkey and gravy, which may have been prepared either at the church or in women's homes and carried to the church. Some or all of the accompaniments—rolls and jelly, green salad with French dressing, toasted St. Johnsbury biscuits, cherry ice cream, coffee, and cake— may also have been prepared in homes, given their more complicated ingredients and preparation requirements. In any event, this church contained a stove, and it is likely that even if the turkey, rolls, biscuits, and cake were not cooked on the premises, they would have been kept warm in a church oven. Coffee, moreover, needed to made be fresh and kept hot. Certainly hot water was needed for the washing up. Ice cream, another popular church supper feature, required cooking several ingredients (which may have been done at home), allowing them to cool, and then churning them in an ice cream freezer (which easily could have been done in the church kitchen). Unfortunately, ascertaining actual church kitchen use requires the kind of descriptive memoir material that is rare.[55]

The importance of women's cooking expertise merged easily with the domestic ideology developing within evangelical religion. According to historian Glenna Matthews, the task of preparing meals carried the sacred meaning of nurturing the family and thus offered a focus for personal satisfaction and pride.[56] The sanctity of the task along with the resulting evidence of the skill and piety of the mother/cook suggest a framework for understanding the desire for kitchens within churches. Because the tasks of baking or cooking could be considered sacred, they were appropriately performed within the church; thus, kitchens could safely be included within the sacred walls of the church. Whether or not such reasoning was used by church designers of the period, it does suggest the intimate connections between the dominant domestic ideology and the subsequent inclusion of kitchens in church buildings. Furthermore, the presence of these kitchens in churches helped to dramatically reorient the role of women as church members, for even if part of the kitchen work itself was relegated to servants (who would have been doing much of it in the homes of middle-class members), the overseeing of meals would have been seen as the duty of the women members of the church. Evidence of correlations between women's domestic cooking and their church lives are abundant, not only in the growing number of church kitchens and corresponding suppers, banquets, and charity dinners, but also in the simultaneous development of what became a stable in the arsenal of church fundraising: the church-sponsored cookbook. In Minnesota, for instance, the 1870s saw publication of a number of such books, including *Valuable Recipes* by the ladies of Westminster Presbyterian Church in Minneapolis.[57] Insofar as cooking and food service were transferred into the church, that building became not only a church home but also an extension of this important facet of women's domestic lives.

In providing space then for women's organizational meetings and domestic work, the evangelical churches stand as eloquent testimony to many of the activities that shaped evangelical women's religious live at the end of the nineteenth century. They also indicate the centrality of these activities within the life of the congregation. Although women's names may not have been routinely posted among the leaders of congregations, the significance of their work was deeply inscribed on the spaces of the church itself. At the same time, the domestic character of the buildings attests to the changing character of evangelical religion itself.

The interiors of these new church homes mirrored aspects of middle-class domestic life beyond their parlors, kitchens, and dining rooms, however, embracing a number of spatial strategies engendered by interest in the technological advances and cultural changes that informed "scientific housekeeping." Storage space, for instance, was an increasingly important element in homes as families put a high premium on the philosophy of "everything in its place."[58] In addition to the pantries and china closets already mentioned, cloakrooms and closets, sometimes designated as men's and women's, became increasingly common in both the homes and the churches of middle-class Americans. These rooms linked the church not only to the home but also to the theatre, another institution that increasingly offered means of stowing coats, hats, and umbrellas during performances. Following the theatre model, the Extension of the Mother Church of Christian Science, an enormous auditorium church in Boston's Back Bay area, contains a semicircle of several coat-check windows, behind which attendants secured worshipers' hats, coats, and umbrellas for the duration of the services.

In addition, vestibules, highly popular in domestic architecture, became de rigueur in churches. Almost every church boasted at least one at each entry, and many plans designated numerous small rooms or hall spaces as "vestibules."[59] These multipurpose spaces played significant roles in both the social and liturgical lives of the congregation. First, like the entrance to a home, a vestibule at the main entrance of a church created a buffer between the outdoors and the sanctuary, blocking both drafts and noise from the street. Because the vestibule was the first space to make an impression upon the visitor, it was intended to present a friendly greeting, perhaps being "furnished with seats and great fireplaces, where the roaring blaze gives a pleasant welcome."[60] Many vestibules required congregants to take a circuitous path to the main auditorium. As one entered Wesley M.E. Church in Minneapolis, for instance, the route to the sanctuary proceeded into a wood-paneled vestibule, up the stairs on either the right or left, through another vestibule, and into the auditorium. Echoing ancient patterns that aimed at obscuring or enhancing the significance of religiously powerful places, these routes emphasized the transition between secular public space and the holy domestic sanctuary.

Vestibules also accommodated new activities within evangelical churches. Weddings and funerals were increasingly held in these buildings, and vestibules provided gathering spaces for those participating in the processionals that increasingly constituted part of these occasions. Unlike the ecclesiastical processions of High Churches, these evangelical processions were performed by the laity. Wedding and funeral parties would gather in the vestibule and enter the church at the appropriate time. To facilitate their entry, architects often specified clear glass windows between vestibules and sanctuaries.[61] In churches such as First Baptist in Minneapolis and Park Church in Elmira, New York, such processions could make highly dramatic entrances from the balcony, approaching the pulpit stage down the sweeping staircases that connected gallery and stage (see fig. 1.5). Vestibules, like the sanctuaries themselves, thus catered to the needs of congregants and indicated the new lay ceremonialism.

Despite their firm connections to the sacred domestic ideals of middle-class society, the inclusion of domestic rooms in churches roused some debate among traditionalists. In 1877 architect R. S. Peabody strongly disparaged the trend toward including "church parlors, lecture-room seatings, cooking-stoves, pantries, and the other adjuncts of a well-regulated meetinghouse" because they detracted from the spiritual purpose of worship. The church, which in his opinion should be "from bottom to top, sacred," was compromised by such facilities.[62] But the rapid inclusion of these rooms in churches and their predominance by the 1880s suggests that Peabody's opinion was in the minority. Indeed, these rooms, as much as the sanctuaries themselves, attested precisely to how the word *sacred* should be interpreted. The domestic ideal of the single family home, having achieved the position of the predominant symbol of Christian piety and social stability, had become the standard against which all churchly sacredness was measured. No longer did the church control what was sacred and what was inappropriate in the church. That which was churchly was domestic.[63]

One last observation must be made about these domestic church homes, however. Regardless of their churchly character, the democratic character of evangelicalism, and the belief in the moral suasion of women, the family church, in the end, housed a patriarchal family circumscribed by perfectly transparent male power. The homelike interiors, the kitchens, the parlors, and the coatrooms remained enveloped in neomedieval facades whose armory-like skin protected these "softer" interior features. If the female sphere, characterized by Christian morality and the loving nurture of family members in a pleasant and safe home, was represented in the overtly domestic interiors, the Richardsonian Romanesque and Romanesque Revival styles indicated the public world of the male sphere, marked by conflict and risk and requiring an aggressive response, a "spiritual armory," in the language of the Reverend M. M. Dana. Through this inside-outside dichotomy, these churches offered an architectural rendering of the social roles of the middle-class family in which a public masculine presence sheltered and confined private feminine activity.

Liberal and Orthodox Protestants and Their Church Homes

Evangelical religion was pulled toward two sometimes complementary, sometimes contradictory poles. On the one hand, revivalism existed at the heart of the evangelical agenda. To spread the gospel to as many people as possible was a critical task of all evangelical denominations during this period. For many congregations of the late nineteenth century, this goal was addressed through evangelizing and missionary work. The formation of interdenominational Foreign and Home Missionary societies and the fundraising efforts undertaken by all members of church families to further the work of missionaries attest to the importance attached to witnessing abroad. On the other hand, once people were converted, their spiritual needs required ongoing support. Family churches—church homes—offered essential opportunities for ongoing worship, pastoral care, and social interaction among Christians.

Yet these two activities—spreading the gospel and addressing the needs of the converted, particularly of families—could conflict, laying bare a number of issues embedded in congregations' missions and social makeup. Evangelical roots lay in revivals, intentionally promiscuous gatherings, but stable churches and congregations tended toward relative social homogeneity. While late nineteenth-century urban churches supported revival efforts and perhaps longed for their own revival, they rarely made sponsoring such events a priority. They would raise money and send missionaries, they might welcome a particular revival preacher into their pulpit, but rarely would they hold a revival within their own buildings. The most successful revivals of the period took place apart from established churches. Dwight L. Moody's 1876 Chicago revival, for instance, was housed in a tabernacle built especially for his use. Sam Porter Jones's revivals took place in Tom Ryman's Union Gospel Tabernacle in Nashville, which was constructed specifically for them. Evangelical church homes were generally not revival churches.[64] Within them, congregations that were more family oriented focused on the needs of already converted members.

The question, then, is whether the categories of *revivalism* and *family ministry* should be linked with the two ideological camps, orthodox and liberal, and whether, by extension, the spaces in which they took place can be so linked as well. Some individuals attempted to do precisely this. As Joseph Siry has pointed out, Unitarian minister Jenkin Lloyd Jones claimed the family church ideal and its architectural rendering in the auditorium church home for liberal religion. "Jones," Siry writes, "reasoned that a church should be like a residence, believing that the congregation 'is the larger family and its building must be made the larger home.'"[65] Conservative minister William Bell Riley of First Baptist Church in Minneapolis similarly saw the family church as a manifestation of liberalism, but in his view, family churches were hardly the welcoming places that that Jones envisioned. Bell saw them as exclusive, wealthy, antidemocratic organizations that existed in opposition to the revival church.

A closer examination of the situation at First Baptist, however, reveals the complexity of the revival and family ministry missions. Riley saw himself gathering crowds of thousands eager to hear the gospel, just as did his idol, George Lorimer, in Tremont Temple in Boston and Moody in Philadelphia and Chicago. A few years after his arrival at First, several lay leaders of the church clashed with Riley over theological matters and the direction of the church, and ultimately 150 original members of the congregation left to form a new church. Testimony from both sides in this heated five-year battle was replete with elevated rhetoric and manipulative intent, but one statement made by Riley is curiously telling. Riley, not noted for restraint or circumspection in his evaluation of those who opposed him, was quoted as saying upon the removal of the opposing members that their new church would "probably be located in a fine residence neighborhood, where their ideas of family church can be realized." Scholars have generally focused on the social-class disparities embedded in this position, arguing that the conservative Riley favored democratic, heterogeneous evangelism over the more insular, family-oriented desires of the wealthy. Riley himself suggested this when he stated that, in his view, a "church should be no respecter of person." To counter the wealthy dissenters, he "advocated a people's church, free pews, etc., visited the poor as often as the rich, advertised in the hotels and boarding houses about us and thus sought attendance."[66] To an extent, Riley's prediction was realized: The new congregation did build in the newly developed and very expensive Lowry Hill area, and among those who left were some wealthy members. Yet many of the wealthiest members of First remained, and Riley remained a welcomed visitor among elite social circles in the city throughout his ministry. This was not a simple conflict between wealth and Riley's notions of evangelical inclusiveness. Scholars' attention to the class issue has obscured the religious differences played out in the struggle over First Baptist, for what was at stake in this conflict was church mission. Should evangelism continue through revivalism or through ministry to the converted?

Despite the fact that Bell saw an alliance among religious liberalism, wealth, and the family church, on the one hand, and orthodoxy, democracy, and revivalism, on the other, the analysis does not hold up when applied to this situation. First Baptist had been growing as a family church for nearly four decades, and many wanted it to remain such. The dissatisfaction with Riley may well have stemmed from the fact that his vision of a revival church threatened the family church itself. The mass meetings he desired could easily have replaced the familiar, more intimate Sunday services and stressed the building itself. The congregation would have had to put up with, and control, all sorts of visitors. More important, however, other actions that Riley took shortly after his arrival may also have been interpreted as threatening the family character of the church. According to an admiring biography of Riley written by his wife, Marie Riley, he despaired of the financing of the church shortly after he arrived and went to the leaders of several of the women's societies to ask them to discontinue their fundraising events—church suppers, bake sales, and the like—arguing that such nickle-and-diming of the wealthy male members disinclined them to contribute more substantial sums to the church. Though Marie Riley states that the women readily submitted to Riley's request, archival sources show that socials and suppers continued to occur in the church.[67] In fact, the use of the church for social functions expanded so quickly in the early twentieth century that the congregation was soon strapped for adequate space. Riley, it seems, had not won this skirmish. Whether or not his request stirred displeasure among the women of the church is unknown, but clearly, any attempt to marginalize women members violated the very foundation of the domestic, family church ideal. Whereas evangelicals championed the moral suasion of women and encouraged their church work to the extent of completely redesigning church space to accommodate it, Riley seems to have exhibited, at least initially, a divergent attitude toward women's participation.[68] Fondness for the family church was deeply rooted in this congregation.

Further, as rancorous as the situation at First Baptist was, it did not reflect a simple revival/orthodox versus family/liberal dichotomy, even though William and Marie Riley attempted to paint it as such. In fact, Riley was not sufficiently orthodox in his preaching for many at First. In leaving to form their own church, the disaffected group cited their theological dissatisfaction with Riley. In particular, they abhorred his willingness to relax his orthodox Calvinism to embrace such innovative new practices and ideas as divine healing and dispensationalism. As they developed their new Trinity Church, they made it not a bastion of liberalism but a moderate-to-conservative evangelical family church. Adopting the orthodox New Hampshire Confession, the new congregation met in the YMCA and YWCA for several months, and in 1905 they called Lathan A. Crandall of Chicago to minister in their new $60,000 church.

In light of this scenario, the argument can be made that the family church ideal functioned similarly to the auditorium space itself: as a factor that tended to keep theologically liberal and conservative evangelicals generally united during the period. Family-centered church homes appealed to both. First Congregational of Minneapolis, an increasingly liberal church closely associated with the University of Minnesota, prided itself on being a family church as much as did the more conservative evangelicals who left First Baptist. Although Riley heralded the revivalist direction and courting of the economically disadvantaged that conservative and fundamentalist religion would ultimately pursue after the turn of the twentieth century, these aspects had not yet sorted themselves out into distinctive theological camps.[69] Under Riley's direction, First Baptist Church did sponsor revivals, but it also maintained all of the characteristics of a family church, updating its domestically informed building in 1924 and continuing to sponsor a variety of programs aimed at all of the members of attending families, including programs for young people and, particularly, programs to bring men into the church.

One final question further indicates the complexity of the challenges of modern life to religious orthodoxy. Given the trend toward showplace churches—costly buildings filled with the latest technical innovations and lush furnishings and décor—one must ask whether evangelical religion was simply colonized by capitalism during the peak of the U.S. industrial revolution. Were these churches merely the gilded totems of a capitalist age? Were they artifacts that furthered the ideology of wealth and consumption, bathing it in a glow of sanctified virtuosity and thus justifying it and the materialistic lifestyle it encouraged as sacred?

Many feared this was precisely the case. As mentioned previously, a Wisconsin bishop invited to dedicate the new Wesley M.E. Church in Minneapolis was appalled at the $150,000 cost of the building, and in a scathing letter declined, saying, "Methodists don't spend money on buildings; they spend money on missions. You have violated that principle and I refuse to come and dedicate that sinful structure."[70] In a similar vein, the *Church Building Quarterly* in 1891 published a warning against "palatial churches," quoting from John Hall's address to the Presbyterian Union in Chicago: "Let the demand be made loud and long that all the churches leave off their trying to rival the world in art and architecture in the name of the Lord, and come down to plain preaching."[71]

Such tension between materialism and Reformed religion was, of course, nothing new. From the early nineteenth century (and perhaps earlier), the question of congregational spending was often rhetorically placed in a zero-sum relationship with missionary work. If congregations were spending their money on impressive buildings, they were neglecting their duty to spread the gospel through the support of missionary work.[72] Lewis Tappan similarly decried the spending of large sums on church buildings, arguing that resources should be used to build "spiritual temples," not those of "brick and mortar."[73] Warnings against the evils of materialism had been common throughout the late eighteenth and early nineteenth centuries, particularly during periods of revival. Finney publicly excoriated and privately warned women and men against showing off their fine clothing at church.

Yet, many were also convinced that it was capitalism itself that brought the opportunity for evangelization. Lewis Tappan and his association colleagues were positioned to launch free churches in New York precisely because of their comfortable financial situations and business expertise. Capital, too, allowed David Hale to "save" the Broadway Tabernacle. By the latter part of the century, Methodists, unused to being economic and social leaders, found themselves in precisely these positions, and they experimented widely to integrate capitalism and evangelical religion. Those experiments, as we have seen, focused, not surprisingly, on real estate and on churches.[74]

Such examples, I think, reveal less of a co-opting of evangelicalism by capitalism than evangelicals' struggle to create something sacred within the expanding capitalist milieu. Surely, these groups did not hesitate to use the tools available to them through capitalism to shape and express their changing religious beliefs. Their choice to sacralize the family and the domestic household was not without difficulties, particularly for those who did not, could not, or simply did not choose to share that value. Their choice to make their devotions more expressive—not only through architecture and visual ornament but through liturgy, hymnody, and art-music as well—expanded the devotional possibilities available while at the same time serving to limit the audience who would find such features relevant.

Does such commingling of economics and religion constitute a false consciousness or impostor faith that is nothing more than class strategy in disguise? For many, the answer is yes: These buildings attest to the final eclipsing of a purer evangelical religion rooted in Calvinist principles or revivalism, not in industrial capitalist culture. But such a conclusion is too simplistic, for religion, any religion, is necessarily rooted in culture. Christians of all stripes have struggled to redefine religious meaning as times have changed. Societies have only the tools of culture with which to fashion religious meaning, to sacralize their world and their existence. This is not to say that tensions did not exist between use and ideals, that all congregations and all individuals refused to use these tools to their own advantage, or that hypocrisy did not exist, for religion itself is, of course, intimately concerned with power. In these buildings occurred a commingling of supernatural, social, and personal power. The churches spoke of God's power, society's power, and individual power, blending all three in a conversation that not only made sense in terms of these Protestants' view of salvation but that, as I will demonstrate in the next chapter, would also, many believed, determine the future of the nation.

7

Building for the Children

Akron Plan Sunday Schools and Institutional Churches

Like the sacralized Christian family, the church home did not necessarily eschew the changing social and public contexts of U.S. society. In some cases, it actually thrived upon them. As a strategy for negotiating position within the public and private worlds, it did not forsake the former for the latter, but used its close association with the domestic familial sphere as a safe foundation from which to make forays into the public realm. Legitimized and bolstered by the familial alliance, congregations throughout the country engaged in a broadly social evangelizing that blended the spiritual message with benevolence and social welfare programs aimed at disadvantaged non-church members. To be an evangelical family church, whether more liberal or more conservative in stripe, meant to give generously of money and often of time in efforts to extend the benefits of the Christian family to those beyond the church doors. Nowhere are these processes more clearly exhibited than in the extraordinary expansion of the function of church buildings beyond providing worship and meeting space into also providing educational and recreational space.

Congregations' forays into these new areas emerged directly from the church home ideal. If a family church were to be successful, it had to minister to every member of the church family, from the eldest to the youngest, and while maintaining the eldest members might not be too difficult, the stakes were high, then as now, in keeping the children of the church within the fold. It comes as no surprise, then, that as congregations planned and erected their new church homes, they were acutely concerned with accommodating the religious education of children and keeping them involved in church activities. Architectural expression of these concerns produced two innovative spaces: the Akron Plan Sunday school and the institutional church. Closely associated with neomedieval auditorium churches, these forms constitute the final architectural components of the church home ideal.

Like almost all other aspects of the evangelical auditorium churches, these new educational elements indicated complex meanings—in that case, meanings well beyond the simple education of children into the faith. While that was a crucial function, the new educational and recreational facilities that sometimes came to dominate the physical plants of evangelical churches also indicated a desire to embrace community outreach as a new part of church mission. At last ostensibly intended for both the children of congregation members and the wider community, these facilities would become the site upon which the tensions between the family ministry mission and the outreach mission would be played out.

Transformation of the Sunday School

The development of Sunday school space in the United States reflects the growing importance that congregations invested in religious education as the nineteenth century progressed. Changing religious ideas about the nature of children and reinterpretations of their relation to the covenant between God and society spurred the creation of the Sunday school. Seventeenth-century Calvinists had viewed children as not only corrupted by original sin but also, due to their ignorance, uniquely vulnerable to Satan's ministrations. Thus, although children shared in the covenant of their parents, they came under strict parental discipline early in their lives. In Plymouth Colony, for instance, parents were to make sure they were "at least to be able duely [sic] to read the Scriptures" and understand "the main Grounds and Principles of Christian Religion."[1] Using the Bible to teach basic literacy skills and catechizing their children, parents regularly fulfilled this duty. They also took their children to worship services, but in the meetinghouse children were relegated to the galleries, where a tithing monitor would keep an eye on them. The religious education of children remained the duty of parents.[2]

The move to place religious education in others' hands began in England during the Arminian revivals of the eighteenth century. For Whitefield and the Wesleys, although children might not possess the maturity required for religious conversion, they urgently needed instruction in the foundations of Christianity in order to be prepared for the possibility of conversion. Education formed a precondition for conversion, a preparing of the soil, so to speak.[3] Thus, preachers of an Arminian cast set about to evangelize children through education, focusing particularly on the children of the poor who lacked the literacy skills needed for minimal conversance with the Bible. Teaching reading and writing through biblical texts, the British Sunday schools founded by interdenominational evangelical organizations were soon imitated by secular groups interested in improving the conditions of the working class.[4]

Devoted to the children of the poor and marginal, and sponsored not by individual congregations but by interdenominational evangelical groups, early Sunday schools were housed separately from churches. The schools met in functional buildings rented or constructed for the purpose with large open rooms and seating arrangements that allowed for the greatest efficiency in monitoring the activities of the pupils. Rarely were these buildings ornamented with any features that would indicate their religious function, for their didactic function did not yet fall under the auspices of the church. These early British schools, though linked to evangelical roots, remained quasi-religious institutions, outside the purview of churches.[5]

In the United States this interdenominational, quasi-religious model was initially followed, although rapidly changing evangelical convictions soon brought modifications. In the early nineteenth-century context of religious voluntarism and denominational competition, Sunday school quickly became an evangelizing tool. Focusing on the unconverted, early nineteenth-century Sunday schools were somewhat akin to open-air revivalism, which was evangelism in the "wilderness" rather than within the church. Here, the wilderness was the city and the beasts to be tamed were the children. In Sunday school, children and adults received a heavy dose of evangelical religion and moral training along with literacy instruction. As biblical knowledge was increasingly stressed, however, church members grew intrigued with the idea of extending the religious education of their own children through such schools. The popular legend is that Lyman Beecher, impressed with his local Sunday school, enrolled his own children to further their religious knowledge. Regardless of the veracity of the story, it is clear that during the 1830s the clientele, the mission, and the physical location of Sunday schools embarked on a slow, but ultimately radical, transformation. Pupils began to come from within the church family, literacy training gave way to Bible study, and Sunday schools moved from outside the walls of the church to inside them.[6]

Although occurring as early as the 1830s, the inclusion of classrooms in church buildings was relatively slow in coming. In 1835 the *New York Evangelist* reported on a newly dedicated African-American church in Troy, New York, which contained two basement rooms, "one designed for the use of the Male and Female Benevolent Societies formed among this people; the other occupied by a day school . . . [and] is also used by the Sabbath school belonging to the society," that is, the congregation that owned the building sponsored the Sunday school.[7] A year later, the Kirtland Temple, erected by Joseph Smith to house his nascent Mormon church, featured two stories, a lower one for worship services and an upper one devoted to education.[8] In 1844, Charles Finney intended to incorporate six recitation rooms behind the pulpit, "three above and three below," in the Oberlin meetinghouse; the building committee, however, relocated these rooms to the basement as they recast the plans.[9] These three examples, however, serve as transitions between the early Sunday schools and the later church schools because they were intended primarily for adult students, not children. The Troy Sabbath school included "Bible classes composed of adults"; the second floor of the Kirtland Temple functioned as a seminary; and the Oberlin meetinghouse rooms were used by the college.

Accommodating children's religious classes within the church soon followed, bringing widespread change to church architecture. In New England, some congregations, eager to expand the square footage of their buildings to accommodate a Sunday school, divided their buildings into two stories. The upper story served as the sanctuary, and the lower became a lecture room for the Sunday school and a handy place for town meetings. Another strategy was to physically lift the church building and excavate a basement or half-basement below it. In other instances, congregations erected separate vestry buildings to house their Sunday school classes and other meetings.[10] At midcentury, most Sunday schools consisted of little more than a single large or two smaller classrooms, one for "infant" classes up to age six and one for older children. Though George Bowler's Methodist-approved *Chapel and Church Architecture* of 1856 encouraged "providing suitable rooms for all the various purposes demanded by congregation of worshipers,—class-rooms, prayer and conference rooms, retiring rooms, &c.,—and we have recommended, as a matter of economy, that all these should be under the same roof," it offered only one plan with designated Sunday school space. In this two-story church, the sanctuary occupied the upper level, and the lower level was divided for a 38-by-40-

foot lecture room and two 12-by-14-foot classrooms, one of which was designated for Bible classes.[11]

Such Sunday school rooms were typically designed and furnished with as much flexibility as possible so that they could serve a variety of purposes. For Sunday school use, chairs were arranged in small semicircles surrounding individual teachers (fig. 7.1). A superintendent's desk might be placed at one end of the room, but this was a level of formalism not adopted by most churches. Some more advanced plans featured means of partitioning space to create two or more smaller rooms out of a larger one. For instance, the Kirtland Temple featured a system of "veils," or large canvas sheets, which could be rolled down from ceiling to floor to partition the room into several segments. Similarly, Finney requested that rolling partitions separate the Sunday school rooms in the Oberlin meetinghouse in order to accommodate groups of differing sizes. Designed with function in mind, these rooms might house the school on Sunday afternoons, a meeting of the deacons later in the week, and even social gatherings when necessary.[12]

While church buildings began to include Sunday school rooms as early as the 1830s, discussion of Sunday school architecture within denominational literature came only in the 1850s. Although many periodicals published drawings of church exteriors with second stories, as did Bowler, most made no mention of specific Sunday school spaces nor illustrated them with plans. In 1859, the *Congregational Quarterly* set a new course with the publication of a written description of Broadway Congregational Church in Norwich, Connecticut. Its basement featured a large Sabbath school room separated from a lecture room one-third its size by a movable partition. It also housed a library, infant school room, and ladies' room.[13] In 1860, the *Congregational Quarterly* described the new and expensive Clinton Avenue Congregational Church in New York City and mentioned that a room at the rear of the building served the pastor, the Sunday school, and weekly meetings. Three years later, the same publication referred in passing to the Sunday school room in the basement of South Church in Andover.[14] Despite such examples, however, published church plans regularly lacked Sunday school space, even as late as the 1870s.

This lack of published Sunday school plans was due only in part to the common practice of not printing basement plans (probably because of space restrictions in periodicals), for criticism of Sunday schools did exist. Some felt that the incorporation of educational space within the church brought into question, indeed skewed, the mission of the church. At a time when congregations were struggling with the shift from revival to family ministry, religious education constituted a particularly ambiguous signifier. If the function of the church were to house and foster worship, many argued, the building should be from "top to bottom churchly"; if classrooms, along with domestic rooms, were necessary, they should be relegated to a separate building. But even those who supported the family church ideal remained wary of Sunday schools, concerned, ironically, that congregationally sponsored Sunday schools threatened the family by usurping parents' responsibility to provide for the religious education of their children.[15] If churches took on this role, lazy parents could shirk their duties and the enthusiasm of more conscientious parents might be jeopardized. Further, in a country suspicious of the power of the church, the idea of handing one's children over to religious teachers irked many.

Sunday school supporters responded energetically to these criticisms, placing the Sunday school squarely within the context of the church home and family religion and

superintendent. The following diagram will show this still more clearly:

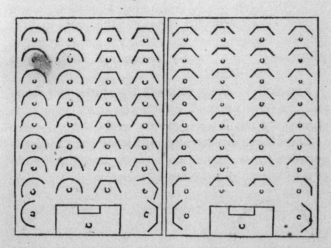

The following cut is made from a photograph of one of these seats:

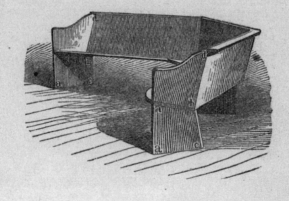

Fig. 7.1. Infant Sunday school seating arrangement. Alice W. Knox and Charles E. Knox, *The Infant Sunday School* (New York: Broughton & Wyman, 1870), 14.

arguing that the church school not only had no intention of usurping parental roles but was, to the contrary, intended as "a complement of the family in the religious instruction and training of children," as H. Clay Trumbull put it.[16] Religious education was cast as a fundamental element of family ministry. The ideology of domestic piety offered fertile ground for a reconception not just of church mission but of the religious nature of children as well. Articulated by Horace Bushnell, the concept of Christian nurture, based in part on the scriptural charge to "bring them up in the nurture and admonition of the Lord" (Eph. 6:4), surmised that, like a clean slate, a child brought up knowing only a Christian life would by necessity grow up to be a Christian. As Bushnell explained, "The child is to grow up a Christian [and never know himself as being otherwise]. . . . the aim, effort, and expectation should be, not, as is commonly assumed, that the child is to grow up in sin, to be converted after he comes to a mature age, but that he is to open on the world as one that is spiritually renewed, not remembering the time when he went through a technical experience, but seeming rather to have loved what is good from his earliest years."[17] Although disputed widely for decades, this view significantly redefined the stakes associated with the parental role of Christian education. Failure to raise children into good Christians now would rest with the domestic environment and, particularly, parents, not original sin.[18] In this high-stakes situation, Bushnell argued in favor of Sunday schools, stating that, in part, the responsibility to raise properly nurtured children "belongs to the church of God, according to the degree of its social power over you and in you and around your children."[19] The church and the family would constitute a partnership for the Christian nurture of children.[20]

A fundamental result of these reconceptualizations was that by the 1870s middle-class congregations had fully embraced Sunday school education for their own children, and the pupils in the Sunday schools housed in middle-class churches were predominantly the children of church members. The use of religious education as an evangelizing tool to reach the unchurched remained a significant part of the missionary work of middle-class churches, but it was pursued not within the church home but within mission churches. Together, evangelicals' embracing of the cult of domesticity, with its conception of domestic piety, and their adoption of the family ministry mission were necessary conditions for the full legitimizing of Sunday schools as an integral part of church life. As the belief in the divinely ordained family gained religious capital and as the stakes rose on children's upbringing, churches needed to participate in, if not firmly guide, this sacred institution. Admittedly, the church home negotiated a fine line between assistance and interference in family matters. Nevertheless, that which had originated outside the church was fully contained within it by the end of the century. By the 1880s, apologists argued that where Sunday schools are strong, so too is family religion, and where Sunday schools are weak, so too is family religion.[21]

Professionalization of the Sunday School and the Akron Plan

Itself a religious innovation, Sunday schools fostered interest in innovative teaching. Just as prescriptive literature for childrearing burgeoned in the latter half of the nineteenth century, so did literature for Sunday schools. Professionalization began to influence Sunday school teaching around the 1860s, influenced by secular education, which was also coming into its own with the development of theories of child psychology aimed at improving teaching strategies. Sunday school educators were at the forefront of these discussions, and periodicals like the previously established Methodist *Sunday School Advocate* (1840) and the newer *Sunday School Journal* (1860) and *Sunday School Classmate* (1870) disseminated the latest teaching strategies and lessons. Training institutes and conferences for teachers, standardized lesson sequences, scientific classroom methods, and, ultimately, though much later, graded progress redefined Sunday school education after the Civil War.[22]

The most critical event of the professionalizing period was the adoption of the International Uniform Lessons in 1872 by the interdenominational American Sunday School Union. Under this plan every class in all participating schools studied the same course lessons throughout the entire year. If the lesson were on temperance, every Sunday school student from the infant class to the seniors studied it. The Uniform Lessons effectively consolidated the power of each church's Sunday school superintendent, whose responsibility it was to catechize students on the previous week's lesson and introduce the new one. Because everyone studied the same lesson, this could now be done more efficiently in a large group recitation and lecture, and the superintendent was no longer required to visit each class separately.[23]

Though some schools had followed similar strategies of large-group introductory exercises followed by small classes previously, the Uniform Lessons made readily apparent the weaknesses of traditional Sunday school spaces. In the typical single-room Sunday schools, with their semicircles of children grouped around the teacher, holding large-group sessions focused on the superintendent's desk required a chaotic and time-consuming rearranging of seats. Even more pressing was the problem of distractions. Maintaining children's attention is difficult under the best of circumstances, but with perhaps a dozen small groups clustered within a single room, all supposedly discussing the same subject, rampant distractions made it all but impossible. While some congregations were able to put infant classes in rooms separate from those of older children, the ideal solution was to give each class its own room.[24] Consequently, innovation in Sunday school curriculum was accompanied by architectural innovation. Some congregations expanded their Sunday schools to three or four individual rooms, but this strategy eliminated valuable large-group space. What was needed was a flexible space that could accommodate the large groups and then be quickly transformed with minimal seat shifting and distractions to accommodate small groups.

Lewis Miller, a businessman and lay minister in the First M.E. Church of Akron, Ohio, took it upon himself to find a solution to the Sunday school space problem. Between 1864, when he took over the superintending duties of that congregation's Sunday school, and 1868, when his distinctive Sunday school building was completed, Miller searched for a functional solution to the space problem. In his travels to various cities to examine Sunday school buildings, Miller was accompanied by Akron builder Jacob B. Snyder, a partner in the Weary, Snyder & Wilcox Manufacturing Company. By training, Snyder was a carpenter, and he had both designed and erected buildings. As a member and trustee of the First M.E. Church and the Akron Board of Education and as superintendent, teacher, and historian of the Sabbath school of First Church, he was also keenly interested in church architecture. Guided by Miller's inspiration and energy, Snyder provided the technical expertise to create a revolution in Sunday school space for the First M.E. Church of Akron.[25]

Emphasizing the principles of spatial efficiency and flexibility, Miller and Snyder developed a Sunday school design that, though expensive to erect, would prove enormously popular and influential. The fundamental spatial theme of what came to be known as the Akron Plan Sunday school, like that of the auditorium sanctuary, was the theatre. Here, however, the prototype was that of the Renaissance, in which tier upon tier of boxes fully encircled a performance oval.[26] First M.E.'s school building consisted of a large semicircular room in which two stories of "gallery boxes" ringed a level parterre (fig. 7.2). The boxes, however, were not theatre boxes but small classrooms. Taking the earlier use of partitioned educational space within churches to a new level, these rooms could be separated from one another and from the main auditorium with recessible partitions (fig. 7.3). With each age group assigned to a different room, the plan fostered the desire for graded classes, yet, with the raising of all of the partitions facing the main auditorium, all grades could participate together in opening and closing exercises. In this way, both small classes and large assemblies were accommodated by the single area, eliminating the need to move students between rooms. Moreover, the partitions eliminated visual contact among students in different classes and significantly reduced aural distractions. As Miller's close friend and nationally known Sunday school educator John H. Vincent explained, the building could "provide for togetherness and separateness;

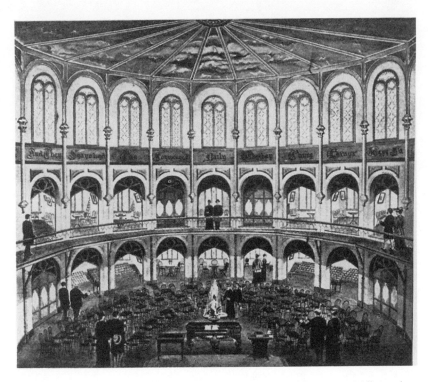

Fig. 7.2. The Sunday school of First M.E. Church, Akron, Ohio. Lewis Miller and Jacob B. Snyder, archs. Lithograph from Ellwood Hendrick, *Lewis Miller: A Biographical Essay* (New York: Putnam's, 1925), following p. 146. Courtesy Chautauqua Institute.

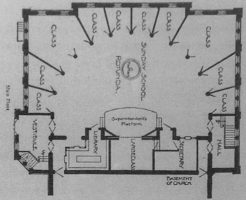

By permission of G. W. Kramer, Architect, New York City

FIG. 1.—The Original Akron Plan. Main Floor

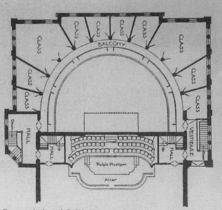

By permission of G. W. Kramer, Architect, New York City

FIG. 2.—The Original Akron Plan. Balcony Floor

Fig. 7.3. The Akron Plan as rendered by George Kramer, arch. Herbert Francis Evans, *The Sunday-School Building and Its Equipment* (Chicago: University of Chicago Press, 1914), 7.

have a room in which the whole school can be brought together in a moment for simultaneous exercises, and with the minimum of movement be divided into classes for uninterrupted class work."[27]

Miller and Snyder's plan was conceived as a building separate from First M.E. Church in Akron, and soon some congregations erected Akron Plan buildings fully apart from their church buildings. Many more, however, kept their Akron Plan Sunday school within the church walls, locating it adjacent to the main sanctuary on a shared wall. This latter arrangement was employed in the first Akron Plan Sunday school featured in the *American Architect and Building News*, the new First M.E. Church at Wilkes-Barre, Pennsylvania, that had been designed by architect Bruce Price, in the 23 September 1876 issue (fig. 7.4). This cruciform Gothic church shared its chancel wall with the Sunday school chapel building. As the article explained the Sunday school plan, "This is in form a semi-dodecagon, whose ground floor is occupied by class-rooms for week-day classes, while the chapel, a large galleried auditorium occupies the second floor. Both upon and under the gallery are class-rooms, separated from the auditorium by sliding glass partitions, in order that, when necessary, they may be used as part of the auditorium, so that it will accommodate about six hundred scholars."[28] Similar arrangements with an Akron Plan chapel/Sunday school building attached to the back wall of the church chancel or to a side wall appear in several other instances. Stanford White's First M.E. in Baltimore, for instance, featured a Sunday school building that shared the chancel wall with the main auditorium. Akron Plan in design, the lecture hall with its ring of classrooms was conceived by the Reverend Goucher and incorporated into White's plans. This also became a favorite strategy of architect George Kramer, who was closely associated with the Akron Plan design.[29]

Interestingly, the characteristic of this new plan that became most universally replicated was not the ring of classrooms but the use of recessible walls and rolling partitions to separate Sunday school spaces from sanctuaries. Churches that housed a Sunday school room at the back or side of the sanctuary could replace the solid wall that separated the two with a recessible wall or folding doors, which could be thrown open to increase the size of the sanctuary on special occasions (fig. 7.5). Whereas the cost of an Akron Plan Sunday school was out of the reach of many congregations, they could replicate to an extent its flexibility of space by installing movable walls.

This feature of recessible walls seems to explain the universalization of the term *Akron Plan* in the twentieth century to mean almost any church sanctuary with an attached room separated by a recessible wall. In particular, diagonal-plan sanctuaries have been called Akron Plan whether or not the church building includes the ring of classrooms encircling a central area. Popularized by architect Warren H. Hayes, the diagonal plan effectively integrated the sanctuary with an Akron Plan Sunday school. With the pulpit located in the corner of the squarish sanctuary, one adjacent wall could be recessed to open up the space of the neighboring Sunday school or fellowship hall. The purpose of this connection was not, however, to expand the Sunday school or make it more efficient but to increase the size of the sanctuary for special occasions. From the corner pulpit, the minister could address a house nearly double the size of the original auditorium.[30]

Among the many examples of this type of church is Hayes's First Congregational in Minneapolis (see figs. 4.8, 5.7, 7.5). When the church was destroyed by fire in 1886,

Fig. 7.4. First M.E. Church, Wilkes-Barre, Pa. Bruce Price, arch. *American Architect and Building News*, 23 Sept. 1876, 307–8. Courtesy Special Collections and Rare Books, University of Minnesota Libraries, Twin Cities.

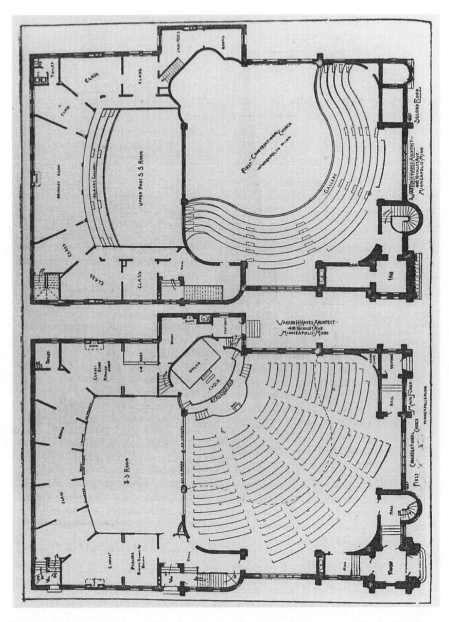

Fig. 7.5. First Congregational Church, Minneapolis, Minn. *Congregational Yearbook 1888*
(Boston: Congregational Publishing Society, 1988), 84.

the congregation planned a new building that could accommodate their educational needs. As the 3 December 1885 minutes of the board of trustees notes, "The question of enlarging the Church for the better accommodation of the Sabbath School was presented and it [aroused] much Enthusiasm."[31] Hayes's plan featured a "Pilgrim Hall" adjacent to the diagonally oriented sanctuary and separated from it by a wall of wooden and glass doors, which recessed into the floor. Small classrooms with rolling partitions ringed the rectangular Pilgrim Hall on both the main level and the gallery level. This building type was to become his signature church and was replicated in the First Presbyterian Church of Peoria, Illinois, Central Presbyterian in St. Paul, Minnesota, Wesley M.E. in Minneapolis, and several others.[32] Similar diagonal-plan sanctuaries with Akron Plan Sunday schools were subsequently used by other architects, including Bullard and Bullard (of Springfield, Illinois) for the First Baptist Church of Red Wing, Minnesota, and the First Baptist Church of Fort Worth, Texas; Pierce and Dockstader (of New York) for the Free Baptist Church of Elmira, New York; and George W. Kramer (of Akron), for St. Paul's M.E. Church of Hartford, Connecticut. In addition, many church design books published during the period included the integrated diagonal sanctuary/Akron Plan design.[33]

Other alternatives also existed for congregations interested in this state-of-the-art Sunday school plan. Trinity M.E. Church in Denver, for instance, whose intention was to serve as a family church for the residents of Capitol Hill, incorporated into its basement a modified Akron Plan Sunday school with classrooms located at each end of a lecture hall. As church historian Peter Winne described it:

> We enter the main Sunday School room, which is 83⅔ feet x 56½ feet and will accommodate 1,000 people in the comfortable chairs with which it is furnished. . . . At the east end of the room is the Superintendent's platform, 11 feet wide and 55 feet long. The room is enclosed at the east end by a rolling partition in four sections, extending across the entire width of the room. Back of these are the parlors. . . . These rooms will also be used as class rooms and contain the Sunday School library. . . . The west end of the main room is also inclosed with rolling partitions, as above described, which cuts off from the main room two class rooms, 23 x 21 each, having entrances from the main hall as above described. . . . These rolling partitions are nine feet high, the space between the top and the ceiling being of glass. They are made of white wood, varnished, and are coiled into the casings overhead. When all are thrown up we have a room 92 x 83⅔, giving a seating capacity of 1,400.[34]

That this space was put to heavy use is apparent from the church bulletin of 13 October 1889, which listed Sunday school class meetings at 9:30 and 12:30 and Bible school service at 2:30.[35]

Manipulation of space is a key element in the architectural, religious, and cultural significance of these Sunday school spaces. The Akron Plan interiors demonstrate that no matter how concerned middle-class evangelical congregations were about the effects of modernization on the social structures and relationships of American life, they were eager and willing to embrace the technological changes that modernization brought. Indeed, Akron Plan interiors encouraged congregations to claim power over their architectural space and manipulate it as they saw fit. Although the sanctuary or even the entire church might increasingly be conceived of as special or even holy space, those meanings did not preclude utilitarianism.

Such manipulation of space became popular in houses at the same time, particularly after the 1876 Centennial Exposition in Philadelphia. It was at this event that Americans were first exposed to Japanese architecture and the Queen Anne–style home popularized in England by Richard Norman Shaw. Japanese houses, with their movable *shoji* screens and free-flowing spaces designed to catch passing breezes, embraced a whole new relationship between space and users. Contrasting directly with the spatial determinism that American needs for heating and privacy had seemingly demanded, Japanese rooms opened onto one another and were thus less restrictive and more conducive to human interaction.[36] The recessible and sliding doors appealed strongly to U.S. designers, and in 1889 the *American Architect and Building News* editorialized to the effect that such were particularly "American pieces of construction" and discussed a recent article admiring them in the French journal *La Semaine*.[37]

At the same time that recessible doors were becoming popular in homes they were also gaining popularity in churches. Thus, the doors may have constituted a further demonstration of the close connection between the home and the church. Given women's important roles in both locations, it is not surprising that trade advertisements for rolling partitions frequently pictured them being raised or lowered by women, presumably Sunday school teachers, to show the ease with which they could be manipulated. One could divide Sunday school space as easily as one pulled a shade in a bedroom or closed a sliding door in the dining room (fig. 7.6). Both highly utilitarian and somewhat domestic, recessible partitions became a standard feature in neomedieval auditorium churches.[38]

In addition to spatial manipulation, the extent to which the Akron Plan allowed for monitoring and manipulating the behavior of the Sunday school students was also critical to its significance. First, the Akron Plan made use of the panopticon qualities of the amphitheatre. It allowed the superintendent, holding forth on the platform or central desk, to see into every classroom (if the partitions were raised) and observe each student and teacher. In some Akron Plan Sunday schools, the floors within the small individual classrooms were actually ranked steps (similar to those in sanctuary galleries) or they simply sloped from the back of the room down to the front. This allowed the superintendent, seated at the desk at the head of the lower lecture room, to see the faces of each

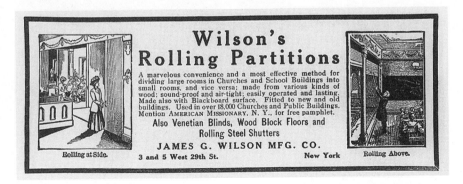

Fig. 7.6. Wilson's rolling partitions advertisement. *American Missionary* 64 (Feb. 1910): 1021.

student in the classrooms when the partitions were raised. This visual capability greatly assisted in maintaining order and discipline during large-group sessions. With the partitions closed, the small classrooms enabled teachers to keep in close contact with each student. Thus, the Akron Plan enhanced and maintained the authority of both superintendent and teacher.[39]

Second, placing the Sunday school in a separate or adjacent building allowed for direct entry into Sunday school rooms either from inside the church or from the outside. Wesley M.E. in Minneapolis, for instance, provided two entries to the church: a main entry that connected to the sanctuary and a smaller entry a few feet down into the Akron Plan space of Lillibridge Hall (fig. 7.7). Having an exterior entrance was seen as more welcoming to children of the community, who might be intimidated by having to enter the main church. At the same time, the separate doors reduced disruptions during services, a problem that many congregations faced. The advisory board of the First Baptist Church in Minneapolis, for instance, voted to post monitors in the church vestibules during services to discourage any youthful exuberance that might be overheard by those worshiping in the sanctuary.[40] With the Akron Plan wing separate from the church, pupils could not disrupt sanctuary services; in fact, they did not need to even set foot in the church (a situation that will be discussed further below). Neither

Fig. 7.7. Wesley (Centenary) M.E. Church, Minneapolis, Minn. 1892. Warren H. Hayes, arch. Photograph by Paul R. Kilde, c. 2000.

did the students encroach upon the sacredness of the sanctuary nor need they be intimidated by the same. In these ways the Akron Plan building placed careful controls and limitations upon the activities of Sunday school students.

Resulting then from the union of the religious educational agenda of the family mission with the professionalization of education, the popular Akron Plan design for Sunday schools not only helped to advance the Sunday school cause and legitimize it as an acceptable feature of family ministry but also served to maintain the Christian family ideal itself. Assessing Methodist Sunday schools in his 1903 history of the denomination, Bishop John Fletcher Hurst concluded, "It has been a blessing to the home."[41] Christian education within churches did indeed aid parents in raising Christian children. In this regard, and in its ubiquity, the Akron Plan Sunday school also attested to the strong links among evangelicals at the turn of the twentieth century. Methodists, Congregationalists, Baptists, and Presbyterians all erected Akron Plan Sunday schools in connection with their neomedieval auditorium churches. They became a characteristic feature of evangelical churches and yet another sign of the solidarity of evangelicalism in the United States.

In a similar vein, historian Anne Boylan has described the Uniform Lessons themselves as a "triumph for . . . interdenominationalism." Adopted by hundreds of evangelical churches, the systematized Sunday school curriculum emphasized a universal evangelicalism not (necessarily) constricted by denominational boundaries. The widespread adoption of the Akron Plan and its architectural offshoots similarly underscored this congruity among evangelicals. Indeed, at stake in the Sunday schools of the turn of the century was nothing less than the future of evangelicalism itself. As Herbert Francis Evans of Grinnell College asserted in his 1914 book on Sunday school buildings, "The type of future members in our churches is being determined everywhere in the Sunday schools of today."[42] Congregations' survival depended, many felt, on raising Christian children and maintaining the Christian family. The new church buildings with their technically advanced Sunday schools assisted in both tasks.

Family Ministry and the Missionary Impulse in the Institutional Church

The merging of specialized Sunday school facilities with the church home ideal launched church architecture in yet another direction in the design of religious space epitomized by the "institutional church," which gained popularity in the late 1880s and 1890s. Generally characterized conceptually by its multiple services intended to aid the poor and working populations within cities, the institutional church was one of the cornerstones of the Social Gospel, a constellation of ideas and methods for applying Christian moral codes to the problems of dislocation, poverty, and despair that middle-class observers saw escalating within the growing urban population, as well as to the exploitation and corruption that seemed to accompany industrial capitalism. Focusing on ameliorating the environmental and structural challenges that suffused urban life in industrial capitalism, Social Gospel practitioners pursued a broad range of ideas and activities: from faith in education and personal betterment that resulted in church libraries being opened as public reading rooms, to belief in the morally purifying power of the fine arts that resulted in music and art appreciation classes, to socialist conceptions of the rights of workers that encouraged unionization efforts.[43] By the turn of the century institutional churches were commonly associated with social welfare services like infirmaries and visiting nurses, facilities for exercise and personal hygiene, employment agencies, English-language classes, clothing distribution, kindergartens, and day nurseries. Their physical plants almost always included a gymnasium, men's and women's shower or bath, locker rooms, reading rooms, classrooms, kitchens, and dining rooms. In addition, game rooms, furnished with billiards, checkers, and other games were popular, as were bowling alleys.[44]

The domestic character of many of these facilities points up the critical connection between the institutional church and the church home. For marginalized urban young people, the institutional church home would provide the amenities, socialization, and Christian nurture that their real homes did not. As social critic Josiah Strong reported in *Religious Movements for Social Betterment*:

> The Institutional Church succeeds because it adopts itself to changing conditions. It finds that the people living around it have in their homes no opportunity to take a bath; it therefore furnishes bathing facilities. It sees that the people have little or no healthful social life; it accordingly opens attractive social rooms, and organizes clubs for men, women, boys and girls. The people know little of legitimate amusement; the church therefore provides it. They are ignorant of house-hold economy; the church established its cooking-schools, its sewing classes, and the like. In their homes the people have few books and papers; in the church they find a free reading-room and library. Their homes afford no opportunity for intellectual cultivation; the church opens evening schools and provides lecture courses. As in the human organism, when one organ fails, its functions are often undertaken and more or less imperfectly performed by some other organ; so in the great social organism of the city, when the home fails, the church sometimes undertakes the functions of the home. Such a church we call "institutional."[45]

For many evangelicals, opening the church home in order to both serve and evangelize the community held attraction. But although many congregations designed their new church buildings with the intention of addressing the needs of the urban community, in some cases, the distance between the family church and the urban community was too far to be easily bridged. Though the doors may have been open, few were entering. While institutional churches have been roundly criticized by twentieth-century historians as tools for social control that imposed self-defeating values upon workers while assuaging the guilt of the exploitative capitalist class that sponsored them, the reality of many of these institutions was that they probably had little impact upon the poor whom they intended to serve. Through the lens of the institutional church building, the tension between family ministry and evangelical mission is made particularly transparent.

Middle-class congregations generally kept family ministry and the evangelical missionary impulse physically separated. Family ministry took place within the church building, filled with its domestic amenities, while evangelizing work resulted in and focused on missions and other institutions, established at some distance from the family church. As discussed in chapter 3, church extension, that is, the financial supporting of new congregations through donating to church building, was a cornerstone of the evangelical work of home missionary societies. Such efforts to strengthen the denomination while spreading the gospel extended to the frontier regions of the western United States. In addition, churches also helped to establish missions closer to home. For instance, when part of the membership of Lawrence Street Church in downtown Denver departed their church to meet in the Tabor Opera House during the construction of the new building that would eventually house them as the Trinity M.E. Church, they sponsored a Sunday school in the former building and about two years after their departure helped to establish a new congregation there called the Church of the Strangers. Trinity also donated to the Railroad Mission, later the People's Tabernacle, and the Haymarket Mission, later the City Temple Institutional Society.[46] Similarly, other congregations supported, often quite generously, mission churches in poorer sections of their cities. First Baptist Church in Minneapolis was a major sponsor of the Berean Mission and the Emerson Street Mission in that city and donated to a number of other mission churches. Although pastors, official church "visitors," and members of home mission committees might actually spend time at such a mission, most congregants' connection to these charitable/evangelizing organizations came in fundraising. Specific Sundays were earmarked for collections for individual missions, and a variety of suppers, fairs, and sales throughout the year raised further funds while used clothing drives brought in-kind aid to the poor. Ideally, a mission church would eventually become self-supporting and graduate from a mission to a church in its own right, perhaps sponsoring another new mission itself. In this way, home missionary work constituted an important tool for evangelizing and, particularly, for the extension of the denomination.

The work of many mission churches, however, particularly those in urban centers, increasingly involved poor relief. Immersed in immigrant and working-class communities, mission churches often struggled to provide resources and services for the physical person—the body—as well as for the soul. Many voices argued that middle-class churches owed a larger debt to society, that financial support offered from such a distance simply maintained the structural social cleavages erected by industrial capitalism. Evangelicalism, with its history of egalitarianism, creed of individual salvation, and code of personal betterment, was uniquely positioned to offer both spiritual and temporal uplift in an industrializing world. Moreover, Christianity, with its model of Christ as sympathizer with the poor, could easily be read as having a third mission: ministering to the physical situation of those in need. Nevertheless, the distance, both physical and social, between middle-class family churches and mission churches would not be easily bridged.

The Sunday school, of course, served as the primary point of interaction between many congregations and the broader community. Even those church members who might not be eager to welcome residents of lower socioeconomic status than themselves into their churches allowed and even encouraged neighborhood children to attend their Sunday schools. Offering free books, refreshments, and other incentives, churches' on-site Sunday schools successfully attracted large numbers of neighborhood children whose names swelled their enrollment lists. Actual attendance numbers (which are much harder to come by than enrollment lists), however, tend to be far smaller, often less than half of the enrollment figure. Clearly, the extent to which these Sunday schools actually engaged the children of nonmembers is questionable.

Such efforts were soon followed by other missionary strategies to bring neighboring nonmembers into the church. In the 1870s, a handful of socially concerned individuals attempted to extend their mission to the poor and marginal beyond Sunday school and church extension/mission efforts. Retaining the evangelical focus on the redemption of the individual, these congregations aimed to apply the idea of Christian nurture on a broader social scale. By bringing the urban population into the church building itself, they felt, evangelical congregations could provide the atmosphere and benefits of Christian nurture on a grand scale. Offering both a physical place and a social community steeped in a moral, Christian lifestyle, churches could counter the negative forces and temptations rampant in the streets and thus offer a route toward redemption for the urban resident. Ministering to both body and soul, these groups sought to harmonize the family ministry model and the missionary impulse.

The Reverend Thomas K. Beecher was among the first to cast his church home as a broad and inclusive family, welcoming and willing to aid any who came. Among the first institutional churches, Beecher's Park Church in Elmira, New York, constructed under his direction and plan in 1876, consisted of three buildings: a family church auditorium, complete with radial arrangement of curved pews, carved proscenium arch springing from slender wooden columns, and dramatic gallery staircase leading to the pulpit stage; a Sunday school building with classrooms downstairs and playroom upstairs; and a social building with reception rooms, parlors, library, infirmary, kitchen, and baths. To this "institution" Beecher encouraged all to come. The sanctuary would provide worship opportunities. The Sunday school, in which Beecher and his wife, Julia Jones Beecher, used theatricals and play to instruct the children, would provide the religious foundation that children were missing in their own homes. The parlors would serve those who had no parlor at home. The library would aid those learning to read and those aiming to educate themselves. And the kitchens would feed the hungry.[47]

Yet, as historian Myra C. Glenn demonstrates, these intentions were probably realized on a much less grand scale than Beecher imagined. In the words of a Park Church usher, the "extremely humble and poor" did attend Beecher's meetings, but they "slipped in under cover of evening shadows."[48] Critics charged that the church remained, in Glenn's words, "more of a social club for the wealthy rather than a church," a place where "fashionably dressed people amused themselves with parlor games, gossip, and plays, and where the pastor indulgently advocated 'a light and easy plan of salvation.'"[49] Such was the tension necessarily created in negotiating between catering to families and to outsiders. Church members easily dominated the facilities and by their mere presence discouraged their use by nonmembers. Moreover, the elaborateness of the spaces and furnishings themselves broadcast readily perceived messages regarding who did and did not belong there regardless of how warm the invitation. As Glenn concludes, achievement of Beecher's goals remained elusive. I would argue further that Beecher's efforts and the resulting situation at Park Church served to portend a pattern that would be repeated among institutional churches throughout the country at the close of the century. For while Park Church grew from its minister's devotion to the Christian socialism gaining favor among liberal Protestants, the attractions of church home recreation strongly appealed to congregants themselves. Repeating the process that had occurred earlier in the century, when churches took over Sunday schools and integrated religious education into the family ministry mission through the idea of Christian nurture, middle-class congregants appropriated institutional space for their own use, precisely because the facilities addressed a pressing need of their own—to keep their children within the church fold during their adolescent years.

Many feared that as the children of the church reached their teen years and became bored by and impatient with the Sunday school routine, they would leave the church. To counter this, congregations reevaluated the position of young people within the church home. Sunday school expert Herbert F. Evans explained, "The leisure hours of our young people are potent for good or evil. The church touches the lives of its young people at too few points. The need of direction of young people's leisure time is recognized and the new architecture is responsive to the need."[50] In his view, Sunday schools should become proactive in keeping children in the church by appealing directly to them. But Sunday school was also part of the problem. Although religious educators encouraged granting teens greater responsibility in the church, lessons that were repeated year after year in continually monitored classrooms were not the stuff to encourage their interest.

Thus, congregations developed a variety of new activities for their young people, and all of them required expanded church space. Meeting rooms were a priority, as congregations experimented with youth organizations, among them the Young People's Society for Christian Endeavor. A national organization, YPSCE chapters could be formed by young adults within their respective churches, and through them they could engage in missionary and church extension projects, fundraising, and a host of other programs. While the YPSCE proved popular, congregations grew increasingly concerned that their young men were not adequately involved. Indeed, female participants dominated the membership rolls (a situation mirrored in full church membership), convincing many that church life must be reorganized to encourage manly interest. Muscular Christianity, a constellation of strategies developed to encourage male religious participation, came into vogue. Many congregations organized Boys' Brigades, quasi-military drill classes, for their pre-adolescent boys. Meeting in the Sunday school lecture rooms, dining halls, or, better, gymnasiums of evangelical churches, Brigade boys practiced marching and, in some cases, rifle drills for an hour or so each week.[51]

Another popular strategy was the formation of Baraca Bible classes for young men. Founded in 1890, the sex-segregated Baraca classes were a step beyond Sunday school and were student- rather than teacher-driven. Students selected their own leaders or teachers and organized the meetings, which focused on their own questions and interests. Popular among all evangelical denominations, by 1905 the Baraca Union of America had a membership of some 100,000.[52] These all-male classes, however, quickly moved beyond Bible study. As Marshall A. Hudson, president of the Baraca Union of America in 1905, explained, the focus on young men revealed to many pastors and teachers that "young men craved social life." Not surprisingly, given the strength of both the ideology of Christian nurture and the concept of the family church, catering to this need in order to keep young men in the church became a significant goal of many churches.

Here, too, space was critical. Bible school and benevolence work combined with recreation as meeting rooms were given over first to reading rooms and then to game rooms. As Hudson explained the situation in Syracuse, "The Baraca room was opened every night, and if a young man had a desire we could fill, we aimed to satisfy him; we had our game night, lecture course, debate or city council, bicycle or ball clubs, rally Sundays, Monday Bible Club, and after a few years a small gymnasium, with basket ball and once a year a Baraca field day and yearly banquet."[53] Such expansion of Baraca classes located the move toward institutionalization squarely within the church home ideology. Congregations were willing to do whatever was needed to keep their young male children within the church home fold, and this often meant expanding the physical plant of the church with specialized rooms. Thus, to maintain adolescent children's interest in church life and fully render the Christian nurture model, institutional facilities became an increasingly significant requirement.[54]

Two distinct impulses then are discernible in the development of institutional churches. On the one hand, congregations led by individuals like Thomas Beecher, who were devoted to the ideals of Christianity as a foundation for social and economic uplift, opened up their physical plants specifically as a service to the nearby nonmember community. Their motivations stemmed from the missionary impulse and the view that the Christ model required Christian responsibility for all of society. These are the congregations that historians have generally explored within the category of "institutional church," many of which were inner-city churches.[55] An evangelical example is Judson Memorial Church in Washington Square in New York, founded in 1890 by Baptist minister Edward Judson and financed by John D. Rockefeller. This church grew from Judson's convictions that evangelical churches had a duty to remain in downtown areas and minister to immigrants struggling to survive in the city. The stakes were high, in Judson's view. Impoverished urban populations threatened the very fabric of U.S. society with their social disorder, disease, intemperance, prostitution, and crime. The gymnasium, classrooms, lecture halls, and health facilities of Judson Memorial served as a missionary stronghold to stem the advance of a fearful enemy.[56]

The second impulse toward institutional facilities came through the family ministry desire to cater to the needs of all members of the congregational family. Congregationalist minister Wallace Nutting of Providence, Rhode Island, articulated this constellation of linked ideas in an article published in the *Church Building Quarterly*. Beginning by interrogating "our right to live in homes better than those in which the Christian Church worships," Nutting argued that church buildings must be designed to address the "drifting away of children." The church should serve as a "light-house," a "life-saving" place, and he urged his reader to build "churches with open doors" precisely where young men are, in order to succor them wherever they wander.[57] Here, too, the stakes were high. If evangelicals could not ensure that their own children would pass on their beliefs, Protestantism itself could succumb, particularly given the growth of the Roman Catholic population. In both cases, no longer would the church simply be a place of worship, a source for the salvation of the soul. Now it would be a resource for temporal reality as well, nurturing and providing for the well-being of the body as well as the spirit. Further, it would give particular attention to young people, for in them rested the future of evangelical religion.

Thus, the missionary and family ministry agenda became entangled, and the democratic impulses of the former came into conflict with the social exclusivity of the latter. In at least some congregations, like that at Park Church, the lack of adequate acknowledgment of the blending of these agendas resulted in either an eclipsing or a diminishing of the missionary goal by family ministry concerns. Another example of the confusion created by this entanglement is that of the Pilgrim Congregational Church in Cleveland. As mentioned in chapter 5, Pilgrim was somewhat unusual in that when the congregation decided to build a new church in the early 1890s, they did not follow the national trend of leaving their neighborhood into which industry and immigrants were moving but chose a site just a few blocks away from the original church in what is still called the Tremont area. Tremont's character had certainly undergone transformation, and by the 1890s the Yankee and German families who had lived there since the 1850s were joined by immigrants from Ireland, Slovenia, and, later, Poland, the Ukraine, Russia, and other Eastern European countries, who worked in the mills along the Cuyahoga River.[58] Attracting immigrants at a rapid rate, this community had a growing need for services, and during a temperance campaign in the early 1870s, Pilgrim participated with other local groups in the founding of a "rest and recreation room" a few blocks from the church for the recreation of young men who had taken oaths against drinking. Games and reading materials were provided, but the rooms were closed in 1875 due to financial problems. A year or two later, the group reopened the reading room at another location and combined it with a sewing school for young girls and a mothers' club for immigrant women.[59]

While these initial efforts in service to the immediate nonmember community paralleled the common pattern of maintaining physical separation between the church and its mission work, the growth of Pilgrim's Sunday school and its expansion to nonmember children shifted the pattern to in-church services in the late 1880s. Out of Sunday school enrollments of more than 900 in 1891, ten students joined the church in 1890 and seventeen did so in 1891.[60] As the 1891 *Yearbook* reported, "It is the constant aim of the Superintendent and Pastor to make the school a great agency in saving lives for the Master."[61] The Sunday school's success in enrolling neighborhood children brought into question the situation of congregational children.[62] The Young People's Association, organized in 1881, experienced an initial membership surge, but by 1888 it had too few members to remain viable. A chapter of the YPSCE was formed, but participation was small. In 1889, this youth group offered to set up and support an on-site reading room and thereby took a critical step toward combining the family ministry concerns for children of the church and the missionary impulse to evangelize and aid outsiders under the roof of the church. Yet the organization remained unstable. The Junior Society, for children ages eight to sixteen, seems to have been more successful, boasting a membership of forty-three with an average attendance at meetings of fifty. In contrast, the Boys' Christian Society had only twenty-five members and did not report its average attendance.[63]

With the shift to in-house programs, space quickly become a critical issue. By 1891 the Sunday school was seriously overcrowded with a total of 961 pupils registered, though average attendance was several hundred fewer than this.[64] In November of that year, the new minister, Charles S. Mills, laid the groundwork for expanding these activities, preaching a sermon titled "Winning Young Men" that argued that the church must serve as a counterattraction to saloons and other "improper places" frequented by young men. By the time the Outlook Committee, charged with examining the question of erecting a new church, began to meet, these agendas were firmly established, and the committee conceived of the new church as an institutional church from the outset. The building was to include a "reading room, reception room and library for young men and women, social room for young men, special room for boys, gymnasium arranged for use by either young men or young women, ladies' parlors, young ladies' parlors, kitchen, cloak rooms, [and] bath rooms."[65] As designed by architect Sidney Badgley, most of these rooms were located on the floor beneath the large auditorium sanctuary or in its contiguous Akron Plan Sunday school (fig. 7.8).[66]

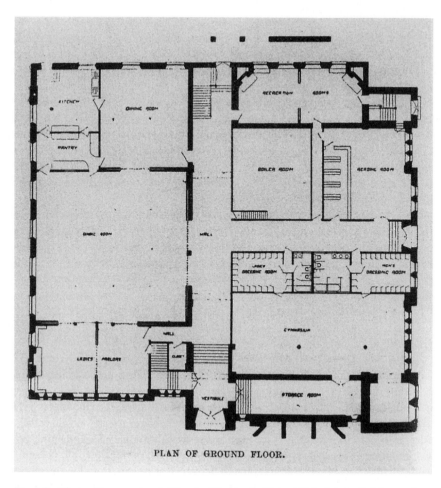

PLAN OF GROUND FLOOR.

Fig. 7.8. Pilgrim Congregational Church, Cleveland, Ohio. 1894. Sidney Badgley, arch. *Church Building Quarterly* 13 (Oct. 1895): 228.

To whom, then, were these facilities actually directed? Members or children of members? Nonmember adults or children within the urban area? In the latter category were the sewing school, in which neighborhood girls were taught basic sewing skills, hemming multitudes of handkerchiefs and towels, and the kitchen garden classes, which followed the sewing school on Saturday afternoons and taught girls the "rudiments of good housekeeping," including "how to make beds, set tables, build fires, wash dishes, sweep, [and] dust."[67] To accommodate the girls in these Saturday afternoon activities, the church offered a kindergarten, apparently to care for the younger siblings for whom these young students were often responsible. Neither of the classes required payment of dues, though "penny collections" were occasionally held. In addition, a mothers' club, offering neighborhood women a venue for discussing housekeeping and childraising, was popular.[68] Springing from the missionary impulse—the concern for salvation of the urban population and the need to train them in the values of Protestantism in order to preserve the country—the on-site programs were apparently held in the large dining room and the Sunday school classrooms above. So located, they challenged the spatial distinction between mission and in-church work that many other congregations retained through the period.

However, these nonmember social programs remained administratively separate from another important set of programs that formed the Pilgrim institutional church.[69] Upon approval of the designs of the new church, the Pilgrim Society, the official governing body of the church, created the Pilgrim Institute to administer the new social and recreational facilities. Only certain activities fell within the jurisdiction of the institute, however. Nonmember programs were not under the purview of the institute, whose efforts were directed generally at members or other individuals with a certain amount of discretionary income. Persons had to pay a membership fee in order to use the institute facilities or attend programs. Among the offerings were gymnasium programs (games and team sports) and general use of the gymnasium, showers, and locker rooms; classes in German, French, and Spanish; piano lessons; classes in business arithmetic, bookkeeping, penmanship; numerous clubs, including the Travel Club, Fine Arts Club, History Club, and Camera Club; a Literary Society; and a Debating Society. These activities were clearly aimed at the young people of the congregation. The use of the recreation room, which offered billiards and games, and the reading room was also overseen by the institute, also suggesting that membership may have been required for their use, though this seems unlikely because the reading room had been founded as a public service. In general, though, the Pilgrim Institute seems to have aimed at enhancing the lives of the members of the congregation, particularly of the teenage members, at least as much, if not more, than it aimed at serving the community at large.[70]

When Social Gospel leader Washington Gladden addressed the Pilgrim congregation to deliver the dedication sermon on 25 November 1894, his concern lay less in defining who would have access to the facilities than in justifying the social nature of the new church building. Castigating those who insisted that religious activities were distinctly unique and separate from secular ones, he argued that the sacred and the secular were identical and "that all common functions and callings are, when rightly understood and rightly performed, in the deepest sense sacred [and this] is a fundamental truth of Christianity."[71] By extension, he argued, it is perfectly correct and necessary for the church to provide for the intellectual, social, and recreational needs of its people. To Gladden, the "exceptional appointments" of the building were "significan[t] and [sacred]." And, in doing the work of Jesus Christ, "the church opens these hospitable doors and expects and desires that the people of this neighborhood, rich and poor, will freely avail themselves, not only of its privileges of worship, but of all these facilities of instruction and recreation." Thus, by responding to criticism that had been leveled at church builders since the earliest auditorium churches were constructed in Chicago—that they were too secular and that the tendency to make provisions for all sorts of auxiliary rooms like kitchen, dining hall, parlors, readings rooms, nurseries, and so on was robbing the church of its sacred nature—Gladden placed the social work of Pilgrim squarely within the evangelical mission.

One denominational publication, *Outlook*, recognized this mixed agenda and commented on Pilgrim's unusual approach. In an announcement titled "Another Institutional Church," the editors praised the Reverend Charles S. Mills as a strong leader in institutional work and announced that his congregation had just dedicated a new building that was "the most complete perhaps in the whole country, and fully adapted for institutional work." The description clarified the type of institutional work to be pursued at Pilgrim, however, explaining, "This differs from most churches of the kind in that it adapts institutional methods to those who are of the upper middle class. The object of the institutional department of this church is to lift toward the highest life those who are already financially able to seek it, but who lack the inspiration to seek the highest ideals."[72] Whether or not this comment was meant ironically to insinuate a corruption of the institutional church, it clearly identified a new connotation for it. Moreover, it anticipated criticism that would be aimed at the YMCA in the twentieth century: that its programs for middle-class participants were masquerading as democratic social welfare efforts.[73]

So who actually used the Pilgrim facilities? To some extent, the answer is probably the children of both members and nonmembers from the surrounding area. Echoing family ministry sentiments, local Sunday school educators predicted that the new facilities would "solve the problem of how to keep the young people in the Sunday school from thinking they were too old to any longer attend."[74] With enrollments of more than 900, it is certain likely that many of these children continued to use the church in their teen years. Church yearbooks and histories clearly show the ongoing participation of members' children in the various youth organizations though never at Sunday school enrollment proportions. Yet as the demographic character of the area changed, with predominantly Catholic immigrants moving in, even the Sunday school numbers were not sustained. A 1913 report of the nearby Merrick Settlement House mentioned that the neighborhood had "no social nor recreational center save Pilgrim church, which stands on the outskirts and can never fully meet the needs of a Catholic community."[75] In 1919–1920, the congregation added a Community House to their physical plant, which contained an updated gymnasium, shower, and bowling alleys. By 1936, a study by the Welfare Federation of Cleveland of religious programs available to boys ages ten to nineteen determined that though the church was considered the "best equipped institutional church in America" when it was built, "only 17 boys from the Area are affiliated with the church and fewer than 30 boys of our age range are entered in any of the church's activities."[76] Programs sponsored by the church did attract younger boys and many girls (some 300 in the Daily Vacation School in the summer), but boys and young men in the neighborhood "felt the equipment could be used to better advantage." The report quoted one young man: "They are afraid we'll bust things up and so we have to go a mile to bowl."[77] The continuing use of the facilities by the children of church members, however, is clear from church yearbooks.

The precise ratio of nonmember users to member users will likely never be ascertained, yet the lesson Pilgrim conveys is that mixed agendas, informed both by the family ministry mission on the one hand and the evangelizing mission on the other, were embedded in institutional churches. While the former tended toward exclusivity, the latter moved toward democratization. Both of these attitudes could be found in congregations that sponsored institutional churches. Though the Social Gospel offered a unique means of combining the two into a theologically legitimate program of social service, it was quite easy for congregation members with such intentions to end up with programs that pertained primarily to their own children's needs. In particular, those congregations that attempted to house institutional elements within a church that maintained an ongoing family ministry likely found blending the missions the most problematic. Park Church in the relatively small city of Elmira and Pilgrim Church in Tremont both attempted this melding of middle- and upper-middle-class congregants and working-class neighbors within their church buildings.

In any event, Pilgrim soon functioned as a model for organizing "physical, social, and intellectual culture" under the administrative auspices of a church institute. By 1896, the Trinity Congregational Church, also in Cleveland but located across the Cuyahoga River in the middle-class Fairfax neighborhood, featured a diagonal-plan auditorium with attached "institute" consisting of an Akron Plan Sunday school on the auditorium level and "a well-equipped gymnasium, with shower-baths, etc., reading-room, library and recreation-rooms, together with a dining-hall capable of seating 225, and a kitchen with all necessary appurtenances" in the basement.[78] Given the character of this middle-class neighborhood, these facilities most likely served the congregation itself, rather than nonmembers. Further, the inclusion of reading rooms, game rooms, gymnasiums, showers, and bowling alleys became increasingly popular whether or not a congregation articulated Social Gospel sentiments.

Such features became standard within well-equipped church homes at the turn of the century just as kitchens had a generation earlier. Social Gospel adherents discussed their function in the context of community service; as the Reverend Philip S. Moxom argued, a city church must have a place to worship, "but still more it needs modern equipment for its enterprise. It must have a home, but it must have also a school, a laboratory, a drill-room, a rallying-place for all the forces—philanthropic, eleemosynary, educational, evangelistic. To fight the saloon it must have a club-room; to fight the playhouse, it must have a place and means for wholesome recreation; to offset the natural deficiency of the public school it must have room and classes for many kinds of study."[79] Institutional facilities were required if the church were to remain vital within local communities.

Thus, congregations followed multiple paths to the formation of institutional churches. Some of those paths emphasized the missionary agenda of evangelical churches, while some emphasized the family ministry agenda. Many congregations, however, blended the two missions, combining social concerns, often closely linked with evangelizing, with a desire to broaden opportunities for their own children. But ministering to the working and the middle classes at once would be difficult. Just keeping everyone comfortable within such clearly bourgeois spaces was a feat. Despite the democratizing agenda that informed many of these efforts, natural interaction among disparate social groups within a church plant was difficult to achieve. Park Church discovered this in the 1870s, and Pilgrim was certainly aware of it by the 1920s. Church buildings were simply not neutral ground on which everyone might feel comfortable. No matter how genuine might be the intentions to provide community services, obtaining the participation of the community could be problematic. Nevertheless, the fact that institutional churches could be justified under either rubric gave great power to the institutional model and contributed to the radical reconceptualization of evangelical church space that developed in the late nineteenth century.

In the development of specialized Sunday school space and institutional church facilities lies yet another example of the close relationship between changes in evangelical religion and changes in architecture. These church buildings indicate the extent to which the bodies and minds of children served as one site upon which Protestant congregations negotiated the territory between evangelism and family ministry. In the new Sunday schools, congregations expressed their desires for their children and those of the broader community by using specialized architectural strategies to manipulate and monitor their activities just as they used specialized curriculums. In the institutional church, they articulated their hopes that the church could affect the physical and vocational training of children as well. These spaces, designed to foster a family-oriented church home spirit for its members and to minister to non-Christians, reveal congregations' struggles to reconcile their desire for family churches with their duty to spread the gospel.

Although the question of precisely which children would participate in these programs revealed some ambiguities regarding church mission, the buildings nevertheless show that the role of children, teens, and young adults within religious and secular society was being addressed with unprecendented energy. In this, the Sunday school and institutional church facilities indicate the strongly progressive and millennial character of evangelical religion during the late nineteenth century. The educational agendas—religious, secular, or vocational—aimed at saving children not only for their own sakes but for the salvation of society and the nation. Providing extensive facilities for young people, these congregations demonstrated an enormous concern for future generations and their continued engagement in the church. As the Reverend H. C. Woods prophesied at the cornerstone-laying ceremony held in 1885 for the new First Baptist Church in Minneapolis, "The children of the youngest that are here tonight will have slept with their fathers before these stones have crumbled."[80] Although the stone walls of these buildings would indeed endure, the twentieth century would bring new transformations to evangelical religion that would render many of their classrooms, gymnasiums, and game rooms obsolete.

8

Meanings in Nineteenth-Century Evangelical Architecture

From Charles Finney's Chatham Street Chapel of 1832 to the fully developed auditorium church with auxiliary institutional spaces of the 1890s, evangelicals helped to define the vanguard of Christian architecture in the nineteenth century. Their willingness to experiment, to take religious architecture in directions never before attempted, grew out of the social change that characterized the United States during the period as well as transformations in religious creed, code, and cultus that marked evangelical religion. For Finney and his associates, the missionary impulse justified a strong public presence for the church and justified, specifically, taking Christianity into the realm of the theatre. In short order, the spatial advantages of the theatre impressed Finney, the revival preacher. The stage accommodated preaching as no physically constricting elevated pulpit could, and the galleries and sloped floor not only helped rivet viewers' attention on the stage but also allowed the preacher to more easily see each listener. The subsequent Broadway Tabernacle, designed under Finney's direction, improved upon these elements, mimicking the amphitheatre and evoking the big tent that welcomed all to the revival. Thus, the seeds of architectural experimentation were planted.

But what to do after the revival? The missionary impulse alone could not sustain a viable religious experience. Converts could not sustain the euphoria of conversion indefinitely. As evangelicals negotiated new religious missions, two distinctive elements emerged to define the heart of congregational life and to transform church architecture. The first of these was a new emphasis on worship as a fundamental element of religious services. Evoked by preaching and consisting of prayers, recitatives, liturgies, responsive readings, and hymn singing, worship became an interaction between the believer and the divine as critical as conversion. These changes in cultus required changes in the spaces in which the new ritual practices were performed. Choir lofts and soaring organ pipes took up their new locations behind and above pulpit stages, and by the end of the century many churches took on the aura of opera houses, with proscenium arches, marquis lighting, opera boxes, and hinged seats housed within large amphitheatres. The second new evangelical mission derived from the sacralization of the Christian family. Viewing the church as a supporting institution for the divinely ordained family, evangelicals recast their churches' missions as ministry to families and redefined the church itself as a proxy home. These new church homes drew heavily on the architectural contexts of the domestic sphere: From kitchen, dining room, and parlor spaces to the decoration of the sanctuary itself, church homes evoked private family homes. Stepping carefully to avoid accusations of usurping familial prerogative, congregations developed voluntarism into a tool for family ministry, offering each family member—mother, father, teen, and toddler—organizations and activities matching his or her particular interests, as well as spaces in which to pursue them. From Sunday schools to drill rooms to gymnasiums, evangelicals recast church architecture to accommodate functions never dreamed of a century earlier.

These new missions did not, however, eclipse that which had traditionally informed evangelicalism: the missionary impulse. Family ministry could be meshed, at least in theory, with ongoing missionizing. As the Reverend Dana had remarked upon laying the cornerstone for First Congregational Church in Minneapolis, these churches, filled with families, were beehives of activity, most of which involved sending the evangelical message abroad, either through raising money for missionary work or through direct benevolence work within the community. The rooms of the institutional church could serve double duty, aiding in family ministry and in reaching out to the broader community.

Thus, by the closing decades of the nineteenth century, a tripartite religious agenda or code characterized evangelical churches—worship, family ministry, and missionizing—and neomedieval auditorium churches physically expressed each of these ongoing functions in their very forms. Their auditoriums with elaborate stages, their parlors and kitchens, their classrooms and reading rooms physically articulated the functions carried on within and, thus, congregations' missions. The semiotic labor of these churches went well beyond this denotative level, however, for neomedieval auditorium churches also embodied and expressed cultural ideas and meanings closely associated with the three agendas. While it is relatively easy to trace the changing religious agendas through the changing spaces, the cultural and social meanings of these buildings are somewhat more elusive. Yet within those meanings is found the significance of these church buildings.

Ideological Messages in Evangelical Churches

Three sociocultural concerns correspond, roughly, to the three mission categories: worship, family ministry, and missionizing. Overlap among these concerns is great, for each sprang from the ideological contexts engendered by the development and growth of a cohesive middle class. First, in cultivating the worship mission, middle-class evangelical Protestants identified themselves with the growing "high culture" industry and, thus, established their claim to sociocultural authority. Second, shifts toward family ministry ushered in means of reconciling the growing ethic of materialism with religious practice. Lastly, the missionary impulse provided a platform from which middle-class congregations could express their fear of the changing U.S. social landscape while at the same time locating their religious agenda within it. Neomedieval churches expressed these ideological concerns—each of which entails some contest for power among competing groups—on an iconographic or connotative level; these are the cultural meanings associated with the buildings and articulated by those who used the churches. Some of these meaning were clearly expressed by users of the period, while others can be inferred from the spatial relationships created by the buildings. Embodying these ideological elements, these churches served as powerful statements on the landscape, reminding those who attended services in them as well as casual passersby that these ideals and the congregations that upheld them were potent players in the U.S. cultural milieu.

Corresponding with changes in worship, the first of these ideological concerns involves the contests for relative influence or power of two different types, the first involving the relative power of worshipers vis-à-vis clergy and the second involving the relative influence of the congregation vis-à-vis society. Negotiations over power within the two matrixes ensued within the context of evolving ideas about democracy, voluntarism, and entertainment. When at midcentury northern evangelicals responded to intracongregational disagreements (particularly those fueled by the issue of slavery) by choosing to emphasize ritual practice through worship, charges that such measures were antidemocratic and infringed upon religious voluntarism might easily have been leveled. After all, in a period of rampant anti-Catholicism, any move toward formalism, much less the borrowing of specific liturgical elements like the Gloria Patri, might have easily provoked outrage. Nevertheless, augmented liturgical elements were adopted. They were performed, however, in the dramatically new ritual setting of the amphitheatre sanctuary. This space, with its emphasis on the corporate body of equals, indicated the power of those gathered, of the congregation, and that power was equal, if not superior, to that of the clerical performer upon the stage. The space itself announced that evangelical worship would tolerate no domineering priesthood. Corroborating this spatial democracy was the fact that outside of the sanctuary, congregations eagerly grasped the power to steer church affairs, participating in congregational organizations and denominational and interdenominational networks on a scale never before seen. These evangelical worshipers owned their churches and their sanctuaries in ways that they never had before.

Despite this strong influence, however, one change in worship—the increased importance of sacred music—threatened to eclipse congregational participation in services entirely. The same amphitheatre features that made manifest the corporate body also encouraged audiences to remain quiet and passive as they focused their attention on the stage. The theatrical spaces equated services with entertainment, and many evangelical churches also served as concert halls, offering organ, choir, and orchestra performances on a regular basis. Further, intercongregational competitions to secure the best musicians and orators raged in many localities, suggesting that the appreciation of virtuoso performance—entertainment—was becoming the raison d'être of religious gatherings. Two novelists of the period described this potential. In William Dean Howells's 1890 novel, *A Hazard of New Fortunes*, the protagonist, Basil March, describes a sudden impulse to attend services at Grace Church in New York City that gripped him and his wife, Isabel: "But no matter how consecrated we feel now, we mustn't forget that we went into the church for precisely the same reason that we went to the Vienna Café for breakfast—to gratify an aesthetic sense, to renew the faded pleasure of travel for a moment, to get back into the Europe of our youth. It was a purely pagan impulse, Isabel, and we'd better know it."[1] The Marches' experience falls within one of several voyeuristic tours of the city, during which they gaze at the city, its people, and its environments but do not become involved in the activities they see occurring. They similarly enjoy the religious spectacle and discuss its aesthetic elements, but they do not participate in it. Though Howells did not have his characters visit an evangelical church, he easily could have, for

New York boasted not just Henry Ward Beecher's newly remodeled Plymouth Congregational Church in Brooklyn, now a typical auditorium sanctuary, but several other evangelical auditorium churches as well.[2] But if fulfilling an aesthetic desire was to become the fundamental purpose of attending services, if religious congregations, passive in their seats, simply watched worship performances, what need was there for the church at all? Novelist Edward Bellamy suggested just this when his characters in *Looking Backward* tune in to a radio-broadcasted Sunday morning sermon in the privacy of their own home and thus become the ultimate, fully passive, nonparticipatory religious audience.

Yet such portents were not fully realized. Services were not reduced to entertainment, for congregations maintained a strong level of participation in worship, but clearly, the entertainment elements of services were important. Again and again, congregations proved their willingness to pay hundreds of dollars to retain excellent musicians or an outstanding preacher and thousands to obtain a state-of-the-art organ. Comparisons between the theatre or opera and the church underscored the performative element of religious services. A particularly renowned preacher or an excellent quartet choir might guarantee a packed house on Sunday morning. And offering highbrow music and oratory could establish the congregation's position within the local social hierarchy. But most evangelical congregations refused to allow the performance aspects of their services to monopolize worship. Clergy and congregants agreed that congregational participation in responsive readings, psalms, recitatives, and hymns was integral to worship, and they eagerly snapped up the many new hymnals produced in the closing decades of the century. Thus, the power of these middle-class audiences was brought to bear in balancing the desire for entertainment with the desire to participate. Middle-class evangelicals were clearly consumers of their Sunday morning shows, but they were also participants in them. In these ways congregations negotiated the related polarities of clerical authority versus congregational democracy and highbrow entertainment versus congregational participation. In so doing, they created worship practices that connected their desire for an experience of transcendent power with the social realities of their everyday lives.

The ideology of domestic piety and the sacralized family also engendered powerful cultural meanings, which infused these buildings and were in turn broadcast by them. Among these, materialism was predominant. Evangelicals infused a strongly material element into their expression of the divine and of their beliefs. This integration of material life and religion is strongly emphasized in the introduction of new technologies, indicative of scientific advancement, into church buildings. From acoustical designs to state-of-the-art heating and cooling systems, from recessible doors and rolling partitions to electric lighting and mechanized cleaning systems, churches were showcases of architectural and mechanical innovation. Much of this entered churches through the intercessory function of the sanctified family and its domestic home, for the comforts and amenities that graced a sanctified home were readily adopted into the church home. In this way evangelicals allied their engagement with contemporary society and its scientific advancement with their religious creed and then announced the alliance to the world. These were not reactionary people clinging to past forms, but progressive ones endeavoring to reconcile or coordinate their belief in a divine being whose Word must be spread via the contemporary contexts in which they lived.

Furthermore, these churches demonstrate that late nineteenth-century evangelicals completely overcame the portion of their Reformed heritage that shunned material expressions of God. The buildings negotiated a new compatibility between the supernatural or divine and human reality, using the sanctity of the family as an intercessory. Just as the individual family might demonstrate its sanctification by acquiring and displaying mass-produced items, from Gothic chairs to paintings of Christ, congregations demonstrated their sanctity through similar means. Stained glass, frescoes, and furnishings, widely advertised in religious literature, infused evangelical churches with multiple references to sacred power. By the 1890s, stained-glass images of Jesus as the Good Shepherd, holding a lamb, or of Jesus "knocking at the door," seeking an individual soul, were particularly popular. In addition to Jesus, one could also find images of Matthew, Mark, Luke, and John in evangelical churches as well as personifications of the cardinal virtues—Faith, Hope, Charity, Mercy, Constancy, Fortitude, Justice, and Humility—as angels.[3]

This materialism was, of course, dependent upon and engendered by industrialization and the burgeoning consumer culture of the Gilded Age. Rapidly transforming manufacturing techniques made a multitude of products available, and congregations were primed to buy. Families demonstrated their sanctity through consumer products, thereby also announcing their socioeconomic status. Similarly, evangelical congregations did both, often demonstrating their social position through their largest material project: their church building. Lavish displays of stone, glass, fresco, polished wood, carpeting, and upholstery, in addition to fully equipped auxiliary rooms, announced not just devotion to God but also the status and taste of the congregation. In a period of intense competition among evangelical denominations, in which congregations openly competed in building bigger and better churches, the intertwining of these religious and secular meanings served a critical function. Using material culture to negotiate a relationship between religious life and secular life, evangelicalism was able to remain viable throughout the development of industrial capitalism.

But were evangelicals trying to "buy" their salvation? Were they perverting Protestant belief systems? Clearly, some believed so. In the 1830s Finney condemned sartorial ostentation in his church. In the 1890s a bishop refused to dedicate Wesley M.E. in Minneapolis because it diverted money from missions. Historians have argued that material religion became a tool by which capitalists legitimized their wealth and deflected criticism of their exploitative practices. John D. Rockefeller, a committed Baptist, funded numerous churches during this period, including Riverside Church and the institutional Judson Memorial, both in New York, and the African-American Antioch Baptist Church in Cleveland. Some congregations, as we have seen, sought ways of making their churches profitable, particularly through the formation of a "business block" church. Clearly, these churches indicate an accord between evangelicalism and capitalism. This reality is not a basis for condemnation, however. The connections between religious meaning and economic circumstances point up the cultural roots of religion itself. No religion is created outside of culture. Late nineteenth-century evangelicalism was the progeny of its time, the result not only of negotiated religious ideas but also of negotiated religious practices, among them church building. The new middle classes that composed many evangelical congregations clearly valued the material life and comforts afforded them and purposely sought to integrate them into their religious value system. Participating in the process of creating meaning, of making sense of the changing world, church buildings aided in sacralizing that which middle-class Protestant society most valued.

Lastly, the missionary impulse carried its own cultural meanings during these years, which were marked by the rapid expansion of the laboring classes and an increasing social distance between capital and labor. Evangelicals viewed the turbulent urban milieu as a kind of battleground in which their position was at once offensive and defensive. Sprinkled throughout the literature of evangelical architecture in the nineteenth century is the language of religious militancy. Echoing Lewis Tappan's statement that founding a free church within the Chatham Theatre would be like "storming a redoubt, or taking cannon & turning them upon the enemy," late nineteenth-century evangelicals saw their building efforts in the context of a great battle between God's forces—Protestant Christians—and the unconverted, who had not turned toward God's saving grace.[4] The prospectus printed in the inaugural issues of the *Church Building Quarterly* solicited material on church architecture from its readers, proclaiming that "if brethren will send on such material, it will arrange itself in battle array for an onslaught of the Kingdom of darkness. The range is long,—from 1000 to 3—miles. 'Smooth bores' will not answer. Rifles serve a better purpose."[5] *Century Illustrated Monthly Magazine* editor Eugene Thayer, in speaking of the importance of filling auditoriums to capacity with worshipers, similarly tapped the militaristic metaphor: "If a church seats five thousand people, there must be five thousand people in it to have any congregational singing in the true and proper sense of the word. Singers may be likened to gunpowder. Condensed in the pistol, the thimbleful of powder may produce marked effect; a barrelful scattered over the lawn will not injure him who may apply a torch to it. Our singers, whether choir or congregation, must be compact and together if we would realize our just expectations."[6] The descriptive phrase *spiritual armory*, which was applied to the First Congregational Church in 1886, would have deeply resonated with evangelicals steeped in such metaphors. Massive audiences, the "gunpowder" of worship, and the spiritual armory were the Christian defense against the "onslaught of the Kingdom of darkness."

These metaphors illuminate the significance of evangelical church architecture during this period on two levels. First, the militarism indicates the remarkable extent to which congruence characterized the semiotic relationship between evangelical ideology and architectural style. The battered stone walls and Romanesque details of these churches did resemble armories, secure fortresses for both offense and defense within urban terrain marked by growing contests between the haves and the have-nots. The buildings announced to the congregants and the public alike that this was indeed a war, not simply a metaphorical struggle but a real battle that occupied the minds and hearts of those within. Second, these church buildings physically concentrated the gunpowder of the specific values and concerns of their middle-class and affluent congregations. Compacted into the architecture of the church building, yet remaining clearly discerniable, these ideals defined the nature of and helped to maintain evangelical religious life at the end of the nineteenth century. As explored throughout this volume, these values included democracy and voluntarism combined with congregational self-determination and audience power; the importance of high culture as aesthetic knowledge; materialism and pride in technological advancement; the values of education, industriousness, thrift, productivity, teamwork, and respect for authority, which so many evangelical congregations taught through their Sunday schools and institutional programs; and an encompassing concern for the family, ordained by God as the fundamental sacred society. Viewing a neomedieval auditorium church, almost any late nineteenth-century resident of North America would have been cognizant of these messages regarding the congregation within.

Perhaps the most important element of the semiotic function of these churches, however, is the extent to which they demonstrated congruence among evangelicals at the end of the century. The eclectic medieval exterior facades (whether accomplished in stone, brick, or wood), the auditorium interiors, and the Sunday schools and institutional rooms defined the evangelical church and indicated that those who built them fully shared a consistent religious and sociocultural world view. Whether erected by Presbyterians, Congregationalists, Methodists, or Baptists, the ubiquitousness of the neomedieval church style announced not simply the existence of a unique evangelical stance but also the hegemony of this shared outlook. The disruption of this outlook, however, would soon bring about a sharp decline in the popularity of this church type.

Gothic Revival of the Early Twentieth Century

Given that it reinforced and broadcast a class- and time-specific ideology, it is not surprising that the neomedieval auditorium church remained popular for only a brief period. Peaking in the 1890s, its popularity diminished steadily after the turn of the twentieth century. Only a handful of examples were completed after 1910. The church type lost its popularity for two reasons: The religious agendas and the evangelical alliances that the buildings embodied and broadcast waned, and at the same time, architects, church art critics, and designers embraced new criteria for both aesthetics and function. By World War I, the concerns that had informed the worship, family, and missionary agendas of these congregations had lost their potency, and the conceptions of cultural authority that had undergirded them were eclipsed by a modern world that no longer located authority in religion or family. The architectural profession, having successfully established itself as not just a technical but also an aesthetic field, engaged once again in the historicization of medieval Gothic architecture as distinctively Christian.

Perhaps foremost among the waning ideological elements was the fading importance of the domestic model of evangelical piety. The connection between church and home, so critical for late nineteenth-century evangelicals, lost much of its relevance after the turn of the century. The ideology of domestic piety waned in part because the family was so fully established as the premier social institution that religious sanction for it was no longer needed. Physical expression of domestic piety in churches waned because congregations no longer needed to legitimize the materialism of their churches. Stained glass, upholstery, frescoing, and mechanical means of maintaining physical comfort were commonplace, as were kitchens, dining halls, and parlors. No longer was a demonstration of the connection between church and the sacralized domicile needed to justify religious materialism. Related to this shift was the increasing irrelevance of the boundary between the private sphere and the public. Education, service, consumerism, and recreation frequently took family members, particularly women and children, outside the private domicile. The need for churches to negotiate between these two spheres slowly vanished.

Related to the decline of the model of domestic piety was the changing position of the middle class within urban contexts. After the turn of the century, many of the threats against middle-class hegemony so acutely perceived in the 1880s were seemingly eliminated or mitigated. Religious institutions no longer needed to establish their legitimacy through being authoritative cultural institutions. Municipal orchestra halls, libraries, and even public restaurants superseded churches as locations for respectable or highbrow entertainment. Nor need churches function as outposts of civil authority. As cities erected municipal armories and police stations, church buildings lost much of their relevance as symbols of social authority and moral order. With the growth of Federalism and a civil religion that implicitly linked civil authority to Christianity, the battles to be played out in the twentieth-century public realm would have little need to establish moral authority through demonstrable religious association.

The collapse of the evangelical consensus around these two points rendered the messages of unity and hegemony conveyed by these buildings ironic. As new religious ideas and missions developed, the neomedieval auditorium church simply lost its centrality within the landscape of Protestant architecture. The unique aspect of the neomedieval auditorium church was the amazing extent to which it had manifested the religious ideals and missions of late nineteenth-century evangelicals. Perhaps never before, and only rarely since, has religious architecture so intimately paralleled ideology. But as those ideological beliefs waned, so too waned the architectural style that had so successfully embodied them.

What replaced the neomedieval auditorium church was a new ecclesiasticism in both religious practice and architecture. The Late Gothic Revival, a return to "accurate" Gothic that swept the nation just after the turn of the twentieth century, ultimately eclipsed the auditorium churches of the previous generation. Architects and designers once again championed the aesthetic preeminence of historicized facades and the functional superiority of clergy-oriented plans. Indications of this new direction in church architecture were evident as early as the mid-1890s. In 1892, the Congregationalist journal *Church Building Quarterly* published an article on the new Winter Hill Church in Somerville, Massachusetts, designed by the firm of Hartwell and Richardson. Describing the building's oblong, "preaching box" sanctuary, the article called it "a room for worship." It continued, "It is a sanctuary and nothing else. No perversity of fancy could construe it as a lecture room or concert hall. In the arrangement of the pews there is suggestion surely of a church—not the faintest of a theatre."[7] Published at the zenith of the auditorium church's popularity, this implied criticism of the auditorium church type foreshadowed the future. Two years later, the same journal published the plans and photographs of the new Central Congregational Church of Providence, Rhode Island, designed by the New York architectural firm of Carrere and Hastings (fig. 8.1). A cruciform building completed in 1890, its plan imitated that of Richardson's famous Trinity Episcopal Church in Boston. Enveloped in a French Renaissance exterior, this Congregational church featured a dome 52 feet in diameter and 73 feet in height over the crossing. Rectilinear pews occupied the nave and transepts, and a divided chancel (not indicated on the published plan) with Communion table positioned in the apse dominated the room. Choir and organ were located in a gallery at the back of the church over the entry vestibule.[8] These formalized spaces emphasized the role of clergy not as preachers, but as priests, officiating over the worship of the divine being. Returning to the spaces of

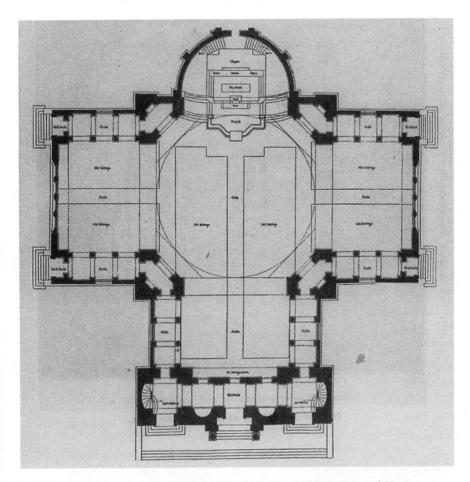

Fig. 8.1. Central Congregational Church, Providence, R.I. 1890. Carrere and Hastings, archs. *Church Building Quarterly* 12 (July 1894): 179.

ecclesiastical religion and to the architectural vocabularies of the Renaissance, this church further demonstrated the design decisions that would ultimately vanquish the neomedieval auditorium church.

In offering their bid for the new direction in church architecture, however, Carrere and Hastings got the architectural style wrong. For although they anticipated the popularity that neo-classicism would soon gain with the World's Columbia Exposition, it would not be neo-classicism that would eclipse the eclectic medieval facades of the evangelical churches, but neo-Gothicism.[9] The Late Gothic Revival began to challenge the hegemony of evangelical auditorium churches in the mid-1890s, and in the early twentieth century it swept through the Protestant denominations. As during the earlier Gothic Revival and the Romanesque Revival, stylistic trends in church architecture paralleled those in domestic architecture, despite the fact that designers of the period disparaged any relationship between the domestic environment and the church. From the early

1890s, the very wealthy had favored for their homes English Gothic facades, a rather loose stylistic approach that included, in the words of architectural historian Donald R. Torbert, "detail or composition that was derived from the Tudor, Jacobean or Elizabethan and realized in stone, brick, half-timber or a combination of the three."[10] But this was also an architect-driven trend, for like the Ecclesiologists a half century earlier, early twentieth-century architects championed the Gothic as the expression of authentic, pure Christianity. At the head of the movement was Ralph Adams Cram, who argued that contemporary architects must begin with the Gothic vocabularies prevalent at the time of the English Reformation in order to develop a creative, new, fully Christian architecture. Cram maintained that Gothic vocabularies grew out of liturgical formalism and therefore were most suited to liturgical, High Church denominations.[11] Nevertheless, Methodists, particularly, but Presbyterians, Congregationalists, and Baptists as well, were well positioned to accept the spatial forms and ornamental features of Gothic architecture given the liturgical additions of the previous generation, the earlier interest in the Gothic during the mid–nineteenth century, and the continued borrowing of Gothic elements throughout the latter decades of the century.

Congregations moving to new suburbs eagerly commissioned Gothic Revival churches. Two general types predominated. First, churches modeled on the rather informal rural English parish type tended to be favored in residential areas. For instance, Andrew-Riverside Presbyterian Church in Minneapolis, designed in 1890 by Charles S. Sedgwick, was reputed to echo sixteenth-century Presbyterian divine John Knox's St. Giles Church in Edinburgh (fig. 8.2). Similarly, when dissenters separated from First Baptist Church in Minneapolis and erected Trinity Church in the new Lowry Hill subdivision, it featured similar rough-hewn, random-laid granite and limestone walls, a long cruciform

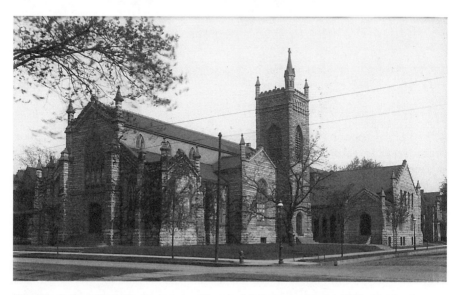

Fig. 8.2. Andrew-Riverside Presbyterian Church, Minneapolis, Minn. 1890. Charles S. Sedgwick, arch. Photograph by Charles J. Hibbard, c. 1911. Courtesy of the Minnesota Historical Society (4547–B).

nave, and a roof supported by trusses. Also echoing the parish-church type, Plymouth Congregational in Minneapolis, designed by the Boston firm of Shepley, Rutan, and Coolidge (successors to Richardson), featured variegated, random-laid, seam-faced granite exterior walls, a massive square tower, and an interior nave with hammerhead beams supporting the roof.

In addition to these parish churches, more formal treatments of the Gothic dominated on major thoroughfares. Often large in scale, the dressed granite facades of these churches echoed English cathedrals, featuring impressive west-end entrances sheltered under sculpted Gothic arches and tracery-filled rose windows, multiple bays divided by buttresses, and massive bell towers often positioned on the English model to the south of the eastern chancel.[12] The Church of the Covenant in Cleveland, designed by Cram and Ferguson in 1909 for a Presbyterian congregation, featured octagonal turrets flanking both sides of a front entrance with a deeply recessed rose window above a dramatic pointed-arch doorway. Four bays compose the vaulted nave, and these were marked on the exterior with buttresses and large windows. A 140–foot-square tower occupied the southeast corner and separated the church from the parish house. House of Hope Presbyterian in St. Paul, Minnesota, designed by Cram, Goodhue, and Ferguson in 1912, is another example, and Baptists adopted the style in Goodhue's Rockefeller Memorial Chapel of 1926-1927, built on the campus of the University of Chicago and featuring a tower rising 207 feet above its 265–foot-long nave.[13] The vast majority of these Gothic Revival churches abandoned both the auditorium seating plans and the pulpit platforms of the earlier evangelical churches. In these longitudinally oriented naves, often featuring vaulting supported by columns, rectilinear pews were divided by a center, processional aisle. A divided chancel typically occupied the east end of the room, which terminated, in many instances, in an apse.

A few exceptions, however, attempted to blend the Gothic Revival with the benefits of the amphitheatre. Hennepin Avenue Methodist in Minneapolis, for instance, consisted of a large octagonal sanctuary, which was modeled after the lantern in Ely Cathedral (see fig. 4.5). This centralized space housed an amphitheatre sanctuary with bowled floor, curved pews, and encircling galleries. While examples like this one point to a period of transition in which auditorium and Gothic Revival churches overlapped, they also demonstrate the steamrollerlike force of the new architectural aesthetic. By 1920 it had gained clear predominance. Neomedieval auditorium churches became the bane of many congregations and, in the opinion of a new flock of commentators on religious art and architecture, the curse of Protestantism and America alike.

Almost all aspects of the neomedieval auditorium churches were held up for ridicule and scorn. The domestic character of the churches came under particular fire. As historian David Bains has pointed out, proponents of the Gothic Revival found the churches of the late nineteenth century "too comfortable and too feminine."[14] Congregationalist-turned-Unitarian minister Von Ogden Vogt of Chicago deplored the "family-at-home feeling" of the auditorium churches, asserting that the proper aesthetic was "stern and rigorous . . . restrained and austere."[15] Although, he argued, a church should have a feeling of "peace and repose," it cannot come from "the mere physical peace of comfortableness." "Sensuousness," he warned, can derive as readily from the richly sweeping gallery and warmly tinted stained glass as it can from the presence of "effigies or shrines."[16]

The rejection of the domestic also took place on a practical level as at least one aspect of the family church came under fire: pew rentals. Opponents of pew rentals in both the liberal and conservative camps associated them with the family church ideal, and their arguments indicate the extent to which this ideal was passing. At Fifth Avenue Presbyterian Church in New York City, families who reserved full pews on the previous family church model drew fire for guarding empty family seats while standing-room-only crowds packed the church. During the Reverend John Henry Jowett's years as senior minister, the Sunday bulletin carried a notice to pew holders to be generous with their space.[17] Much more conservative than Jowett, William Bell Riley, as we have seen, argued against family pews as undemocratic and associated them with wealth and privilege.

This rejection of the domestic sphere as a source for architectural strategies paralleled the rejection of domestic piety as a model for the Christian experience. "A church," Vogt argued, "cannot be like a theatre or a drawing room, it must ever call for the mortification of the flesh and the regnancy of the conscience."[18] Bains rightly argues that this new perspective was strongly gendered toward masculinity, a point that he illustrates by citing Elbert Conover's opinion that the church should be a "place where one could imagine a knight keeping 'the vigil from which great quests were followed.'"[19] It is important to clarify, however, that what is being rejected in the curved galleries and cushioned seats is not masculinity's opposite, femininity, for this was not a category used to describe churches; rather, it is the domestic, the homelike quality. The shift here constitutes a realignment of the church with the public world. The centrality of the sheltering, defensive character of the home and its nurturing of Christian spirit yielded to a more aggressive, public quest for communion with God. The church should not be a comfortable retreat, but a place from whence the spiritual quest commences—and comfort does not precipitate quests. For Conover, the best church interiors incorporated the "qualities of sincerity, nobility and greatness."[20]

Similarly, the theatre-derived aspects of the auditorium space came under fire as what had been modest increases in the liturgical elements within services in the nineteenth century evolved into a widespread and influential liturgical movement that came to characterize liberal Protestanism. Vogt criticized Protestant liturgy as characterized by "artistic confusion and prevalent ugliness," at the same time as he condemned church architecture as "ugly," "disagreeable," and born of "ignorance."[21] He leveled his greatest vitriol at the auditorium and, particularly, the diagonal-plan auditorium with the adjacent Sunday school room: "No invention was ever more frightful. No artist would dream of focusing attention to the corner of a square room. Sitting askew of the cardinal points puts a slant into your very morals. And the circular pews make one feel as through he were in a clinical laboratory. The prominence of organ pipes on one side and the dreary, barren waste of folding doors on the other constitute a composition in disharmony and impropriety almost positively demoralizing."[22] A concern for formalism infuses Vogt's writing, and in his view practical desires had overshadowed proper expression. The auditorium arrangement, he concluded, could not "remotely be connected with the world of the fine arts."[23]

Congregationalist writer and editor of *Advance* John R. Scotford also criticized the auditorium sanctuary, but his concern centered on its panopticon character:

> Many churches built between 1890 and 1920 are wide and shallow with the pews curving in a great circle. Whether so intended or not, the result is to make it easy for every

worshiper to see every other worshiper. The individual achieves the maximum prominence. As a result, most people take the back seats, while anyone who is beguiled into
one of the front center pews is made exceedingly uncomfortable by the many eyes which
are focused upon him. He dare not sneeze, cough or even move. Although he may not
detect the reason, he knows that he has had a disagreeable experience, and is discouraged
from repeating it.[24]

Constant surveillance by fellow audience members, a feature praised a generation earlier for its fostering of congregational unity, turned twentieth-century services into exercises in self-consciousness. The mutual voyeurism created by the location of minister
and choir facing the audience exacerbated this feeling. As Scotford observed, choir
members not only became self-conscious under the scrutiny of audiences, but the minister too occupied an awkward position that, in essence, indicated the wrong type of
authority: "Often he sits on a rocky promontory jutting out into the congregation like a
king on [his] throne or a school teacher at his desk. He is a presiding officer rather than
a leader of worship. He is too omnipresent." For Scotford, the solution was to "rel-
egate" the choir and minister "to positions of comparative inconspicuousness."[25] The
performative authority that late nineteenth-century evangelical ministers eagerly claimed
was thus strongly disparaged by the mid–twentieth century. Emphasis during services
in the new church was to be on worship, on higher thoughts of the sacred, and consequently, lofty spaces in which symbolic stained glass rather than other people's faces
drew the attention gained favor. The old auditorium sanctuaries, Thomas A. Stafford
argued, were simply "all-purpose buildings that make little or no contribution to worship." Continuing his disparagement of the buildings, he asserted, "If the services of
worship in them are uplifting, it is generally in spite of the uninspiring surroundings.
Many of these buildings are positively depressing in their effect on a sensitive mind."[26]

Having their auditorium churches thus relegated to the ash heap of regrettable architecture, many congregations radically remodeled their sanctuaries at midcentury. Critics
and architects alike championed the liturgically facilitative "split chancel" as the most
desirable arrangement. As explained at midcentury by Richard H. Ritter, the split chancel balanced the four primary symbolic representations of God's revelation held by Protestants: the Bible, the table, the pulpit, and the cross. Balance among these symbols
was achieved by placing the cross on the far wall at the back of the chancel, centering
the table in the chancel on the longitudinal axis but several feet out from the wall, placing the lectern holding the Bible on one side of the axis, and positioning the pulpit on
the other. Through this arrangement, Ritter argued, "The sacrifice and fellowship of
the Sacrament, and the historicity and prophetical vigor of the Word are kept in equi-
poise, all showing forth the infinite greatness of our God."[27]

Conover similarly championed the split chancel arrangement, and his 1948 book,
The Church Builder, offered suggestions for remodeling along these lines with before
and after photographs. As in the case of First Presbyterian Church in Knoxville, Tennessee, these images demonstrate the removal of the pulpit platform, choir, organ
pipes, and proscenium and the creation of a divided chancel (figs. 8.3, 8.4). Curved
pews have been replaced with rectilinear ones, and they have been reoriented in the
room to form a center aisle. Lighting has also been altered. Frescoing and dark wainscoting were replaced by painted wood in a light color. These discussions emphasized
processionals, the taking of Communion at altar rails, and worshipful reverence. Preach-

Fig. 8.3. First Presbyterian Church, Knoxville, Tenn. 1903. Photograph, c. 1946. Courtesy of the C. M. McClung Historical Collection (A9265).

ing and hearing and seeing the preacher, primary concerns in the 1880s, were mentioned only to be dismissed, often with logic that directly contradicted that of the earlier builders.[28]

Akron Plan features also came under fire. As we have seen, the diagonally oriented sanctuary and the recessible walls that separated it from the Sunday school hall were particularly disparaged. Mechanisms for raising and lowering the wall were temperamental, and congregations found that few occasions warranted throwing open the wall to join both rooms.[29] The crowds of thousands envisioned by congregations that boasted only 300 to 400 members often did not materialize. Sunday school officials also criticized the Akron Plan itself, arguing that while the rolling partitions between classrooms and lecture rooms served well to shut out visual distractions, they offered very little soundproofing, and the odd-shaped rooms that resulted from the ring arrangement proved challenging to use, as did the risers within these classrooms. Perhaps the most important factor contributing to the decline of the Akron Plan Sunday school, however, was the widespread adoption of graded classes in the 1910s. Graded classes were divided into departments—primary, junior, and senior—and each of these needed lecture space. In the opinion of Henry Tralle and George Merrill, the Akron Plan was "wholly unsuited to the needs of the modern, graded departmentalized school."[30] Nevertheless, the processes that the Akron Plan had begun, that is, the separation of the Sunday school

Fig. 8.4. First Presbyterian Church, Knoxville, Tenn. 1903. Photograph c. 1947. Courtesy of the C. M. McClung Historical Collection (B546).

from the church building and the specialization of space to facilitate curriculum, continued despite the fact that the progenitor was discredited.

Thus, by 1910, the eclipsing of the neomedieval auditorium church type by the new Gothic Revival type and new institutional facilities was rapidly progressing. It is with this advent of the Late Gothic Revival that an architectural expression of the schism between Protestant liberals and fundamentalists becomes evident. Those who embraced the Gothic Revival in the twentieth century were by and large liberal-leaning congregations. Vogt, who echoed mid–nineteenth-century arguments when he hailed the new Gothic style as a means of fostering Christian unity, in effect acknowledged that growing schism. He felt that the Gothic style and liturgical worship practice could unite all Christians into a new ecumenical alignment indicative of the advancing Christian culture.[31] All Protestants, however, did not share this progressive agenda.

Liberal-Fundamentalist Schism and Religious Auditoriums in the Twentieth Century

The rise of Protestant fundamentalism in the early 1920s decisively severed the nineteenth-century evangelical alliance. Combining traditional evangelicalism with the relatively new perspectives of dispensational premillennialism, holiness, and Pentacostalism, fundamentalism coalesced as a religiously based sociopolitical alternative to the progressive modernism of liberal religion. These origins brought two critical religious missions into tension. On the one hand, fundamentalists inherited, and for the most part claimed, the traditional duty to proselytize, to evangelize the nation. On the other hand, strong separatist leanings, fueled particularly by the cultural marginalization that conservatives experienced during the evolution battles of the 1920s, urged conservative Protestants to isolate themselves from a society they perceived as increasingly corrupt.[32]

Diversity of belief characterized conservative Protestantism on the congregational level, however. Here the heritage of revivalism held strong, and the inheritance of the architectural space of revival religion is evident. Not only did conservatives trace their theological history back through the work of Moody, Finney, and Whitefield, but in retaining the amphitheatre form, they traced their architecture back through this same heritage. Drawing upon the architectural lineage that extended from the Broadway Tabernacle to the Tremont Temple to Central Music Hall and the Ryman Auditorium, twentieth-century churches like Aimee Semple McPherson's Angelus Temple in Los Angeles (1923), the Moody Memorial Church in Chicago (1925), and the Boston Avenue Methodist Church in Tulsa (1929) replicated the amphitheatre plan to procure huge audience-seating capacities and to facilitate performance-centered services.

Maintaining the functional concerns of late nineteenth-century evangelicals, each of these buildings was designed to accommodate the physical needs of as large a congregation as possible, and in so doing, each replicated the strategies developed a generation earlier. The Angelus Temple, for instance, designed as a huge oval to seat some 5,300 people (and often accommodating hundreds more on its main floor and in the double galleries), broadcast an encompassing welcome to the urban community. Its ample stage provided an appropriately theatrelike setting for McPherson's services, and each Sunday it was filled with scenery and props used in the dramatizations that McPherson wrote and presented to teach her gospel lessons. Using characters that ranged from motorcycle cops to Indian princesses, Sister Aimee's skits underscored the theatrical origins of the religious amphitheatre. The Moody auditorium (fig. 8.5), designed in 1924 by John R. Fugard, similarly offered a huge audience area, seating more than 4,000 people, and featured a single cantilevered gallery encircling three sides of the room. Its pulpit stage, outlined by a double proscenium, located the choir and organ at the back, replicating the late nineteenth-century church precisely. Boston Avenue Methodist in Tulsa (fig. 8.6), designed by Adah Robinson and built in 1929 by the firm of Rush, Endacott, and Rush, also featured a round amphitheatre with a cantilevered gallery facing a pulpit stage. In addition to these amphitheatre features, each of these churches provided individual theatre seats to ensure the comfort of each visitor.

Generally, the decor of these 1920s religious auditoriums tended toward modernism rather than toward the domestic piety of the previous generation. Though the Angelus Temple used stained glass, frescoing, and warm chandelier and marquis lighting to achieve a certain intimacy, the exterior classical loggia and the huge dome supported by a ring of narrow, horizontal windows projected a strong modernism to the street. With its massive radio towers, spotlights, and searchlights, the temple appeared as a huge spaceship landed in Los Angeles. Boston Avenue Methodist championed modernism even more thoroughly. Its stark, Moderne exterior was composed of a circular mass ringed

Fig. 8.5. Moody Memorial Church, Chicago, Ill. 1926. Courtesy Archives of the Billy Graham Center, Wheaton, Ill.

Fig. 8.6. Boston Avenue Methodist Church, Tulsa, Okla. 1929. Adah Robinson, designer. Photograph by Robert Yarnell Richie. Courtesy Boston Avenue United Methodist Church.

with narrow, rectangular windows and large square projections at the compass points, defining the entries. Inside, the tall, clear windows let in unfiltered light under a ceiling ornamented with an abstract circular pattern.[33] In contrast to these buildings, Chicago's Moody Memorial replicated the domestic aesthetic of the late nineteenth-century churches with its abundant stained glass, frescoing, polished wood, and carpeting.

Although conservative in outlook, these congregations did not eschew contemporary aesthetics. By and large they avoided the traditional architectural vocabularies that liberal Protestants were embracing (particularly Gothic) and chose the more plain and utilitarian aesthetic of modernism. While liberals generally returned to the historicizing sleight of hand achieved by the Gothic and, by the 1920s, Colonial Revival architectural styles, conservatives tended to make aesthetic choices in accordance with the flourishing architectural litany "form follows function" while, at the same time, downplaying connotative semiotic labor. Conservative evangelical churches minimized and even eliminated ornament, returning at least in ambience to the plainstyle aesthetic of the colonial period.

Many conservative congregations, however, remained within their late nineteenth-century churches and, like liberals, they too remodeled their buildings. The 1920s, for instance, saw the remodeling of fundamentalist leader William Bell Riley's First Baptist Church in Minneapolis. Riley and his building committee began with ambitious plans, originally intending to build a new church in conjunction with a huge new Sunday school. Gradually, between 1919 and 1924, it became increasingly obvious that financial realities would limit these plans. A reduction of the church lot caused by street widening further necessitated modification of their desires. Ultimately, Riley proposed the enlarging of the existing audience room, rather than the construction of a new church. The new goal was carried out under the direction of the Kees and Coburn architectural firm. The original diagonal orientation of First Baptist was shifted forty-five degrees to relocate the pulpit platform, complete with choir loft and organ case, against the west wall of the sanctuary in a recess that added some 20 feet to the length of the room. The new sanctuary accommodated 2,500 people on its sloped main floor and gallery, a sizable increase over the original seating capacity of around 900.[34]

The Southern Baptists also remained comfortable with the church architecture of the previous generation. The denomination published a book of church and Sunday school designs in 1920 that recommended auditorium arrangements of the sanctuary as the only satisfactory means of "building for evangelism." Recommending large auditoriums with sloping floors and curving pews, the author, P. E. Burroughs, argued, as had his earlier evangelical counterparts, that the space of the sanctuary and its arrangement would "lend assistance to evangelism." Several diagonal plan churches were featured and numerous illustrations emphasized elaborate prosceniums sheltering impressive organ pipes and choir seating. Further, while the Southern Baptists did adopt graded classrooms, Burroughs recommended the use of sliding partitions to separate them.[35]

Thus, whereas liberals frequently remodeled their churches to eliminate the auditorium elements, conservatives generally carried on the connection between amphitheatre space and the evangelical tradition of preaching as the centerpiece of the religious service. Generally speaking, services among these evangelical congregations still focused on preaching and musical performance. The liturgical elements often remained those of the previous generation: hymn singing, prayer, and scriptural reading. In some cases, however, fundamentalists minimized liturgical features. For instance, at Riley's urging, First Baptist eliminated Communion in its Sunday services, moving the sacrament to the first Thursday evening after the first Sunday in every month.[36] Thus while liberals fostered a liturgical revival that located power within the minister (and within the divided chancel) and the sacraments, evangelicals fostered new means of individual power, particularly through holiness and Pentecostal means. As liberal congregations were enhancing ecclesiasticism in their services, conservative and fundamentalist ones either retained the late nineteenth-century balance of worship and preaching or moved to reduce ecclesiastical observances. The focus in these services remained on the preacher and the Word, though it is likely that the pulpit stages of these twentieth-century auditorium churches also accommodated additional revivalist features, including the altar calls and demonstrations of divine healing popularized by fundamentalists.[37]

The liberalism/Gothic and conservatism/auditorium alignments were far from universal, however, and should be viewed as a general means of understanding the architecture of the twentieth century. One exception, for instance, is the relatively late construction of St. Paul's M.E. Church in Cedar Rapids, Iowa. Designed by George Grant Elmslie, who modified a proposed plan by Louis Sullivan, the brick semicircular building completed in 1914 conveyed a distinctly modernist feeling, and the interior was outfitted with the radial plan, curvilinear pews, and pulpit stage of the early auditorium churches.[38] Thus this fairly liberal congregation countered the general trends identified above.

The Megachurch; or, The New Religious Auditorium

The intimate connection between evangelicalism and the amphitheatre space once again asserted itself on the national scene at the end of the twentieth century with the development of the megachurch. These huge religious complexes, usually located in suburbs, number their members in the thousands and attract thousands more to Sunday services each week. Their physical plants include not just a massive auditorium, often seating several thousand individuals, but also snack bars or food courts; bookstores and memorabilia shops; meeting, counseling, and prayer rooms; Sunday school facilities; nurseries and preschool playrooms; lounges and social rooms; and recreational facilities like gymnasiums and game rooms. Though hailed by many as indicating an unprecedented turn in religious architecture, these church complexes are, in fact, firmly rooted in the history of evangelical spaces. From their use of amphitheatre space to their integration of state-of-the-art technology to their rooms and services for every member of the family, these churches carry on the strategies that evangelical churches adopted in the 1870s and 1880s, though they do so in decidedly late twentieth-century language. Moreover, just like their nineteenth-century counterparts, these buildings articulate messages specifically designed to appeal to a broad middle class. As did their progenitors, these churches help to spread the evangelical message by offering an attractive religious haven within a turbulent world.

Megachurches were born of the desire to bring middle-class white Protestants who likely grew up within a church but had abandoned it as adults "back" to the church. The question that faced pastors was how to do this. The oft-told story of Willow Creek

Community Church founder Bill Hybels going door to door to ascertain just what would appeal to suburban Chicago residents in a church is emblematic of the utilitarian bent of the megachurch movement: identify the needs and desires of the target group and fulfill them. In Hybels's case, the research showed that while people did not know exactly what they wanted in a church, they definitely knew what they did not want. Thus, the megachurch mission grew from a negative model. The new church would *not* be like traditional churches. There would be no pleas for money during services. There would be no belaboring of abstruse theology or exegesis of irrelevant scriptural passages, no emphasis on troubling elements like sin and guilt. There would be no religious symbols designed to overawe worshipers. The new church would minimize social class and not make people feel they needed to dress or behave in certain ways when inside the building. It would not pressure members into becoming involved in committees or programs. Most of all, the new church would not evoke an otherworldliness that made people uncomfortable. It would be an institution marked by its familiarity, not its distinctiveness.[39]

The new church would locate itself precisely at the junction between everyday life and religion. It would be a place in which the kinds of questions that arise in family and work life are placed in the context of biblical advice. It would offer means of community involvement and individual counseling but maintain them on a strictly voluntary basis. It would make services entertaining, with modern music, skits, and ministers who were ordinary, down-to-earth people, who spoke about the issues people faced on a day-to-day basis. Most of all, it would be relevant to the lives of middle-class people. Thus, the megachurch phenomenon is admittedly consumer oriented. Church organizers following Hybels's model regularly engage marketing experts in assessing the desires of their target audiences, and in designing their religious product, they fully intend to satisfy those desires.

While such strategies might take to a new extreme those formulated by evangelicals as early as the eighteenth century—bringing religion to the people, making it relevant to their lives, presenting the religious message in an entertaining way—they are certainly grounded in evangelical history. This demand-supply relationship exists not only between the activities and services megachurches offer to satisfy their congregations' needs, but also between the buildings and those needs. Just as in neomedieval auditorium churches, in the new megachurches, we can read the meanings and values that inform contemporary life.

The amphitheatre plan of megachurches caters to the same physical needs and desires in the late twentieth century as it did in the late nineteenth. Hearing and seeing in a comfortable setting remain paramount. As the Reverend Lee Strobel, a pastor at Willow Creek, pointed out about St. Paul's Cathedral in London, "The lighting is bad, you can't hear the guys up front, and it's uncomfortable." He continued, "We wanted Willow Creek to be more functional."[40] The strategies used to accommodate this requirement vary widely. Among the earliest examples of the megachurch was Robert Schuller's Crystal Cathedral, designed in 1980 by architect Philip Johnson (fig. 8.7). Echoing the late nineteenth-century willingness to experiment with the shape of auditorium space, the sanctuary is in the shape of a four-pointed star with banks of rectilinear amphitheatre seating and galleries in three segments and a preaching stage in the fourth. Seating in each of these sections points directly down to the stage. Somewhat more traditional is

Fig. 8.7. Crystal Cathedral, Garden Grove, Calif. 1980. Philip Johnson, arch. Courtesy Robert Schuller's Ministries.

the hexagonal auditorium of Willow Creek (fig. 8.8). On the main floor, banks of theatre seats on a gently sloping floor curve around a thrust stage. Above, a cantilevered gallery encircles the room. In it, as in so many nineteenth-century galleries as well as in Finney's sketch, the seating is placed upon steps.

In addition to these traditional strategies to aid hearing and seeing, megachurch auditoriums employ the latest technologies to further facilitate reception of the service. Microphones and amplifiers are prevalent, having been introduced into churches as early as the 1920s. Video screens enhance audiences' view of the stage. In Willow Creek, video screens built into friezes near the ceilings of the galleries (three or four per section) provide clear pictures for those people seated in what would be called the "nosebleed" seats in a sports arena. If one cannot clearly see the performers on the stage, a glance at the video screen reveals a close-up of the action.

Maintaining audience attention is also critical, and these congregations, like their earlier counterparts, turn to entertainment to accomplish this. In the late nineteenth century the entertaining elements consisted of oratory, musical performance, and, especially, visual spectacle created by the stage arrangement and lighting techniques, and in the late twentieth century these elements remained very much intact with the addition of dramatizations. Modifications designed to suit the tastes of contemporary audiences are, of course, evident. Contemporary sermons emphasize not only vernacular language

Fig. 8.8. Willow Creek Community Church, South Barrington, Ill. 1981. Photograph by Paul R. Kilde, 2001. Courtesy Willow Creek Association.

but also vernacular situations, and the music, still performed by professional musicians, is no long classical art-music but soft rock or country. Visual spectacle, provided in the nineteenth century through the elaboration of the stage with proscenium arch, choir loft, and organ pipes, is replicated in some new auditorium churches. Wooddale Church just outside of Minneapolis, for instance, features a pulpit stage, choir loft, baptistry, and hovering organ, which closely replicate nineteenth-century strategies. All that is missing is the proscenium.

On the other hand, many new religious auditoriums eschew such architectural spectacle as too indicative of traditional churches and opt instead for other means of creating an entertaining visual spectacle. Willow Creek, devoid of permanent decoration, relies upon movable scenery and props to enhance performances. Giant video screens flanking the stage can be used to project images that illustrate the oratorical performance. For instance, during a service in May 1998, Hybels read a children's book aloud as a part of his sermon and projected the images from the book on these screens. In addition, theatrical lighting techniques are used to transform musical numbers into visual light shows. Similarly, skits are enhanced with video projections and lighting. Visual spectacle then remains a critical element in evangelical services, and while contemporary church leaders might speak much more freely about the need to entertain their audiences than did their late nineteenth-century counterparts, their goals remain quite similar.

Contemporary megachurches also offer a wide variety of facilities and services within their physical plants, all designed to address the needs of middle-class families. The food courts, counseling programs, preschools, and video game rooms are twentieth-century versions of the institutional church facilities of the late nineteenth century. But while the late nineteenth-century evangelicals may have had trouble distinguishing between the functions of their similar facilities as instigated by Social Gospel desires to reach out to their urban communities and their own desire to keep their children within the church, late twentieth-century megachurches have little similar angst. These facilities are clearly intended for church participants and are often strong attractions for nonmembers to join.

The fact that institutional church facilities were originally connected (however loosely) to the Social Gospel mission of community service brings into question the mission of the megachurches. If family ministry, worship, and spreading the gospel competed within late nineteenth-century evangelical churches, what missions inform late twentieth-century megachurches, which draw so heavily upon the earlier buildings? Clearly, attracting a broad middle class into the religious institution is the fundamental mission of the churches. This religious institution, however, plays down its relationship to the rest of the world; megachurches pride themselves on being "havens," "oases," or "refuges" from the tumultuous everyday lives of their members.

There are, of course, similarities here to the nineteenth-century situation in which churches drew upon the ideology of the sanctified home in defining themselves as places of sanctuary, as spiritual armories, in a turbulent society. The family home at the time, however, actually vied with the church in offering the most attractive respite from the world. In the late twentieth century, the megachurch locates itself on a separate plane of respite outside of the stresses of everyday life by identifying with other contemporary places of peace, places where people spend their leisure hours (hopefully) untroubled by the cares of the world: the shopping mall, the sports arena, the movie theatre. The church home is no longer relevant, but the mall provides the feeling of worry-free comfort for which the megachurch strives.[41] Whereas the spiritual armory stood within an ongoing dialectic with the surrounding community and national cultural context, the megachurch emphasizes refuge, a withdrawal from the world. While spiritual armories filled with fighting minions aimed to bring about the salvation of the nation, many modern churchgoers (or nonchurchgoers) felt less burdened by such responsibilities, so megachurches minimize pressure on the individual. They provide a space, time, and place in which one might get away from it all. Attending a service is an activity akin to going to a movie: One need not dress up, worry about the kids misbehaving, or be upset by a depressing message.[42] While community service programs are available for interested members, no such overall mission defines these congregations. Further, these are generally not revival churches. Overt proselytizing, an activity that places a great deal of pressure on audiences, is simply antithetical to their mission.

The use of religious auditoriums, however, is not isolated within the nondenominational megachurch movement. Just as in the late nineteenth century, hundreds of congregations, building new churches in the newest ring of suburbs now quite distant from their urban centers, now choose the amphitheatre form. Circular, wedgelike, oblong, or free form, these new auditoriums are easily read from the exterior, unlike their late nineteenth-century ancestors. Yet the congregations they house may be anything from Baptist to Lutheran to Roman Catholic. The fundamental appeal of this sanctuary form, however, remains the same today as in 1832: The amphitheatre space can accommodate a large audience in a way that allows everyone gathered to hear and see the performances taking place upon the stage. Analysis of the full ramifications of the reemergence of this desire to satisfy audiences' requirements—physical, psychological, social, and spiritual—must await another study; nevertheless, the contemporary revival of the evangelical auditorium underscores the significance of its development a century earlier. The audience-centered nature of evangelical worship is aptly expressed by this architectural form, and the buildings themselves attest to the slow emergence of interest in audience satisfaction in worship in the nineteenth century, its zenith in the auditorium churches of the 1880s and 1890s, its rapid decline in the early twentieth century, and its reemergence in the 1970s and 1980s.

Notes

1. On Wren's and Hawksmoor's churches, see Christopher Hibbert, *London's Churches* (London: Macdonald, 1988).

2. The ornamental balustrade that runs the length of the roof of First Church of Christ was not typical of the period, though it did echo a similar feature of St. Martin-in-the-Fields. On First Church of Christ, New Haven, see J. Frederick Kelly, *Early Connecticut Meetinghouses: Being an Account of the Church Edifices Built before 1830 Based Chiefly on Town and Parish Records* (New York: Columbia University Press, 1948), 2:3-21.

3. See Kelly, *Early Connecticut Meetinghouses*, 3-21. On the evolution from the colonial meetinghouse to the more churchly building type, see Peter W. Williams, "Metamorphoses of the Meetinghouse: Three Case Studies," in *Seeing beyond the Word: Visual Arts and the Calvinist Tradition*, edited by Paul Corby Finney, 479-505 (Grand Rapids, Mich.: Eerdmans, 1999); Peter Benes and Philip D. Zimmerman, *New England Meeting House and Church: 1630-1850* (Boston: Boston University for the Dublin Seminar for New England Folklife, 1979); and Edmund W. Sinnott, *Meetinghouse & Church in Early New England* (New York: McGraw-Hill, 1963). For interpretive analyses of the Federalist buildings, see Gretchen Townsend Buggeln, "Elegance and Sensibility in the Calvinist Tradition: The First Congregational Church of Hartford, Connecticut," in Finney, *Seeing beyond the Word*, 429-56; and James F. White, "From Protestant to Catholic Plain Style," in Finney, *Seeing beyond the Word*, 457-77.

4. For an early description of the church, see "The Minneapolis Dedication," *Minneapolis Daily Tribune*, n.d., clipping located in First Baptist Church Archives, Minneapolis, Minn.; and "A Visit to Minneapolis" (Chicago) *Standard*, 19 Dec. 1886.

5. On the idea that "the sacred" carries in-dwelling supernatural power while "the profane" does not, see Mircea Eliade, *The Sacred and the Profane: The Nature of Religion* (New York: Harcourt, Brace, 1959), 20-65. Smith, in contrast, places sacralization in the cultural context of the negotiation of power or, more specifically, in the political context of hierarchy reification. Ritual, he claims, whether negotiating differentiation (read: hierarchy) in terms of status based upon a purity-impurity distinction or power based upon a sacred-profane distinction, forces one to pay attention precisely to the critical differentiation. Space defines the boundaries of this attention: "When one enters a temple, one enters marked-off space . . . in which, at least in principle, nothing is accidental; everything, at least potentially, demands attention. The temple serves as a focusing lens, establishing the possibility of significance by directing attention, by requiring the percep-

tion of difference. Within the temple, the ordinary becomes significant, becomes 'sacred,' simply by being there. A ritual object or action becomes sacred by having attention focused on it in a highly marked way. From such a point of view, there is nothing that is inherently sacred or profane. These are not substantive categories, but rather situational ones. Sacrality is, above all, a category of emplacement." Jonathan Z. Smith, To Take Place: Toward Theory in Ritual (Chicago: University of Chicago Press, 1987), 103–5. The quotation appears on p. 104. For a further clarification of these perspectives, see David Chidester and Edward T. Linenthal, "Introduction," in American Sacred Space, edited by David Chidester and Edward T. Linenthal (Bloomington: Indiana University Press, 1995), 1–42.

6. On culture as the process of creating meaning and the role of religion in this process, see Clifford Geertz, "Religion as a Cultural System," in his The Interpretation of Cultures (New York: Basic, 1973), 87–125; Victor W. Turner, The Ritual Process: Structure and Anti-Structure (New York: Aldine, 1969), Dramas, Fields, and Metaphors: Symbolic Action in Human Society (Ithaca, N.Y. Cornell University Press, 1974), 23–59, and "Images and Reflection: Ritual, Drama, Carnival, Film, and Spectacle in Cultural Performance," in his The Anthropology of Performance (New York: PAJ, 1986), 21–32. My approach to architectural space has also been influenced by poststructuralism. See Umberto Eco, "Function and Sign: The Semiotics of Architecture," in Signs, Symbols, and Architecture, edited by Geoffrey Broadbent, Richard Bunt, and Charles Jencks (New York: Wiley, 1980), 11–69; and Charles Jencks, "The Architectural Sign," in the same volume, pp. 71–118. For my approach to the sociopolitical dynamics of space, I am indebted to Thomas A. Markus, Buildings and Power: Freedom and Control in the Origin of Modern Building Types (London: Routledge, 1993); Charles Goodsell, The Social Meaning of Civic Space (Lawrence: University of Kansas Press, 1988); Henri Lefebvre, The Production of Space, translated by Donald Nicholson-Smith (Cambridge: Blackwell, 1991); Jürgen Habermas, The Structural Transformation of the Public Sphere: An Inquiry into a Category of Bourgeois Society, translated by Thomas Burger and Frederick Lawrence (Cambridge, Mass.: MIT Press, 1989); and Amos Rapoport, The Meaning of the Built Environment: A Nonverbal Communication Approach (Beverly Hills, Calif.: Sage, 1982).

7. On the visual nature of the Eucharist service, see Eamon Duffy, The Stripping of the Altars: Traditional Religion in England, c. 1400–c. 1580 (New Haven, Conn.: Yale University Press, 1992), 91–130; and Joseph A. Jungmann, The Mass of the Roman Rite: Its Origins and Development, translated by Francis A. Brunner (London: Burns and Oates, 1959), 81–96. See also Francois Amiot, History of the Mass (New York: Hawthorne, 1959). On iconoclasm, see Duffy, Stripping of the Altars; and Stanford E. Lehmberg, The Reformation of Cathedrals: Cathedrals in English Society, 1485–1603 (Princeton, N.J.: Princeton University Press, 1988), 69–76. St. Peter's, an enormous statement of human wealth, clerical power, and artistic achievement, drew the censure of Martin Luther, who denounced the use of indulgences to finance the building; yet Luther did not favor iconoclasm and came out of seclusion in 1522 in part to denounce the destruction of churches by Karlstadt's followers. See Richard Marius, Martin Luther: The Christian between God and Death (Cambridge, Mass.: Harvard University Press, 1999), 317–35.

8. While good acoustics emerged as a new design principle, it should be noted that the science of acoustics was in its infancy and would not claim a significant role in architectural design until the eighteenth century.

9. This is not to say that the Protestant ministry had the exclusive authority to interpret Scripture, a power claimed by the Catholic magisterium. Protestants allowed individual interpretation—to a point. The role of the sermon was to illustrate the thinking processes of those most knowledgeable and educated in theology. Sermons began with the reading of a scriptural text, proceeded into a long analysis of the text in abstract terms, and then concluded with an application of the text to everyday life.

10. On revealing and concealing in the Mass, see Duffy, *Stripping of the Altars*, 91–130; and William Anderson and Clive Hicks, *The Rise of the Gothic* (Salem, N.H.: Salem House, 1985), 167.

11. On Anglican pulpits, see Dell Upton, *Holy Things and Profane: Anglican Parish Churches in Colonial Virginia* (Cambridge, Mass.: MIT Press, 1986), 133–38. On Puritan pulpits, see Benes and Zimmerman, *New England Meeting House*, 35–47.

12. For examples of Puritan religious objects, see Benes and Zimmerman, *New England Meeting House*, 69–105. On hourglasses, see Benes and Zimmerman, 47.

13. Patricia Bonomi, *Under the Cope of Heaven: Religion, Society, and Politics in Colonial America* (New York: Oxford University Press, 1986).

14. On the guildhall as the prototype for Puritan meetinghouses, see Marian Card Donnelly, *The New England Meeting Houses of the Seventeenth Century* (Middletown, Conn.: Wesleyan University Press, 1968), 91–108. On colonial Anglican churches, see Upton, *Holy Things and Profane*; and Sinnott, *Meetinghouse & Church*. For a discussion of the transformation of Anglican churches in England after the Reformation, see G. W. O. Addleshaw and Frederick Etchells, *The Architectural Setting of Anglican Worship* (London: Faber and Faber, 1948), 22–63.

15. Richard Biedrzynski, *Kirchen Unserer Zeit* (Munich: Hirmer Verlag, 1958), 29–33.

16. Donnelly, *New England Meeting Houses*, 24–29. The quotation is from p. 29.

17. Donnelly, *New England Meeting Houses*, 27.

18. See Peter Müller, *Die Frauenkirche in Dresden: Baugeschichte, Vergleiche, Restaurierungen, Zerstörung, Wiederaufbau* (Weimar: Böhlau Verlag, 1994); and Hans-Joachim Kuke, *Die Frauenkirche in Dresden: Ein Sankt Peter der wahren evangelischen Religion* (Worms: Wernersche Verlagsgesellschaft, 1996). See also *Die Dresdner Frauenkirche: Geschichete–Zerstörun–Rekonstruktion* (Dresden: Dresdner Hefte, 1993). Other examples include the Lutherische Kirche in Amsterdam (1666–1668) and the Theatrekirche in Munich.

19. On the panopticon and the function of surveillance in maintaining authority, see Michel Foucault, *Discipline and Punish: The Birth of the Prison*, translated by Alan Sheridan (New York: Vintage, 1979), 200–209; and Markus, *Buildings and Power* 71–77.

20. John Wesley, *The Journal of the Rev. John Wesley, A.M.*, edited by Nehemiah Curnock (London: Culley, 1909–1916), 5:187. Gwennap Pit was reconstructed in 1806, making it difficult to ascertain its original form. See C. C. Vyvyan, *Our Cornwall* (London: Westaway, 1948), 98–101; and Daphne du Maurier, *Vanishing Cornwall* (Garden City, N.Y.: Doubleday, 1967), 118–21. On Whitefield in Cornwall, see Arnold A. Dallimore, *George Whitefield: The Life and Times of the Great Evangelist of the Eighteenth-Century Revival* (Edinburgh: Banner of Truth Trust, 1980), 2:284. On Wesley, see also John Wesley, *The Works of John Wesley*, edited by W. Reginald Ward and Richard P. Heitzenrater, vol. 21 (Nashville, Tenn.: Abingdon, 1992). Wesley's 20,000 estimate is debatable. See John S. Simon, *John Wesley: The Master-Builder* (London: Epworth, 1927), 200.

21. On evangelical tabernacles and meetinghouses in England, see Christopher Stell, *An Inventory of Nonconformist Chapels and Meeting-Houses in the North of England* (London: Her Majesty's Stationary Office, 1994), "Puritan and Nonconformist Meetinghouses in England," in Finney, *Seeing beyond the Word*, 49–83, and "Chapels and Meeting-Houses in Greater Manchester," *Archaeological Journal* 144 (1987): 7–11; and John Betjeman, "Nonconformist Architecture," *Architectural Review* 88 (Dec. 1940): 160–74. On Whitefield's tabernacles in London and Bristol, see Dallimore, *George Whitefield*, 2:355–63; and James Paterson Gledstone, *The Life and Travels of George Whitefield* (London: Longmans, Green, 1871), 441–42.

22. Furthermore, because amphitheatres, as will be argued in a later chapter, encourage a kind of audience cohesion that renders them a corporate group in counterpoint to the speaker, this spatial plan directly countered the individualism of the holiness practices. A more sugges-

tive development was the practice of building camp-meeting tabernacles circular in form. Finney himself used a large canvas tent in his early years in Oberlin to house meeting audiences. See Charles G. Finney, *The Memoirs of Charles G. Finney*, edited by Garth M. Rosell and Richard A. G. Dupuis (Grand Rapids, Mich.: Academie, 1989), 383–84; and James H. Fairchild, *Oberlin: The Colony and the College, 1833–1883* (Oberlin, Ohio: Goodrich, 1883), 73.

23. Wesley, *Works*, 388. Another striking illustration of the use of elevation to demonstrate and enhance religious power appears in the *Narrative of Sojourner Truth*. One evening during a camp meeting in Northampton that Sojourner Truth was attending, a group of rowdy young men attempted to interrupt the holy proceedings. Truth first huddled in her tent, fearful of the boisterous shouts of the crowd and concerned that she would be a target given that she was the only black person present. She soon rallied, however, and decided to not let pass an opportunity to defend the Lord. She left her tent and strode to the "top of a small rise of ground" where she began to sing a hymn. Her elevation, though slight in a landscape described as "open fields," was important enough to mention, and the image of this small, black woman, elevated a bit above an angry crowd while steadfastly singing about Christ, was an image well-designed to move nineteenth-century audiences. Margaret Washington, ed., *Narrative of Sojourner Truth* (New York: Vintage, 1993): 93–95.

24. Whitefield biographer Arnold Dallimore claims that the preacher in this engraving is Whitefield and that the scene is in Cornwall. There is little evidence, however, to substantiate these claims. On Whitefield in Cornwall, see Dallimore, *George Whitefield*, 2:284. Multiple attempts to ascertain information about this engraving have proved unsuccessful. The artist, the subject, and the location of the original remain unknown.

25. Talbot Hamlin, *Benjamin Henry Latrobe* (New York: Oxford University Press, 1955), 319–22. On other camp meetings, see Ellen Weiss, *City in the Woods: The Life and Design of an American Camp Meeting on Martha's Vineyard* (New York: Oxford University Press, 1987); and Charles A. Johnson, *The Frontier Camp Meeting: Religion's Harvest Time* (Dallas, Tex.: Southern Methodist University Press, 1955). On camp-meeting plans, see Steven D. Cooley, "Manna and the Manual: Sacramental and Instrumental Constructions of the Victorian Methodist Camp Meeting during the Mid-Nineteenth Century," *Religion and American Culture: A Journal of Interpretation* 6 (Summer 1996): 131–60.

26. See Francis Ward, *An Account of Three Camp-Meetings Held by the Methodists, at Sharon, Litchfield County, Connecticut; at Rhinebeck, in Dutchess County; and at Petersburgh, in Rensselaer County, New-York State* (Brooklyn, N.Y.: Robinson & Little, 1806), 3, 12. The author is indebted to Lester Ruth for this source. Reference to the Millerite camp meeting appears in "The Millerites at Long Branch," *Boston Courier*, 24 July 1843, 3.

27. Though these four evangelical denominations clearly dominated the congregations constructing this type of religious building, the Christian exceptions I have found also share the evangelical outlook. Among these are Evangelical Lutherans and German Evangelicals. In addition, this general building type—an amphitheatre interior with a Richardsonian Romanesque facade sans the lofty steeple—was also adopted for synagogues. Jewish architect Dankmar Adler, who used the type in a Methodist amphitheatre and the formerly Presbyterian Central Music Hall in Chicago, used it as well in the Kehilath Anshe Ma'ariv Temple (1891) and Temple Isaiah (1899) in the same city. These buildings are discussed in Charles E. Gregersen, *Dankmar Adler: His Theatres and Auditoriums* (Athens: Swallow Press and Ohio University Press, 1990).

Chapter 2

1. Immigration figures are from the U.S. Immigration and Naturalization Service, 1991, as quoted in George B. Tindall and David E. Shi, *America: A Narrative History*, 3d ed., brief (New York: Norton, 1993), 40–41. New York population figures are from *King's Handbook of New*

York City, 2d ed. (Boston: Moses King, 1893), 47. See also Nan A. Rothschild, *New York City Neighborhoods: The 18th Century* (New York: Academic, 1990), 108. For descriptions of the growing city, see "City Rambles," *New York Mirror and Ladies Literary Gazette*, 12 May 1832, 358–59; and Edward Ruggles, *A Picture of New York in 1846* (New York: Francis, 1846). See also Betsy Blackmar, "Re-walking the 'Walking City': Housing and Property Relations in New York City, 1780–1840," *Radical History Review* 21 (Fall 1979): 131–48; Edward Pessen, *Riches, Class, and Power before the Civil War* (Lexington, Mass.: Heath, 1973), 169–204; and Jay Dolan, *The Immigrant Church: New York's Irish and German Catholics, 1815–1865* (Baltimore, Md.: Johns Hopkins University Press, 1975).

2. Jürgen Habermas, *Jürgen Habermas on Society and Politics: A Reader*, edited by Steven Seidman (Boston: Beacon, 1989), 231–36, and *The Structural Transformation of the Public Sphere: An Inquiry into a Category of Bourgeois Society*, translated by Thomas Burger and Frederick Lawrence (Cambridge, Mass.: MIT Press, 1989), 89–102. On the U.S. public in this period, see Mary P. Ryan, "Gender and Public Access: Women's Politics in Nineteenth-Century America," in *Habermas and the Public Sphere*, edited by Craig Calhoun (Cambridge, Mass.: MIT Press, 1992), 267–71.

3. On Protestant denominations' relationship to political parties of the period, see Richard J. Carwardine, *Evangelicals and Politics in Antebellum America* (New Haven, Conn.: Yale University Press, 1993), 121–32. On similar challenges faced by Episcopalian and Dutch Reformed congregations, see Jonathan Greenleaf, *A History of the Churches of All Denominations in the City of New York, from the First Settlement to the Year 1846* (New York, French 1846), 171.

4. Led by silk merchants Arthur and Lewis Tappan, the group also included Moses Allen, David Low Dodge, Silas Holmes, Eleazar Lord, Zachariah Lewis, Peletiah Perit, Anson G. Phelps, Judge Jonas Platt and his son Zaphania Platt, and Knowles Taylor. Their motivations were multiple and complex. Although members of Presbyterian churches in New·York, they all had previous experience with Congregational organizations in New England, and they found the ecclesiastical nature of the presbytery stifling, particularly as they became increasingly interested in religious responses to societal ills. Stymied in their attempts to organize Congregational churches in the city, the men looked to alternatives within the presbytery for addressing social issues. See letter from Tappan to Finney, 22 Mar. 1832, CGFP, Oberlin College Archives; Keith J. Hardman, *Charles Grandison Finney, 1792–1875: Revivalist and Reformer* (Grand Rapids, Mich.: Baker Book House, 1987), 175–91; exhaustive notes by Rosell and Dupuis in Charles G. Finney, *The Memoirs of Charles G. Finney*, edited by Garth M. Rosell and Richard A. G. Dupuis (Grand Rapids, Mich.: Academie, 1989), 356–62; Henry Fowler, *The American Pulpit* (New York: Fairchild, 1856), 32–38; Joseph P. Thompson, *The Last Sabbath in the Broadway Tabernacle: A Historical Discourse* (New York: Calkins & Stiles, 1857), 7–14; Susan Hayes Ward, *History of the Broadway Tabernacle Church* (New York: Broadway Tabernacle Church, 1901), 22–31; and L. Nelson Nichols, *The History of the Broadway Tabernacle of New York City* (New Haven, Conn: Tuttle, Morehouse and Taylor, 1940), 41–57.

5. It should be noted that the term *free church* has been used in a variety of ways by various Protestant religious groups. For instance, some, like the Free Methodists, have used the phrase to indicate congregational independence from denominational ties while remaining associated with the denomination. Others, like the Evangelical Free Church, have used it to indicate complete denominational independence. The term *free church* is also applied to German pietist groups like the Amish, Mennonites, and Hutterites.

6. Although some auctioned pews went for as much as $1,300 per year, the average was about $250, still well out of reach of the working and artisan classes. See Charles C. Cole, Jr., "The Free Church Movement in New York City," *New York History* 34 (July 1953): 284–85.

7. Gardiner Spring, *The Danger and Hope of the American People: A Discourse on the Day of the Annual Thanksgiving, in the State of New-York* (New York: Trow, 1843), 18–19. See also Clifford S. Griffin, "Religious Benevolence as Social Control, 1815–1860," *Mississippi Valley Historical*

Review 44 (Dec. 1957): 436; and Amy Bridges, *A City in the Republic: Antebellum New York and the Origins of Machine Politics* (New York: Cambridge University Press, 1984), 89.

8. For historical analyses of revivalism, see Bernard A. Weisberger, *They Gathered at the River: The Story of the Great Revivalists and Their Impact upon Religion in America* (Boston: Little, Brown, 1958); William G. McLoughlin, Jr., *Modern Revivalism: Charles Grandison Finney to Billy Graham* (New York: Ronald Press, 1959); and Nathan O. Hatch, *The Democratization of American Christianity* (New Haven, Conn.: Yale University Press, 1989), 195–201. For Finney's views on revivalism, see Charles G. Finney, *Lectures on Revival of Religion*, edited by William G. McLoughlin (Cambridge, Mass.: Harvard University Press, Belknap Press, 1960). An excellent account of the opposition to Finney's revivals appears in Hardman, *Finney*, 104–32.

9. See Finney, *Lectures on Revival*. On the new measures, see Richard Carwardine, "The Second Great Awakening in the Urban Centers: An Examination of Methodism and the 'New Measures,'" *Journal of American History* 59 (1972): 327–40. On Finney's theology, see Charles E. Hambrick-Stowe, *Charles G. Finney and the Spirit of American Evangelicalism* (Grand Rapids, Mich.: Eerdmans, 1996), 79–82.

10. On Finney's early revivals and his relationship with the New York ministers and the Association of Gentlemen, see Hardman, *Finney*, 150–86.

11. Charles Hambrick-Stowe, "The American Evangelicalism of Charles G. Finney," paper presented at the spring meeting of the American Society of Church History, Oberlin, Ohio, Mar. 1994, 5.

12. Marianne Perciaccante argues that the selection of Finney did not necessarily indicate a full-blown antiformalism but represented a negotiated middle ground between traditional Presbyterian formalism and Arminian antiformalism. See Perciaccante, "The Demographics of Diversity in the Burned-Over District," paper presented at the American Society for Church History Annual Spring Meeting, 24–26 Mar. 1994, Oberlin, Ohio. See also her "Calling Down Fire: Charles Grandison Finney and Revivalism in Jefferson County, New York, 1800–1840" (Ph.D. diss., Univ. of Virgina, 1992). On the Association of Gentlemen and its agenda, see Bertram Wyatt-Brown, *Lewis Tappan and the Evangelical War against Slavery* (Cleveland, Ohio: Press of Case Western Reserve University, 1969), 60–62. On Tappan's early moral reform activities, see Wyatt-Brown, 52–55.

13. In England, both Wesley and Whitefield had addressed this question in the late eighteenth century. See Arnold A. Dallimore, *George Whitefield: The Life and Times of the Great Evangelist of the Eighteenth-Century Revival* (Edinburgh: Banner of Truth Trust, 1980), 2:355–63; Christopher Stell, "Puritan and Nonconformist Meetinghouses in England," in *Seeing beyond the Word: Visual Arts and the Calvinist Tradition*, edited by Paul Corby Finney (Grand Rapids, Mich.: Eerdmans, 1999), 49–81; Stell, *An Inventory of Nonconformist Chapels and Meeting-Houses in the North of England* (London: Her Majesty's Stationary Office, 1994); and John Betjeman, "Nonconformist Architecture," *Architectural Review* 88 (Dec. 1940): 160–74.

14. *New York Evangelist*, 29 May 1830, 35. See also Hardman, *Finney*, 183, 186–90. The free churches were supported primarily through donations made during meetings, but the organizers, particularly the Tappans, Anson G. Phelps, and William Green, came to the rescue when offerings did not meet expenses.

15. For instance, revival meetings held by the Reverend Joel Parker, Finney's associate from Rochester, initially met in a small lecture room but soon moved into Broadway Hall, one of the largest meeting rooms in the city. See Thompson, *Last Sabbath*, 9; Nichols, *History*, 51. For building descriptions, see Lewis Tappan, "History of the Free Churches in the City of New York," *New York Evangelist*, 21 Feb. 1835, 29–30.

16. Other denominations as well as the Presbyterians used whatever space was available. As early as 1801, a Presbyterian group may have met in the Angus Long Room, a building used for "city assemblies," or dances. See Henry Dickinson Stone, *Personal Recollections of the Drama; or, Theatrical Reminiscences* (1873; repr. New York: Benjamin Blom, 1969), 21.

17. Tappan, "History"; Fowler, *American Pulpit*, 34. It is interesting to note that a dissenting segment of the congregation lamented the loss of revenue that would result from prohibiting liquor sales on the premises.

18. For descriptions of the Pearl Street area, see Asa Greene, *A Glance at New York* (New York: Greene, 1837), 2–3, and, *The Perils of Pearl Street* (New York: Betts and Anstice, 1834). Nearly bankrupt, Chatham Street Theatre lessee William Blanchard, a circus owner, had sublet the property to actor/manager Thomas Hamblin. For details of the sale, see Joseph N. Ireland, *Records of the New York Stage, from 1750–1860* (New York: Morrell, 1867), 2:33; Tappan's letters to Finney dated 16 and 22 Mar. 1832, CGFP, Oberlin College Archives; and Hardman, *Finney*, 475 n28. Tappan and Green had also negotiated with the owners of the Bowery Theatre, apparently at the encouragement of Finney, but it proved too costly, and Tappan felt the location of the Chatham Theatre was more advantageous. See Tappan to Finney, 16 Mar 1832, CGFP.

19. Although not the first time that Protestant services had been held in a theatre, this did, however, start something of a trend in New York City. As moral reform groups increasingly denounced the theatre as a haven for immoral behavior, several theatres became the targets of "conversion." Under the headline "Another Theatre Converted," the Presbyterian *New York Observer* described the sale of the Norfolk Theatre to a Methodist Protestant congregation (4 May 1833). In 1835 Lewis Tappan secured the middle-class Niblo's Saloon for a Finney meeting (Cole, "Free Church Movement," 293). The Pearl Street Theatre was sold to the St. Paul's Episcopal congregation, which used it for a church from 1839 to 1862 (Stone, *Personal Recollections*, 9).

20. Evangelicals had condemned the theatre with tracts, sermons, and newspaper articles that denounced the immorality that characterized both the actors' performances and the audiences' activities. See Bruce A. McConachie, *Melodramatic Formations: American Theatre and Society, 1820–1870* (Iowa City: University of Iowa Press, 1992), 161–97; and Harrold C. Shiffler, "The Opposition of the Presbyterian Church in the United States of America to the Theatre in America, 1750–1891" (Ph.D. diss., State University of Iowa, 1953), 159–64.

21. On the problems of ascertaining the precise status of the women who occupied the third tier, see Rosemarie K. Bank, "Hustlers in the House: The Bowery Theatre as a Mode of Historical Information," in *The American Stage: Social and Economic Issues from the Colonial Period to the Present*, edited by Ron Engle and Tice L. Miller (New York: Cambridge University Press, 1993), 47–64. See also Bruce A. McConachie, "Museum Theatre and the Problem of Respectability for Mid-Century Urban Americans," in the same volume, 65–80; Richard Butsch, "Bowery B'hoys and Matinee Ladies: The Re-Gendering of Nineteenth-Century American Theater Audiences," *American Quarterly* 46 (Sept. 1994): 374–405; and David Grimsted, *Melodrama Unveiled: American Theater and Culture, 1800–1850* (Chicago: University of Chicago Press, 1968).

22. For a description of the Chatham (Garden) Theatre, see William C. Young, *Documents of American Theater History* (Chicago: American Library Association, 1973), 1:72–74; see also George C. D. Odell, *Annals of the New York Stage* (New York: Columbia University Press, 1928), 3:533. The *New York Mirror* cites competition as a key factor in the Chatham's decline, suggesting that the city cannot "adequately support three [respectable] theatres." See "The Drama," *New York Mirror*, 2 May 1831, 358. See also McConachie, *Melodramatic Formations*, 121.

23. Quoted in a letter from Lewis Tappan to Finney, 16 Mar. 1832, CGFP.

24. Tappan to Finney, 16 Mar. 1832, CGFP. For the context of Finney's fears, see Hardman, *Finney*; 183–238.

25. Tappan to Finney, 22 Mar. 1832, CGFP. See also Fowler, *American Pulpit*, 35.

26. Thompson, *Last Sabbath*, 11. Thompson served as the fourth pastor of the Broadway Tabernacle, which succeeded the Chatham Street Chapel, and cannot be considered a wholly impartial witness.

27. This process of meaning negotiation was acknowledged by a close friend of Finney, Herman Norton: "The Theatre we trust is taken out of the hands of the Devil & will hereafter become a Bethesda. Your voice will one day I hope be heard there proclaiming salvation where have stood the Gates of Hell." Letter from Norton to Finney, 10 Apr. 1832, CGFP.

28. "Chatham Theatre," *New York Mirror and Ladies Literary Gazette,* 14 Oct. 1826, 95. On actor-audience relationships and the role of managers in the early theatre, see Bruce A. McConachie, "Pacifying American Theatrical Audiences, 1820–1900," in *For Fun and Profit: The Transformation of Leisure into Consumption,* edited by Richard Butsch (Philadelphia: Temple University Press, 1990), 47–70.

29. For early accounts of theatre riots, see Odell, *Annals,* 548–50; and Philip Hone, *The Diary of Philip Hone, 1828–1851* (New York: Dodd, Mead, 1889), 39–41. For historical analyses, see Richard Butsch, "American Theater Riots and Class Relations, 1754–1849," *Theatre Annual* 48 (1995): 41–59; Paul A. Gilje, *The Road to Mobocracy: Popular Disorder in New York City, 1763–1834* (Chapel Hill: University of North Carolina Press and Institute of Early American History and Culture, 1987), 246–52; Sean Wilentz, *Chants Democratic: New York City & the Rise of the American Working Class, 1788–1850* (New York: Oxford University Press, 1984); McConachie, *Melodramatic Formations;* J. T. Headley, *The Great Riots of New York, 1712–1873* (New York: Treat, 1873; facsimile ed. Miami, Fla.: Mnemosyne, 1969); and Leonard L. Richards, *"Gentlemen of Property and Standing": Anti-Abolition Mobs in Jacksonian America* (New York: Oxford University Press, 1970).

30. Tappan to Finney, 16 Mar. 1832, CGFP. Tappan, "History," 29–30.

31. Although Tappan emphasized that "We see what wonderful success our Methodist brethren have had by alluring to their houses of worship the middling classes of society, 'firing low,' as their great leader, Wesley, enjoined it upon them," the free churches were partly supported by the collection plate (with the assistance of wealthy supporters), so attracting members of financial means was advantageous. See Tappan, "History." For a discussion of class identification in this period, see Stuart Blumin, *The Emergence of the Middle Class: Social Experience in the American City, 1760–1900* (New York: Cambridge University Press, 1989).

32. Part of the appeal of these groups lay precisely in their antiformalism, which could be interpreted as a critique of respectability itself. For rural and laboring classes suspicious of those higher on the economic scale, antiformalist religion justified their position by condemning the lifestyles of elites. On religion and respectability among Methodists and Baptists, see Hatch, *Democratization,* 201–6; and Janet Moore Lindman, "Ritual Practice and the Creation of Baptist Orthodoxy in Eighteenth-Century America," paper presented at the American Studies Association Annual Meeting, 11 Nov. 1998, Pittsburgh. See also Richard L. Bushman, *The Refinement of America: Persons, Houses, Cities* (New York: Knopf, 1992), 325–26.

33. In the context of competition for religious audiences, Tappan considered the possibility that the chapel would siphon members from Gardiner Spring's Brick Church and concluded, in the spirit of the new breed of religious entrepreneur, so be it. "Would it be murdering souls to draw away half of Dr. Spring's congregations?" he asked, only partly facetiously. Letter from Tappan to Finney, 16 Mar. 1832, CGFP.

34. Letter from Tappan to Finney, 19 Apr. 1832, CGFP. See also letter from Tappan to Finney, 11 Apr. 1832, CGFP. In England, the term *chapel* carried strong connotations of dissenting religious perspectives. While no direct evidence suggests that this association informed the free church's selection, such a connection is not improbable.

35. *New York Mirror,* 15 May 1824. See also Young, *Documents,* 73.

36. "Chatham Theatre," *New York Mirror and Ladies' Literary Gazette,* 14 Oct. 1826, 95.

37. Odell chronicles the changes and decline of the Chatham Street Theatre in *Annals,* 119–21, 278, 355, 469, 527, 533, 590. See also "American Opera House," *New York Mirror and Ladies' Literary Gazette,* 6 June 1829, 383. The *New York Mirror,* first published in 1826, also

served as a means of encouraging the "respectable" theatre. Reviews printed in the *Mirror* endorsed shows that were aimed at mixed-sex audiences and assured female readers of the appropriateness of their attendance. For more on the encouragement of female audiences, see McConachie, "Pacifying American Theatrical Audiences," 47–70; and Robert C. Allen, *Horrible Prettiness: Burlesque and American Culture* (Chapel Hill: University of North Carolina Press, 1991), 61–75.

38. McConachie, "Pacifying American Theatrical Audiences," 53–60.

39. On actors' authority, see McConachie, "Pacifying American Theatrical Audiences," 47–70. Despite the potential for property damage that theatre demonstrations carried, theatre owners were often hesitant to jeopardize box office receipts by calling in the police to suppress demonstrations. Accustomed to using architectural strategies to attract wealthy patrons, theatre owners began to manipulate their auditoriums with an eye toward discouraging rowdy behavior and encouraging self-control among their patrons. The Chatham's attempt to attract women is an example. On the development of the proscenium theatre, see Christos G. Athanasopulos, *Contemporary Theatre: Evolution and Design* (New York: Wiley, 1983), 71–98.

40. Letter from Tappan to Finney, 16 Mar. 1832, CGFP.

41. The free-church Presbyterians spent about $7,000 on the remodeling. See Young, *Documents*, 72–74, for the earliest description of the theatre. One can only wonder whether the Presbyterians removed the bas-relief ornaments of the proscenium (including figures of Thalia, the Muse of comedy, and Melpomene, the Muse of tragedy, and the aforementioned busts of Washington, Jefferson, Franklin, and Jackson with their encircling wreaths of gold), the statues of Shakespeare and Garrick, and the Italian alabaster vases that had graced the stage. Several people were quite concerned about the safety of the supports under the tiers. As the tiers held the bulk of the theatre audience, the strength of the supports was critical. The potential deficiencies of such tier supports were frequently described in journalistic accounts of the openings of new or newly renovated theatres, suggesting that a number of collapses occurred. On the remodeling, see letters from Tappan to Finney, 16 Mar. 1832, 22 March 1832, 11 Apr. 1832, and 19 Apr. 1832, CGFP; Finney, *Memoirs*, 360; and Fowler, *American Pulpit*, 36–37.

42. *New York Evangelist*, 12 May 1832. According to this article, footsteps in the uncarpeted aisles and hallways, along with the opening and shutting of gallery doors, created a great deal of superfluous noise in the room during the heavily attended opening services. Finney biographer Keith Hardman surmises that the extraneous noise was a serious detriment and a contributing factor in the decision to build a new church (Hardman, *Finney*, 252–53, 301). I have not found any other evidence to suggest that superfluous noise was problematic. Given Parker's satisfaction with the space and Finney's later attempts to replicate aspects of the Chatham interior, I suspect that measures were taken to suppress excess noise, perhaps by imposing behavior restrictions on visitors or by the installation of carpets. Testimony to the chapel's amenities comes from Joel Parker, who declared upon seeing the building and the close proximity of the seating to the pulpit, "If I were to build a church it should be in this form" (Tappan to Finney, 22 Mar. 1832, CGFP). An account of the initial meeting, held on 6 May 1832, appeared in the *New York Evangelist*, 12 May 1832. See also Hardman, *Finney*, 251–52.

43. In his excellent study of the relationships between revival religion and democratizing impulses, Nathan Hatch calls this the "Copernican revolution" in U.S. religious history, which made "religious life audience-centered," a process that "blurred the distinction between pulpit and pew" (*Democratization*, 197, 226). Hatch's argument that by "conveying the indigenous methods of popular culture to the middle class," Finney "introduced democratic modifications into respectable institutions" (199) informs much of my analysis of the Chatham Street Chapel. Yet, while Hatch sees Finney as playing a transitional role in a process of chronological change, I find that focusing on his (temporary) role as a negotiator among diverse discourses is more helpful, precisely because many of the changes Finney instigated were soon abandoned by re-

spectable congregations precisely because they were rooted in popular discourse. For instance, Finney himself abandoned his critique of an educated clergy, taking a position as professor of theology at Oberlin College in 1835 and making quite sharp distinctions between "pulpit and pew." See Hatch, *Democratization*, 193–209.

44. That Finney routinely scanned his audiences for familiar faces, for anxious faces, and for faces that suggested sinful activity is made abundantly clear in his *Memoirs*; see, for instance, 432–37. For Finney's use of confederates in the tiers, see his *Memoirs*, 360.

45. Michael Schwarzer, "The Social Genesis of the Public Theater in Germany," in *Karl Friedrich Schinkel: The Drama of Architecture*, edited by John Zukowsky (Chicago: Art Institute of Chicago, 1994), 58. See also Athanasopulos, *Contemporary Theatre*, 71–98.

46. A further consequence of the proscenium theatre was the erection of the "fourth wall," the convention that audiences are merely eavesdropping on a (real) scene through an invisible wall separating viewers from performers. The decorum gradually associated with this fourth-wall convention ultimately put an end to the interactions between performers and audience members. While, technically, preaching erects no such wall, the convention of passive attention grew strong, particularly among elite congregations, which associated such behavior with refinement. Religious performers like Finney, who needed to maintain more than the audience's gaze, used their performances and the New Measures to elicit audience participation. See James H. Johnson, *Listening in Paris: A Cultural History* (Berkeley: University of California Press, 1995); and John F. Kasson, *Rudeness and Civility: Manners in Nineteenth-Century Urban America* (New York: Hill and Wang, 1990), 216–56.

47. For descriptions of Finney's preaching style, see Weisberger, *They Gathered at the River*, 101–3; Hardman, *Finney*, 99–100; Robert Samuel Fletcher, *A History of Oberlin College: From Its Foundation through the Civil War* (Oberlin, Ohio: Oberlin College, 1943), 1:575–79; and R. A. Cheesebro, "The Preaching of Charles G. Finney" (Ph.D. diss., Yale University, 1948), 146–67.

48. Fletcher, *History of Oberlin College*, 16. Fletcher is quoting from John Ware, *Memoir of the Life of Henry Ware, Jr.* (Boston: Munroe, 1846), 179–81.

49. Theatre actors were contending with similar issues of authority during this period, but they approached them as a group that had never enjoyed much authority. McConachie argues that theatre owners and managers encouraged and guided the development of the "star" system, which allowed particular actors to gain great authority over audiences in much the same way that Finney did. See McConachie, "Pacifying American Theatrical Audiences," 53–60.

50. Letter from Mrs. C. L. Brown to Finney, 12 June 1834, CGFP.

51. On other ways Finney merged these, see Hatch, *Democratization*, 193–201. It should also be noted that despite the signal role of charismatic authority, much of the rhetoric of the clergy remained embedded in traditional views of access to authority, i.e., through divine office. The "Principles" of the Broadway Tabernacle Church, the Chatham Street Chapel's successor, stated, "The ministry is of divine origin, intended for the sanctification of believers, for the conversion of sinners, and the reproof of the wicked, and to continue to the end of the world." *New York Evangelist*, 23 Apr. 1836, 65.

52. That charisma was vital and architecture alone could not produce clerical authority is apparent in the sudden decline of the Chatham congregation during Finney's absence from the chapel for health reasons in 1834. The Reverend John Ingersoll, who served in the pulpit in his stead, lacked his engaging style. Letters to Charles and Lydia Finney during this period contain criticism of Ingersoll and his tedious preaching style, and Finney was dismayed to see upon his return how the congregation had shrunk. See Finney, *Memoirs*, 365–67 nn. 39, 43; C. L. Brown to Mrs. Charles G. Finney, 12 June 1834, CGFP; and William Green to Finney, 3 Sept. 1834, CGFP.

53. Here I draw upon the conceptualization of the private as that having to do with the personal and domestic, within the Greek *oikos* rather than the *polis*. See Habermas, *Structural Transformation*, 3–5 and 43–51.

54. See Habermas, *Structural Transformation*, 19. He draws upon Hannah Arendt, *The Human Condition* (Chicago: University of Chicago Press, 1958), 46. He also points out that "subjectivity, as the innermost core of the private, was always already oriented to an audience (*Publikum*)" (49).

55. A plea for members to be generous in their financial contributions appears in *Church Manual for the Communicants of the Second Free Presbyterian Church, Worshipping at the Chatham-Street Chapel* (New York: Dorr and Butterfield, 1834), 35–36.

56. For a full list of organizations, see *New York Evangelist*, 3 May 1835, 2. See also Hardman, *Finney*, 185.

57. On clerical support for colonization, see John R. Bodo, *The Protestant Clergy and Public Issues, 1812–1848* (Princeton, N.J.: Princeton University Press, 1954), 139–42.

58. Finney's position on issues of race was less clear-cut, again because of his ultimate concern for salvation, not worldly existence. He did require African-American participants at his meetings to sit segregated on one side of the chapel. Nevertheless, he denounced slavery from the pulpit and routinely refused to serve Communion to slaveholders. See Hardman, *Finney*, 262, 273–75. See also the Communion exclusions in the *Church Manual*, 46.

59. The white audience did not allow Brown the authority to make a regular speech; instead a panel quizzed him on his experiences in Liberia. Questions could be asked from the floor, but they also had to be submitted in writing and signed by the questioner. A transcription of the examination appears in the *New York Evangelist*, supp., 9 and 10 May 1834.

60. Finney was not present during the July 1834 riots, having left New York City in January for a trip through the Mediterranean; he returned to Boston on 14 July but did not return to New York and Chatham Street until later in the year (Finney, *Memoirs*, 362 n29, 365 n39, 366 n43). On Lewis Tappan's response, see his letter to Theodore Weld, 10 July 1834, in *Letters of Theodore Dwight Weld, Angelina Grimké Weld and Sarah Grimké*, edited by Gilbert H. Barnes and Dwight L. Dumond (Gloucester, Mass.: Peter Smith, 1965), 1:153–56; Lewis Tappan, "Fourth of July in New York," *Emancipator*, 7 July 1834; and Lewis Tappan, *The Life of Arthur Tappan* (New York: Hurd and Houghton, 1870), 205–9. For further primary accounts sympathetic to the antislavery cause in the series of riots during this month, see the *Emancipator and Journal of Public Morals*, 7, 22, 29 July 1834. For views opposing the antislavery cause, see the Presbyterian newspaper the *New York Observer*, 12 July 1834; the *Courier and Enquirer*, 8, 18, 22 July 1834; and the *Commercial Advertiser*, 5 and 8 July 1834. Historical analyses appear in Headley, *Great Riots*, 79–96; Gilje, *Road to Mobocracy*, 162–69; and Linda K. Kerber, "Abolitionists and Amalgamators: The New York City Race Riots of 1834," *New York History* 48 (Jan. 1967): 28–39.

61. The *Journal of Commerce*, quoted in the *New York Observer*, 12 July 1834, 111.

62. *Emancipator*, 29 July 1834, 3.

63. See Habermas, *Structural Transformation*, 1–26.

64. I echo Stewart's language here. See James Brewer Stewart, "Modernizing 'Difference': The Political Meanings of Color in the Free States, 1776–1840," *Journal of the Early Republic* 19 (Winter 1999): 702–3. For an excellent discussion of the politics of race during this period, see the issue of the *Journal of the Republic* 18 (Summer 1998) devoted to the topic, which includes Stewart's essay "The Emergence of Racial Modernity and the Rise of the White North, 1790–1840" (181–217), with comments by Jean L. Soderlund, James Oliver Horton, and Ronald G. Walters.

65. David Zaret, "Religion, Science, and Printing in the Public Spheres in Seventeenth-Century England," in *Habermas and the Public Sphere*, edited by Craig Calhoun (Cambridge, Mass.: MIT Press, 1993), 221, 223.

66. Habermas, quoted in Zaret, "Religion, Science, and Printing," 223.

67. Zaret, "Religion, Science, and Printing," 223.

68. Finney, Memoirs, 364 n35. This scheme may have been conceived as a means of keeping Finney, who had since the spring of 1835 also served as head of the newly formed Oberlin College, in New York City. According to Hardman, Finney originally intended to return to New York each winter to preach (Finney, 298-99). Green and Dimond provided the bulk of financial support. Their dedication to the project stemmed from a variety of sources: Dimond, who had trained as a mechanic and had grown wealthy as a jeweler coterminous with his conversion to Christianity, had pledged his life and wealth to Christian causes; Green, an ardent abolitionist, had contributed to the creation of the Chatham Street Chapel and hoped to expand its anti-slavery influence. Finney himself was becoming increasingly engaged in efforts to provide education for the up-and-coming free-church ministry, having moved on from his earlier disparagement of educated clergy during the 1820s.

69. Finney, Memoirs, 367. See also Nichols, History, 59-60; and Ward, History of Broadway Tabernacle, 27-30.

70. Finney, Memoirs, 354.

71. After the congregation moved even farther uptown in 1857, the church came to be known as the Worth Street Church when Anthony Street was renamed Worth. See Nichols, History, 58-60.

72. Old School (Calvinist) Presbyterians, beleaguered by the increasingly popular modified Calvinism of the New Haven theology, tried several Yale ministers for heresy in the mid-1830s. Finney, who had flirted with Arminianism for a decade, was a likely candidate for such charges. Frustrated with the Third Presbyterian Synod (and it with him), he transferred his ordination to Congregationalism. On the development of the Broadway Tabernacle, see Ward, History of Broadway Tabernacle, 27-33, which includes the Broadway Tabernacle's "Principles and Rules" (224-26) and "Articles of Christian Faith and Church Government" (226-29). See also Nichols, History, 58-64; Finney, Memoirs, 361-62 n25; and Hardman, Finney, 311.

73. Dissenting chapels in England did include some of the distinctive amphitheatre features, specifically, ranked seating within galleries that encircled preaching rooms. Whitefield's chapel in Tottenham Court, London, was the best known. Finney, however, would not visit England until 1849. Free-church leader Anson Phelps had visited England in 1833 though it is not known whether he had any input on the design. See Hardman, Finney, 398. On dissenting chapels, see John Betjeman, "Nonconformist Architecture," 160-74; Stell, North of England; Christopher Stell, An Inventory of Nonconformist Chapels and Meeting-Houses in Central England (London: Her Majesty's Stationary Office, 1986), and "Chapels and Meeting-Houses in Greater Manchester," Archaeological Journal 144 (1987): 7-11.

74. Finney, Memoirs, 367.

75. Joseph Thompson repeats these figures in a number of his writings; see, for instance, Memoir of David Hale (New York: Wiley, 1850), 62.

76. The earliest sketch published in Frank Leslie's Illustrated Newspaper, 15 Mar. 1856, 212, indicates a level floor. An 1857 sketch based on the Leslie's illustration indicates a raked, or sloped, floor. See Thompson, Last Sabbath, frontispiece; also Nichols, History, 59.

77. The quote is from Charles Goodsell, The Social Meaning of Civic Space (Lawrence: University of Kansas Press, 1988), 38; see also 51, 198. See also Rudolf Arnheim, The Dynamics of Architectural Form (Berkeley: University of California Press, 1977), 269. For this reason, the form was increasingly being used to house governing bodies, including the Council Chamber of New York City Hall, completed in 1812 and located a few blocks down Broadway from the tabernacle. See the 1830 sketch in I. N. Phelps Stokes, The Iconography of Manhattan, 1498–1909 (New York: Dodd, 1915), 3:598 plate 101b. The self-reflexive corporate nature of this type of space led German architect Karl Friedrich Schinkel to attempt to bring the intimacy of the amphitheatre auditorium to the upper-class theatre in the early nineteenth century. See Schwarzer, "Social Genesis of the Public Theater," 56-59.

78. Finney, *Memoirs*, 367.

79. Fletcher, *History of Oberlin College*, 31. See also Fowler, *American Pulpit*, 36–37.

80. Fletcher, *History of Oberlin College*, 31.

81. In the 1840s, theatres began to offer morality plays like W. H. Smith's *The Drunkard; or, The Fallen Saved*, in order to appeal to the same morally concerned, middle-class sector that also composed the tabernacle audience. Allen, *Horrible Prettiness*, 62–63. See also McConachie, *Melodramatic Formations*, 175–86.

82. This paralleled changes taking place in theatres and concert halls as entertainment managers sought ways to reduce audience activity and create passive stage-watchers. See Allen, *Horrible Prettiness*, 70; McConachie, "Pacifying American Theatrical Audiences," 62–63; and Johnson, *Listening in Paris*.

83. For instance, in May 1837, anniversary meetings were held in the tabernacle by the New York Congregational Society, the American Seaman's Friend Society, the New York Sunday School Union, the American Moral Reform Society, the American Home Missionary Society, the American Bible Society, the Presbyterian Education Society, and the American Board of Foreign Missions. See *New York Evangelist*, 13 May 1837, 1, 8; 27 May 1837, 1.

84. On social and political agendas among formalist evangelicals, see Curtis Johnson, *Redeeming America: Evangelicals and the Road to the Civil War* (Chicago: Dee, 1993), 86–154.

85. Peter Williams, *America's Religions: Traditions and Cultures* (New York: Macmillan, 1990), 170–71.

86. Charles Sellers, *The Market Revolution: Jacksonian America, 1815–1846* (New York: Oxford University Press, 1991), 30. For an analysis of the correspondences between revivalism and democratic politics, particularly their challenges to authority, see Hatch, *Democratization*, 3–46. See also Daniel Walker Howe, "The Market Revolution and the Shaping of Identity in Whig-Jacksonian America," in *The Market Revolution in America: Social, Political and Religious Expressions, 1800–1880*, edited by Melvyn Stokes and Stephen Conway (Charlottesville: University Press of Virginia, 1996), 259–81. Whereas Sellers has argued that relationship to the market divided Americans into two distinct and opposing groups (rural yeoman democrats, who resisted market forces and engaged in a communally based religious revivalism, and urban, market-oriented federalists, who disparaged enthusiastic religion), Howe problematizes this antipodal synthesis in a way that acknowledges the multiplicity of interests (economic, political, and religious) and the variety of combinations thereof that contributed to the identities of citizens in the early republic. See also Paul E. Johnson, *A Shopkeeper's Millennium: Society and Revivals in Rochester, New York, 1815–1837* (New York: Hill and Wang, 1978).

87. Hatch, *Democratization*, 199.

88. Finney experienced the lack of facilities immediately upon his arrival at Oberlin, when he began organizing a revival. With no suitable space available to house the meetings, he asked the Tappans for some means of shelter. Arthur Tappan arranged for the construction of a huge circular canvas tent, 100 feet in diameter. With a banner reading "Holiness to the Lord" streaming like a gigantic flag from the top of the centerpole, the tent could house 3,000 people. See Finney, *Memoirs*, 383–84.

89. The quote appears in the Ledger of the First Church, Oberlin Society, 13 Aug. 1841. See also Ledger of the First Church, Oberlin Society, 25 Mar. 1841, Oberlin College Archives, Oberlin, Ohio. Society member Henry Platt was initially superintending the building process and was instructed by the society to contact Sears. Ledger of the First Church, Oberlin Society, 24 July 1841. For further information on the Oberlin meetinghouse (variously called the Oberlin Congregational Church and the First Congregational Church of Oberlin), see Fletcher, *History of Oberlin College*, 572–75; Delevan L. Leonard, *The Story of Oberlin: The Institution, the Community, the Idea, the Movement* (Boston: Pilgrim Press, 1898), 180–212; and James H. Fairchild, *Oberlin: The Colony and the College, 1833–1883* (Oberlin, Ohio: Goodrich, 1883).

90. The former private rooms of the Chatham Street Chapel had been converted into prayer rooms, and Finney had subsequently urged the creation of similar meeting space in the basement of the Broadway Tabernacle. The new Oberlin plan designated four small recitation rooms behind the pulpit area, which could be opened to the audience room through means of sliding doors. The completed building eliminated the pews behind the pulpit, brought the gallery down to a level some seven feet above the main floor, and enclosed the ground floor space into classrooms not accessible from the audience room, a scheme similar to that in the Broadway Tabernacle.

91. Ledger of the First Church, Oberlin Society, 12 Nov. 1841.

92. Bond was a founding member of the short-lived National Society of Architects (superseded by the American Institute of Architects). His major works include Gore Hall on the Harvard campus and Bowdoin Square Baptist Church, Boston. See Henry Withey, *Biographical Dictionary of American Architects* (Los Angeles, Calif.: New Age, 1956), 65. I am indebted to Stephen Jerome of the Brookline Historical Society for details of Bond's life and work.

93. Bond wrote, "The [illegible] rear ranges of seats at both ends of the house are designed to rise one above the other end, the nearer one to rise one foot above the seats in the centre of the house which will require the floor of the Vestibule to be rais'd one foot above the center of the house. The rising of the floors may be effected by [firming] up on the joist or by [firming] the joist above the timbers" (Plan for Oberlin Meetinghouse, Oberlin Archives).

94. See John Scott Russell, "Elementary Considerations of Some Principles in the Construction of Buildings Designed to Accommodate Spectators and Auditors," *Edinburgh New Philosophical Journal* 27 (Apr.-Oct. 1839): 131–36. For a discussion of Russell's ideas on the isacoustic curve, see Charles E. Gregersen, *Dankmar Adler: His Theatres and Auditoriums* (Athens: Swallow Press and Ohio University Press, 1990), 11.

95. Keith Hardman implies that the scheme presented in the line drawing on the Bond plan informed Finney's vision regarding the design of the Broadway Tabernacle in 1835–1836. Given its profound similarity to the 1839 Russell drawing and its placement on the back of the 1841 plan, I feel this is unlikely, though the intention to maintain eye contact may well have been a priority for Finney, particularly given his experience in the Chatham Street Chapel (Hardman, *Finney*, 302, 482 n37).

96. On Bentham, see Thomas A. Markus, *Buildings and Power: Freedom and Control in the Origin of Modern Building Types* (London: Routledge, 1993), 66–69. On lecture halls, see S. Forgan, "Context, Image and Function: A Preliminary Enquiry into the Architecture of Scientific Societies," *British Journal for the History of Science* 19 (Mar. 1986): 89–113; and Markus, *Buildings and Power*, 53–84, 229–44.

97. It is also possible that Sears drew the sketch. The knowledgeable editors of Finney's memoirs, Garth Rosell and Richard Dupuis, suggest that the handwriting matches Finney's, but expert analysis has not been done. For further information on Sears, see Finney, *Memoirs*, 402 n84.

98. Fletcher, *History of Oberlin College*, 575; Ledger of the First Church, Oberlin Society, 19 Aug. 1844.

99. Oberlin did have a growing music program. See Fletcher, *History of Oberlin College*, 784–88.

100. On the building committee's concerns about plainness and cost, see the *Oberlin Evangelist* (3 Mar. 1841): 39, (2 July 1842): 111, and (7 June 1843): 95.

Chapter 3

1. This is not to say that earlier American churches were devoid of ornament. Though the term *plain style* is often used to describe a Puritan or Protestant aesthetic, James F. White has demonstrated that, in fact, English Puritans and Protestants more generally did not strive to eliminate beauty from their churches. Ornamentation was lavished particularly on pulpits, the

major liturgical center of services, and on doorways, the entry to religious space. See White, "From Protestant to Catholic Plain Style," in *Seeing beyond the Word: Visual Arts and the Calvinist Tradition*, ed. Paul Corby Finney (Grand Rapids, Mich.: Eerdmans, 1999), 457–76. Nevertheless, the repeated use of the phrase throughout the latter half of the nineteenth century—both by those nostalgic for an earlier, simpler time and by those scornful of the architecture of previous generations—suggests that even if it did not accurately characterize colonial churches, it does reveal the values of the nineteenth century. This idealized imagined past of Calvinist austerity suggests a certain cultural equivocation precisely as material displays came into the reach of more congregations and grew increasingly attractive to them.

2. Richard L. Bushman, *The Refinement of America: Persons, Houses, Cities* (New York: Knopf, 1992), 339–48; and Phoebe Stanton, *The Gothic Revival & American Church Architecture: An Episode in Taste, 1840–1856* (Baltimore, Md.: Johns Hopkins University Press, 1968). For similar interpretations, see Calder Loth and Julius Trousdale Sadler, Jr., *The Only Proper Style: Gothic Architecture in America* (Boston: New York Graphic Society, 1975); and Julius Melton, *Presbyterian Worship in America: Changing Patterns since 1787* (Richmond, Va.: Knox, 1967): 65–69.

3. Upon leaving the tabernacle, Duffield went to First Presbyterian Church in Detroit, where he remained active in denominational matters and played a major role in the termination of the Plan of Union. Later, he was noted for his millenarian beliefs. On Duffield's New School thought, see George M. Marsden, *The Evangelical Mind and the New School Presbyterian Experience: A Case Study of Thought and Theology in Nineteenth-Century America* (New Haven, Conn.: Yale University Press, 1970), 52–56; on his theological differences with Finney, see Charles Grandison Finney, *The Memoirs of Charles G. Finney*, edited by Garth M. Rosell and Richard A. G. Dupuis (Grand Rapids, Mich.: Academie, 1989), 404 n95, 470 nn19, 20. See also L. Nelson Nichols, *The History of the Broadway Tabernacle of New York City* (New Haven, Conn.: Tuttle, Morehouse and Taylor, 1940), 68; and Mark Y. Hanley, *Beyond a Christian Commonwealth: The Protestant Quarrel with the American Republic, 1830–1860* (Chapel Hill: University of North Carolina Press, 1994), 49, 153.

4. Joseph P. Thompson, *Memoir of David Hale* (New York: Wiley, 1850), 63, and *The Last Sabbath in the Broadway Tabernacle: A Historical Discourse* (New York: Calkins & Stiles, 1857), 19–20. Compare with the union statement by David Hale, reprinted in Susan Hayes Ward, *The History of the Broadway Tabernacle Church: From Its Organization in 1840 to the Close of 1900, Including Factors Influencing Its Formation* (New York: Broadway Tabernacle Church, 1901), 36.

5. This merging of a Congregationalist church and a Presbyterian one brought together two different types of polity under one roof. Presbyterian congregations were governed by a centralized, hierarchical organization composed of elders, deacons, and trustees from the immediate congregation, a presbytery of elders from several churches in a region, a state conference, and a national general assembly. Congregationalists, on the other hand, were governed only on the congregational level, by elders elected by the membership. No centralized denominational bodies existed, although representatives from independent Congregational churches had, from time to time, come together to make decisions (suggestions, technically) regarding policies that affected them all. The 1801 Plan of Union between the two denominations served as the foundation for such union agreements as that suggested by the Third Presbytery.

The Broadway Tabernacle Plan of Union stipulated that "the two churches [are] to be connected with the Third presbytery of New York, *it being understood that such principles of the Congregational order shall be engrafted* AS SHALL BE APPROVED BY THE UNITED CHURCHES" (emphasis in original). See Ward, *History of Broadway Tabernacle*, 36; Lewis Tappan, *Proceedings of the Session of Broadway Tabernacle against Lewis Tappan* (New York: n.p., 1839), 4; and Nichols, *History*, 70.

6. Parker, a friend of Finney, had urged Finney to come to New York in the spring of 1831. Parker to Finney, 4 Apr. 1831, CGFP, Oberlin College Archives, Oberlin, Ohio.

7. Lewis Tappan implied that Duffield was railroaded. He complained that a "self-appointed committee" of the tabernacle urged Duffield's resignation although the minister was unwilling to leave without a full vote of the membership. Rather than submit the issue to the membership, however, the committee convinced him to submit a qualified resignation that, along with Helffenstein's resignation, the members accepted. The polity question here revolves around the relative power of the full congregration membership (which the Congregationalist model imbues with power) and the representative committees (composed of elders in the Presbyterian model). A primary account of the merger and the following situation in the tabernacle appears in Tappan, Proceedings, 4. Joseph Thompson, who served as pastor at the tabernacle from 1845 to 1871, but who was not present in New York during the events of the late 1830s, wrote about the situation secondhand in Thompson, Memoir of David Hale, 61–63, and Last Sabbath, 17–19. For historical accounts, see Ward, History of Broadway Tabernacle, 34–37; and Nichols, History, 65–71.

8. These sentiments perhaps made the tabernacle a target for arson. On 16 Dec. 1835, a great fire swept though lower Manhattan, and the interior and roof of the unfinished tabernacle were consumed. Finney biographer Keith Hardman is sympathetic to Finney's memory that the fire was set deliberately and that firefighters stood by and watched the building burn due to their disdain for the rumored "amalgamation" agenda. Nichols, however, argues that the tabernacle was somewhat distant from the burned area of the city. Keith J. Hardman, Charles Grandison Finney, 1792–1875: Revivalist and Reformer (Grand Rapids, Mich.: Baker Book House, 1987), 303; Nichols, History, 61; and Finney, Memoirs, 371.

9. Ward, History of Broadway Tabernacle, 38.

10. On anticolonization activity at the chapel, see the New York Evangelist, supp. 9 and 10 May 1834.

11. Tappan had supported the successful election of a black man, Mr. Van Ranslear, to the position of trustee in the Chatham Street Chapel and had written numerous articles urging Christian equality between the races. Lewis Tappan, Journal, 23 Feb. 1836, Papers of Lewis Tappan (PLT) (Washington, D.C.: Library of Congress, 1975), microfilm. On the Ultraist movement, see Curtis D. Johnson, Islands of Holiness: Rural Religion in Upstate New York, 1790–1860 (Ithaca, N.Y.: Cornell University Press, 1989), 113–33.

12. John R. Bodo, The Protestant Clergy and Public Issues, 1812–1848 (Princeton, N.J.: Princeton University Press, 1954), 140–42.

13. The presbytery referred the situation back to the Broadway Tabernacle Session, charging the leaders to settle the matter themselves. The Session issued a statement in July that it would withdraw the charges if Tappan would leave the church. He refused and complained to the synod. On 16 Oct. 1839, a special committee of the synod called together the Session and Tappan and worked out an agreement: the Session would withdraw the charges without requiring Tappan's removal from the church. Tappan, however, made it clear that he would unite with another church in the near future. Tappan, Journal, 16 Oct. 1839, PLT. Primary accounts of the trial and the appeals to the presbytery and to the general assembly appear in Tappan, Journal, 16 Dec. 1838, 10 Apr 1839, and 7 May 1839, PLT; Tappan, Proceedings; and Thompson, Memoir of David Hale, 63–94. The New York Evangelist also printed some of the testimony of the trial and appellate processes. Historical treatments are available in Ward, History of Broadway Tabernacle, 37–41; and Nichols, History, 71–72.

Tappan's dispute with the Presbyterians probably had religious bases as well. Although a staunch supporter of the free-church movement, Tappan's credentials were likely seen as suspect from his earliest days in New York. In the 1820s this Boston native was well known as a Unitarian lay leader. Active in the Federal Street Church of Ellery Channing, he spearheaded the founding and construction of the Chamber Street Church in 1823 and the Purchase Street Church in 1826. He also served as treasurer and Sunday school superintendent. In the late summer of 1827, his brother, Arthur, offered him a generous partnership in a highly successful

New York mercantile business, on the condition that Lewis refrain from his Unitarian activities. Having recently met Lyman Beecher and become interested in the evangelical movement, Lewis underwent a prolonged and difficult crisis of conscience during the fall of 1827. Within a few months he had resolved the issue, approving of the trinitarian position. (Tappan's wife, Susan Aspinwall Tappan, remained staunchly Unitarian, a position that, while dismaying Lewis, may also have had a bearing on his decision to move to New York alone for about a year prior to moving his family. Susan did convert to "the orthodox position" upon her arrival in New York in the fall of 1829.) Converted, Lewis Tappan quickly became involved, with Beecher's urging, in the movement to colonize New England religion (Congregationalism) within New York, and to this end, he helped to organize the free-church movement. That this Unitarian-turned-New School orthodox newcomer had the audacity to not only criticize Presbyterian power within the city but also threaten it directly by building Congregational churches could not have endeared the man to the presbytery. See Tappan, Journal, Aug. 1827 through 1838, PLT; and Bertram Wyatt-Brown, *Lewis Tappan and the Evangelical War against Slavery* (Cleveland, Ohio: Press of Case Western Reserve University, 1969), 17–36.

14. Letter from [illegible] Brown to Finney, 28 Jan. 1839, CGFP.

15. Angelina Grimké articulated Ultraist frustration with church leadership in a letter to Theodore Weld and John Greenleaf Whittier dated 20 Aug. 1837. She wrote: "Men and Women will have to go out on their own responsibility, just like the prophets of old and declare the *whole* counsel of God to the people. The whole Church government must come down, the clergy stand right in the way of reform, and I do not know but this stumbling block too must be removed *before* Slavery can be abolished, for the system is supported by *them*; it could not exist without the Church as it is called. This grand principle must be mooted." Gilbert H. Barnes and Dwight L. Dumond, eds., *Letters of Theodore Dwight Weld, Angelina Grimké Weld, and Sara Grimké, 1822–1844* (Gloucester, Mass.: Peter Smith, 1965), 431.

16. Hale, who had joined the Seventh Presbyterian Church in New York in 1827 after accepting the position of editor of the *Journal of Commerce* from its founder, Lewis Tappan, likely found himself in a difficult position. No great sympathizer with abolitionism or Tappan, he nonetheless had good reason to maintain a cordial relationship with Tappan. The path of least resistance clearly was to remain silent during the proceedings, yet he had a growing reputation as the editor of the *Journal* and as a commentator on religious matters. In this context, Hale's appeal to procedure, rather than identifying with one side in the Ultraism debate, was a clearly diplomatic course. Tappan, however, implies that Hale's sympathies lay with him, stating that Hale specifically asked him (Tappan) to not leave the tabernacle. Tappan, Journal, 6 June 1839, PLT. Thompson, however, expresses little sympathy for Tappan in his admiring memoir of Hale and thus suggests a more equivocal stance on Hale's part.

17. Specifically, Hale argued that though Tappan was ultimately convicted of contumacy, he had not been charged with it at the beginning of the trial; that his rights had been violated when his request to have the proceedings recorded was denied and when he was not allowed to explain his words; and that, in convicting Tappan, the elders handed down a sentence that did not fit the offense, for while contumacy was a crime against the Session, excommunication was a punishment for crimes against God. Thompson, *Memoir of David Hale*, 77–82.

18. Thompson, *Memoir of David Hale*, 77, 80–81. See also Tappan, *Proceedings*, 42, 61–64.

19. Hale was no theologian. As Mark Hanley points out, ambivalence toward democracy and republicanism characterized formalist evangelicals during the antebellum period. Horace Bushnell, for instance, specifically rejected democracy as no more immune to injustice than any other form of polity. Hanley, *Christian Commonwealth*, 32–48.

20. See Hanley, *Christian Commonwealth*, 52. This excellent study of Protestant critiques of liberalism also examines the positions of well-known Congregationalist ministers Horace Bushnell (43–46) and Mark Hopkins (78–79).

21. On the consequences of the sectional conflict for denominations, see C. C. Goen, *Broken Churches, Broken Nation: Denominational Schisms and the Coming of the American Civil War* (Macon, Ga.: Mercer University Press, 1985), 68–78.

22. Thompson, *Memoir of David Hale*, 66.

23. Green, Isaac Dimond, and other mortgage holders seem to have been carrying the tabernacle financially since it opened. Payments on the mortgages had not been met, severely jeopardizing all of the supporters but Dimond most particularly. See letter from [illegible] Brown to Finney, 28 Jan. 1839, CGFP; and letter from Stephen Brown to Finney, 24 Feb. 1838, CGFP.

24. Several years of examining the records of congregations has impressed upon the author the pervasiveness of such eleventh-hour schemes to save financially jeopardized churches. Often the stories include references to conversions of the heart or even to dreams or visions that impress upon the saving agents their duty to rescue the church. The veracity of such stories is difficult to ascertain. It is clear, however, that these stories function in congregational lore to illustrate God's hand ensuring the ongoing existence of the congregation.

25. Thompson, *Memoir of David Hale*, 102; Ward, *History of Broadway Tabernacle*, 53.

26. Thompson, *Memoir of David Hale*, 102.

27. Thompson, *Memoir of David Hale*, 102–3.

28. Finney's "cooling" toward the slavery issue was defended by Ultraist Theodore Weld, who reasoned that Finney's obsession with revivals of religion meant that he did not work toward specific social goals—temperance, moral reform, antislavery—but that his goal was converting the individual. See letter from Weld to Lewis Tappan, 17 Nov. 1835, in Barnes and Dumond, *Letters*, 242–44. Finney himself wrote to Weld that while making "every new convert . . . an abolitionist" would be good, he found that the "absorbing abolitionism [that] has drunk up the spirit of some of the most efficient moral men" was particularly "alarming," and he feared that if it were allowed to continue, "the church and world, ecclesiastical and state leaders, will become embroiled in one common infernal squabble that will roll a wave of blood over the land." Barnes and Dumond, 319. Discussion of the ramifications of these ideas for reform societies appears in a letter from James A. Thome to Weld of 13 Aug. 1836. Barnes and Dumond, 328.

In his history of the Broadway Tabernacle, Thompson takes pains to distance the congregation from Finney's perfectionism, stating repeatedly that the congregation was a "conservative" one that was "not . . . *perfect* either in its pulpit or in its pews." Thompson, *Last Sabbath*, 16.

29. Quoted in Thompson, *Memoir of David Hale*, 79.

30. Congregationalists and Presbyterians both engaged in similar reconstructions of Pilgrim and Puritan history at midcentury, always in attempts to claim legitimacy for new ideas and directions. Marsden, *Evangelical Mind*, 140–41. See also Emory Washburn, "A Free Church, a Free Gospel, a Free Government," *Congregational Quarterly* 2 (July 1860): 313–29; and Abijah P. Marvin, "Keeping Our Own Vineyard," *Congregational Quarterly* 2 (Oct. 1860): 390–401.

31. The passage is worth reproducing in its entirety: "At this critical and perilous juncture in our nation, when the most radical and revolutionary doctrines are proclaimed from the high places of the land, and from the solemn bench of justice; doctrines that undermine the constitution of the Union and the liberties of the people; doctrines that belie the history of the nation and the sentiments of our fathers; doctrines that repudiate the everlasting decrees of Providence, and the teachings of the Son of God; in these days of radical and rampant wickedness and outrage in public life; and while some church organizations are lending their machinery to be worked by a *radicalism* that subverts the family, contemns [sic] God's word, and tramples justice in the street; we rejoice that Congregationalism, through thousands of churches having no organic connection with this iniquity, may exert its healthful *conservativism* for truth, for order, for freedom, and for righteousness." Thompson, *Last Sabbath*, 34–35.

32. Goen, *Broken Churches*, 95, quoting the minutes of the General Missionary Convention as reported in Arthur T. Foss and Edward Mathews, comps., *Facts for Baptist Churches: Collected, Arranged, and Reviewed* (Utica, N.Y.: American Baptist Free Mission Society, 1850), 21.

33. Goen, *Broken Churches*, 77–78, quoting *The Presbyterian Enterprise: Sources of American Presbyterian History*, edited by Maurice W. Armstrong, Lefferts A. Loetscher, and Charles A. Anderson (Philadelphia: Westminster, 1956), 200. Another example of an individual congregation struggling with this issue appears in Howard J. Conn, *The First Congregational Church of Great Barrington, 1743–1943* (Great Barrington, Mass.: Berkshire Courier, 1943), 27–28. George Marsden notes that after the schism of 1837, New School Presbyterians refused to take a stand on the slavery issue: "At every Assembly slavery was the primary subject of debate. At some almost nothing else was discussed. At none was decisive action taken. In deference to its small minority of Southern members, the Assembly voted in 1839 to leave the matter to the discretion of the local synods. In 1843 the commissioners again refused to make any pronouncements. In 1846 they condemned the institution of slavery but not the individuals who supported it." Marsden, *Evangelical Mind*, 119.

34. *Religious Herald* (Richmond, Va.), 24 Oct. 1844, as quoted in Goen, *Broken Churches*, 95.

35. James Henley Thornwell, "Relation of the Church to Slavery," in *The Collected Writings of James Henley Thornwell*, edited by John B. Adger and John L. Girardeau (Richmond, Va.: Presbyterian Committee of Publication, 1871–1873), 4:394–96, quoted in Goen, *Broken Churches*, 75.

36. The move for Christian unity should be viewed as separate from that for united Evangelicalism, which preceded it. The evangelicalism of the 1830s produced a number of important ecumenical organizations, most notably the many benevolence and reform societies and the American Tract Society, which formed, in the words of historian Charles I. Foster, an "evangelical united front" propelled by a shared belief in the coming millennium to be ushered in by a unified army of Christian soldiers. It is precisely the failure of this unified evangelicalism (spurred by Ultraist challenges) that resulted in arguments like Hale's for a new kind of Christian unity of worship, not action. On united Evangelicalism and its decline, see Marsden, *Evangelical Mind*, 104–27. On union efforts, see Lefferts A. Loetscher, "The Problem of Christian Unity in Early Nineteenth-Century America," *Church History* 32 (Mar. 1963): 3–16; Johnson, *Islands of Holiness*, 137–44; Hanley, *Christian Commonwealth*, 54–57, 73–74; Kenneth Scott Latourette, "Serving Overseas," in *They Seek a Country: The American Presbyterians, Some Aspects*, edited by Gaius Jackson Slosser (New York: Macmillan, 1955); and Richard J. Carwardine, *Evangelicals and Politics in Antebellum America* (New Haven, Conn.: Yale University Press, 1993), 129–30. On various organizations, see John Von Rohr, *The Shaping of American Congregationalism, 1620–1957* (Cleveland, Ohio: Pilgrim Press, 1992), 294–96.

Among the more successful organizations was the Evangelical Alliance, which focused primarily on countering Roman Catholicism. In the summer of 1846, it took its agenda to London to establish the Christian Alliance, but there the Americans were caught short by the strength of the antislavery feeling among British evangelicals. Yet they did agree on the anti-Catholic stance. As Hanley points out, their "Overture for Christian Union," published in 1846, did call for the unification of the Christian community in the goal of "evangelizing the world" (Hanley, *Christian Commonwealth*, 73). Although several U.S. religious leaders, including Lyman Beecher, signed the doctrinal statement developed at the Christian Alliance meetings, criticism mounted. For instance, David Hale criticized the premise that the Christian ministry was of divine origin and reasoned that if justification was by faith alone, as one premise asserted, then that would require welcoming *all* who professed to be faithful into the fold, including "Quakers, Czerski, and even Papists." In Hale's opinion, although the attempt by the alliance toward unity was admirable and though "real union has been increased" by the efforts, the goal itself would remain highly complex and, likely, elusive. David Hale, "Christian Union—The Evangelical Alliance," in Thompson, *Memoir of David Hale*, 337–44. The quotes are found on pp. 340 and 344. On the alliance, see Philip D. Jordan, *The Evangelical Alliance for the United States of America, 1847–1900: Ecumenicism, Identity, and the Religion of the Republic* (New York: Mellen, 1982). On evangelical anti-Catholicism, see Bodo, *Protestant Clergy*, 69–81.

37. "Forms of Worship," *Princeton Review* 18 (Oct. 1846), 488. This piece was likely written by John W. Yeomans. On one level, the author is directing his words exclusively to the Presbyterian debate over liturgy, yet we must assume that the intentional use of inclusive language— "Christian principles" rather than "Presbyterian"—was meant to broaden the scope of the discussion. Surely the writer intended a parochial claiming of Presbyterianism as synonymous with Christian, yet the inclusive language acknowledges that all Protestant denominations were facing similar questions.

The Disciples of Christ, founded by Alexander Campbell on the principle of the unity of primitive and Bible-based Christianity, specifically disavowed "liturgical traditions as divisive human conventions." Hanley, *Christian Commonwealth*, 56.

38. J. C. Webster, "The Worship of the Christian Sanctuary," *Congregational Quarterly* 4 (July 1862): 259–65. See also [Yeomans], "Forms of Worship," 487–514; and "Christianity and the Fine Arts," *Crayon* 6 (Oct. 1859): 307–8.

39. See, for instance, "Presbyterian Liturgies," *Biblical Repertory and Princeton Review* 27 (July 1855): 445–67; and Leonard Woolsey Bacon, "Suggestions Concerning the Ritual of a Puritan Church," *Congregational Quarterly* 5 (July 1863): 242–47.

40. Because the organizational elements of the Presbyterian church tended to respond to frontier situations more aggressively than did the Congregationalist polity, Congregationalists felt themselves at a severe disadvantage as white populations pushed westward. As early as 1846 midwestern Congregationalists had declared their opposition to the Plan of Union. See Marsden, *Evangelical Mind*, 125. Many Congregationalists, however, feared that any national Congregationalist organization would compromise the fundamental premise of congregational independence.

41. *Proceedings of the General Convention of Congregational Ministers and Delegates in the United States, Held at Albany, N.Y., 5th–8th of October, 1852* (New York: Benedict, 1852), 27, quoted in Von Rohr, *American Congregationalism*, 275.

42. New School Presbyterians were in a similar situation: desirous of maintaining and enhancing a theological identity distinct from the Old School while eschewing separation. See Marsden, *Evangelical Mind*, 128–41.

43. This site suggests the importance of the new mission of ministry, particularly ministry to families. It also supports the aesthetic interpretation of the Gothic, given the centrality of the site within one of the trendiest new neighborhoods in the city.

44. Joseph P. Thompson, "Historical Sketch of the Broadway Tabernacle, New York City," *Congregational Quarterly* 2 (Jan. 1860): 64–67.

45. Thompson, "Historical Sketch," 65–66.

46. Thompson, "Historical Sketch," 66.

47. While in her landmark study of the Gothic Revival architectural historian Phoebe Stanton argued that the embracing of Gothic forms by U.S. architects for Episcopalian churches grew primarily from new aesthetic conceptions and standards, she did not examine the influence of the Gothic taste beyond Episcopalianism. Stanton, *Gothic Revival*.

48. James White has argued that the British Ecclesiologists embraced the Gothic as a means of historicizing and legitimizing British nationalism. For the English Ecclesiologists, antiquarianism carried a strong nationalism most evident in a disdain for "foreign" medieval styles and

a strong preference for "our own branch of the Catholick Church," i.e., the English church. In its attempt to recapture a "great past age," the Ecclesiologists' resurrection of the Gothic served as a means for the growing educated middle classes to lay claim to and reassert a nationalist cultural and ideological hegemony. James F. White, *The Cambridge Movement: The Ecclesiologists and the Gothic Revival* (Cambridge: Cambridge University Press, 1962), 31–32. In their adoption of the stylistic aesthetic of the Ecclesiologists, U.S. designers also eagerly absorbed the nationalism of the British. The extent to which the U.S. public could convince itself that any English heritage meant English/Puritan heritage completed a sleight of hand that linked, at least tangentially, the medieval historicization with the construction of an American Puritan history, so evident in the religious and secular literature of the period.

49. Stanton argues that among the first important articulations of this idea was that of the Reverend George Ayliffe Poole in his book *The Appropriate Character of Church Architecture* (Leeds and London: Green and Rivington's, 1842). Poole states, "So entirely did this style arise out of the strivings of the church to give a bodily form to her teaching, that it seems to have clothed her spirit, almost as if the invisible things had put forth their energies, unseen, but powerful and plastic, and gathered around them on all sides the very forms and figures which might best serve to embody them to the eye of sense. . . . A Gothic church, in its perfections, is an exposition of the distinctive doctrines of Christianity, clothed upon with a material form; and is, as Coleridge has more forcibly expressed it, 'the petrification of our religion.'" Poole, quoted in Stanton, *Gothic Revival*, 8–9.

50. The English Ecclesiologists did realize they were on relatively shaky ground, however, a fact to which the abundance of discussion on the Catholic origins of the Gothic attests. As Phoebe Stanton argues, Pugin ultimately found himself marginalized within the movement he began precisely due to his Roman Catholic beliefs. In the United States, however, where architects were less concerned with the ideological aspects of building, Pugin's *The True Principles of Pointed or Christian Architecture*, which appeared in 1841, was welcomed. See Stanton, *Gothic Revival*, 26–27, 168; and White, *Cambridge Movement*, 86–87, 90–91.

51. Stanton, *Gothic Revival*, 168, citing "Rural Church Edifices," *New York Review* 9 (July 1841). Stanton's book is the definitive study of the Episcopalian adoption of the Gothic Revival in the United States.

52. Henry Russell Cleveland, "American Architecture," *North American Review* 43 (Oct. 1836): 372, quoted in Stanton, *Gothic Revival*, 164.

53. Arthur Gilman, "Architecture in the United States," *North American Review* 58 (Apr. 1844): 436–80; and Stanton, *Gothic Revival*, 64–65, 176–77. The view of Gothic architecture as uniquely connected to Christianity had been articulated as early as 1821 in an anonymous review of *An Attempt to Discriminate the Styles of English Architecture from the Conquest to the Reformation*, by Thomas Rickman, and *Chronological and Historical Illustrations of the Ancient Architecture of Great Britain*, by John Britton, *Quarterly Review* 25 (Apr. 1821): 145–47.

54. On the important relationship between Ecclesiology and the professionalization of architecture in the United States, see Stanton, *Gothic Revival*, 320–32.

55. Leopold Eidlitz, "Christian Architecture," *Crayon* 5 (Feb. 1858): 53. See also Eidlitz, "On Style," *Crayon* 5 (May 1858): 139–40. These arguments are essentially restatements of those presented by the British Ecclesiologists in the 1840s.

56. Eidlitz, "Christian Architecture," 53–54.

57. Eidlitz, "Christian Architecture," 54. Eidlitz was a Reform Jew, and it is interesting to note that a few synagogues drew upon the Gothic Revival style during this period.

58. J. Coleman Hart, "Unity in Architecture," *Crayon* 6 (Mar. 1859): 86. Hart's history is inaccurate. The Gothic feature of pointed arches originated in Muslim Spain, and the basilica plan so closely associated with Gothic church architecture was Roman.

59. Hart, "Unity in Architecture," 88. The *Crayon* reported that after this paper was read to the AIA, Eidlitz "concurred fully with the author" and added that "the Renaissance was but a blind return to the Classic styles," that "Michael Angelo did great harm to architecture," and that "the churches of St. Peter in Rome, and St. Paul in London, had injured the cause of architecture more than any buildings that had ever been erected." Hart, 88.

60. Hart, "Unity in Architecture," 86, 88.

61. Hart, "Unity in Architecture," 88.

62. [William A. Dod and Albert Dod], "Church Architecture," *Biblical Repertory and Princeton Review* 27 (Oct. 1855): 625–49. The quote appears on p. 626.

63. [Dod and Dod], "Church Architecture," 640.

64. However, the writers noted, this alternative pointed up the larger problem of Protestant architecture: apart from the parallelogram space (the preaching box), Protestant requirements had been insufficiently theorized to allow for a new, Protestant style to be developed. An ornamented preaching box was not Protestant architecture; the writers deemed the task of "impress[ing] a character of beauty upon that which has not sufficient character to take up the impression" to be futile. Only through a new theory of Protestant architecture could a new style emerge, and the Dods go on to discuss the requirements: auxiliary rooms for governing bodies and space in the sanctuary for presbyters; a large, well-proportioned lecture room with good acoustics and free from intrusions upon sightlines; and an atmosphere of "sacred rest," "tranquillity," and "nature at rest," which would indicate "reverence." Such a Protestant architecture would mirror the timelessness of the Catholic Gothic but would emphasize the "severe," the "simple," and the "enduring." Most important, the new church would "look like a church," with a spire that marked, not through reference to heaven but simply through its presence, the building as Christian. [Dod and Dod], "Church Architecture," 644–45.

65. [Dod and Dod], "Church Architecture," 644–45.

66. "Dr. Spring's Church," *Crayon* 5 (Jan. 1858): 22. A notice regarding the removal of the Brick Church congregation from their former building appeared under the title "The Brick Church in New York," *Presbyterian Magazine* 6 (July 1856): 334.

67. For the architects, as Stanton argues, these concerns about style and its appropriateness for specific uses constituted but the initial absorption of the English Ecclesiologists' work. In the pages of the *Crayon* quoted above, U.S. architects within the AIA were developing a new approach to architectural style, a position "not opposed to the styles themselves, but rather to the use that had been made of them." Stanton, *Gothic Revival,* 325. While the Ecclesiologists continued to explore the "rules of aesthetics" of Christian Gothic and its appropriateness for a renewed Anglo-Catholic worship, the Americans, in Stanton's estimation, viewed the Gothic as "that style of architecture which teaches construction adapted to purpose and organization, with ornamentation to express that construction" (326). By focusing on the philosophy of construction rather than on the layers of embedded ideology, U.S. Gothicists avoided the problem of assigning a Roman Catholic style to Protestant buildings. Concerns about the purpose of the buildings led eventually to questions regarding the differences between Protestant and Anglo-Catholic worship practices and their differing spatial requirements.

68. The popularity of not only the Gothic but of church architecture in general is shown by the inclusion of drawings and descriptions of new churches in the pages of general interest magazines of the period. *Frank Leslie's Illustrated Newspaper,* for instance, carried features on church design in several issues, including 29 Dec. 1855, 1 Mar. 1856, 8 Mar. 1856, 24 May 1856, 5 July 1856, 26 July 1856, 29 July 1856, and 29 Dec. 29, 1858. Most of the churches featured were Gothic. The hegemony of ecclesiastical Gothic is also indicated by the fact that iconoclastic designers who used Gothic vocabularies on nonecclesiastical buildings were held in contempt by some religious writers. See [Dod and Dod], "Church Architecture," 625–49, esp. 626–30.

69. E. W. Gilman, "The American Congregational Union," *Congregational Quarterly* 1 (Jan. 1859): 59-61.

70. Gilman, "American Congregational Union," 60.

71. At the 1855 annual meeting of the Presbyterian General Assembly, the Board of Missions presented a report on the topic of church extension and the advisability of creating a Committee of Church Extension to replace the Board of Church Extension created in 1844. The report details the activities of the board since its creation and appears in "Church Extension and a Fifth Board," *Biblical Repertory and Princeton Review* 27 (July 1855): 509-40. See also Marsden, *Evangelical Mind*, 129.

72. John Fletcher Hurst, *The History of Methodism* (New York: Eaton & Mains, 1903), 3:1040-41.

73. The Gothic buildings were First Presbyterian, Albany (Mar. 1851); First Presbyterian, Cincinnati (June 1852); Second Presbyterian, Princeton (Feb. 1853); First Presbyterian, New York City (Apr. 1853); Seventh Presbyterian, Cincinnati (June 1853); First Presbyterian, Richmond (Sept. 1853); and Fifth Presbyterian, New York City (Oct. 1853). The other buildings illustrated featured a variety of classical vocabularies. Issues from these three years, the first three years of the publication of *Presbyterian Magazine*, contained the largest percentage of church illustrations. After 1853, the magazine contained few church illustrations, with none appearing in 1854 or 1855 and only one in 1856.

74. The two buildings presented in the July and October 1859 *Congregational Quarterly* featured Romanesque and classical facades, respectively. The medieval revival (Romanesque) Broadway Church in Norwich, Conn., had a slender spire that hinted at Gothic despite its round-headed gables. The Winnisimmet Congregational Church of Chelsea, Mass., was a Greek Revival building. In January 1862, the periodical featured the Classical Revival Mount Vernon Church, Boston, but all other featured churches sported medieval elements.

75. "Clinton Avenue Congregational Church," *Congregational Quarterly* 2 (Apr. 1860): 212-14. Such statements as this, which, in historian Julius Melton's words, illustrate an "innocen[t] . . . unabashed espousal of elegance and popular appeal as criteria for the design of a church building," have been interpreted by Melton and others (following Stanton's lead) as an indication that the primary reason for the hegemony of the Gothic during this period was that of changing taste. Melton further argues that Presbyterians were not particularly reflective on the ideological ramifications of their use of the Gothic and that because "styles of architecture were emotionally neutral matters for most American laymen," most Presbyterians were "not certain why they built Gothic churches." Melton, *Presbyterian Worship*, 68, 70. While I agree that the vast majority of descriptions of churches in periodicals at this time used similar language, extolling the "beauty," "richness," and "harmony" of the buildings, I would not dismiss the serious discussions of the style carried on by both architects and Presbyterian writers as readily as does Melton. The Gothic style was acceptable because it carried religious meaning.

76. "Church Architecture" advertisement, *Congregational Quarterly* 1 (July 1859): back flyleaf. See also Isaac P. Langworthy, "Ventilation of Churches," *Congregational Quarterly* 1 (Oct. 1859):369-72, and H. M. Dexter, "Meeting-Houses: Considered Historically and Suggestively," *Congregational Quarterly* 1 (Apr. 1859): 186-214.

77. Review of *Chapel and Church Architecture* in the *Crayon* 5 (Aug. 1858): 223.

78. On the use of Gothic Revival architecture to advance domestic religion, see Colleen McDannell, *The Christian Home in Victorian America, 1840-1900* (Bloomington: Indiana University Press, 1986), 28-49. Bowler's book was panned in an AIA review in the *Crayon*. Quoting long passages from the book with little commentary, the reviewer assumed (probably correctly) that Bowler's imperfect knowledge of historical styles (including his inaccurate chronology) would be self-evident to *Crayon* readers. Spare comments on the designs themselves were remarkably charitable, however. See Review of *Chapel and Church Architecture*, 223-28.

79. For specific examples, see J. S. Clark, "A Lesson from the Past: Early Methods of Church Extension," *Congregational Quarterly* 1 (Jan. 1859): 53–59; Washburn, "A Free Church," 313–29; and Marvin, "Keeping Our Own Vineyard," 390–401.

80. It should be kept in mind that the British also used the Gothic to lend historical legitimacy to the ideological construction of Anglo-nationalism. See n48 above.

81. Von Rohr, *American Congregationalism*, 166.

82. Quoted in Von Rohr, *American Congregationalism*, 231.

83. Von Rohr, *American Congregationalism*, 232.

84. Von Rohr, *American Congregationalism*, 229. Compare this to the 1787 Presbyterian order of worship: prayer of adoration; invocation and preparation; Scripture reading; singing of praise; long prayer of adoration, confession, thanksgiving, supplication, and intercession; Lord's Prayer; sermon; (Lord's Supper when celebrated); prayer; psalm; offering; and blessing. Melton, *Presbyterian Worship*, 21–22.

85. C. Q., "The Old Square Pew," *Presbyterian Magazine* 2 (Feb. 1852): 58.

86. Lewis Tappan, Journal, 25 Dec. 1820, PLT. Seating in churches also continued to undergo change as the practice of seating men and women on opposite sides of the room, which had been slowly supplanted through the eighteenth century by family seating, continued to decline. Tappan does mention attending an ordination service in which the seating was sex-segregated, however (30 June 1823). The growing popularity of family seating is also indicated by George Bowler, who included dividers placed at varying lengths within slip pews to accommodate families of different sizes. Bowler also favored kneelers, to eliminate the practice of having individuals turn to face their seats when kneeling during prayers, and "church sofas," by which he probably means slips. George Bowler, *Chapel and Church Architecture with Designs for Parsonages* (Boston: Jewett, 1856), 13, and design 15, n.p.

87. On the frontier tradition, see James F. White, *Christian Worship in North America: A Retrospective, 1955–1995* (Collegeville, Minn.: Liturgical Press, 1997), 27–29.

88. See Von Rohr, *American Congregationalism*, 299–302.

89. [Dod and Dod], "Church Architecture," 641, 643. Thus, while the architectural vocabularies and sometimes even the spatial forms of the new buildings were Gothic, the arrangement of the furnishings within those spaces linked congregations to the goal-oriented evangelical revivals, not to a liturgical heritage. A Gothic exterior did not predict interior usage or arrangement. Moreover, the disjunction between church exterior facades and interior arrangements is even more evident in the fact that the preaching platform with slanted seats arrangement became standard in Congregational churches of all styles, from Gothic to Classical Revival.

90. See, for instance, McDannell, *Christian Home*; and Ann Douglas, *The Feminization of American Culture* (New York: Anchor, 1988).

91. [John] H[all], "Psalmody and Liturgy," *Presbyterian Magazine* 1 (Apr. 1851): 20.

92. The *Presbyterian Magazine* carried a number of lamentations on worshipers' indecorum. See, for instance, "The Gentleman at Church" (Apr. 1856): 190; and "On Sleeping in Church" (Feb. 1854): 62.

93. H[all], "Psalmody and Liturgy," 159.

94. H[all], "Psalmody and Liturgy," 160. A similar New School condemnation of liturgies appeared in J. F., "Uniformity of Worship," *Presbyterian Magazine* 1 (June 1851): 260–62.

95. H[all], "Psalmody and Liturgy," 160.

96. H[all], "Psalmody and Liturgy," 161.

97. W. H. H., "Congregational Singing in Dr. Alexander's Church, New York," *Presbyterian Magazine* 5 (Oct. 1855): 475.

98. For a similar point of view, see Henry C. Fish, *Primitive Piety Revived; or, The Aggressive Power of the Christian Church* (Boston: Congregational Board of Publication, 1855).

99. [Charles Hodge], Review of *Eutaxia; or, The Presbyterian Liturgies: Historical Sketches*, by Charles Baird, *Biblical Repertory and Princeton Review* 27 (July 1855): 445–67.

100. Melton, *Presbyterian Worship*, 67.

Chapter 4

1. Marian Card Donnelly, *The New England Meeting Houses of the Seventeenth Century* (Middletown, Conn.: Wesleyan University Press, 1968), 7–9. Donnelly also demonstrates that the Puritans of the Massachusetts Bay Company made no mention of public buildings in their charter though they had discussed the "building of churches & ffortyfycacons" (9).

2. Paul Boyer and Stephen Nissenbaum, *Salem Possessed: The Social Origins of Witchcraft* (Cambridge, Mass.: Harvard University Press, 1974).

3. Dell Upton, *Holy Things and Profane: Anglican Parish Churches in Colonial Virginia* (Cambridge, Mass.: MIT Press, 1986), 13–14.

4. George Bowler, *Chapel and Church Architecture with Designs for Parsonages* (Boston: Jewett, 1856), 8.

5. Bowler, *Chapel and Church Architecture*, 8.

6. Bowler, *Chapel and Church Architecture*, 8–9. In the post–Civil War period, church pattern books frequently included comments on location and siting. H. Hudson Holly, for instance, in his book *Church Architecture, Illustrated with Thirty-five Lithographic Plates, from Original Designs* (Hartford, Conn.: Church Press and Mallory, 1871), expresses frustration that urban congregations must often accept whatever site they can get; nevertheless, he advises, a corner lot is preferable (79). See also Francis J. Parker, *Church-Building and Things To Be Considered, Done, or Avoided in Connection Therewith* (Boston: Cupples, Upham, 1886), 20–24.

7. Bowler, *Chapel and Church Architecture*, 8–9.

8. On the rise of the middle class, see Stuart Blumin, *The Emergence of the Middle Class: Social Experience in the American City, 1760–1900* (New York: Cambridge University Press, 1989). On the development of suburbs, see Robert Fishman, *Bourgeois Utopia: The Rise and Fall of Suburbia* (New York: Basic, 1987); Sam Bass Warner, *Streetcar Suburbs: The Process of Growth in Boston, 1870–1900* (Cambridge, Mass.: Harvard University Press, 1962); David Schuyler, *The New Urban Landscape: The Redefinition of City Form in Nineteenth-Century America* (Baltimore, Md.: Johns Hopkins University Press, 1986); Gwendolyn Wright, *Building the Dream: A Social History of Housing in America* (New York: Pantheon, 1981); and Kenneth T. Jackson, *Crabgrass Frontier: The Suburbanization of the United States* (New York: Oxford University Press, 1985).

9. The last third of the century experienced something of a church-building boom. Methodists, for instance, reported an increase of 4,974 church buildings in the period 1865–1874, for an increase in property values of $45,268,013. An incomplete yearly breakdown showed 420 new churches in 1866, 477 in 1868, 1,325 in 1870, 67 in 1871, 569 in 1872, 490 in 1873, and 460 in 1874. *Methodist Almanac 1877* (New York: Nelson and Phillips, 1877), 35.

10. That these three examples are all taken from Methodist Episcopal sources is largely coincidental. While I would like to represent other denominations here, I have found few congregations that have preserved their discussions associated with relocation in the late nineteenth century. Further, excellent historical studies exist of each of the three churches discussed. While Methodists, as Finke and Stark have demonstrated, were particularly adept at winning members and thus developed well-honed competitive skills, the fact that neither the locations they chose nor the churches they built differed from those of Presbyterians, Baptists, and Congregationalists suggests that all of these congregations belonging to many different evangelical denominations experienced similar decisionmaking processes. Thus, the conclusions here about Methodists can be extrapolated with some confidence to other evangelical congregations of the period.

On denominational competition and Methodist strategies, see Roger Finke and Rodney Stark, *The Churching of America, 1776–1900: Winners and Losers in Our Religious Economy* (New Brunswick, N.J.: Rutgers University Press, 1992).

11. In this section, I am deeply indebted to the primary historical research on Lovely Lane performed by David Gilmore Wright and presented as "Conception and Realization: An Historic Building Statement," in the excellent book *The Restoration of the Lovely Lane Church, Baltimore City Station* (Baltimore, Md.: Trustees of the Methodist Episcopal Church, 1980), 1–85.

The First Methodist Episcopal Church congregation existed under a variety of names. Organized in 1784 in the Lovely Lane Meetinghouse, the congregation soon erected a brick church, which they named the Light Street M.E. Church after its location. This church was dedicated by Bishop Francis Asbury, the "founder of American Methodism," on 21 May 1786. After a move, it took the name First M.E. Church of Baltimore in 1872. This name was used through the period under examination in this study and so will be used throughout. In November 1954 the congregation changed its name once again, this time harking back to its point of origin and taking the name Lovely Lane United Methodist Church. See Wright, "Conception and Realization," 2–4, 95.

12. Sherry H. Olson lists the cost as $325,000 in her history of the city, *Baltimore: The Building of an American City* (Baltimore, Md.: Johns Hopkins University Press, 1980), 193–94. Wright lists the cost of the Mount Vernon Place Church as $375,000 in "Conception and Realization," 3.

13. Wright, "Conception and Realization," 12.

14. Wright, "Conception and Realization," 7.

15. Wright, "Conception and Realization," 4. These, like all congregationally produced membership figures, should be approached with caution. It is not clear whether the figure designates 300 families (i.e., 300 male heads of households whose families also attended) or whether it includes all adult male and female members. I have found no earlier membership figures with which to compare this 300 figure.

16. Wright, "Conception and Realization," 12.

17. Wright, "Conception and Realization," 10 n1.

18. Wright, "Conception and Realization," 4.

19. Wright, "Conception and Realization," 5, 16.

20. Wright, "Conception and Realization," 6.

21. The statement echoes the familiar, if paternalistic, rhetoric of the previous generations of Methodist and other revivalists, who considered converting sinners the primary evangelical mission.

22. Wright, "Conception and Realization," 13.

23. It is not certain that all the male members were unaware of Goucher's intentions. Indeed, it is likely that many supported Goucher and his scheme from the beginning. Wright, "Conception and Realization," 12.

24. Wright, "Conception and Realization," 13.

25. Wright, "Conception and Realization," 16. The board of trustees did take the precaution, however, of consulting an attorney on the legality of such a move to the country. Charles W. Ridgley reported that, in his opinion, the word *precincts*, which limited the jurisdiction of the Baltimore Conference, could be interpreted to include all of the "environs" or "suburbs" of Baltimore. The purchase was made, and Goucher himself simultaneously negotiated for several adjacent lots, which he donated in 1885 to the Methodist church for the establishment of a women's college.

26. "Strange Doings—First M.E. Church," *Baltimore Pioneer*, 1 Jan. 1884, 4.

27. This cost figure is an estimate. Wright quotes the *Baltimore American* as estimating the cost at between $240,000 and $250,000, figures that include the cost of the land donated by

Goucher. Such estimates may well have been inflated by boosterism. Wright, "Conception and Realization," 41.

28. See Walter Carlock, *History of Wesley Church: The First 125 Years* (Minneapolis, Minn.: Wesley United Methodist Church, 1977), 39.

29. In this section, I am indebted to historian Linda K. Kirby's excellent congregational history, *Heritage of Heroes: Trinity United Methodist Church, 1859–1988* (Denver, Colo.: Trinity United Methodist Church, 1988).

30. Kirby, *Heritage of Heroes*, 42–44.

31. Kirby, *Heritage of Heroes*, 57.

32. Kirby, *Heritage of Heroes*, 51.

33. Lyle W. Dorsett, *The Queen City: A History of Denver* (Boulder, Colo.: Pruett, 1977), 57.

34. *Rocky Mountain Daily News*, quoted in Gunther Barth, "Metropolism in the Far West," in *The Age of Industrialism in America*, edited by Frederic Cople Jaher (New York: Free Press, 1968), 172–173.

35. Dorsett, *Queen City*, 89; Kirby, *Heritage of Heroes*, 70.

36. Kirby, *Heritage of Heroes*, 72.

37. The quote refers to a plan to turn the site into a business block, which is mentioned later in this chapter. Peter Winne, *Historical Gleanings* (Denver, Colo.: Trinity United Methodist Church, 1915–1916), 72–73.

38. Kirby, *Heritage of Heroes*, 72.

39. Kirby cites a 1929 letter by Bishop Earl M. Cranston (minister at Lawrence Street from 1878 to 1881) to Trinity Church in which the salary range is from $2,500 to $3,500 with the rent-free use of the parsonage, a package that ranked among the best in the country for Methodist ministers. Kirby, *Heritage of Heroes*, 57, 66, 68.

40. Kirby, *Heritage of Heroes*, 72.

41. Winne, *Historical Gleanings*, 74.

42. Kirby, *Heritage of Heroes*, 70.

43. Winne, *Historical Gleanings*, 70. Trustees included John A. Clough, J. B. Avery, John Evans, E. Milleson, J. B. Wightman, Samuel H. Elbert, and W. P. Mills [Miller?]. Winne, 69. Church incorporation was not new. Trinity Church in New York City had centralized its control over its property in a "corporation" in 1814. Its activities during the latter half of the nineteenth century rival secular corporations in terms of avarice and arrogance. See Robert Cross, ed., *The Church and the City* (Indianapolis, Ind.: Bobbs-Merrill, 1967).

44. Alan Trachtenberg, *The Incorporation of America: Culture and Society in the Gilded Age* (New York: Hill and Wang, 1982), 82.

45. Winne, *Historical Gleanings*, 72.

46. Winne, *Historical Gleanings*, 72.

47. Charles E. Gregersen, *Dankmar Adler: His Theatres and Auditoriums* (Athens: Swallow Press and Ohio University Press, 1990), 38, 98. On Methodists' success in attracting members, see Finke and Stark, *Churching of America*. The trend toward congregational ownership of commercial property grew rapidly, making the practice fairly common by the early twentieth century.

48. Kirby, *Heritage of Heroes*, 83–84.

49. *Minneapolis Journal*, 21 Jan. 1891. See also 28 Jan. 1893.

50. The more common usage of the term *mission church* was to designate the establishment of a church in a poor or frontier area in which the residents did not have the wherewithal to do so on their own.

51. Hill was actually the second minister called to Fowler. See John Wesley Hill, *Twin City Methodism: A History of the Methodist Episcopal Church in Minneapolis and St. Paul, Minn.* (Minneapolis, Minn.: Price Bros., 1895), 36–37; and "Fowler M.E. Church—A Part of Hennepin's Past," 37, typescript located in the Scottish Rite Temple Archives, Minneapolis, Minn.

52. Hill, *Twin City Methodism*, 36.

53. Hill, *Twin City Methodism*, 36.

54. Hill, *Twin City Methodism*, 37.

55. Hill, *Twin City Methodism*, 37–38.

56. Quoted in the Reverend Dennis Alexander, "Serving the Downtown Community: Wesley Church," 17 Jan. 1988, Wesley United Methodist Church Archives, Minneapolis, Minn. Perhaps this scolding explains why the conference and Hennepin Avenue Methodist were so careful to call the church they initiated in Lowry Hill a "mission."

57. "Dedication: Fowler Methodist Episcopal Church, Minneapolis", 8 Dec. 1907, Scottish Rite Temple Archives, Minneapolis, Minn.

58. Hill, *Twin City Methodism*, 39.

59. Hill, *Twin City Methodism*, 30.

60. Fowler membership figures appear in "Fowler M.E. Church—A Part of Hennepin's Past," 40, Scottish Rite Temple Archives.

61. *Congregational Yearbook* (Boston: Congregational Publishing Society, 1879), 19; and Methodist Episcopal Church Board of Extension, *Sample Pages of Catalogue of Architectural Plans for Churches and Parsonages* (Philadelphia: Board of Church Extension, 1884), 1–10.

62. This claim was put forth in an article originally published in the *New York Evening Post* and reprinted in an architectural trade serial. Discussing the "conversion of churches in Philadelphia," the brief note asserts that as congregations moved out of that city's business district, having "begun their migration to the residential districts," not only were some able to "erect more pretentious edifices," but "in some cases [were able] to establish an endowment-fund." It further notes that congregations were merging as they migrated out of town: "By the end of the year five of the largest, wealthiest, and most influential of the old-time churches in the city, now located on central Broad Street, will have been abandoned. One of the resultant new churches, the First Baptist, will be the wealthiest institution of its denomination in the country." See "Conversion of Churches in Philadelphia," *AA&BN*, 17 Dec. 1898, 100.

63. See Paul Clifford Larson and Susan M. Brown, eds., *The Spirit of H. H. Richardson on the Midland Prairies: Regional Transformations of an Architecture Style* (Minneapolis, Minn.: University Art Museum, and Ames: Iowa State University Press, 1988).

64. On Warren H. Hayes, see Hill, *Twin City Methodism*, 93–95, 335–36; and Peter Jursik, "Warren H. Hayes," 4 June 1980, typescript in the Minneapolis History Collection, Minneapolis Public Library and Information Center, Minneapolis, Minn.

65. Winne, *Historical Gleanings*, 104.

66. Wright, "Conception and Realization," 7.

67. "The Mother Church of Minnesota Methodism," 11. Original document located in the Wesley United Methodist Church Archives, Minneapolis, Minn.

68. Montgomery Schuyler, *American Architecture and Other Writings* (Cambridge, Mass.: Belknap, 1961), 1:213–14. For further criticism of the church, see F. S. Barnum, Letter to Editor, *AA&BN*, 21 May 1887, 251. A brief defense appears in Clarence O. Arey, Letter to Editor, *AA&BN*, 4 June 1887, 275.

69. One congregationally produced history asserts that while the design for Wesley M.E. Church was attributed to Hayes, Frederick Heath of Tacoma, Wash., returned to the church in 1947 (at the age of 92) and claimed that as a young architect working for Hayes, he had actually designed the building, including the complex center dome. While it is quite likely that Hayes's employees contributed to his projects, Heath's grandiose claim cannot be substantiated. See Carlock, *History of Wesley Church*, 38.

70. For an analysis of the cultural meanings of the late nineteenth-century medieval revival, see T. J. Jackson Lears, *No Place of Grace: Antimodernism and the Transformation of American Culture, 1880–1920* (New York: Pantheon, 1981).

71. Alan Gowans, *Images of American Living: Four Centuries of Architecture and Furniture as Cultural Expression* (Philadelphia: Lippincott, 1964), 354.

72. On Richardson's buildings, see Jeffrey Karl Ochsner, *H. H. Richardson: Complete Architectural Works* (Cambridge, Mass.: MIT Press, 1982).

73. On Stickney and this church, see "The Seventy-Fifth Anniversary Program of the First Congregational Church, Pueblo, Colorado, 1878-1953," 18-25 Oct. 1953. First Congregational Church Archives, Pueblo, Colo.

74. "A Congregational Corner Stone," *Minneapolis Tribune*, 28 Sept. 1886, 5.

75. In the absence of a Congregational minister, Dana, a Presbyterian minister from St. Paul, performed this service under the Union agreement of the region.

76. "Congregational Corner Stone," 5.

77. "Congregational Corner Stone," 5.

78. On municipal armories, see Robert M. Fogelson, *America's Armories: Architecture, Society, and Public Order* (Cambridge, Mass.: Harvard University Press, 1989).

Chapter 5

1. John Durand, "Henry Ward Beecher on Church Architecture," *Crayon* 6 (May 1859): 154-57. The quote appears on p. 156.

2. John Durand, "The Competition Plans for the Plymouth Church," *Crayon* 6 (Dec. 1859): 374-77. The quote appears on pp. 374-75. See also Durand, "Henry Ward Beecher," 154.

3. The terms *auditorium, audience room*, and *sanctuary* were all commonly used during the last third of the nineteenth century to designate the main worship room of evangelical churches. Adopting the term *sanctuary*, Congregationalists and Presbyterians indicated the extent to which the interest in liturgics and more High Church worship forms popularized during the Gothic Revival period had achieved a lasting place in their religious symbol system. The first article in the inaugural issue of *Church Building Quarterly* addressed the use of the term *sanctuary*, presenting arguments in favor of it ranging from biblical justification to the idea that the sanctuary is ordained by God and within it he dwells. See T. K. Noble, "The Sanctuary, in Its Relation to the Material, Moral, and Spiritual Life of the Community," *Church Building Quarterly* 1 (Jan. 1883): 13.

The question of which was the first auditorium church is one that I have avoided because it is so difficult to isolate the origins of any architectural phenomenon. The four 1860s examples I cite as the earliest were, of course, preceded by the Broadway Tabernacle, and isolated British and European examples also occurred. Even so, it was not until the buildings of the 1860s that the auditorium sanctuary became a distinct church type.

4. For a description of First Baptist, see "First Baptist Church, New Completion—A Model Edifice," *Chicago Tribune*, 16 Mar. 1866, 4. The floor of this church was not inclined as an amphitheatre. For a description of First Congregational, see "A Church Burned," *Chicago Daily Tribune*, 17 Jan. 1873, 4. A list, by no means exhaustive, of fifty-eight auditorium churches is found in Jeanne Halgren Kilde, "Spiritual Armories: A Social and Architectural History of Neo-Medieval Auditorium Churches in the U.S., 1869-1910" (Ph.D. diss., University of Minnesota, 1991), 218-25.

5. Catherine L. Albanese, *America: Religions and Religion*, 3d ed. (Belmont, Calif.: Wadsworth, 1999), 8-10.

6. Individual congregations of the period often had a dozen or more internal committees as well as societies and organizations formed by members, and several studies of this "age of association" exist. See, for instance, Evelyn Brooks Higginbotham, *Righteous Discontent: The Women's Movement in the Black Baptist Church, 1880-1920* (Cambridge, Mass.: Harvard University Press, 1993); and Ruth Bordin, *Women and Temperance: The Quest for Power and Liberty, 1873-1900* (Philadelphia: Temple University Press, 1981).

7. Pilgrim Congregational Church, Cleveland, Ohio, "Forty Years in Pilgrim Church, 1859–1899: A Brief Account of the Celebration of the Fortieth Anniversary, the Historical Paper, the Sermon of the Pastor the Following Sunday, and Other Historical Data," Western Reserve Historical Society, Cleveland, Ohio (pamphlet C669). See also *1891 Yearbook of the Jennings Avenue Congregational Church*, Pilgrim Congregational Church Archives, Cleveland, Ohio.

8. Quoted in Francine Haber, Kenneth R. Fuller, and David N. Wetzel, *Robert S. Roeschlaub: Architect of the Emerging West, 1843–1923* (Denver: Colorado Historical Society, 1988), 72. This congregation, of course, had decided to relocate and rebuild because it felt its vitality failing, and the idea of attracting people by building a large auditorium made sense, even if it were a bit risky. More conservative advice was offered by the Reverend W. P. Fisher of Brunswick, Maine, who warned that a congregation of 200 should build an audience room for 500. See W. P. Fisher, "The Size and Shape of the Church Edifice," *Church Building Quarterly* 1 (Oct. 1883): 104–5.

9. Quoted in William T. Euster, *The Philosophy of Church Building: How to Build a Beautiful Modern Church or Parsonage at Half Price* (Pendleton, Oreg.: Pendleton Printery, Jack Huston, 1908), 25. Euster also encouraged the construction of audience rooms as large as the congregation could afford.

10. Editorial, *AA&BN*, 10 Nov. 1877, 357.

11. John A. Faxon, "Modern Church Building I, " *AA&BN*, 15 Feb. 1879, 50–52, and "Modern Church Building II," *AA&BN*, 1 Mar. 1879, 66–67.

12. See E. C. Gardner, *Common Sense in Church Building, Illustrated by Seven Original Plates* (New York: Bicknell & Comstock, 1880). See also a review of this book, which points out that not all Protestant services are so heavily based on sermonizing as are the Congregationalists about whom Gardner writes. The reviewer further argues that the centralized amphitheatre plan encouraged by Gardner is not appropriate for all denominations. Review of *Common Sense in Church Building*, by E. C. Gardner, *AA&BN*, 20 Mar. 1880, 120.

13. A. F. Oakley, "Notes on Modern Church Building," *AA&BN*, 21 Aug. 1880, 88–89.

14. Unsigned letter from Stanford White to John Franklin Goucher, Sept. 1886, Lovely Lane Church Archives, Baltimore, Md., quoted in David Gilmore Wright, "Conception and Realization: An Historic Building Statement," in *The Restoration of the Lovely Lane Church, Baltimore City Station* (Baltimore, Md.: Trustees of the Methodist Episcopal Church, 1980), 48. See also Richard M. Hunt, "The Church Architecture That We Need," *AA&BN*, 1 Dec. 1877, 384–85; and Emlen Littell, "The Church Architecture That We Need," *AA&BN*, 12 Jan. 1878, 10–12.

15. Shortly after completing First Congregational Church in Oak Park, Adler began a serious study of acoustics and the use of the isacoustic curve to enhance viewers' reception of stage performances. His study culminated in another church project, the Central Music Hall (1880), a building commissioned by supporters of popular preacher David Swing to house his new nondenominational congregation. Gregersen argues that Adler developed most of the acoustical principles that ultimately resulted in his national reputation during his work on Central. See Charles E. Gregersen, *Dankmar Adler: His Theatres and Auditoriums* (Athens: Swallow Press and Ohio University Press, 1990), 10–17, 38–49.

16. For further discussion of acoustics and church amphitheatres during the period, see Oakley, "Notes on Modern Church Building," 88–89. Amphitheatres were used regularly in college and university lecture halls, perhaps harking back to their use as dissecting theatres in the early seventeenth century. The strong association between education and the amphitheatre may have discouraged its use in the entertainment field. Further study is needed in this area.

17. On Castle Garden Theatre, see Stanley T. Lewis, "The New York Theatre: Its Background and Architectural Development, 1750–1853" (Ph.D. diss., Ohio State University, 1953), 165–88. On the Beyreuth Festspielhaus and other amphitheatres designed by Gottfried Semper and Karl Schinkel, see Nikolaus Pevsner, *A History of Building Types* (Princeton, N.J.: Princeton University Press, 1976), 86–87; and Donald C. Mullin, *The Development of the Playhouse: A*

Survey of Theatre Architecture from the Renaissance to the Present (Berkeley: University of California Press, 1970), 142–46.

18. See "M.E. Church at Lodi, N.Y.," *AA&BN*, 29 July 1882, 344. It is not clear whether this church featured an auditorium interior. Other published examples include First Congregational Church, Minneapolis, Minn., *Congregational Yearbook 1888* (Boston: Congregational Publishing Society, 1888), 83–85; First Congregational, Appleton, Wis., *Congregational Yearbook 1889*, 82–83; New Union Congregational, Rockville, Conn., *Congregational Yearbook 1891*, 8–9; First Congregational, Salt Lake City, Utah, *Congregational Yearbook 1892*, 82–83; Plymouth Congregational, Oshkosh, Wis., *Congregational Yearbook, 1895*, 520; and Congregational Church, Eagle Grove, Iowa, *Congregational Yearbook 1896*, 10. See also First Presbyterian, Peoria, Ill., *AA&BN*, 7 July 1888, 7; and Centenary M.E., Minneapolis, Minn., *AA&BN*, 25 Oct. 1890, following p. 60. Probably due to his repeated use and modification of the diagonal plan, Hayes has been credited as the originator of this plan. See "Our Church Cut," *Church Building Quarterly* 6 (Apr. 1888): 54–55; and Henry F. Withey and Elsie R. Withey, *Biographical Dictionary of American Architects* (Los Angeles, Calif: New Age, 1956), 274. Instances prior to these known ones by Hayes did occur, however. Tilden published a diagonally oriented "Village Church" in the *AA&BN*, 22 May 1880, 224; and William H. Brearley published a diagonal-plan auditorium in his *Improved Bible-School Building and Church Edifice Combined* (Detroit, Mich.: n.p., 1881), 4–5. Minneapolis architects Louis Long and Frederick Kees completed their diagonally oriented First Baptist Church in 1886.

Diagonal plans became quite common in the architectural literature by the late 1880s. See Twelfth Baptist Church, Boston, *AA&BN*, 23 Mar. 1889, plate following p. 140; Mission Chapel, Minneapolis, Minn. (Orff and Orff, architects), *AA&BN*, 24 Aug. 1889, following p. 86; and First Baptist Church in Elmira, N.Y. (Pierce and Dockstader, architects), *AA&BN*, 22 Feb. 1890, 126. See also William H. Brearley, *Brearley's Improved Church Plans* (Detroit, Mich.: n. p., 1883); Sidney J. Osgood, *Churches* (Grand Rapids, Mich.: Dean, 1893); George W. Kramer, *The What, How, and Why of Church Building* (New York: n.p., 1897); Euster, *Philosophy of Church Building*; and William Wallace Martin, *Manual of Ecclesiastical Architecture* (Cincinnati, Ohio: Curts & Jennings, 1897), 391–92. The diagonal plan was particularly suitable for those congregations that wanted a Sunday school attached to their sanctuaries. See chap. 7 on the Akron Plan Sunday school.

19. Curtains were used in late eighteenth- and early nineteenth-century churches as a background to elevated pulpits; thus, their use in the new performance platforms, although clearly quoting from theatrical venues, was not unprecedented in religious spaces.

20. Often donated by individual benefactors, church organs were invariably showered with praise. The Roosevelt organ of Denver's Trinity M.E. was declared "the greatest organ in America and one of the greatest in the world" for its "amazing power and volume." Linda K. Kirby, *Heritage of Heroes: Trinity United Methodist Church; 1859–1988* (Denver, Colo.: Trinity United Methodist Church, 1988), 90. In Minneapolis, the $5,500 Steere & Turner organ that Governor Pillsbury donated to First Congregational Church was "pronounced a very fine instrument" by "musical experts of [Minneapolis]." "Dedicated to God," *Minneapolis Tribune*, 5 Mar. 1888, 5.

21. This formalist message may have been considered at odds with evangelical worship a generation earlier, but by the end of the century would be considered perfectly acceptable. It should also be noted that, particularly in the pipe-fence arrangement, not all of the visible pipes are functional. On the history of this important instrument, see Orpha Ochse, *The History of the Organ in the United States* (Bloomington: Indiana University Press, 1975).

22. Simon Tidworth, *Theatres: An Architectural and Cultural History* (New York: Praeger, 1973), 170.

23. See Christos G. Athanasopulos, *Contemporary Theatre: Evolution and Design* (New York: Wiley, 1983), 106–7.

24. Haber et al., *Roeschlaub*, 76.

25. For descriptions, see Emma E. Newman, Diary, vol. 10, 19 Oct. 1876, quoted in Randi Jones Walker, *Emma Newman: A Frontier Woman Minister* (Syracuse, N.Y.: Syracuse University Press, 2000), 103. See also Darrel M. Robertson, *The Chicago Revival, 1876: Society and Revivalism in a Nineteenth-Century City* (Metuchen, N.J.: Scarecrow, 1989), 50–51; and "Mr. Moody's Temple," *AA&BN*, 24 June 1876, 208.

26. The lighting in First M.E. is described in the *Baltimore Sun*, 7 Nov. 1887.

27. Haber et al., *Roeschlaub*, 152 n46. The use of marquis lighting was by no means an exclusively Protestant practice. Isaac Meyer Wise's Plum Street Synagogue in Cincinnati, Ohio, included marquis lights, and Dankmar Adler's K. A. M. (Kehilath Anshe Ma'ariv) Temple in Chicago featured a frieze of six-pointed stars, each with a center marquis light, running throughout the audience room. Religious buildings were also among the first to use exterior lighting. Wesley (Centenary) M.E. in Minneapolis, for instance, displayed a five-foot-high lighted, electric cross on the cap of its massive tower in 1892.

28. I have not found pew rental plans for any of these three churches. On Trinity's invalid boxes, see Haber et al., *Roeschlaub*, 72. On the use of boxes to indicate social distinction, see Marvin Carlson, *Places of Performance: The Semiotics of Theatre Architecture* (Ithaca, N.Y.: Cornell University Press, 1989), 135–56.

29. For instance, Free Church Baptists in Boston bought the Tremont Theatre in 1843 in a move that echoed the New York Presbyterian free churchers.

30. On the opera house service, see George T. Peck, "Historical Account of the Fifth Avenue Presbyterian Church," in *A Noble Landmark of New York: The Fifth Avenue Presbyterian Church, 1808–1958* (New York: Fifth Avenue Presbyterian Church, 1960), 37. On Thomas Beecher, see Myra C. Glenn, *Thomas K. Beecher: Minister to a Changing America, 1824–1900* (Westport, Conn.: Greenwood, 1996), 126–29. Glenn points out that Beecher was strongly criticized by other clergy in Elmira for holding his meetings in the opera house. On Moody, see J. C. Pollock, *Moody: A Biographical Portrait of the Pacesetter in Modern Mass Evangelism* (New York: Macmillan, 1963), 79. On the Methodists at the Metropolitan Opera House, see Roger Finke and Rodney Stark, *The Churching of America, 1776–1990* (New Brunswick, N.J.: Rutgers University Press, 1992), 162–63. On David Swing, see Daniel Bluestone, *Constructing Chicago* (New Haven, Conn.: Yale University Press, 1991), 99–103.

31. "The Things of Heaven," *Rocky Mountain News*, 1 Apr. 1888.

32. The use of opera seats should not be confused with the use of individual chairs, which had long been the standard in British cathedrals. Small, rural congregations that used their sanctuaries for Sunday school as well as for worship services were advised to furnish the room with folding seats, which could be reconfigured to suit each need. See "Design No. 29," *Church Building Quarterly* 1 (July 1883): n.p.

33. J. C. Worthington, *The Building of a Church* (Philadelphia: Architectural Pen-Points, 1887), 4.

34. Many descriptions of churches published in the trade literature during this period focus on technical and mechanical innovations. An excellent example is "The Illustrations: Fifth Avenue Presbyterian Church, New York, N.Y., Mr. Carl Pfeiffer, Architect, New York, N.Y.," *AA&BN*, 24 Mar. 1883, 139–40. A discussion of the integration of technology into churches in the first half of the nineteenth century appears in Jane C. Nylander, "Toward Comfort and Uniformity in New England Meeting Houses, 1750–1850," in *New England Meeting House and Church: 1630–1850*, ed. Peter Benes and Philip D. Zimmerman (Boston: Boston University for the Dublin Seminar for New England Folklife, 1979), 86–100.

35. "The Changes in Preaching," *Scribner's Monthly Magazine* 14 (June 1877): 255–56. The quote appears on p. 255.

36. William G. T. Shedd, *Homiletics and Pastoral Theology*, 8th ed. (New York: Scribner, Armstrong, 1875). For a discussion of the goals of seminary education at this time, see Kathleen

A. Mahoney, "The Concept of Time in the Secularization of the Academy," paper delivered at the 168th meeting of the American Society of Church History, Boston, 7 Jan. 2001. Several articles on preaching appeared in *Scribner's Monthly*, indicating the public nature of this discussion. On Moody and other evangelists, see "Mr. Moody and His Works," *Scribner's Monthly* 11 (Nov. 1875): 124–25. See also "'God's Word through Preaching,'" *Scribner's Monthly* 11 (Dec. 1875): 294–95, an editorial evaluating preaching education at Yale and praising the publication of the Reverend John Hall's lectures delivered under the Lyman Beecher lectureship. On the delivery and impending publication of the Beecher lectures by the Rev. Dr. R. S. Storrs, see "'Preaching without Notes,'" *Scribner's Monthly* 11 (Dec. 1875): 295. See also "Modern Preaching," *Scribner's Monthly Illustrated Magazine* 4 (Sept. 1872): 628–29; "Revivals and Evangelists," *Scribner's Monthly* 11 (Apr. 1876): 887; "A New Departure," *Scribner's Monthly* 12 (June 1876): 268–69; "The Changes in Preaching," *Scribner's Monthly* 14 (June 1877): 255–56; and S. L. Blake, "Extempore Preaching," *Congregational Quarterly* , 2d ser., 2 (July 1870): 378–91.

37. Such motivations, of course, also informed the construction of the Broadway Tabernacle. Plymouth Church in Brooklyn, built in 1850, was informed by similar motivations.

38. Later in his career, Euster published *The Philosophy of Church Building*, which included plans and drawings for several types of church buildings (including several square and diagonally oriented auditorium sanctuaries) and advice on furnishings, interior decoration, ventilation, and acoustics. Euster was assigned to a new congregation approximately every three years, following the Methodist church rules for assigning ministers. Architect H. N. Black apparently followed Euster, providing the building expertise and plans for churches in Great Falls and Anaconda, Mont.; Moscow and Lewiston, Idaho; and Pendleton and Portland, Oreg.

39. Prior to coming to First Methodist, Goucher had gained church-building experience guiding the relocation of Baltimore's Gilmore Street Methodist congregation and the erection of their new church near Harlem Park, an area that attracted upper-middle-class residents. See Sherry H. Olson, *Baltimore: The Building of an American City* (Baltimore, Md.: Johns Hopkins University Press, 1980), 191. In 1880, he was called to the Strawbridge M.E. Church where his first sermon, "Rise and Build," spurred the congregation into a building project that resulted in the completion of a new church in 1882. Given his successful track record as both an inspiring preacher and accomplished church builder, it was probably not coincidental that Goucher was called to First M.E. in 1883, when that congregation was vacillating on the question of whether to build a new church. Goucher's experience and knowledge proved critical to the final product, as he not only proved an energetic and charismatic fundraiser but he also developed alternate plans for the chapel and Sunday school areas of the church that were subsequently incorporated into architect Stanford White's design. See Wright, "Conception and Realization," 7–8, 20. Similarly, Buchtel had established a reputation as both a preacher and a church builder prior to his call to Trinity Church in Denver. See Kirby, *Heritage of Heroes*, 80. In both cases, the arrival (likely carefully planned by factions in each congregation) of a dynamic preacher and experienced church builder proved to be the catalyst that an uncertain congregation needed to take action. In both cases, the result was a monumental auditorium church. Preachers such as Buchtel and Goucher were uniquely capable of inspiring congregations' enthusiasm for the building project, cohesion around a single plan of action, and willingness to donate time and money. Stories of inspiring fundraising sermons survive in the lore of several congregations. The tone is often one of awe as conscientious newspaper reporters and church historians recorded the vast sums that ministers coaxed out of members' pockets during a single service. Most notable is the *Denver Republican's* coverage of the remarkable Easter Sunday service of 1 Apr. 1888, during which Buchtel raised more than $60,000 for Trinity Church. Kirby, 86.

40. An alternative interpretation is offered by Bruggink and Droppers, who attribute the Protestant shift away from the raised pulpit toward the lectern to a growing interest in the personality of ministers rather than in the message, an emphasis they interpret as an expectation of a moving

performance by an individual. Donald J. Bruggink and Carl H. Droppers, *Christ and Architecture: Building Presbyterian Reformed Churches* (Grand Rapids, Mich.: Eerdmans, 1965), 399.

41. Shedd, *Homiletics*, 296.

42. Shedd maintains that "eloquence" is the fundamental quality of preaching, and the bulk of his text is devoted to it. While he gives relatively short shrift to the three elements he places in the liturgical category—scriptural reading, hymns, and prayer—he does assert that certain elements of Latin and medieval liturgies can be productively included in evangelical Protestant services, particularly the use of "such grand chants as the *Gloria in excelsis*, and the *Te Deum laudamus*, [which] if frequently read and meditated in the sounding and rhythmical Latin, lift up the mind for praise and adoration, like the pealing tones of an organ, and impart a craving for simple and lofty verse, in the sanctuary." Shedd, *Homiletics*, 306.

43. Lyman Abbott, "Report of the Committee on the Improvement of Worship," *Minutes of the National Council of the Congregational Churches in the United States*, 8th sess. Minneapolis, Minn. (Boston: Congregational Sunday School and Publishing Society, 1893), 93.

44. Abbott, "Report of the Committee," 93. Abbott self-deprecatingly claimed that his suggestions were simply offered "for public discussion" and were not to be taken as a call for greater liturgicism in Congregational churches. Whether he did this to assuage those who disliked interference by the national council in local congregational decisions or to assuage those who disliked the growing interest in liturgy is not clear.

45. See, for instance, Leonard Woolsey Bacon, "Suggestions Concerning the Ritual of a Puritan Church," *Congregational Quarterly* 5 (July 1863): 242–46. Bacon suggests the following order for morning service: introit (chanting of passage of Scripture by choir), invitation to confession and prayer (read by minister), confession and invocation (by minister), Lord's Prayer (congregation), Gloria Patri (congregation), reading of Scripture (minister), anthem, prayer, hymn, sermon, prayer, hymn, and benediction. The 1900 *Manual* of the First Congregational Church in Minneapolis included the following order of service: organ prelude, Sanctus, invocation, Lord's Prayer, responsive reading, anthem, reading of the Scriptures, offering, prayer, sermon, hymn, benediction, and organ postlude. The 23 Feb. 1902 anniversary service of Central Presbyterian Church in St. Paul included the following order of service: organ voluntary, doxology, invocation, responsive psalm reading, anthem, hymn, Scripture lesson, prayer, offertory, duet, hymn, sermon, prayer, hymn, benediction, and postlude. First Baptist Church of Minneapolis worshiped on Sunday, 23 Nov. 1919, with the following order of service: organ prelude, doxology, hymn, responsive reading, Gloria Patri, violin solo, Scripture lesson, solo, pastoral prayer, offertory, hymn, sermon, hymn, benediction, and organ postlude.

The term *doxology* is used in the general sense to indicate a hymn of praise to God and most likely refers to "Praise God from Whom All Blessings Flow." This is in distinction to the Roman Catholic "greater doxology," or the hymn Gloria in Excelsis Deo, performed at the Eucharist and the "lesser doxology," Gloria Patri, sung after each psalm in the liturgy. The Gloria Patri remains common in United Church of Christ (Congregational) services today. (The author has standardized the spelling of this title, which appears both as Gloria Patri and Gloria Patria.) The Te Deum (Te Deum Laudamus, or "Thee, God, We Praise") is a Latin hymn traditionally said to have been improvised by St. Ambrose as he baptized St. Augustine in 386 c.e.. Scholarship, however, attributes it to Niceta, bishop of Remesiana (d. c. 414 c.e.). See the *Wordsworth Dictionary of Phrase and Fable* (Ware, Hertfordshire, U.K.: Wordsworth, 1993).

46. R. S. Peabody, quoted in "Modern Church Architecture," *AA&BN*, 8 Dec. 1877, 393.

47. For instance, B. Waugh and T. Mason, eds., *A Collection of Hymns, for the Use of the Methodist Episcopal Church, Principally from the Collection of the Rev. John Wesley, A.M.*, rev. ed. (New York: Lane & Tippett, 1845).

48. This, however, was also changing as new hymns addressed sinners and the unconverted, exhorting them to become Christian. Early Presbyterian discussions of church music appear in

"Church Music, Considered in Reference to Its Original Design and Its Present State," *Biblical Repertory and Princeton Review* 5 (1829): 410-29; "Thoughts on Church Music," *Presbyterian Magazine* 4 (July 1854): 303-8; "Praise-Singing: A Duty and a Means of Grace," *Presbyterian Magazine* 4 (June 1854): 266-70; and "Singing the Praises of God," *Presbyterian Magazine* 5 (July 1855): 335.

49. Josiah Holland ridiculed hymns that went beyond praise to express human concerns regarding the end time, judgment, death, mourning, and passing time. These sentiments, he argued, were not "naturally" expressed in music. See Holland, "Church Music," *Scribner's Monthly* 18 (1879): 134-35. For a brief summary of American hymnody, see Charles Hamm, *Music in the New World* (New York: Norton, 1983), 263-78.

50. Henry Theophilus Finck, *My Adventures in the Golden Age of Music* (New York: Funk and Wagnalls, 1926), 33-38, quoted in Lawrence W. Levine, *Highbrow/Lowbrow: The Emergence of Cultural Hierarchy in America* (Cambridge, Mass.: Harvard University Press, 1988), 133. See also Ellis Gray [Louisa T. Cragin], "The Mission of Music," *Harper's New Monthly Magazine* 51 (Oct. 1875): 736-44.

51. See Joseph A. Mussulman, *Music in the Cultured Generation* (Evanston, Ill.: Northwestern University Press, 1971).

52. This section relies heavily on the catalog presented by Mussulman in appendices 1-4 (Mussulman, *Music in the Cultured Generation*, 200-273), which list all of the articles on music from the *Atlantic Monthly*, 1857-1900; *Harper's New Monthly Magazine*, 1850-1900; *Scribner's Monthly/Century Illustrated Monthly*, 1871-1900; and *Scribner's Magazine*, 1887-1900. I have supplemented this list with examinations of denominational literature.

53. Shedd, *Homiletics*, 309. While some argued that didactic hymns were not appropriate because the natural expression for teaching is not singing, Shedd allowed for the use of didactic hymns.

54. Robinson initially made the case against art-music and professional musicians in "Artistic Help in Divine Service," *Century Illustrated Monthly Magazine* 27 (Feb. 1884): 632-34. The phrase *worship by proxy* was suggested in a response letter from "W. H. S." in "In Re: Church Music," *Century Illustrated Monthly Magazine* 28 (July 1884): 471. See also Charles S. Robinson, "Organs and Orchestras in Church," *Century Illustrated Monthly Magazine* 27 (Mar. 1884): 787-89; and "Worshiping by Proxy," *Century Illustrated Monthly Magazine* 27 (Apr. 1884): 946-48.

55. Mrs. A. B. Blake, "Church Music in America," *Harper's New Monthly Magazine* 58 (Apr. 1879): 737. See also "The Singing Seats," *Harper's Weekly* (19 Aug. 1876): 676, 678.

56. Not surprisingly, the sanctuary plan that Parker suggested in his book was the traditional cruciform of the Anglican church. See Francis J. Parker, *Church Building and Things To Be Considered* (Boston: Cupples, Upham, 1886), 85.

57. Charles S. Robinson, "What the Choirs Say," *Century Illustrated Monthly Magazine* 28 (June 1884): 307. Local discussion of these questions was also common. See, for instance, "Incongruities in Music," *Rocky Mountain News*, 9 Dec. 1888, 9.

58. Blake, "Church Music in America," 739. Demonstrating the immorality of professional musicians, Robinson relates the story of a "prominent soprano in New York, who immediately after Sabbath evening service was over, went to a beer-drinking saloon to sing at the concert." Robinson, "What the Choirs Say," 307. See also Robinson, "Artistic Help," 623-34; Robinson, "Organs and Orchestras," 787-89; Robinson, "Worshiping by Proxy," 946-48; Charles S. Robinson, "The Minister and the Man," *Century Illustrated Monthly Magazine* 28 (July 1884): 468-71; W. H. S., "In Re: Church Music," 471; Fred W. Wodell, "An Ideal Church," *Century Illustrated Monthly Magazine* 28 (July 1884): 471; "Church Music: A Letter to the Rev. Dr. Robinson," *Century Illustrated Monthly Magazine* 28 (July 1884): 472; Eugene Thayer, "Congregational Singing," *Century Illustrated Monthly Magazine* 28 (July 1884):

950-52; "A Word from the Organ-loft," *Century Illustrated Monthly Magazine* 29 (Nov. 1884): 156-57; and Edward Witherspoon, "Church Music: A Voice from the Choir-Loft," *Century Illustrated Monthly Magazine* 29 (Nov. 1884): 474-76.

Congregations and clergy were also criticized for compromising the solemnity of services, as a statement by R. Brown illustrates: "I went to the morning service in a new church in the fashionable Back Bay district of Boston. Behind the comfortable seat to which I was shown were some people talking evidently about secular matters. There was handshaking and much general conversation. Finally, the service began. The music seemed quite a feature and was chiefly confined to the choir of three or four young people who, nattily dressed, occupied a very prominent position directly over the pulpit. They warbled sweetly and frequently, so that at times one could almost imagine that a concert of sacred music was in progress, especially as the congregation were only once permitted to have any share in the vocal part of the service. The clergyman read a long string of notices, and made a mild attempt at a joke about one of these. He next suggested that a committee be appointed to transact some business, and, to my surprise, a baldheaded gentleman arose and named three or four persons. I felt apprehensive lest there might be a debate, but fortunately there was no dissent." See R. Brown, Jr., "What Our Architecture Lacks," *AA&BN*, 30 June 1888, 304.

59. Wodell, "Ideal Church," 471; Shedd, *Homiletics*, 301-9; Blake, "Church Music in America," 737-40; and Thayer, "Congregational Singing," 950-52.

60. Josiah G. Holland, "Church Music," *Scribner's Monthly* 28 (1879): 134-35.

61. Josiah G. Holland, "The Music of the Church," *Scribner's Monthly* 10 (1875): 243.

62. Mussulman, *Music in the Cultured Generation*, 188.

63. Levine, *Highbrow/Lowbrow*, 104-46, 226-31. As Levine argues, the sacralization of European art-music justified elites' near complete possession and control of it: only they, in their own estimation, were capable of performing it correctly and understanding it fully. Possession, however, did not preclude the possibility of wider dissemination, for with the sacralization of music came the corollary that it was capable of uplifting "lower" elements of society, a view that fueled the creation of "working people's" and popular concerts by various symphony orchestras. See also Mussulman, *Music in the Cultured Generation*, 70-83. A related musical movement was the jubilees, which were initially conceived by Patrick S. Gilmore, whose National and World Peace Jubilees were held in Boston in 1869 and 1872. During the initial jubilee, close to 40,000 spectators filled a specially erected auditorium to witness an orchestra of 900 pieces and a chorus of 20,000 voices. Gilmore, a bandleader who willingly bridged the chasm between art-music and more popular fare, created a program that included religious compositions by Mozart and Bach, popular hymns such as "A Mighty Fortress Is Our God," patriotic tunes, and popular operatic pieces. The jubilee idea caught on quickly, and similarly gigantic music festivals were held in New York, Chicago, and elsewhere throughout the United States in the 1870s and 1880s. The music presented at these events was predominantly religious. See H. W. Schwartz, *Bands of America* (Garden City, N.Y.: Doubleday, 1957); and Marwood Darlington, *Irish Orpheus: The Life of Patrick S. Gilmore, Bandmaster Extraordinary* (Philadelphia: Olivier, Maney, Klein, 1950).

64. Holland, "Music of the Church," 243. Elite congregations, such as San Francisco's First Presbyterian Church, could boast of a professional choir of ten. Robert Stevenson, *Protestant Church Music in America: A Short Survey of Men and Movements from 1564 to the Present* (New York: Norton, 1966), 112-14.

65. Blake, "Church Music in America," 737.

66. Holland, "Church Music," 135. Plymouth Church in Brooklyn, under the leadership of Henry Ward Beecher, was cited as a noted exception by Holland, for it did integrate congregational singing into its worship services. He excused the congregation for the practice, however, on several grounds: the organ was capable of drowning out the voices, the church did hire some

professional singers, and (because seats in the church were difficult to acquire) the guaranteed seats in the choir attracted excellent volunteer singers. See Holland, "Music of the Church," 243.

67. Mussulman, *Music in the Cultured Generation*, 187.

68. Mussulman, *Music in the Cultured Generation*, 57–69. Although Mussulman acknowledges that middle-class critics interpreted European art-music as inherently containing important messages about morality, about how people should live, and about spiritual inspiration, these meanings are not integrated into his analysis of the sacred-secular polarity that he sees between the church sanctuary and the opera house.

69. The opening service was held on Sunday, 23 Dec. 1888. The bulletin for the opening Sunday in the auditorium and the order of service for 13 October 1889 appear in Kirby, *Heritage of Heroes*, 88 and 102, respectively.

70. "Easter Services at First Baptist Church, Minneapolis, Minn.," 29 Mar. 1891, First Baptist Church Archives, Minneapolis, Minn.; and First Baptist Church Bulletin, 23 Nov. 1919, Minnesota Historical Society Archives, St. Paul, Minn.

71. Destroyed by fire in 1852, rebuilt and again burned in 1879, and again rebuilt and burned in 1893, the temple's architectural history must be considered in serial fashion. The 1879 and 1893 incarnations reflected the auditorium sanctuary trend, with its oblong audience room filled with curved pews, double gallery tiers, and elaborate stages. Individuals appearing on the Tremont Temple stage during this period included Frederick Douglass, Charles Dickens, Henry Ward Beecher, Mary Baker Eddy, Dwight L. Moody, Evangeline Booth, and Billy Sunday. Under pastor George C. Lorimer's leadership, the temple served as a center for evangelism, and William B. Riley was so impressed with the thousands gathered to hear Lorimer's preaching that his experience there continued to inspire him for decades.

72. See Bluestone, *Constructing Chicago*, 101–3.

73. See Papers of the First Baptist Church, Minnesota Historical Society Archives, St. Paul, Minn.

74. "Festival Opening," *Rocky Mountain Daily News*, 21 Dec. 1888. I have regularized the spellings of these titles and composers. The event was well advertised, and tickets sold for $1.50 each. Fifteen hundred people attended the concert in which "the cream of the musical circles of Denver, fully half of them . . . well-known soloists," as well as guest organists from Chicago and Salt Lake City presented sacred and secular art-music. Kirby, *Heritage of Heroes*, 90.

75. "The Great Organ: A Popular Concert at Trinity Methodist Last Night," *Rocky Mountain Daily News*, 22 Dec. 1888. Compare Levine on people's concerts, *Highbrow/Lowbrow*, 120–23, 130–31.

76. The largest hall in Denver until 1908, Trinity Church continued to be used for concerts and other public gatherings. Kirby, *Heritage of Heroes*, 103. Pilgrim Congregational Church in Cleveland also opened its new building with an organ recital in November 1894. Tickets to this event went for fifty cents and similarly included both religious and secular numbers. See Advertisement, "Organ Concert," *Cleveland Plain Dealer*, 24 Nov. 1894, 5; and "The New Organ," *Cleveland Plain Dealer*, 25 Nov. 1894, 15.

77. Nonetheless, jeremiads lamenting a perceived decline in religious enthusiasm were common, as the following passage from the editors of the *Chautauquan* illustrates: "In those days [of the Reformation] religious earnestness was at its maximum; we seem to be passing through a period when it is at a minimum. How far the seeming is accurate, it may not be easy to determine; but appearances are against the modern church. All our religious services lack in spirituality. The lack is in the sermon, the song, the prayer." Editorial, *Chautauquan* (Apr. 1885): 423–24.

78. Shedd refuses to designate an ideal length for sermons, instead mentioning in passing options of thirty, forty-five, and sixty minutes. Shedd, *Homiletics*, 141. Strong criticism came, however, from ministers who disliked the trend toward shorter sermons. Comparative studies

of congregational participation are needed. Historians have too often taken the public moanings of those convinced that religiosity was declining as accurate, ignoring the appeal of the jeremiad as a rhetorical strategy regardless of its truth.

79. On liberal Protestantism, see Kenneth Cauthen, *The Impact of American Religious Liberalism*, 2d ed. (Lanham, Md.: University Press of America, 1983); William R. Hutchinson, *The Modernist Impulse in American Protestantism* (Cambridge, Mass.: Harvard University Press, 1976); and Paul A. Carter, *The Spiritual Crisis of the Gilded Age* (Dekalb: Northern Illinois University Press, 1971). On more orthodox or conservative evangelicalism, see George W. Marsden, *Fundamentalism and American Culture: The Shaping of Twentieth-Century Evangelicalism, 1870–1925* (New York: Oxford University Press, 1980), and *Understanding Fundamentalism and Evangelicalism* (Grand Rapids, Mich.: Eerdmans, 1991), 9–61. On biblical inerrancy, see Ernest R. Sandeen, *The Roots of Fundamentalism: British and American Millenarianism, 1800–1930* (Chicago: University of Chicago Press, 1970), 103–31. For a more comparative analysis, see Ferenc Morton Szasz, *The Divided Mind of Protestant America, 1880–1930* (University: University of Alabama Press, 1982), 42–67.

80. Marsden, *Understanding Fundamentalism*, 38–39. There were, of course, exceptions. First Baptist in Minneapolis experienced five rancorous years of struggle between moderates and conservatives before the former split from the church in 1902. See William Vance Trollinger, *God's Empire: William Bell Riley and Midwestern Fundamentalism* (Madison: University of Wisconsin Press, 1990), 14–23; and Marie Acomb Riley, *The Dynamic of a Dream* (Grand Rapids, Mich.: Eerdmans, 1938), 65–88.

81. Albert C. Knudson, "The Evolution of Modern Biblical Study," *Methodist Review* 93 (1911): 910, quoted in Szasz, *Divided Mind*, 41.

82. See Guy Stanton Ford and Dora V. Smith, *The First Congregational Church of Minnesota: A Retrospect of Eighty Years* (Minneapolis, Minn.: n.p., 1952).

83. Joseph Siry, "Frank Lloyd Wright's Unity Temple and Architecture for Liberal Religion in Chicago, 1885–1909," *Art Bulletin* 73 (June 1991): 257–59.

84. Bluestone, *Constructing Chicago*, 99.

85. Bluestone, *Constructing Chicago*, 99–100.

86. Exceptions, which will be examined in the next chapter, generally focused on the domestic and familial nature of the church.

87. On the Union Gospel Tabernacle, see Jerry Eugene Henderson, "A History of the Ryman Auditorium in Nashville, Tennessee: 1892–1920" (Ph.D. diss., Louisiana State University, 1962); and William U. Eiland, *Nashville's Mother Church: The History of the Ryman Auditorium* (Nashville, Tenn.: Opryland, 1992).

88. For a Unitarian perspective disapproving of church auditoriums and supporting more ecclesiastical churches, see "Unitarian Church Building," *AA&BN*, 22 Nov. 1884, 248–49.

89. Trinity M.E. in Denver offered 1,650 regular seatings although some 2,000 could pack into it on special occasions. Kirby, *Heritage of Heroes*, 90. Wesley M.E. in Minneapolis accommodated some 1,300; First Congregational in Manistee, Mich., 1,200; and Union Park Congregational in Chicago, 1,500. To further escalate audience size, several auditorium sanctuaries contained multiple gallery tiers. Central Music Hall in Chicago featured two horseshoe-shaped galleries, and Mary Baker Eddy's First Church of Christian Science Extension (1906) in Boston had double tiers in the transepts adjacent to the stage and triple tiers opposite the stage. Another popular means of expanding auditorium space was the placement of a large Sunday school assembly room adjacent to the main auditorium. Separated by a recessible wall, the auditorium and the assembly room could be unified into a single continuous space with the removal of the wall. Particularly effective with diagonal-plan sanctuaries, this strategy has often been mislabeled as the Akron Plan, a term originally designating a specific Sunday school arrangement (see chap. 7).

Large seatings, however, did not guarantee large congregations. First Congregational in Minneapolis, for instance, seating 800, never did attract sufficient members to warrant the construction of the gallery in the original plan. This church, which featured a diagonal-plan sanctuary and an adjacent Akron Plan section called the Pilgrim Hall, accommodated 1,400 with the wall recessed. See description in the *Minneapolis Tribune*, 5 Mar. 1888, 3.

90. Faxon is clearly referring to curved seating here as well as a ramped audience room. See his 1879 series of articles on the U.S. theatre printed in the *AA&BN* beginning on 19 July 1879, 20–21, and continuing through several issues. The quote is from 2 Aug. 1879, 36.

91. On Pilgrim Congregational, see *1891 Yearbook of the Jennings Avenue Congregational Church*, 29, Pilgrim Congregational Church Archives, Cleveland, Ohio. I place this congregation in the moderate-to-liberal category on the basis that they invited well-known liberal Washington Gladden to dedicate their new church and on published sermons of the period by their minister, Charles S. Mills. See "Sermon Preached at the Fiftieth Anniversary of the Founding of Pilgrim Church," *Souvenir of the Jubilee and Directory, 1859–1909*, Cleveland, Ohio, 1909, Cleveland Public Library. On Swing, see Bluestone, *Constructing Chicago*, 100.

92. Riley is quoted in Riley, *Dynamic of a Dream*, 68. See also Trollinger, *God's Empire*, 17–18. Whether or not Riley actually eliminated pew rentals is in some doubt. His statement regarding the antidemocratic nature of rentals was made in the context of a heated power struggle within the church. Shortly after his arrival, he was challenged in his position by a faction of the congregation that disapproved of his interest in and preaching on divine healing, the Second Coming, and the power of the devil, elements that became increasingly important in Riley's fundamentalism. Various administrative moves were made on both sides to consolidate congregational power with the result being the departure of some 150 long-time members, who formed Trinity Baptist Church in 1903. Riley asserted that the dissenting group consisted of disaffected wealthy members who had formerly wielded decisive power in the church, and that among the changes he moved to institute and to which they were opposed were pew rentals. Their opposition to Riley on this topic demonstrated, he charged, their aristocratic outlook. That this argument was most likely elevated rhetoric presented to sway public opinion in the press (which was closely covering the dispute) is suggested by the fact that First Baptist does not appear to have eliminated rents when the dissenting group left. Both the 1910 and 1911 *Manual* include the ambiguous category "rents" in the receipts section of the church's financial statements. While it is possible that this means rent collected from leasing the buildings, another category called "use of church building" seems to cover this area. More definitively, however, the new Trinity Baptist congregation, organized by the folks who supposedly opposed eliminating pew rents, does not seem to have instituted rents in their new church building erected in 1907; their 1910 financial statement lists only collections and pledges under receipts, no pew rents. See "Trinity Baptist Church, Officers and Statistical Report," 1910, Minnesota History Center; and First Baptist Church, Minneapolis, Minn., *Manual*, 1901-2, 1910, 1911, Minnesota History Center. For a personal analysis of the situation, see that of Riley's wife: Riley, *Dynamic of a Dream*, 68–89. For a more scholarly treatment, see Walter Edmund Warren Ellis, "Social and Religious Factors in the Fundamentalist-Modernist Schisms among Baptists in North America, 1895–1934" (Ph.D. diss., University of Pittsburgh, 1974); and Trollinger, *God's Empire*, 16–23. Both Trollinger and Ellis downplay the religious issues at stake, interpreting the conflict as Marie Riley did, as a struggle over class ideologies in which First Baptist's wealthy elite was threatened by Riley's inclusive, democratic vision of transforming the church into an evangelistic church drawing in lower-middle- and working-class parishioners. A collection of local newspaper clippings on the conflict is housed with the Trinity Baptist Church Records, Minnesota History Center.

93. Kirby, *Heritage of Heroes*, 118. Precisely how the congregation members linked their pledges to their seats prior to the 1891 announcement is not clear; however, a sentence in the announcement reminding people that once the minister had taken the pulpit all seats were free indicates

that they indeed did. This practice of declaring the seats free once the service had begun was widespread. Any seats not occupied at that time could be taken by visitors.

94. See Fisher, "Size and Shape of the Church Edifice," 104. As early as 1861, congregations were concerned about the cost of pews. First Congregational in Winchester, Mass., for instance, wanted to minimize the financial burden of their new church in regard to their "poor" members and so lowered the price of their cheapest pews to $15 per year. This did not adequately allow "the poorest man in the congregation an opportunity of owning a pew, if he wished," so assessment was refigured, and pews costing less than $1.50 were made available. See "First Congregational Church, Winchester, MS," *Congregational Quarterly* 3 (Oct. 1861): 337–40.

95. Nathan O. Hatch, "Evangelicalism as a Democratic Movement," in *Evangelicalism and Modern America*, edited by George Marsden (Grand Rapids, Mich.: Eerdmans, 1984), 71–82. See also Henry Martyn Dexter, *A Hand-Book of Congregationalism* (Boston: Congregational Publishing Society, 1880), esp. chap. 2. For democracy and equality themes in architectural discussions, see George F. Magoun, "Church Architecture and the Masses," *Congregational Quarterly* 4 (Jan. 1862): 25–36, esp. 34; and Faxon, "Modern Church Building I," 50–51.

96. Rachel Wild Patterson, *The Long-Lost Rachel Wild; or, Seeking Diamonds in the Rough* (Denver, Colo.: Reed, 1905), 213.

97. Having attended services in a number of amphitheatre auditoriums, I can attest to the temptation to "people watch" encouraged by the seating fan. The feeling of being watched by others, in turn, can be unsettling.

98. Szasz, *Divided Mind*, 42–67.

Chapter 6

1. R. Brown, Jr., "What Our Architecture Lacks," *AA&BN*, 30 June 1888, 304. For more of Brown's description of the service, see chap. 5, n58. Another notice in the *AA&BN* related, "The other day we went by a new building, which, to our practiced eye, could be nothing else than a pumping-station. 'That's the new branch of the water-works,' we said, very oracularly. 'No such thing,' bluntly responded the friend walking with us. 'That is a gymnasium.' He proved his point by the windows, high up and small, and evidently intended to prevent people looking in, or out, for that matter. We proved our position by the smoke-stack and the 'altogether' of the edifice. Presently we asked a little street-urchin whom we met, and he said: 'That? Why that's the new — Church.' And so it proved to be." See the *Chicago Interior*, quoted in "The Chicago Church," *AA&BN*, 11 Jan. 1896, 24.

2. T. K. Noble, "The Sanctuary in Its Relation to the Material, Moral, and Spiritual Life of the Community," *Church Building Quarterly* 1 (Jan. 1883): 17–18.

3. Noble, "The Sanctuary," 17.

4. Noble, "The Sanctuary," 18.

5. Maxine Van De Wetering, "The Popular Concept of 'Home' in Nineteenth-Century America," *Journal of American Studies* 18 (1984): 12.

6. Colleen McDannell, *The Christian Home in Victorian America, 1840–1900* (Bloomington: Indiana University Press, 1986), 77–78.

7. For further discussion of the public-private nuances of families, see Stephanie Coontz, *The Way We Never Were: American Families and the Nostalgia Trap* (New York: Basic, 1992), 96–115. See also Mary Ryan, *Cradle of the Middle Class: The Family in Oneida County, New York, 1790–1865* (Cambridge: Cambridge University Press, 1981), 98–104, 135–65.

8. H. Clay Trumbull, *The Sunday-School: Its Origin, Mission, Methods, and Auxiliaries* (Philadelphia: Wattles, 1896), 146.

9. Horace Bushnell, *Christian Nurture* (New York: Scribner, 1861). Portions of this work appeared as early as 1847 under the title *Views of Christian Nurture* (Hartford, Conn.: Hunt).

10. See McDannell, *Christian Home*; and Colleen McDannell, *Material Christianity: Religion and Popular Culture in America* (New Haven, Conn.: Yale University Press, 1995), 17–102.

11. McDannell, *Christian Home*, 153. See also Gwendolyn Wright, *Moralism and the Model Home: Domestic Architecture and Cultural Conflict in Chicago, 1873–1913* (Chicago: University of Chicago Press, 1980), 45.

12. Further analysis of the sacralized home is found in Clifford E. Clark, Jr., *The American Family Home, 1800–1960* (Chapel Hill: University of North Carolina Press, 1986), 19–28; John Maass, *The Victorian Home in America* (New York: Hawthorn, 1972); Van De Wetering, "Popular Concept of 'Home,'" 14; and Harvey Green, *The Light of the Home: An Intimate View of the Lives of Women in Victorian America* (New York: Pantheon, 1983).

13. John F. W. Ware, *Home Life in America: What It Is and What It Needs* (Boston: n.p., 1864), 124–25. See also C. E. Sargent, *Our Home; or, The Key to a Nobler Life* (Springfield, Mass.: King, Richardson, 1894), 23–34.

14. Edward Bellamy, *Looking Backward* (1888; reprint, New York: Signet Classic, 1960), 182–94.

15. This is not to discount the important public role of domestic evangelicalism, which is discussed in chap. 4. These churches, like middle-class homes, did not shrink from making distinctive public, architectural statements. Those statements, though, often contained ambivalence, like that embedded in the simultaneously offensive and defensive character of the "spiritual armory" metaphor. See Clifford E. Clark, Jr., "Domestic Architecture as an Index to Social History: The Romantic Revival and the Cult of Domesticity in America, 1840–1870," *Journal of Interdisciplinary History* 7 (Summer 1976): 33–56.

16. George F. Magoun, "Architecture and Christian Principle," *Congregational Quarterly* 1 (Oct. 1859): 373.

17. "The Plymouth Church, Cleveland, O.," *Congregational Quarterly* 3 (Apr. 1861): 181. An alternative view was offered by the Reverend Thomas Beecher, who specifically extended the church home idea beyond the middle classes, arguing that his church home would be "'family on a large scale,' where the strongest and wealthiest members would nurture and protect the smallest and poorest in their community." His Park Church in Elmira, N.Y., constructed to include a variety of social and recreational facilities, was one of the first institutional churches in the United States. See Myra C. Glenn, *Thomas K. Beecher: Minister to a Changing America, 1824–1900* (Westport, Conn.: Greenwood, 1996), 148, 210 n6. See also chap. 7; and William Wallace Martin, *Manual of Ecclesiastical Architecture* (Cincinnati, Ohio: Curts & Jennings, 1897), 393.

18. W. P. Fisher, "The Size and Shape of the Church Edifice," *Church Building Quarterly* 1 (October 1883): 105.

19. "Designs in Church Architecture," *Congregational Yearbook 1881* (Boston: Congregational Publishing Company, 1881), 5. The concept of the church home was also used to encourage support for home missionary and church extension work. See Isaac P. Langworthy, "A Congregational Home," *Congregational Quarterly* 5 (Oct. 1863): 286–92; and D. Burt, "Congregationalism in Minnesota," *Congregational Quarterly* 2 (Jan. 1860): 67–72.

20. L. P. Rose, "The Union's Place and Power," *Church Building Quarterly* 4 (Mar. 1886): 7–8.

21. See Perry Miller, *Errand into the Wilderness* (Cambridge, Mass.: Belknap, 1956); and Catherine Albanese, *Nature Religion in America: From the Algonkian Indians to the New Age* (Chicago: University of Chicago Press, 1990).

22. John Heyl Vincent, *The Chautauqua Movement* (Boston: Chautauqua Press, 1886), 10.

23. Gwendolyn Wright, *Building the Dream: A Social History of Housing in America* (New York: Pantheon, 1981), 104–7; see also Martha Crabill McClaugherty, "Household Art: Creating the Artistic Home, 1868–1893," *Winterthur Portfolio* 18 (Spring 1983): 10–15.

24. The fresco technique had gained favor in domestic decorating in the 1860s. An article by Philadelphia frescoer and painter Charles Bremer published in an 1868 issue of *Sloan's Architectural Review and Builders' Journal* traced the use of fresco from ancient Rome through the Renaissance to modern times, urging its use as an ideal solution to several crucial home interior problems. Most important, he argued, frescoes provided homeowners a clean and safe means of lavishly decorating their walls. Fresco, not being "subject to chemical reaction," was "perfectly healthy," a concern generated from fears that wallpaper collected dirt and filth. Furthermore, frescoes did not "smell in wet or damp weather," nor did they attract "those pestiferous insects, that perpetually infest dwellings covered with wall paper." The popularity of frescoing was emphasized in "Interior Decoration," *Scribner's Monthly* 11 (June 1876): 283.

25. McClaugherty, "Household Art," 14; Clark, *American Family Home*, 93–95. See also Russell Lynes, *The Tastemakers* (New York: Harper and Bro., 1955), 170–72.

26. "Dedicated to God," *Minneapolis Tribune*, 5 Mar. 1888, 5.

27. As quoted in "An Extraordinary Dedication," *Christian Advocate* (N.Y.), 10 Nov. 1887, 733.

28. For descriptions of early evangelical churches with stained glass, see "The Seventh Presbyterian Church," *Presbyterian Magazine* 3 (June 1853): 288–89; Isaac P. Langworthy, "Ventilation of Churches," *Congregational Quarterly* 1 (Oct. 1859): 369–72; Joseph P. Thompson, "Historical Sketch of the Broadway Tabernacle, New York City," *Congregational Quarterly* 2 (Jan. 1860): 64–67; and "Clinton Avenue Congregational Church," *Congregational Quarterly* 2 (Apr. 1860): 212–14. Debate on this issue characterized the period, however. In his 1856 book, George Bowler argued that "[because] the purer forms of religious worship and the liberty of a nobler faith have dawned upon us, we do not need to excite our superstitious emotions by contact with gloomy associations; rather, we hail the light, in all its diffusive beauty, as an emblem of our holy hopes." He did acknowledge, however, that some "subduing" of midday glare is helpful and could be accomplished with shades, lattices, or lead glass panes. See George Bowler, *Chapel and Church Architecture with Designs for Parsonages* (Boston: Jewett, 1856), 13. The Reverend George Magoun similarly argued in 1859 that Congregational churches should strive for "the effect of the truth" and not include stained-glass windows. See Magoun, "Architecture and Christian Principle," 378.

29. Examples include Lyndhurst, a villa in Terrytown, N.Y., originally designed in 1838 by Alexander Jackson Davis for former New York mayor William Paulding, and Burholme, a Philadelphia mansion built in 1859 for Robert W. Ryerss. See Clark, *American Family Home*, 25.

30. "The Use of Stained Glass," *Inland Architect and Builder* 1 (May 1883): 52. See also Sharon S. Darling's excellent book *Decorative & Architectural Arts in Chicago, 1871–1933* (Chicago: Chicago Historical Society and University of Chicago Press, 1982). This work dates the increase in the use of stained glass in places of business and domestic buildings in Chicago as following the Great Fire of 1871. Darling documents the processes, artisans, and patrons of stained glass and also provides several excellent illustrations of representative works.

31. McClaugherty, "Household Art," 17.

32. "Use of Stained Glass," 52.

33. See Charles A. Cole, "Painted Glass in Household Decoration," *Harper's New Monthly Magazine* 59 (Oct. 1879): 655–64.

34. "Dedicated to God, 5." Published lists of Tiffany-produced windows do show that "ornamental windows" were installed in the church, but whether this includes the original banks is unclear. The reason for uncertainty is that the term "Tiffany glass" was often applied to all opalescent glass imitative of that produced by Louis C. Tiffany, whose success stemmed in part from his ability to make and market his trademark opalescent glass on a large scale. Tiffany manufactured large amounts of the glass, stockpiled it, and, drawing upon an entire factory of

glass cutters and artisans, filled orders from across the country, particularly those of wealthy clients in Boston and New York. See Robert Koch, *Louis C. Tiffany: Rebel in Glass*, 2d ed. (New York: Crown, 1966), 87–118; and John Gilbert Lloyd, *Stained Glass in America* (Jenkintown, Pa.: Foundation, 1963), 56–61. With the imprimatur of the wealthy, Tiffany windows became a statement of aesthetic taste that indicated the social prestige of the owners, be they a family or an entire congregation. Several firms produced glass similar to Tiffany's signature opalescent window glass, which resulted in many unsubstantiated claims to Tiffany windows in churches across the United States. For instance, the windows in Denver's Trinity Church were for years regarded as Tiffany windows because the prestige of the Tiffany name had eclipsed that of the original designers, Healy and Millet. Fairly complete lists of windows produced by the Tiffany Company do exist. See Alistair Duncan, *Tiffany Windows* (New York: Simon and Schuster, 1980).

35. The reason that the large windows were never filled with stained glass is unclear. While it may simply be that the congregation ran out of money—and indications of this include their decision to delay building the gallery intended for the sanctuary—this university-oriented congregation may have harbored some scruples about an elaborate display of stained glass, harking back to the earlier Low Church use of clear glass.

36. Several of Trinity's windows are reproduced in Linda K. Kirby, *Heritage of Heroes: Trinity United Methodist Church, 1859–1988* (Denver, Colo.: Trinity United Methodist Church, 1988), between pages 265 and 266. The 1882 lecture tour of Oscar Wilde stimulated the U.S. Arts and Crafts movement. See Gillian Naylor, *The Arts and Crafts Movement: A Study of Its Sources, Ideals and Influence on Design Theory* (Cambridge, Mass.: MIT Press, 1971); Isabelle Anscombe and Charlotte Gere, *Arts and Crafts in Britain and America* (New York: Rizzoli, 1978); and Darling, *Decorative & Architectural Arts*.

37. McClaugherty, "Household Art," 10.

38. From the *Baltimore American*, 5 Nov. 1887, quoted in David Gilmore Wright, "Conception and Realization: An Historic Building Statement," in *The Restoration of the Lovely Lane Church Baltimore City Station* (Baltimore, Md.: Trustees of the Methodist Episcopal Church, 1980), 35.

39. Wright, *Building the Dream*, 106.

40. This church appears in *Church Building Quarterly* 8 (Oct. 1890): 219–20.

41. Wright, *Building the Dream*, 106.

42. Ernest Greene, "Hints on Church Building II: The Interior," *Church Building Quarterly* 9 (Jan. 1891): 40.

43. Francine Haber, Kenneth R. Fuller, and David N. Wetzel, *Robert S. Roeschlaub: Architect of the Emerging West, 1843–1923* (Denver: Colorado Historical Society, 1988), 64.

44. Quoted in Wright, "Conception and Realization," 48.

45. Clark, *American Family Home*, 40–43. On parlors as female space, see Karen Halttunen, *Confidence Men and Painted Women: A Study of Middle-Class Culture in America, 1830–1870* (New Haven, Conn.: Yale University Press, 1982), 56–65.

46. In 1892, First Congregational of Minneapolis, a congregation of about 400, listed more than fifteen such organizations, including the Bible School, the Ladies Benevolent Society, the Women's Foreign Missionary Society, the Women's Home Missionary Society, the Young Ladies Union, the Heart and Hand Society, the Senior Young People's Society for Christian Endeavor (YPSCE), the Junior YPSCE, the Earnest Workers, the King's Daughters, the Bethesda Branch, and the Brotherhood of Andrew and Philip. See Guy Stanton Ford and Dora V. Smith, *The First Congregational Church of Minnesota: A Century of Service* (Minneapolis: n.p., 1952), 18. In 1895, Central Presbyterian Church of St. Paul fielded the following organizations, exclusive of the many church committees that managed the day-to-day functioning of the church: YPSCE, Women's Foreign Missionary Society, Women's Home Missionary Society, Women's Society for Church Work, Young Women's Foreign Missionary Society, Young People's Home Missionary Society, the Little Flock (children's band), and the Boys'

Brigade (drill team). The same year, Dayton Avenue Presbyterian in St. Paul claimed ten church committees: Finance, Library, Spiritual Interests, Temperance, Reception, Supplies, Music, Missionary, Visiting, and Social. See *Official Yearbook and Directory of the Presbyterian Churches of St. Paul, Minn.* (St. Paul, Minn.: n.p., 1895), Minnesota Historical Society Archives. Such lists were replicated in Methodist and Baptist congregations as well.

47. Women's non–church-associated organizations were often located in houselike buildings, similarly called "homes." Hull House and the settlement movement itself are prime examples, as are the many benevolence homes founded and run by women. On domestic architecture in women's colleges, see Helen Lefkowitz Horowitz, *Alma Mater: Design and Experience in the Women's Colleges from Their Nineteenth-Century Beginnings to the 1930s* (New York: Knopf, 1984).

48. Of the forty interior plans shown in the *AA&BN*, ten designate one parlor, four designate two parlors, and five designate a ladies' parlor, for a total of twenty-three. At roughly 56 percent of the churches shown, this is a remarkably high figure given the fact that parlors were, like kitchens, relegated to basement levels whose plans were often not published. In addition, a clear majority of the hundreds of plans published in the *Church Building Quarterly* between 1883 and 1909 included at least one parlor and often a ladies' parlor.

49. Halttunen, *Confidence Men and Painted Women*, 59. See also Katherine Kish Sklar, *Catherine Beecher: A Study in American Domesticity* (New Haven, Conn.: Yale University Press, 1973), 95–97.

50. Lizabeth A. Cohen, "Embellishing a Life of Labor: An Interpretation of the Material Culture of American Working-Class Homes, 1885–1915," in *Material Culture Studies in America*, edited by Thomas J. Schlereth (Nashville, Tenn.: The American Association for State and Local History, 1982), 293. Cohen demonstrates that the grand formality of the parlor, even when available to immigrant families and those of modest income, was often forsaken for the cozy informality of the kitchen (299–301).

51. Women's toilets frequently were reached only through these parlors (or sometimes through kindergarten rooms). Men's toilets generally opened onto main hallways.

52. Isaac P. Langworthy, "Ventilation of Churches," *Congregational Quarterly* 1 (Oct. 1859): 370.

53. A small lean-to kitchen appears in the plan for the $5,000 Queen Anne–style Trinity Congregational Church, Normal Park, Ill. See *Church Building Quarterly* 8 (Oct. 1890): 219–20. For an example of a half-basement, see First Congregational Church, Evanston, Ill., *Church Building Quarterly* 6 (July 1888): 94–95. Other good descriptions of auxiliary rooms appear in "Central Congregational Church, Worcester, Mass.," *Church Building Quarterly* 6 (Apr. 1888): 56–57; "Bethlehem Church, Chicago, Illinois," *Church Building Quarterly* 8 (Oct. 1890): 221–23; and "Plymouth Church, Milwaukee, Wisconsin," *Church Building Quarterly* 8 (Oct. 1890): 226–29.

54. For instance, six days before Christmas 1888, the Minneapolis Centenary M.E. congregation offered a "New England dinner" to "all strangers who have no place of regular church attendance." Wesley United Methodist Church Archives, Minneapolis, Minn.

55. The menu for First Congregational Church's banquet is found in "Washington's Birthday Banquet, February 22, 1906," First Congregational Church Papers, 1883–1931, Minnesota Historical Society Archives, St. Paul, Minn.

56. See Glenna Matthews, *"Just a Housewife": The Rise & Fall of Domesticity in America* (New York: Oxford University Press, 1987), 14–17.

57. On church cookbooks in Minnesota, see Marjorie Kreidberg, *Food on the Frontier: Minnesota Cooking from 1850 to 1900 with Selected Recipes* (St. Paul, Minn.: Minnesota Historical Society Press, 1975), 191–94.

58. See Matthews, *"Just a Housewife."* See also David P. Handlin, *The American Home: Architecture and Society, 1815–1915* (Boston: Little, Brown, 1979).

59. The term *vestibule* is used rather loosely on interior plans. Some are closetlike rooms with single entries, and others are passages between other rooms (for instance, those rooms that guide entry into the sanctuary).

60. Greene, "Hints on Church Building II: The Interior," 39. A similar suggestion is made in Normand S. Patton, "How to Secure a Good Church Plan: The Advice of an Architect," *Church Building Quarterly* 10 (Apr. 1892): 99.

61. See, for instance, Greene, "Hints on Church Building II: The Interior," 40.

62. R. S. Peabody, quoted in "Modern Church Architecture," *AA&BN*, 8 Dec. 1877, 393–94.

63. Some congregations did take care to physically separate the church's domestic facilities from the sanctuary. Lovely Lane M.E. in Baltimore, for instance, housed the kitchen, parlors, and ladies' toilet in the basement of the Sunday school building adjacent to but contiguous with the sanctuary building. Growing desire for such distinctions mark, in part, the decline of the church home movement; see chap. 8.

64. Some commentators indicate that the process of building itself could spark a revival and thus result in the filling of the new sanctuary with masses of new people. This may explain in part the propensity for overbuilding that was common during the period; many congregations built churches with sanctuaries that would seat two, three, or even four times their usual Sunday attendance figures. Much of this overbuilding, however, stemmed from congregations' perception that they were building for future generations—for their children and their children's children.

65. Jenkin Lloyd Jones, quoted in Joseph Siry, "Frank Lloyd Wright's Unity Temple and Architecture for Liberal Religion in Chicago, 1885–1909," *Art Bulletin* 73 (June 1991): 258.

66. For Riley's comments, see "Wishes Them Success" (no newspaper title, n.d.), Clipping File, Trinity Baptist Church, Minneapolis, Minnesota History Center, St. Paul, Minn.

67. Marie Acomb Riley, *The Dynamic of a Dream: The Life Story of Dr. William B. Riley* (Grand Rapids, Mich.: Eerdmans, 1938), 70–71.

68. Betty DeBerg argues that while conservatives strongly disapproved of women's ordination at this time and widely debated their participation in the pulpit as orators, churches were so dependent upon women's financial contributions that fundamentalist leaders did not "declare a desire to remove women from church work altogether." Betty A. DeBerg, *Ungodly Women: Gender and the First Wave of American Fundamentalism* (Minneapolis, Minn.: Fortress, 1990), 80. Riley himself seems to have quickly abandoned attempts to curtail women's participation, for within a few years he encouraged his advisory board to allow women to serve on it, and he defended women's capacity to evangelize, if not be ordained. See William Bell Riley, "Women in the Ministry," *Christian Fundamentalist* 1 (May 1928): 21.

69. One reason for the delay was that, apart from Unitarians, theological liberalism had not yet coalesced on the congregational level.

70. Quoted in Dennis Alexander, "Serving the Downtown Community: Wesley Church," 17 Jan. 1988, Wesley United Methodist Church Archives, Minneapolis, Minn.

71. "Palatial Churches," *Church Building Quarterly* 9 (Oct. 1891): 174–75.

72. See, for instance, "Expensive Churches," *New York Evangelist*, 31 July 1830, 72.

73. Lewis Tappan to Charles G. Finney, 16 Mar. 1832, CGFP, Oberlin College Archives, Oberlin, Ohio.

74. In 1873, Chicago Methodists erected a four-story commercial building in which the middle floors housed a congregation and worship space, while the lower floor was rented to seven merchants and the upper floor housed sixteen offices, which were made available for lease. Trinity

Church in Denver contemplated this option as the members began their discussions for the need of a new church in the early 1880s. On the Chicago building, see Charles E. Gregersen, *Dankmar Adler: His Theatres and Auditoriums* (Athens: Swallow Press, and Ohio University Press, 1990), 38, 104. On both buildings, see chap. 5.

Chapter 7

1. William Brigham, *The Compact with the Charter and Laws of the Colony of New Plymouth* (Boston, 1836), 270–71, quoted in John Demos, *A Little Commonwealth: Family Life in Plymouth Colony* (New York: Oxford University Press, 1970), 104.

2. On Puritan views of the religious lives of children, see Edmund S. Morgan, *The Puritan Family: Religion and Domestic Relations in Seventeenth-Century New England*, rev. ed. (New York: Harper & Row, 1966), 87–108, 135–40. See also Ross W. Beales, Jr., "The Child in Seventeenth-Century America," in *American Childhood: A Research Guide and Historical Handbook*, edited by Joseph M. Hawes and N. Ray Hiner (Westport, Conn.: Greenwood, 1985), 15–56. Material on seventeenth- and eighteenth-century children appears in Constance B. Schulz's historiographic essay "Children and Childhood in the Eighteenth Century," 57–109, in the same volume. On children in meetinghouses, see H. Clay Trumbull, *The Sunday-School: Its Origin, Mission, Methods, and Auxiliaries* (Philadelphia: Wattles, 1896), 174n.

3. For the similar situation in the United States, see Schulz, "Children and Childhood," 60–63. See also H. Shelton Smith, "Editor's Introduction," in *Horace Bushnell*, edited by H. Shelton Smith (New York: Oxford University Press, 1965), 3–39. On the view of evangelicals in the seventeenth and eighteenth centuries, see Philip J. Greven, Jr., *The Protestant Temperament* (New York: Knopf, 1977).

4. Scholars disagree on the motivations of these Sunday school organizers with respect to the working classes. The classic treatments are E. P. Thompson, *The Making of the Working Class* (New York: Vintage, 1966), 375–79, which argues that the Sunday schools were tools of a hegemonic bourgeoisie used to indoctrinate workers in ethical patterns and beliefs counter to the workers' interests; and Thomas Walter Laqueur, *Religion and Respectability: Sunday Schools and Working-Class Culture, 1780–1850* (New Haven, Conn.: Yale University Press, 1976), 187–241, which counters that while a few Sunday schools were clearly exploitative, the values championed by Sunday schools—"honesty, orderliness, punctuality, hard work, refinement in manners and morals" (239)—were not a monopoly of a particular (capitalist) class and that these values united all working people and distinguished them from those who were idle. In Laqueur's opinion, many working-class people who supported and taught in Sunday schools embraced these values and taught them to others without reservation. Clearly, Sunday schools provided students access to socialization that might otherwise have been unavailable. For a discussion of this dispute, see Anne M. Boylan, *Sunday School: The Formation of an American Institution, 1790–1880* (New Haven, Conn.: Yale University Press, 1988), 37–39.

5. On British Sunday school buildings, see Thomas A. Markus, *Buildings and Power: Freedom and Control in the Origin of Modern Building Types* (London: Routledge, 1993), 48–53.

6. The Beecher story is mentioned in Boylan, *Sunday School*, 18. Contemporary scholarly work on Sunday schools, apart from Boylan, is scarce. Other early treatments of the origins and subsequent transformation of Sunday schools in the United States include Marianna C. Brown, *Sunday School Movements in America* (New York: Revell, 1901); *The Development of the Sunday-School, 1780–1905*, edited by W. N. Hartshorn, George R. Merrill, and Marion Lawrance (Boston: International Sunday-School Association, 1905); Marshall A. Hudson, "Bible Class Work for Men," 275–78, in the same volume; Edwin Wilbur Rice, *The Sunday-School Movement and the American Sunday-School Union, 1780–1917* (Philadelphia: American Sunday-School Union, 1917); and Addie Grace Wardle, *History of the Sunday School Movement in*

the *Methodist Episcopal Church* (New York: Methodist Book Concern, 1918). See also "Sabbath Schools," *Calvinistic Magazine* 3 (Mar. 1829); "American Sunday School Union," *Calvinistic Magazine* 4 (July 1830): 221–24; and "A Plea for Sabbath Schools," *Calvinistic Magazine* 5 (Aug. 1831): 238–54.

7. Letter from Justitia, "For the New York Evangelist," *New York Evangelist*, 10 Jan. 1835, 6.

8. For an early description of the Kirtland Temple, see Letter from James H. Eells, *New York Evangelist*, 9 Apr. 1836, 59. See also Laurel Brana Blank Andrew, *The Early Temples of the Mormons: The Architecture of the Millennial Kingdom in the American West* (Albany: State University of New York Press, 1978); and W. Ray Luce, "Building the Kingdom of God: Mormon Architecture before 1847," *Brigham Young University Studies* 30 (Spring 1990): 33–45.

9. See "Church for Oberlin," *Oberlin Evangelist*, 3 Mar. 1841, 39; and "Oberlin Meeting House," *Oberlin Evangelist*, 7 June 1843, 95.

10. On early meetinghouses remodeled for Sunday schools, see Edmund W. Sinnott, *Meetinghouse & Church in Early New England* (New York: McGraw-Hill, 1963), 141–74. A description of an early church basement appears in Justitia, "For the New-York Evangelist." By midcentury, the term *vestry* came into vogue to designate such multi-purpose rooms. This is a recasting of the Roman Catholic use of the term as a robing room for the priest and of the Episcopalian use as a room used by the "vestry," or congregational advisors to the priest.

11. See design 4 in George Bowler, *Chapel and Church Architecture with Designs for Parsonages* (Boston: Jewett, 1856), n.p.

12. Sliding-door schemes were reported in the following articles: "The First Presbyterian Church, Richmond, VA," *Presbyterian Magazine* 3 (Sept. 1853): 426–28; and "Central Congregational Church, Lawrence, MS [Mass.]," *Congregational Quarterly* 3 (Jan. 1861): 18–20. See also Boylan, *Sunday School*, 162.

13. John P. Gulliver, "Sketch of the Broadway Church, Norwich, Conn., with Particular Reference to Ventilation," *Congregational Quarterly* 1 (July 1859): 300–308.

14. "Clinton Avenue Congregational Church," *Congregational Quarterly* 2 (Apr. 1860): 212–14; and "The South Church, Andover, MS.," *Congregational Quarterly* 5 (Jan. 1863): 20–22.

15. See Trumbull, *Sunday-School*, 148–51.

16. Trumbull, *Sunday-School*, 150.

17. Smith, *Horace Bushnell*, 378–79.

18. Glenna Matthews, *"Just a Housewife": The Rise & Fall of Domesticity in America* (New York: Oxford University Press, 1987), 18–19.

19. Smith, *Horace Bushnell*, 380.

20. Boylan argues that the paradoxical goals of Christian nurture and conversion coexisted within many Sunday schools and Sunday school publications through much of the late nineteenth century. She further asserts that Christian nurture offered a comfortable context in which congregations could shift their focus from public evangelizing through educating poor children to a more "tribal" focus on their own children. Living apart from wholesome, Christian homes, she argues, prevented poor children from having access to Christian nurture. See Boylan, *Sunday School*, 47–51. While the former point is persuasive—and clearly by midcentury the focus is on churched children—many congregations continued to welcome unchurched children into their Sunday schools. Fully convincing figures, one way or the other, have not yet been gathered.

21. See Trumbull, *Sunday-School*, 158–84. For other criticisms of the Sunday school movement, including the charge that its efforts to impose an evangelical perspective on U.S. citizens was antidemocratic, see Rice, *Sunday-School Movement*, 130–334.

22. The theories of Swiss educator Johann Pestalozzi, who challenged the hegemony of rote learning in the late eighteenth century, were of particular interest to Sunday school educators. See Boylan, *Sunday School*, 150–51; Rice, *Sunday-School Movement*, 116–19; and Trumbull, *Sunday-School*, 83–84 n3.

23. On the Uniform Lessons, see Boylan, *Sunday School*, 98–99.

24. See E. Morris Fergusson, *Historic Chapters in Christian Education in America* (New York: Revell, 1935), 126.

25. On the inception of the Akron Plan, see Ellwood Hendrick, *Lewis Miller: A Biographical Essay* (New York: Putnam's, 1925), 146–47; "History of the First Methodist Episcopal Church and Sunday School," typescript, Lewis Miller Papers, Chautauqua Institute Archives, Chautauqua, N.Y; Samuel A. Lane, *Fifty Years and Over of Akron and Summit County* (n.p., n.d.), 487, 511; and Herbert Francis Evans, "Architecture, Sunday School," in *The Encyclopedia of Sunday Schools and Religious Education*, edited by John T. McFarland and Benjamin S. Winchester (New York: Nelson & Sons, 1915), 29–30.

26. This spatial form had gained popularity during the Renaissance period and was replicated in such Elizabethan theatres as the Rose and the Globe. By the nineteenth century, American entrepreneurs used it to house circuses. Rickett's Amphitheatre in New York was a well-known example.

27. John H. Vincent, quoted in Evans, "Architecture, Sunday School," 30.

28. "The Illustrations," *AA&BN*, 23 Sept. 1876, 308.

29. Some have attributed the Akron Plan design to architect George Kramer, who designed hundreds of Akron Plan churches and modified the plan to accommodate separate departments, but he contradicted this suggestion in his book *The What, How, and Why of Church Building* by acknowledging his debt to Snyder and Miller. Kramer may have known Snyder personally, for his architectural partner, Frank O. Weary, was the son of Snyder's manufacturing partner, Simon Weary. The confusion surrounding the origin of the Akron Plan was furthered by the *New York Times* obituary of Kramer (21 Oct. 1938), which inaccurately reported that he developed the plan between 1879 and 1885. See George W. Kramer, *The What, How, and Why of Church Building* (New York: n.p., 1897). Illustrations and plans for several Kramer churches and Sunday schools are included in *What, How, and Why*. Similar plans are also featured in W. T. Euster's *The Philosophy of Church Building* (Pendleton, Oreg.: Pendleton Printery, Jack Huston, 1908). For examples by L. B. Valk, see illustrations of the First Presbyterian Church of Perrysburgh, Ohio, and the Baptist Church of Bennington, Vt., in *AA&BN*, 25 May 1878, plate following p. 80. See also the Baptist Church of Bennington, Vt., by Arthur Vinal (*AA&BN*, 5 Jan. 1878, plate following p. 4; and Puritan Congregational Church of Wilkes-Barre, Pa., by Albert H. Kipp (*AA&BN*, 6 Aug. 1887, plate following p. 68. On Lovely Lane, see David Gilmore Wright, "Conception and Realization: An Historic Building Statement," in *The Restoration of the Lovely Lane Church, Baltimore City Station* (Baltimore, Md.: Trustees of the Methodist Episcopal Church, 1980), 20.

30. On the attribution of the diagonal plan, see chap. 5, n18. On First Congregational Church, see *Congregational Year Book, 1888* (Boston: Congregational Publishing Society, 1888), 83–85.

31. First Congregational Church, Record 1880–1890, MS, 154, Minnesota Historical Society Archives, St. Paul, Minn.

32. For First Congregational of Minneapolis, see *Scientific American: Architects and Builders Edition*, Jan. 1887, 16. For Wesley (Centenary) Methodist of Minneapolis, see *AA&BN*, 25 Oct. 1890, plate follows p. 60. For First Presbyterian of Peoria, Ill., see *AA&BN*, 7 July 1888, 7. See also First Congregational Church, Minneapolis, Minn., *Church Building Quarterly* 6 (Apr. 1888): 54–55; First Congregational Church, Menomonie, Wisc., *Church Building Quarterly* 9 (July 1891): 148; and First Congregational Church, St. Joseph, Mo., *Church Building Quarterly* 8 (Oct. 1890): 216.

33. For Bullard and Bullard's First Baptist Church, see Willard B. Robinson, *Texas Public Buildings of the Nineteenth Century* (Austin: University of Texas, 1974), 142. For Hayes's Elmira Free Baptist Church, see *AA&BN*, 22 Feb. 1890. For Kramer's St. Paul's M.E. of Hartford, see the National Register of Historical Places Inventory: Nomination Form (Washington, D.C.: National Register of Historical Places).

34. Peter Winne, *Historical Gleanings*, Trinity United Methodist Church Archive (Denver, Colo.: 1915–1916), 105.

35. This bulletin is found in Linda K. Kirby, *Heritage of Heroes: Trinity United Methodist Church, 1859–1988* (Denver, Colo.: Trinity United Methodist Church, 1988), 102.

36. Marcus Whiffen and Frederick Koeper, *American Architecture* (Cambridge, Mass.: MIT Press, 1983), 2:294–96.

37. Editorial, *AA&BN*, 31 Aug. 1889, 94.

38. The large number of advertisements for rolling partitions appearing in building jour-nals and denominational literature during the 1880s and 1890s attests to the popularity of these apparatuses. See, for example, the advertisement for partitions made by the J. Godfrey Wilson Company of New York that appeared in the *Church Building Quarterly* 22 (July 1904): endpapers.

39. For an excellent study of the panopticon qualities of British Sunday schools and their use in instilling order and discipline in pupils, see Markus, *Buildings and Power*, 48–75. The congregation of Wesley M.E. in Minneapolis remodeled their Hayes-designed Akron Plan Lillibridge Hall in 1908 to eliminate this feature. Walter Carlock, *History of Wesley Church* (Minneapolis, Minn.: Wesley United Methodist Church, 1977), 46.

40. Advisory Board Meeting Minutes, 21 May 1915, First Baptist Church Archives, Minne-apolis, Minn. First Baptist at this time had a very small Akron Plan wing connected to the sanctuary.

41. John Fletcher Hurst, *The History of Methodism* (New York: Eaton & Mains, 1903), 2:885.

42. Herbert Francis Evans, *The Sunday-School Building and Its Equipment* (Chicago: Univer-sity of Chicago Press, 1914), 1.

43. See, for instance, Jacob Dorn's comparative analysis of three Social Gospel spokesmen, "The Social Gospel and Socialism: A Comparison of the Thought of Francis Greenwood Peabody, Washington Gladden, and Walter Rauschenbusch," *Church History* 62 (Mar. 1993): 82–100.

44. Bowling alleys in churches appear as early as 1896, when the Congregation House of the Congregational Church in Adams, Mass., designed by the architectural firm of Gardner, Pyne and Gardner, included bowling alleys in the basement. *Church Building Quarterly* 14 (June 1896): 63–64. See also John T. McFarland and Benjamin S. Winchester, eds., *The Encyclopedia of Sunday Schools and Religious Education* (New York: Nelson & Sons, 1915), 36–40.

45. Josiah Strong, *Religious Movements for Social Betterment* (New York: Baker and Taylor, 1900), 46–48. On the role of the church in social betterment, see also "Human Society and the Relations of Jesus Christ Thereto," *Cleveland Plain Dealer*, 26 Nov. 1894; Frank J. Goodwin, "The Church as a Center of Civil Life," *Church Building Quarterly* 23 (July 1905): 131–40; Frank S. Fitch, "The Church in Relation to the Christian Development of America," *Church Building Quarterly* 23 (July 1905): 140–43; and Frank Newhall White, "The Leavening Power of the Church in City and Country," *Church Building Quarterly* 25 (Oct. 1907): 201–9.

46. Kirby, *Heritage of Heroes*, 107–14.

47. In this section, I am indebted to Myra Glenn's excellent discussion of Beecher's inten-tions for Park Church and the actual work of the church itself. Myra C. Glenn, *Thomas K. Beecher: Minister to a Changing America, 1824–1900* (Westport, Conn.: Greenwood, 1996), 147–61.

48. Quoted in Glenn, *Thomas K. Beecher*, 159.

49. Glenn, *Thomas K. Beecher*, 159.

50. Evans, *Sunday-School Building*, 1.

51. Mention of Boys' Brigades appears in the records of many of the churches cited throughout this study. The Boys' Brigade at Pilgrim Congregational in Cleveland was directed by a Civil War veteran. The groups were the targets of some criticism, particularly from organizations like the Woman's Christian Temperance Union, which had strong peace agendas. Concern for adolescent boys and young men was widely shared among evangelicals and social reformers of

the period. The YMCA, founded in 1869, widely promoted values like "hard work, cooperation, and respect for authority" to middle-class children who paid membership fees. Soon, programs for urban youth of more modest socioeconomic circumstances developed, but they had varying success in attracting working children with their middle-class ideologies. See Steven A. Riess, *City Games: The Evolution of American Urban Society and the Rise of Sports* (Urbana: University of Illinois Press, 1989), 151–68.

52. Hudson, "Bible Class Work for Men," 277–78.

53. Hudson, "Bible Class Work for Men," 276–77.

54. Upon taking over the pulpit of First Baptist Church in Minneapolis in 1897, William Bell Riley quickly initiated special evening meetings for men. He remained deeply concerned with providing social and educational opportunities for the young men of his church. First Baptist Church, Minneapolis, Advisory Board Meeting Minutes, 23 Aug. 1897, 11 Oct. 1897, and 30 Dec. 1897. For an excellent analysis of the politics of masculinity during this period, see Gail Bederman, *Manliness and Civilization: A Cultural History of Gender and Race in the United States, 1880–1917* (Chicago: University of Chicago Press, 1995).

55. On the institutional church, see *The Church and the City,* edited by Robert Cross (Indianapolis, Ind.: Bobbs-Merrill, 1967), 331–52.

56. On the Judson Memorial Church, see Joan Jacobs Brumberg, *Mission for Life* (New York: Free Press, 1980), 180–91. A photo of the church appeared in *AA&BN,* 13 May 1893.

57. Wallace Nutting, "Address on Church Building," *Church Building Quarterly* 14 (Apr. 1896): 151–54.

58. The area of south Cleveland that became known as Tremont seems to have not been experiencing the rapid change that downtown Cleveland, for instance, was experiencing. Somewhat isolated across the river from downtown Cleveland, the area was always rather suburban. Until the 1880s, the highland region was predominantly German, with both Catholic and Protestant faiths well represented. Quite likely, the German immigrants who were building churches in the area by the 1860s and the native-born American migrants from the East (particularly the Connecticut Colony, from whence came Thomas and Samuel Sessions and Isaac P. Lamson, leading industrialist supporters of Pilgrim, who owned a large factory in the area) blended fairly easily.

59. Pilgrim Congregational Church, *120th Anniversary, 1859–1979,* Cleveland, Ohio, 11 Nov. 1979, n.p., Pilgrim Congregational Church Archives, Cleveland, Ohio.

60. Most of these enrollments would have been neighborhood children rather than children whose parents were church members. Whether those who actually joined had family who were already members is not indicated in church records. Temperance and abstinence were particularly encouraged among the children enrolled in the sewing school and the Sunday school. See *Souvenir of the Jubilee and Directory, 1859–1909* (Cleveland, Ohio: Pilgrim Congregational Church, 1909), 20. For Sunday school enrollment and conversion figures, see *Yearbook of the Jennings Avenue Congregational Church, Cleveland Ohio, 1891* (Cleveland, Ohio: Jennings Avenue Congregational Church and Rogers, 1892), 7, 39.

61. Pilgrim Church, *Yearbook, 1891,* 7.

62. In 1891, the congregation boasted a residential membership of 314, which included 300 "families or parts of families." Pilgrim Church, *Yearbook, 1891.*

63. Pilgrim Church, *Souvenir,* 21. On the YPSCE see *Yearbook, 1891,* 42. This is not to say that the off-site work ended. The congregation financially supported Congregational home and foreign missionary programs as well as a number of local institutions, including the Jones Home for Friendless Children, which they had helped to found. See Pilgrim Church, *Yearbook, 1891.*

64. Pilgrim Church, *Yearbook, 1894,* and Pilgrim Church, *Yearbook, 1895,* record attendance figures and averages. The *Yearbook, 1891,* places Sunday school enrollment at "almost 1000," with 300 members signed up in 1891 alone (7).

65. Pilgrim Church, *Yearbook, 1891,* 31, 33.

66. The original plan appears in "Pilgrim Congregational Church, Cleveland, O.," *Church Building Quarterly* 13 (Oct. 1895): 226-30. Descriptions appear in "Magnificent: The New Pilgrim Church Almost Ready for Dedication," *Cleveland Plain Dealer*, 22 Nov. 1894, 2. Accounts of the various meetings during the week-long dedication period include "Church Services: Full Program for the Dedication of Pilgrim Church," *Cleveland Plain Dealer*, 24 Nov. 1894, 5; "Prayer Meetings: They Were Discussed at the New Pilgrim Church," *Cleveland Plain Dealer*, 1 Dec. 1894, 2; "Pilgrim Church Organ," *Cleveland Plain Dealer*, 24 Nov. 1894, 10; "The New Organ," *Cleveland Plain Dealer*, 25 Nov. 1894, 15; "An Offering to God," *Cleveland Leader*, 26 Nov. 1894, 5; and "Last Service: Dedicatory Exercises at the New Pilgrim Church Concluded," *Cleveland Plain Dealer*, 3 Dec. 1894, 2. See also "Services in Dedication of Pilgrim Church, Cleveland, Ohio, Nov. 24-Dec. 2, 1894," vertical file, folder 1, Western Reserve Historical Society, Cleveland, Ohio.

67. Pilgrim Church, *Yearbook, 1897*, 31.

68. The kindergarten expanded to weekly morning sessions in 1895, with a fee of ten cents per week per child. Pilgrim Church, *Yearbook, 1895*, 31.

69. Pilgrim's yearbooks reflect the distinction, listing institute work separately from that of the sewing school, Sunday school, and other classes.

70. Pilgrim's programs are cited in several sources; see Jeannette Hart, "A History," in *Pilgrim Church: History and Directory, 1859-1929* (Cleveland, Ohio: Pilgrim Congregational Church, 1929), 7-22, located in Pilgrim Congregational Church Archives. Curiously, this early history, while ambiguously mentioning that the new building was "the finest church of its kind in the country," does not mention the phrase *institutional church* nor allude to any programs sponsored within the building. See also Pilgrim Congregational Church, *Our First One Hundred Years* (Cleveland, Ohio: Pilgrim Congregational Church, 1959), 6-7.

Plymouth Church in Indianapolis used a similar institute model. Located in the heart of Indianapolis, Plymouth's institutional programs were conceived by Oscar C. McCulloch, a fairly widely known Social Gospel minister and worker. According to historian Genevieve C. Weeks, in 1884, Plymouth's classes in "literature, French, German, current history, stenography, bookkeeping, drawing, and elocution" attracted some 179 students, reported to be "young men and women who worked in stores, offices, shops, and factories." Weeks, "Oscar C. McCulloch Transforms Plymouth Church, Indianapolis, into an 'Institution' Church," *Indiana Magazine of History* 64 (June 1968): 87-108. The quote appears on p. 103.

71. "Dedicated amid Impressive Scenes, Pilgrim Church Is Given to God," *Cleveland Plain Dealer*, 26 Nov. 1894, 6. Washington Gladden's dedicatory sermon is reprinted in full in this article.

72. "Another Institutional Church," *Outlook*, 1 Dec. 1894, 932.

73. See Riess, *City Games*, 156-57.

74. "Dedicated," *Cleveland Plain Dealer*, 26 Nov. 1894.

75. Susan Ellen Tenney, *Annual Report–1913, Tremont School Branch* 473 (Cleveland, Ohio: Merrick House, 1914).

76. Congregational histories report that the commission of the Paris Exposition of 1899 requested photographs and information on the church. These materials are not cited in catalogs of the exposition, however, so they may not have actually been displayed. See Hart, "A History," 21. A number of other church histories also exist in the Pilgrim Church Archives.

77. Charles E. Hendry and Margaret T. Svendsen, *Between Spires and Stacks* (Cleveland, Ohio: Welfare Federation of Cleveland, 1936), 31-32.

78. "Trinity Congregational Church, Cleveland, Ohio," *Church Building Quarterly* 15 (Jan. 1897): 46-49. The quotation appears on p. 49.

79. Philip S. Moxom, "Church Work in Our Cities," *Church Building Quarterly* 22 (Oct. 1904): 209-12. The quote appears on p. 212. Moxom's opinion was not universal. Preceding

his article, two other articles lamented the weakened state of evangelical churches. As the Reverend Frank T. Bayley of Denver stated, the weakness in the church "is not lack of men or money. It lies deeper, in the immeasurable loss, out of our hearts, our homes, our colleges, and seminaries, and our very pulpits, of the Gospel." In this view, facilities alone would not resolve the problems, whether they were seen as the need to retain the children of members or the need to bring in new members through evangelizing. See Frank T. Bayley, "Church Building as a Factor in Christianizing America," *Church Building Quarterly* 22 (Oct. 1904): 192–99.

80. "Laying the Corner Stone," typescript, First Baptist Church Archives, Minneapolis, Minn.

Chapter 8

1. William Dean Howells, *A Hazard of New Fortunes* (1890; reprint, New York: New American Library, 1980), 47.

2. Plymouth Church had been remodeled into an auditorium church by 1883. It retained its classical revival exterior, however. Neomedieval auditorium churches in New York included New York Presbyterian Church at 151 West 128th Street (1885, John Rochester Thomas, arch.; 1890 auditorium, Richard R. Davis, arch.); Madison Avenue M.E. Church at 60th Street (R. H. Robertson, arch.), featured in *AA&BN*, 5 Jan. 1884, 6 and plate 419, and 17 Aug. 1889, plate 712; Fifth Avenue Presbyterian Church (1875, Carl Pfeiffer, arch.), featured in *AA&BN*, 24 Mar. 1883, 139–40; Park Avenue M.E. Church at 86th Street (J. D. Cady, arch.), featured in *AA&BN*, 16 Apr. 1892, frontispiece; First M.E. Church, Brooklyn (John Welch, arch.), featured in *AA&BN*, 18 Feb. 1893, plate following p. 112; West End Presbyterian Church, Amsterdam Avenue and 105th Street (Henry F. Kilburn, arch.), featured in *AA&BN*, 7 Jan. 1893, frontispiece; and First Reformed Church, Yonkers (J. W. Northrop, arch.), featured in *AA&BN*, 30 Mar. 1895, plate following p. 140.

3 See, for instance, John Lyman Faxon, "First Congregational Church, Detroit, Mich.," *Church Building Quarterly* 11 (Jan. 1893): 56–58. An example of the Good Shepherd appears in "Elkhart, Indiana," *Church Building Quarterly* 25 (July 1907): 137–39. Female personifications of Love, Hope, Memory, and Faith appear in architect Harry Jones's Memorial Chapel (1908, nondenominational) in Lakewood Cemetery, Minneapolis, Minn; see Mame Osteen, *Haven in the Heart of the City: The History of Lakewood Cemetery* (Minneapolis, Minn.: Lakewood Cemetery, 1992), 101–12.

4. Free church organizer Lewis Tappan made this point in a letter to Charles Finney. See chap. 2, n24.

5. "Prospectus," *Church Building Quarterly* 1 (Jan. 1883): i. Later that summer, the editors of the periodical pleaded for donations, arguing that "our [Congregationalists'] lack of building enthusiasm gives the enemy of all good his best chance to sow the quick-sprouting seed of sectarianism." *Church Building Quarterly* 1 (July 1883): 59.

6. Eugene Thayer, "Congregational Singing," *Century Illustrated Monthly Magazine* 28 (July 1884): 950.

7. "Winter Hill Church, Somerville, Mass.," *Church Building Quarterly* 10 (July 1892): 148–51.

8. "Central Congregational Church, Providence, RI," *Church Building Quarterly* 12 (July 1894): 179–81. Similarly, the changing interior aesthetic had some early proponents. Architect John Jager, for instance, dismissed "false-golden wallpaper and mock mouldings, and cheap bric-a-brac" in his *Fundamental Ideas of Church Architecture* (Minneapolis, Minn.: Great Western, 1903), 7.

9. While the neoclassical style became widely popular for municipal buildings, it was used infrequently for Protestant church buildings. Christian Scientists are a major exception, however, for they adopted it widely, in part as a means of establishing and announcing their legitimacy in the urban landscape. See Paul Eli Ivey, *Prayers in Stone: Christian Science Architecture in*

the United States, 1894–1930 (Urbana: University of Illinois Press, 1999). Catholics also favored neoclassical styles at the turn of the century.

10. Donald R. Torbert, *Significant Architecture in the History of Minneapolis* (Minneapolis, Minn.: Minneapolis Planning Commission and Minneapolis Chapter, American Institute of Architects, 1969), 100. New York architect Richard Morris Hunt was among the popularizers of domestic Gothic during the 1890s.

11. See Ralph Adams Cram, *Church Building: A Study of the Principles of Architecture in their Relation to the Church* (Boston: Small, Maynard, 1901), *The Gothic Quest* (New York: Baker and Taylor, Company, 1907), and *Convictions and Controversies* (Boston: Marshall Jones, 1935). On Cram's work, see Douglass Shand-Tucci, *Ralph Adams Cram: Life and Architecture* (Amherst: University of Massachusetts, 1995); and Robert Muccigrosso, *American Gothic: The Mind and Art of Ralph Adams Cram* (Washington, D.C.: University Press of America, 1980).

12. Particularly in the United States, the geographical directions do not necessarily refer to the actual siting of these churches; rather, they refer to the traditional siting of a cathedral with the nave running from the west door to the east chancel.

13. On Plymouth Congregational in Minneapolis, see Torbert, *Significant Architecture*, 92–93. It is also listed in David Gebhard and Tom Martinson, *A Guide to the Architecture of Minnesota* (Minneapolis: University of Minnesota Press, 1977), 64. The Church of the Covenant in Cleveland is listed in Foster Armstrong, Richard Klein, and Cara Armstrong, *A Guide to Cleveland's Sacred Landmarks* (Kent, Ohio: Kent State University Press, 1992), 48–49. On House of Hope Presbyterian, see Gebhard and Martinson, *Guide*, 104; and on Rockefeller Memorial Chapel, see George A. Lane, *Chicago Churches and Synagogues* (Chicago: Loyola University Press, 1981), 182–83.

14. David Ralph Bains, "The Liturgical Impulse in Mid-Twentieth-Century American Mainline Protestantism" (Ph.D. diss., Harvard University, 1999), 73. I am indebted to Bains for his work in this area and for his helpful comments on this section.

15. Von Ogden Vogt, *Art and Religion* (New Haven, Conn.: Yale University Press, 1921), 203, 208, quoted in Bains, "Liturgical Impulse," 73.

16. Vogt, *Art and Religion*, 206.

17. *A Noble Landmark of New York: The Fifth Avenue Presbyterian Church, 1808–1958* (New York: Fifth Avenue Presbyterian Church, 1960), 72.

18. Vogt, *Art and Religion*, 208.

19. Elbert M. Conover, *Building the House of God* (New York: Methodist Book Concern, 1928), 15, quoted in Bains, "Liturgical Impulse," 74.

20. Elbert M. Conover, *The Church Builder* (New York: Interdenominational Bureau of Architecture, 1948), 41.

21. Vogt, *Art and Religion*, 45–46.

22. Vogt, *Art and Religion*, 45.

23. Vogt, *Art and Religion*, 46.

24. John R. Scotford, *The Church Beautiful: A Practical Discussion of Church Architecture* (Boston: Pilgrim Press, 1945), 16–17.

25. Scotford, *Church Beautiful*, 19. See also Conover, *Church Builder*, 57–58.

26. Thomas Albert Stafford, *Christian Symbolism in the Evangelical Churches* (New York: Abingdon-Cokesbury, 1942), 106.

27. Richard H. Ritter, *The Arts of the Church* (Boston: Pilgrim Press, 1947), 41. Ritter, ordained in the Presbyterian church, served variously in Congregationalist, Methodist, and Baptist pulpits and on a nondenominational campus. His book presents the work of the Congregational Christian Arts Guild.

28. Before and after photos are found in Conover, *Church Builder*, 57, 59, 65; and after photos are included in Scotford, *Church Beautiful*, 16, 18. Several photos of divided chancels

also appear in Stafford, *Christian Symbolism*, 118, 120, 125, 130. Conover argues that the long, narrow nave is acoustically superior to the broader auditorium type, which he loathes. See Conover, 79–80.

29. Henry E. Tralle and George Earnest Merrill, *Building for Religious Education* (New York: Century, 1926), 119–20.

30. Tralle and Merrill, *Building*, 7. These authors did not spare their criticism, claiming that the recessible doors were "wholly undesirable, because they provide only partial separation; they are unsightly and interfere with attractive room-furnishings and wall-decorations; they are more expensive than plaster partitions; their manipulation is difficult and sometimes impossible; their moving is detrimental to order and reverence; their benefits are imaginary; and they are unnecessary when the church building is properly planned" (119–20).

31. Bains, "Liturgical Impulse," offers an excellent in-depth analysis of the concerns driving the liturgical movement during this period and its architectural expression. See also James F. White, *Protestant Worship and Church Architecture: Theological and Historical Concerns* (New York: Oxford University Press, 1964).

32. On the evangelical schism, see George M. Marsden, *Understanding Fundamentalism and Evangelicalism* (Grand Rapids, Mich.: Eerdmans, 1991), 9–61. On liberal Protestantism, see William R. Hutchinson, *The Modernist Impulse in American Protestantism* (Cambridge, Mass: Harvard University Press, 1976); and Ferenc Morton Szasz, *The Divided Mind of Protestant America, 1880–1930* (University: University of Alabama Press, 1982).

33. On the Angelus Temple, see Edith L. Blumhofer, *Aimee Semple McPherson: Everybody's Sister* (Grand Rapids, Mich.: Eerdmans, 1993), 232–80. On the Moody Memorial Church, see Lane, *Chicago Churches and Synagogues*, 172. On the Boston Avenue Methodist Church, see Robert C. Broderick, *Historic Churches of the United States* (New York: Wilfred Funk, 1958), 202–6; and Peter W. Williams, *Houses of God: Region, Religion, and Architecture in the United States* (Urbana: University of Illinois Press, 1997), 215–26.

34. Riley juggled the desire for a new, spacious auditorium with the desire for the expansion of the Sunday school into a Bible college. Construction on the latter, Jackson Hall, commenced in 1922. This four-story building contained forty-six classrooms and seven offices. The next year, the congregation began the rebuilding of the church with Frederick Kees, who had designed the original church, directing the project. The building committee's discussions appear from 1 Sept. 1919 through 27 Feb. 1924 in First Baptist Church, Advisory Board Minutes, First Baptist Church Archives, Minneaplis, Minn. See also *Dedication of First Baptist Church, Minneapolis*, 6 Jan. 1924, in the same archives.

35. P. E. Burroughs, *Church and Sunday-School Buildings* (Nashville, Tenn.: Sunday School Board, Southern Baptist Convention, 1920), 67, 68, 41–46.

36. First Baptist Church, Advisory Board Minutes, 26 Apr. 1922.

37. On these differences, see White, *Protestant Worship*, 118–22. Catholic architecture developed an interesting footnote to this general trend among Protestants in the 1960s. In its effort to increase the relevance of religion for young people, Vatican II fostered liturgical experimentation and, as a consequence, architectural innovation. Blending liturgical and audience-centered spaces, several Catholic congregations chose the theatre-in-the-round model, locating the altar at the center of a square of pews. For instance, architect Marcel Breuer's St. John's Abbey Church (1954–1961), constructed for the Benedictines of St. John on their campus in Collegeville, Minn., expertly anticipated this plan, directing a shaft of light onto the altar from a skylight overhead. In addition to several Catholic churches that adopted this plan in the 1960s and early 1970s, some Protestant churches were also constructed along this plan, among them Eero Saarinen's North Christian Church in Columbus, Ohio, a town noted for its fostering of architectural excellence. Although Saarinen's seating arrangement sloped like a Greek amphitheatre, it abandoned the curvilinear form, dividing the hexagonal space into banks of

rectilinear pews fully surrounding a central pit occupied by the Communion table. Organ pipes and the pulpit placed within one of these banks distinguished it as a secondary focal point.

38. On St. Paul's in Cedar Rapids, see Marilyn J. Chiat, *America's Religious Architecture: Sacred Places for Every Community* (New York: Wiley, 1997), 159. Recent work interrogating the efficacy of the bipolar liberal-conservative model holds great promise for interpreting the varieties of architectural expression in the twentieth century. See *Re-forming the Center: American Protestantism, 1900 to the Present*, edited by Douglas Jacobsen and William Vance Trollinger, Jr. (Grand Rapids, Mich.: Eerdmans, 1998).

39. On Hybels and the conceptualization of the church, several journalistic accounts offer useful information. See Barbara Dolan, "Full House at Willow Creek; A Multimedia Appeal to the 'Unchurched Harrys,'" *Time*, 6 Mar. 1989, 60; Cyndee Miller, "Churches Turn to Research for Help in Saving New Souls," *Marketing News*, 11 Apr. 1994, 1, 3; Gustav Niebuhr, "Where Religion Gets a Big Dose of Shopping-Mall Culture," *New York Times*, 16 Apr. 1995, 1; Gustav Niebuhr, "The Minister as Marketer Learning from Business," *New York Times*, 18 Apr. 1995, 1; Michael Lewis, "The Capitalist: God Is in the Packaging," *New York Times*, 21 July 1996, 94; and Bill Hybels, "Bill Hybels on a Megachurch Ministry," interview by A. M. Banks, *Christian Century*, 14 May 1997, 484. Scholarly discussion of the megachurch phenomenon remains sparse; see Scott Thumma, "Exploring the Megachurch Phenomenon: Their Characteristics and Cultural Contexts," Center for Social and Religious Research, Hartford Seminary, http://www.hartsem.edu/csrr/people/slt/megachurch.htm, and the accompanying bibliography at http://www.hartsem.edu/csrr/people/slt/megabiblio.htm.

40. Quoted in Paul Goldberger, "The Gospel of Church Architecture, Revised," *New York Times*, 20 Apr. 1995, C1.

41. This raises the question of whether contemporary culture is sacralizing recreation and recreational space. Analyses of the shopping mall as sacralized space and sacred centers have been advanced. Thus far, I see few attempts to sacralize such space, however. And megachurches draw upon these connections not for their religious connotations, as neomedieval auditorium churches drew upon domestic piety, but precisely for their more comforting secular connotations.

42. Services still might be challenging, however. Often focused on relationships, these sermons cover a gamut of emotions, offering an emotional rollercoaster ride much like that intended by family movies. In these services, individuals might assess their own lives and relationships through the guidance of a scriptural passage.

Bibliography

Primary Source Collections

Finney, Charles Grandison. Papers. Oberlin College Archives, Oberlin, Ohio. (abbreviated as CGFP)

First Baptist Church, Minneapolis. Papers. First Baptist Church Archives, Minneapolis, Minn.

First Baptist Church, Minneapolis. Papers. Minnesota Historical Society Archives, St. Paul, Minn.

First Church, Oberlin Society. Papers. Oberlin College Archives, Oberlin, Ohio.

First Congregational Church, Pueblo. Papers. First Congregational Church Archives, Pueblo, Colo.

First Congregational Church. Papers. Minnesota Historical Society Archives. St. Paul, Minn.

Fowler M.E. Church, Minneapolis. Papers. Scottish Rite Temple Archives, Minneapolis, Minn.

Miller, Lewis. Papers. Chautauqua Institute Archives, Chautauqua, N.Y.

National Register of Historic Places, Washington, D.C.

Pilgrim Congregational Church, Cleveland. Papers. Pilgrim Congregational Church Archives, Cleveland, Ohio.

Pilgrim Congregational Church, Cleveland. Papers. Western Reserve Historical Society, Cleveland, Ohio.

Tappan, Lewis. Papers. Library of Congress, Washington, D.C., Microfilm, 1975. (abbreviated as PLT)

Trinity United Methodist Church, Denver, Colo. Papers. Trinity United Methodist Church Archives, Denver, Colo.

Wesley United Methodist Church, Minneapolis. Papers. Wesley United Methodist Church Archives, Minneapolis, Minn.

Primary Source Journals

American Architect and Building News (abbreviated as *AA&BN*)
Atlantic Monthly
Biblical Repertory and Princeton Review
Calvinistic Magazine
Century Illustrated Monthly Magazine
Chautauquan
Christian Advocate

Church Building Quarterly
Cleveland Leader
Cleveland Plain Dealer
Congregational Quarterly
Congregational Yearbook
Crayon
Frank Leslie's Illustrated Newspaper
Harper's New Monthly Magazine
Inland Architect and Builder
Journal of Commerce
Methodist Almanac
Minneapolis Journal
Minneapolis Tribune
New York Evangelist
New York Mirror and Ladies' Literary Gazette
New York Times
North American Review
Oberlin Evangelist
Presbyterian Magazine
Princeton Review (Biblical Repertory and Princeton Review)
Rocky Mountain News (Denver)
Scribner's Monthly Magazine
Sloan's Architectural Review and Builders' Journal

Other Primary Sources

Abbott, Lyman. "Report of the Committee on the Improvement of Worship." *Minutes of the National Council of the Congregational Churches in the United States*, 8th sess., Minneapolis, Minn. Boston: Congregational Sunday School and Publishing Society, 1893.

Bacon, Leonard Woolsey. "Suggestions Concerning the Ritual of a Puritan Church." *Congregational Quarterly* 5 (July 1863): 242–47.

Barnes, Gilbert H., and Dwight L. Dumond, eds. *Letters of Theodore Dwight Weld, Angelina Grimké Weld, and Sara Grimké, 1822–1844.* Gloucester, Mass.: Peter Smith, 1965.

Bayley, Frank T. "Church Building as a Factor in Christianizing America." *Church Building Quarterly* 22 (Oct. 1904): 192–99.

Bellamy, Edward. *Looking Backward.* 1888. Reprint. New York: Signet Classic, 1960.

Blake, Mrs. A. B. "Church Music in America." *Harper's New Monthly Magazine* 58 (Apr. 1879): 737.

Blake, S. L. "Extempore Preaching." *Congregational Quarterly.* 2d ser., 2 (July 1870): 378–91.

Bowler, George. *Chapel and Church Architecture with Designs for Parsonages.* Boston: Jewett, 1856.

Brearley, William H. *Improved Bible-School Building and Church Edifice Combined.* Detroit, Mich.: n.p., 1881.

Brown, R., Jr. "What Our Architecture Lacks." *AA&BN* (30 June 1888): 304–5.

Burroughs, P. E. *Church and Sunday-School Buildings.* Nashville, Tenn.: Sunday School Board, Southern Baptist Convention, 1920.

Burt, D. "Congregationalism in Minnesota." *Congregational Quarterly* 2 (Jan. 1860): 67–72.

Bushnell, Horace. *Christian Nurture.* New York: Scribner, 1861.

———. *Views of Christian Nurture.* Hartford, Conn.: Hunt, 1847.

"The Changes in Preaching." *Scribner's Monthly Magazine* 14 (June 1877): 255–56.

Church Manual for the Communicants of the Second Free Presbyterian Church, Worshipping at the Chatham-Street Chapel. New York: Dorr and Butterfield, 1834.

Clark, J. S. "A Lesson from the Past: Early Methods of Church Extension." *Congregational Quarterly* 1 (Jan. 1859): 53–59.

Cleveland, Henry Russell. "American Architecture." *North American Review* 43 (Oct. 1836): 372.

Cole, Charles A. "Painted Glass in Household Decoration." *Harper's New Monthly Magazine* 59 (Oct. 1879): 655–64.

Conover, Elbert M. *Building the House of God.* New York: Methodist Book Concern, 1928.

———. *The Church Builder.* New York: Interdenominational Bureau of Architecture, 1948.

Cram, Ralph Adams. *Church Building: A Study of the Principles of Architecture in Their Relation to the Church.* Boston: Small, Maynard, 1901.

———. *Convictions and Controversies.* Boston, Marshall Jones, 1935.

———. *The Gothic Quest.* New York: Baker and Taylor, 1907.

"Designs in Church Architecture." In *Congregational Yearbook 1881.* Boston: Congregational Publishing Company, 1881, 5.

Dexter, H. M. "Meeting-Houses: Considered Historically and Suggestively." *Congregational Quarterly* 1 (Apr. 1859): 186–214.

Dexter, Henry Martyn. *A Hand-Book of Congregationalism.* Boston: Congregational Publishing Society, 1880.

[Dod, William A., and Albert Dod]. "Church Architecture." *Biblical Repertory and Princeton Review* 27 (Oct. 1855): 625–49.

Durdand, John. "The Competition Plans for the Plymouth Church." *Crayon* 6 (Dec. 1859): 374–77.

———. "Henry Ward Beecher on Church Architecture." *Crayon,* 6 (May 1859): 154–57.

Eidlitz, Leopold. "Christian Architecture." *Crayon* 5 (Feb. 1858): 53–55.

———. "On Style." *Crayon* 5 (May 1858): 139–42.

Euster, W. T. *The Philosophy of Church Building: How to Build a Beautiful Modern Church or Parsonage at Half Price.* Pendleton, Oreg.: Pendleton Printery, Jack Huston, 1908.

Evans, Herbert Francis. "Architecture, Sunday School." In *The Encyclopedia of Sunday Schools and Religious Education.* Edited by John T. McFarland and Benjamin S. Winchester. New York: Nelson & Sons, 1915. 29–30.

———. *The Sunday-School Building and Its Equipment.* Chicago: University of Chicago Press, 1914.

Faxon, John A. "Modern Church Building I." *AA&BN* (15 Feb. 1879): 50–52.

———. "Modern Church Building II." *AA&BN* (1 Mar. 1879): 66–67.

Finck, Henry Theophilus. *My Adventures in the Golden Age of Music.* New York: Funk and Wagnalls, 1926.

Finney, Charles G. *Lectures on Revivals of Religion.* Edited by William G. McLoughlin. Cambridge, Mass.: Harvard University Press, Belknap Press, 1960.

———. *The Memoirs of Charles G. Finney.* Edited by Garth M. Rosell and Richard A. G. Dupuis. Grand Rapids, Mich.: Academie, 1989.

Fish, Henry C. *Primitive Piety Revived; or, The Aggressive Power of the Christian Church.* Boston: Congregational Board of Publication, 1855.

Fisher, W. P. "The Size and Shape of the Church Edifice." *Church Building Quarterly* 1 (Oct. 1883): 104–5.

Fitch, Frank S. "The Church in Relation to the Christian Development of America." *Church Building Quarterly* 23 (July 1905): 140–43.

Foss, Arthur T., and Edward Mathews, comps. *Facts for Baptist Churches: Collected, Arranged, and Reviewed.* Utica, N.Y.: American Baptist Free Mission Society, 1850.

Fowler, Henry. *The American Pulpit.* New York: Fairchild, 1856.

Gardner, E. C. *Common Sense in Church Building, Illustrated by Seven Original Plates.* New York: Bicknell & Comstock, 1880.

General Congregational Convention. *A Book of Plans for Churches and Parsonages.* New York: Daniel Burgess, 1853.

Gilman, Arthur. "Architecture in the United States." *North American Review* 58 (Apr. 1844): 436–80.

Gilman, E. W. "The American Congregational Union." *Congregational Quarterly* 1 (Jan. 1859): 59–61.

Goodwin, Frank J. "The Church as a Center of Civic Life." *Church Building Quarterly* 23 (July 1905): 131–40.

Gray, Ellis [Louisa T. Cragin]. "The Mission of Music." *Harper's New Monthly Magazine* 51 (Oct. 1875): 736–44.

Greene, Asa. *A Glance at New York.* New York: Greene, 1837.

———. *The Perils of Pearl Street.* New York: Betts and Anstice, 1834.

Greene, Ernest. "Hints on Church Building II: The Interior." *Church Building Quarterly* 9 (Jan. 1891): 39–42.

Greenleaf, Jonathan. *A History of the Churches of All Denominations in the City of New York, from the First Settlement to the Year 1846.* New York: French, 1846.

Gulliver, John P. Sketch of the Broadway Church, Norwich, Conn., with Particular Reference to Ventilation." *Congregational Quarterly* 1 (July 1859): 300–308.

H[all, John]. "Psalmody and Liturgy." *Presbyterian Magazine* 1 (Apr. 1851): 20.

Hart, J. Coleman. "Unity in Architecture." *Crayon* 6 (Mar. 1859): 84–89.

Hartshorn, W. N., George R. Merrill, and Marion Lawrance, eds. *The Development of the Sunday-School, 1780–1905.* Boston: International Sunday-School Association, 1905.

Hendry, Charles E., and Margaret T. Svendsen. *Between Spines and Stacks.* Cleveland, Ohio: Welfare Federation of Cleveland, 1936.

Hill, John Wesley. *Twin City Methodism: A History of the Methodist Episcopal Church in Minneapolis and St. Paul, Minn.* Minneapolis, Minn.: Price Bros., 1895.

[Hodge, Charles]. "Review of *Eutaxia; or, The Presbyterian Liturgies: Historical Sketches,* by Charles Baird." *Biblical Repertory and Princeton Review* 27 (July 1855): 445–67.

[Holland, Josiah C.] "Church Music." *Scribner's Monthly* 18 (1879): 134–35.

———. "The Music of the Church." *Scribner's Monthly* 10 (1875): 242–43.

Holly, H. Hudson. *Church Architecture, Illustrated with Thirty-five Lithographic Plates, from Original Designs.* Hartford, Conn.: Church Press and Mallory, 1871.

Hone, Philip. *The Diary of Philip Hone, 1828–1851.* New York: Dodd, Mead, 1889.

Howells, William Dean. *A Hazard of New Fortunes.* 1890. Reprint. New York: New American Library, 1980.

Hudson, Marshall A. "Bible Class Work for Men." In *The Development of the Sunday-School, 1780–1905.* Boston: International Sunday-School Association, 1905. 275–78.

Hunt, Richard M. "The Church Architecture That We Need." *AA&BN* (1 Dec. 1877): 384–85.

Ireland, Joseph N. *Records of the New York Stage, from 1750–1860.* 2 vols. New York: Morrell, 1867.

Jager, John. *Fundamental Ideas of Church Architecture.* Minneapolis, Minn.: Great Western, 1903.

J. F. "Uniformity of Worship." *Presbyterian Magazine* 1 (June 1851): 260–62.

Knox, Alice W., and Charles E. Knox. *The Infant Sunday School.* New York: Broughton & Wyman, 1870.

Kramer, George W. *The What, How, and Why of Church Building.* New York: n.p., 1897.

Langworthy, Isaac P. "A Congregational Home." *Congregational Quarterly* 5 (Oct. 1863): 286–92.

———. "Ventilation of Churches." *Congregational Quarterly* 1 (Oct. 1859): 369–72.

Latourette, Kenneth Scott. "Serving Overseas." In *They Seek a Country: The American Presbyterians, Some Aspects*. Edited by Gaius Jackson Slosser. New York: Macmillan, 1955.

Littell, Emlen. "The Church Architecture That We Need." *AA&BN* (12 Jan. 1878): 10-12.

Magoun, George F. "Architecture and Christian Principle." *Congregational Quarterly* 1 (Oct. 1859): 373-85.

—— "Church Architecture and the Masses." *Congregational Quarterly* 4 (Jan. 1862): 25-36.

Martin, William Wallace. *Manual of Ecclesiastical Architecture, Comprising a Study of Its Various Styles, the Chronological Arrangement of Its Elements, and Its Relation to Christian Worship*. Cincinnati, Ohio: Curts & Jennings, 1897.

Marvin, Abijah P. "Keeping Our Own Vineyard." *Congregational Quarterly* 2 (Oct. 1860): 390-401.

Methodist Episcopal Church Board of Extension. *Sample Pages of Catalogue of Architectural Plans for Churches and Parsonages*. Philadelphia: Board of Church Extension, 1884.

Moxom, Philip S. "Church Work in Our Cities." *Church Building Quarterly* 22 (Oct. 1904): 209-12.

Noble, T. K. "The Sanctuary in Its Relation to the Material, Moral, and Spiritual Life of the Community." *Church Building Quarterly* 1 (Jan. 1883): 13-20.

Nutting, Wallace. "Address on Church Building." *Church Building Quarterly* 14 (Apr. 1896): 151-54.

Oakley, A. F. "Notes on Modern Church Building." *AA&BN* (21 Aug. 1880): 88-89.

Osgood, Sidney J. *Churches*. Grand Rapids, Mich.: Dean, 1893.

Otis, Adams. *The First Presbyterian Church, 1833-1913*. 2d rev. ed. Chicago: Revell, 1913.

Parker, Francis J. *Church-Building and Things To Be Considered, Done, or Avoided in Connection Therewith*. Boston: Cupples, Upham, 1886.

Patterson, Rachel Wild. *The Long-Lost Rachel Wild; or, Seeking Diamonds in the Rough*. Denver, Colo.: Reed, 1905.

Patton, Normand S. "How to Secure a Good Church Plan: The Advice of an Architect." *Church Building Quarterly* 10 (Apr. 1892): 99.

"Pilgrim Congregational Church, Cleveland, O." *Church Building Quarterly* 13 (Oct. 1895): 226-30.

Poole, George Ayliffe. *The Appropriate Character of Church Architecture*. Leeds and London: Green and Rivington's, 1842.

"Presbyterian Liturgies." *Biblical Repertory and Princeton Review* 27 (July 1855): 445-67.

Proceedings of the General Convention of Congregational Ministers and Delegates in the United States, Held at Albany, N.Y., 5th-8th of October, 1852. New York: Benedict, 1852.

Pullan, Richard Popplewell. *Elementary Lectures on Christian Architecture*. London: Stanford, 1879.

Review of *An Attempt to Discriminate the Styles of English Architecture from the Conquest to the Reformation*, by Thomas Rickman, and *Chronological Historical Illustrations of the Ancient Architecture of Great Britain*, by John Britton. *Quarterly Review* 25 (1821): 112-47.

Rice, Edwin Wilbur. *The Sunday-School Movement and the American Sunday-School Union, 1780-1917*. Philadelphia: American Sunday-School Union, 1917.

Riley, Marie Acomb. *The Dynamic of a Dream: The Life Story of Dr. William B. Riley*. Grand Rapids, Mich.: Eerdmans, 1938.

Riley, William Bell. "Women in the Ministry." *Christian Fundamentalist* 1 (May 1928): 21.

Ritter, Richard H. *The Arts of the Church*. Boston: Pilgrim Press, 1947.

Robinson, Charles S. "Artistic Help in Divine Service." *Century Illustrated Monthly Magazine* 27 (Feb. 1884): 632-34.

——. "The Minister and the Man." *Century Illustrated Monthly Magazine* 28 (July 1884): 468-71.

——. "Organs and Orchestras in Church." *Century Illustrated Monthly Magazine* 27 (Mar. 1884), 787-89.

——. "What the Choirs Say." *Century Illustrated Monthly Magazine* 28 (June 1884): 306-9.

——. "Worshiping by Proxy." *Century Illustrated Monthly Magazine* 27 (Apr. 1884): 946-48.

Rose, L. P. "The Union's Place and Power." *Church Building Quarterly* 4 (Mar. 1886): 7-8.

Ruggles, Edward. *A Picture of New York in 1846.* New York: Francis, 1846.

Russell, John Scott. "Elementary Considerations of Some Principles in the Construction of Buildings Designed to Accommodate Spectators and Auditors." *Edinburgh New Philosophical Journal* 27 (Apr.-Oct. 1839): 131-36.

Sargent, C. E. *Our Home; or, The Key to a Nobler Life.* Springfield, Mass.: King, Richardson, 1894.

Scotford, John R. *The Church Beautiful: A Practical Discussion of Church Architecture.* Boston: Pilgrim Press, 1945.

Shedd, William G. T. *Homiletics and Pastoral Theology.* 8th ed. New York: Scribner, Armstrong, 1875.

Spring, Gardiner. *The Danger and Hope of the American People: A Discourse on the Day of the Annual Thanksgiving, in the State of New-York.* New York: Trow, 1843.

Stafford, Thomas Albert. *Christian Symbolism in the Evangelical Churches.* New York: Abingdon-Cokesbury, 1942.

Stokes, I. N. Phelps. *The Iconography of Manhattan, 1498-1909.* 6 vols. New York: Dodd, 1915.

Stone, Henry Dickinson. *Personal Recollections of the Drama; or, Theatrical Reminiscences.* 1873. Reprint. New York: Benjamin Blom, 1969.

Strong, Josiah. *Religious Movements for Social Betterment.* New York: Baker and Taylor, 1900.

Tappan, Lewis. "History of the Free Churches in the City of New York." *New York Evangelist* (21 Feb. 1835): 29-30.

——. *The Life of Arthur Tappan.* New York: Hurd and Houghton, 1870.

——. *Proceedings of the Session of Broadway Tabernacle against Lewis Tappan.* New York: n.p., 1839.

Tenney, Susan Ellen. *Annual Report—1913, Tremont School Branch.* Cleveland, Ohio: Merrick House, 1914.

Thayer, Eugene. "Congregational Singing." *Century Illustrated Monthly Magazine* 28 (July 1884): 950-52.

Thompson, Joseph P. "Historical Sketch of the Broadway Tabernacle, New York City." *Congregational Quarterly* 2 (Jan. 1860): 64-67.

——. *The Last Sabbath in the Broadway Tabernacle: A Historical Discourse.* New York: Calkins & Stiles, 1857.

——. *Memoir of David Hale, Late Editor of the Journal of Commerce, with Selections from His Miscellaneous Writings.* New York: Wiley, 1850.

Thornwell, James Henley. "Relation of the Church to Slavery." In *The Collected Writings of James Henley Thornwell.* 4 vols. Edited by John B. Adger and John L. Girardeau. Richmond, Va.: Presbyterian Committee of Publication, 1871-1873. 381-97.

Tralle, Henry E., and George Earnest Merrill. *Building for Religious Education.* New York: Century, 1926.

Trumbull, H. Clay. *The Sunday-School: Its Origin, Mission, Methods, and Auxiliaries.* Philadelphia: Wattles, 1896.

Vincent, John Heyl. *The Chautauqua Movement.* Boston: Chuatauqua Press, 1886.

Vogt, Von Ogden. *Art and Religion.* New Haven, Conn.: Yale University Press, 1921.

Ward, Francis. *An Account of Three Camp-Meetings Held by the Methodists, at Sharon, Litchfield County, Connecticut; at Rhinebeck, in Dutchess County; and at Petersburgh, in Rensselaer County, New-York State.* Brooklyn, N.Y.: Robinson & Little, 1806.

Wardle, Addie Grace. *History of the Sunday School Movement in the Methodist Episcopal Church.* New York: Methodist Book Concern, 1918.

Ware, John. *Memoir of the Life of Henry Ware, Jr.* Boston: Munroe, 1846.

Ware, John F. W. *Home Life in America: What It Is and What It Needs*. Boston: n.p., 1864.

Washburn, Emory. "A Free Church, a Free Gospel, a Free Government." *Congregational Quarterly* 2 (July 1860): 313-29.

Washington, Margaret, ed. *Narrative of Sojourner Truth*. New York: Vintage, 1993.

Waugh, B., and T. Mason, eds. *A Collection of Hymns, for the Use of the Methodist Episcopal Church, Principally from the Collection of the Rev. John Wesley, A. M.*, rev. ed. New York: Lane & Tippett, 1845.

Webster, J. C. "The Worship of the Christian Sanctuary." *Congregational Quarterly* 4 (July 1862): 259-65.

Wesley, John. *The Journal of the Rev. John Wesley, A. M.* 8 vols. Edited by Nehemiah Curnock. London: Culley, 1909-1916.

———. *The Works of John Wesley*. Vol. 21. Edited by W. Reginald Ward and Richard P. Heitzenrater. Nashvile, Tenn.: Abingdon, 1992.

W. H. H. "Congregational Singing in Dr. Alexander's Church, New York. "*Presbyterian Magazine* 5 (Oct. 1855): 475.

White, Frank Newhall. "The Leavening Power of the Church in City and Country." *Church Building Quarterly* 25 (Oct. 1907): 201-9.

W. H. S. "*In Re*: Church Music." *Century Illustrated Monthly Magazine* 28 (July 1884): 471.

Winne, Peter. *Historical Gleanings*. Denver, Colo.: Trinity United Methodist Church, 1915-1916.

Witherspoon, Edward. "Church Music: A Voice from the Choir Loft." *Century Illustrated Monthly Magazine* 29 (Nov. 1884): 474-76.

Wodell, Fred W. "An Ideal Church." *Century Illustrated Monthly Magazine* 28 (July 1884): 471.

Worthington, J. C. *The Building of a Church*. Philadelphia: Architectural Pen-Points, 1887.

[Yeomans, John W]. "Forms of Worship." *Princeton Review* 18 (Oct. 1846): 488.

Young, William C. *Documents of American Theater History*. 2 vols. Chicago: American Library Association, 1973.

Secondary Sources

Addleshaw, G. W. O., and Frederick Etchells. *The Architectural Setting of Anglican Worship*. London: Faber and Faber, 1948.

Albanese, Catherine L. *America: Religions and Religion*. 3d. ed. Belmont, Calif.: Wadsworth, 1999.

———. *Nature Religion in America: From the Algonkian Indians to the New Age*. Chicago: University of Chicago Press, 1990.

Alexander, Dennis. Serving the Downtown Community: Wesley Church." 17 Jan. 1988. Wesley United Methodist Church Archives. Minneapolis, Minn.

Allen, Robert C. *Horrible Prettiness: Burlesque and American Culture*. Chapel Hill: University of North Carolina Press, 1991.

Amiot, Francois. *History of the Mass*. New York: Hawthorne, 1959.

Anderson, William, and Clive Hicks. *The Rise of the Gothic*. Salem, N.H.: Salem House, 1985.

Andrew, Laura Brana Blank. *The Early Temples of the Mormons: The Architecture of the Millennial Kingdom of the West*. Albany: State University of New York Press, 1978.

Andrews, Mildren Tanner. *Seeking to Serve: The Legacy of Seattle's Plymouth Congregational Church*. Dubuque, Iowa: Kendall/Hunt, 1988.

Anscombe, Isabelle, and Charlotte Gere. *Arts and Crafts in Britain and America*. New York: Rizzoli, 1978.

Armstrong, Foster, Richard Klein, and Cara Armstrong. *A Guide to Cleveland's Sacred Landmarks*. Kent, Ohio: Kent State University Press, 1992.

Armstrong, Maurice W., Lefferts A. Loetscher, and Charles A. Anderson, eds. *The Presbyterian Enterprise: Sources of American Presbyterian History.* Philadelphia: Westminster, 1956.

Arndt, Hannah. *The Human Condition.* Chicago: University of Chicago Press, 1958.

Arnheim, Rudolf. *The Dynamics of Architectural Form.* Berkeley: University of California Press, 1977.

Athanasopulos, Christos G. *Contemporary Theatre: Evolution and Design.* New York: Wiley, 1983.

Bains, David Ralph. "The Liturgical Impulse in Mid-Twentieth-Century American Mainline Protestantism." Ph.D. diss., Harvard University, 1999.

Bank, Rosemarie K. "Hustlers in the House: The Bowery Theatre as a Mode of Historical Information." In *The American Stage: Social and Economic Issues from the Colonial Period to the Present.* Edited by Ron Engle and Tice L. Miller. New York: Cambridge University Press, 1993. 47-64.

Barth, Gunther. "Metropolism in the Far West." In *The Age of Industrialism in America.* Edited by Frederic Cople Jaher. New York: Free Press, 1968. 158-87.

Beales, Ross W., Jr. "The Child in Seventeenth-Century America." In *American Childhood: A Research Guide and Historical Handbook.* Edited by Joseph M. Hawes and N. Ray Hiner. Westport, Conn.: Greenwood, 1985. 15-56.

Bederman, Gail. *Manliness and Civilization: A Cultural History of Gender and Race in the United States, 1880-1917.* Chicago: University of Chicago Press, 1995.

Benes, Peter, and Philip D. Zimmerman. *New England Meeting House and Church: 1630-1850.* Boston: Boston University for the Dublin Seminar for New England Folklife, 1979.

Betjeman, John. "Nonconformist Architecture." *Architectural Review* 88 (Dec. 1940): 160-74.

Biedrzynski, Richard. *Kirchen Unserer Zeit.* Munich: Hirmer Verlag, 1958.

Blackmar, Betsy. "Re-walking the 'Walking City': Housing and Property Relations in New York City, 1780-1840." *Radical History Review* 21 (Fall 1979): 131-48.

Bluestone, Daniel. *Constructing Chicago.* New Haven, Conn.: Yale University Press, 1991.

Blumhofer, Edith L. *Aimee Semple McPherson: Everybody's Sister.* Grand Rapids, Mich.: Eerdmans, 1993.

Blumin, Stuart. *The Emergence of the Middle Class: Social Experience in the American City, 1760-1900.* New York: Cambridge University Press, 1989.

Bodo, John R. *The Protestant Clergy and Public Issues, 1812-1848.* Princeton N.J.: Princeton University Press, 1954.

Bonomi, Patricia. *Under the Cope of Heaven: Religion, Society, and Politics in Colonial America.* New York: Oxford University Press, 1986.

Bordin, Ruth. *Women and Temperance: The Quest for Power and Liberty, 1873-1900.* Philadelphia: Temple University Press, 1981.

Boyer, Paul, and Stephen Nissenbaum. *Salem Possessed: The Social Origins of Witchcraft.* Cambridge, Mass.: Harvard University Press, 1974.

Boylan, Anne M. *Sunday School: The Formation of an American Institution, 1790-1880.* New Haven, Conn.: Yale University Press, 1988.

Bridges, Amy. *A City in the Republic: Antebellum New York and the Origins of Machine Politics.* New York: Cambridge University Press, 1984.

Broderick, Robert C. *Historic Churches of the United States.* New York: Wilfred Funk, 1958.

Brown, Marianna C. *Sunday School Movements in America.* New York: Revell, 1901.

Bruggink, Donald J., and Carl H. Droppers. *Christ and Architecture: Building Presbyterian Reformed Churches.* Grand Rapids, Mich.: Eerdmans, 1965.

Brumberg, Joan Jacobs. *Mission for Life.* New York: Free Press, 1980.

Buggeln, Gretchen Townsend. "Elegance and Sensibility in the Calvinist Tradition: The First Congregational Church of Hartford, Connecticut." In *Seeing beyond the Word: Visual Arts* and the Calvinist Tradition. Edited by Paul Corby Finney. Grand Rapids, Mich.: Eerdmans, 1999. 429–56.

Bushman, Richard L. The Refinement of America: Persons, Houses, Cities. New York: A. Knopf, 1992.

Butsch, Richard. "American Theater Riots and Class Relations, 1754–1849." Theatre Annual 48 (1995): 41–59.

——. "Bowery B'hoys and Matinee Ladies: The Re-Gendering of Nineteenth-Century American Theater Audiences." American Quarterly 46 (Sept. 1994): 374–405.

Carlock, Walter. History of Wesley Church: The First 125 Years. Minneapolis, Minn.: Wesley United Methodist Church, 1977.

Carlson, Marvin. Places of Performance: The Semiotics of Theatre Architecture. Ithaca, N.Y.: Cornell University Press, 1989.

Carter, Paul A. The Spiritual Crisis of the Gilded Age. Dekalb: Northern Illinois University Press, 1971.

Carwardine, Richard J. Evangelicals and Politics in Antebellum America. New Haven, Conn.: Yale University Press, 1993.

——. "The Second Great Awakening in the Urban Centers: An Examination of Methodism and the 'New Measures.'" Journal of American History 59 (1972): 327–40.

Cauthen, Kenneth. The Impact of American Religious Liberalism. 2nd ed. Lanham, Md.: University Press of America, 1983.

Cheesebro, R. A. "The Preaching of Charles G. Finney." Ph.D. diss., Yale University, 1948.

Chiat, Marilyn J. America's Religious Architecture: Sacred Places for Every Community. New York: Wiley, 1997.

Chidester, David, and Edward T. Linenthal, eds. American Sacred Space. Bloomington: Indiana University Press, 1995.

Clark, Clifford E., Jr. The American Family Home, 1800–1960. Chapel Hill: University of North Carolina Press, 1986.

——. "Domestic Architecture as an Index to Social History: The Romantic Revival and the Cult of Domesticity in America, 1840–1870." Journal of Interdisciplinary History 7 (Summer 1976): 33–56.

Cohen, Lizabeth A. "Embellishing a Life of Labor: An Interpretation of the Material Culture of American Working-Class Homes, 1885–1915." In Material Culture Studies in America. Edited by Thomas J. Schlereth. Nashville, Tenn.: American Association for State and Local History, 1982. 289–305.

Cole, Charles C., Jr. "The Free Church Movement in New York City." New York History 34 (July 1953): 284–97.

Conn, Howard J. The First Congregational Church of Great Barrington, 1743–1943. Great Barrington, Mass.: Berkshire Courier, 1943.

Cooley, Steven D. "Manna and the Manual: Sacramental and Instrumental Constructions of the Victorian Methodist Camp Meeting during the Mid-Nineteenth Century." Religion and American Culture: A Journal of Interpretation 6 (Summer 1996): 131–60.

Coontz, Stephanie. The Way We Never Were: American Families and the Nostalgia Trap. New York: Basic, 1992.

Cross, Robert, ed. The Church and the City. Indianapolis, Ind.: Bobbs-Merrill, 1967.

Dallimore, Arnold A. George Whitefield: The Life and Times of the Great Evangelist of the Eighteenth-Century Revival. 2 vols. Edinburgh: Banner of Truth Trust, 1980.

Darling, Sharon S. Decorative & Architectural Arts in Chicago, 1871–1933. Chicago: Chicago Historical Society and University of Chicago Press, 1982.

Darlington, Marwood. Irish Orpheus: The Life of Patrick S. Gilmore, Bandmaster Extraordinary. Philadelphia: Olivier, Maney, Klein, 1950.

DeBerg, Betty A. *Ungodly Women: Gender and the First Wave of American Fundamentalism.* Minneapolis, Minn.: Fortress, 1990.

Demos, John. *A Little Commonwealth: Family Life in Plymouth Colony.* New York: Oxford University Press, 1970.

Dolan, Barbara. "Full House at Willow Creek: A Multimedia Appeal to the 'Unchurched Harrys.'" *Time* (6 Mar. 1989): 60.

Dolan, Jay. *The Immigrant Church: New York's Irish and German Catholics, 1815–1865.* Baltimore, Md.: Johns Hopkins University Press, 1975.

Donnelly, Marian Card. *The New England Meeting Houses of the Seventeenth Century.* Middletown, Conn.: Wesleyan University Press, 1968.

Dorn, Jacob. "The Social Gospel and Socialism: A Comparison of the Thought of Francis Greenwood Peabody, Washington Gladden, and Walter Rauschenbusch." *Church History* 62 (Mar. 1993): 82–100.

Dorsett, Lyle W. *The Queen City: A History of Denver.* Boulder, Colo.: Pruett, 1977.

Douglas, Ann. *The Feminization of American Culture.* New York: Anchor, 1988.

Duffy, Eamon. *The Stripping of the Altars: Traditional Religion in England, c. 1400–c. 1580.* New Haven, Conn.: Yale University Press, 1992.

Du Maurier, Daphne. *Vanishing Cornwall.* Garden City, N.Y.: Doubleday, 1967.

Duncan, Alistair. *Tiffany Windows.* New York: Simon and Schuster, 1980.

Eco, Umberto. "Function and Sign: The Semiotics of Architecture." In *Signs, Symbols, and Architecture.* Edited by Geoffrey Broadbent, Richard Bunt, and Charles Jencks. New York: Wiley, 1980. 11–69.

Eiland, William U. *Nashville's Mother Church: The History of the Ryman Auditorium.* Nashville, Tenn.: Opryland, 1992.

Eliade, Mircea. *The Sacred and the Profane: The Nature of Religion.* New York: Harcourt, Brace, 1959.

Ellis, Walter Edmund Warren. "Social and Religious Factors in the Fundamentalist-Modernist Schisms among Baptists in North America, 1895-1934." Ph.D. diss., University of Pittsburgh, 1974.

Fairchild, James H. *Oberlin: The Colony and the College, 1833–1883.* Oberlin, Ohio: Goodrich, 1883.

Fergusson, E. Morris. *Chapters in Christian Education in America.* New York: Revell, 1935.

Finke, Roger, and Rodney Stark. *The Churching of America, 1776–1900: Winners and Losers in Our Religious Economy.* New Brunswick, N.J.: Rutgers University Press, 1992.

Finney, Paul Corby, ed. *Seeing beyond the Word: Visual Arts and the Calvinist Tradition.* Grand Rapids, Mich.: Eerdmans, 1999.

Fishman, Robert. *Bourgeois Utopia: The Rise and Fall of Suburbia.* New York: Basic, 1987.

Fletcher, Robert Samuel. *A History of Oberlin College: From Its Foundation through the Civil War.* 2 vols. Oberlin, Ohio: Oberlin College, 1943.

Fogelson, Robert M. *America's Armories: Architecture, Society, and Public Order.* Cambridge, Mass.: Harvard University Press, 1989.

Ford, Guy Stanton, and Dora V. Smith. *The First Congregational Church of Minnesota: A Retrospective of Eighty Years.* Minneapolis, Minn.: n.p., 1952.

Forgan, S. "Context, Image and Function: A Preliminary Enquiry into the Architecture of Scientific Societies." *British Journal for the History of Science* 19 (Mar. 1986): 89–113.

Foucault, Michel. *Discipline and Punish: The Birth of the Prison.* Translated by Alan Sheridan. New York: Vintage, 1979.

Gebhard, David, and Tom Martinson. *A Guide to the Architecture of Minnesota.* Minneapolis, Minn.: University of Minnesota Press, 1977.

Geertz, Clifford. *The Interpretation of Cultures.* New York: Basic, 1973.

Gilje, Paul A. *The Road to Mobocracy: Popular Disorder in New York City, 1763-1834.* Chapel Hill: University of North Carolina Press and Institute of Early American History and Culture, 1987.

Gledstone, James Paterson. *The Life and Travels of George Whitefield.* London: Longmans, Green, 1871.

Glenn, Myra C. *Thomas K. Beecher: Minister to a Changing America, 1824-1900.* Westport, Conn.: Greenwood, 1996.

Goen, C. C. *Broken Churches, Broken Nation: Denominational Schisms and the Coming of the American Civil War.* Macon, Ga.: Mercer University Press, 1985.

Goldberger, Paul. "The Gospel of Church Architecture, Revised." *New York Times,* 20 Apr. 1995, C1.

Goodsell, Charles. *The Social Meaning of Civic Space.* Lawrence: University of Kansas Press, 1988.

Gowans, Alan. *Images of American Living: Four Centuries of Architecture and Furniture as Cultural Expression.* Philadelphia: Lippincott, 1964.

Green, Harvey. *The Light of the Home: An Intimate View of the Lives of Women in Victorian America.* New York: Pantheon, 1983.

Gregersen, Charles E. *Dankmar Adler: His Theatres and Auditoriums.* Athens: Swallow Press and Ohio University Press, 1990.

Greven, Philip J. Jr. *The Protestant Temperament.* New York: Knopf, 1977.

Griffin, Clifford S. "Religious Benevolence as Social Control, 1815-1860." *Mississippi Valley Historical Review* 44 (Dec. 1957): 423-44.

Grimsted, David. *Melodrama Unveiled: American Theater and Culture, 1800-1850.* Chicago: University of Chicago Press, 1968.

Haber, Francine, Kenneth R. Fuller, and David N. Wetzel. *Robert S. Roeschlaub: Architect of the Emerging West, 1843-1923.* Denver: Colorado Historical Society, 1988.

Habermas, Jürgen. *Jürgen Habermas on Society and Politics: A Reader.* Edited by Steven Seidman. Boston: Beacon, 1989.

———. *The Structural Transformation of the Public Sphere: An Inquiry into a Category of Bourgeois Society.* Translated by Thomas Burger and Frederick Lawrence. Cambridge, Mass.: MIT Press, 1989.

Halttunen, Karen. *Confidence Men and Painted Women: A Study of Middle-Class Culture in America, 1830-1870.* New Haven, Conn.: Yale University Press, 1982.

Hambrick-Stowe, Charles. "The American Evangelicalism of Charles G. Finney." Paper presented at the spring meeting of the American Society of Church History, Oberlin, Ohio, Mar. 1994.

———. *Charles G. Finney and the Spirit of American Evangelicalism.* Grand Rapids, Mich.: Eerdmans, 1996.

Hamlin, Talbot. *Benjamin Henry Latrobe.* New York: Oxford University Press, 1955.

Hamm, Charles. *Music in the New World.* New York: Norton, 1983.

Handlin, David P. *The American Home: Architecture and Society, 1815-1915.* Boston: Little, Brown, 1979.

Hanley, Mark Y. *Beyond a Christian Commonwealth: The Protestant Quarrel with the American Republic, 1830-1860.* Chapel Hill: University of North Carolina Press, 1994.

Hardman, Keith J. *Charles Grandison Finney, 1792-1875: Revivalist and Reformer.* Grand Rapids, Mich.: Baker Book House, 1987.

Hart, Jeannette. "A History." In *Pilgrim Church: History and Directory, 1859-1929.* Cleveland, Ohio: Pilgrim Congregational Church, 1929. 7-39.

Hatch, Nathan O. *The Democratization of American Christianity.* New Haven, Conn.: Yale University Press, 1989.

——. "Evangelicalism as a Democratic Movement." In *Evangelicalism and Modern America.* Edited by George Marsden. Grand Rapids, Mich.: Eerdmans, 1984. 71–82.

Headley, J. T. *The Great Riots of New York, 1712–1873.* New York: Treat, 1873. Facsimile ed. Miami, Fla.: Mnemosyne, 1969.

Henderson, Jerry Eugene. "A History of the Ryman Auditorium in Nashville, Tennessee: 1892–1920." Ph.D. diss., Louisiana State University, 1962.

Hendrick, Ellwood. *Lewis Miller: A Biographical Essay.* New York: Putnam's, 1925.

Hibbert, Christopher. *London's Churches.* London: Macdonald, 1988.

Higginbotham, Evelyn Brooks. *Righteous Discontent: The Women's Movement in the Black Baptist Church, 1880–1920.* Cambridge, Mass.: Harvard University Press, 1993.

Horowitz, Helen Lefkowitz. *Alma Mater: Design and Experience in the Women's Colleges from Their Nineteenth-Century Beginnings to the 1930s.* New York: Knopf, 1984.

Howe, Daniel Walker. "The Market Revolution and the Shaping of Identity in Whig-Jacksonian America." In *The Market Revolution in America: Social, Political and Religious Expressions, 1800–1880.* Edited by Melvyn Stokes and Stephen Conway. Charlottesville: University Press of Virginia, 1996. 259–81.

Hurst, John Fletcher. *The History of Methodism.* 7 vols. New York: Eaton & Mains, 1902–1904.

Hutchinson, William R. *The Modernist Impulse in American Protestantism.* Cambridge, Mass.: Harvard University Press, 1976.

Hybels, Bill. "Bill Hybels on a Megachurch Ministry." Interview by A. M. Banks. *Christian Century* (14 May 1997): 484.

Ivey, Paul Eli. *Prayers in Stone: Christian Science Architecture in the United States, 1894–1930.* Urbana: University of Illinois Press, 1999.

Jackson, Kenneth T. *Crabgrass Frontier: The Suburbanization of the United States.* New York: Oxford University Press, 1985.

Jacobsen, Douglas, and William Vance Trollinger, J., eds. *Re-forming the Center: American Protestantism, 1900 to the Present.* Grand Rapids, Mich.: Eerdmans, 1998.

Jaeger, A. Robert. "The Auditorium and Akron Plans: Reflections on a Half Century of American Protestantism." M.A. thesis, Cornell University, 1984.

Jencks, Charles. "The Architectural Sign." In *Signs, Symbols, and Architecture.* Edited by Geoffrey Broadbent, Richard Bunt, and Charles Jencks. New York: Wiley, 1980. 71–118.

Johnson, Charles A. *The Frontier Camp Meeting: Religion's Harvest Time.* Dallas, Tex.: Southern Methodist University Press, 1955.

Johnson, Curtis D. *Islands of Holiness: Rural Religion in Upstate New York, 1790–1860.* Ithaca, N.Y.: Cornell University Press, 1989.

——. *Redeeming America: Evangelicals and the Road to the Civil War.* Chicago: Dee, 1993.

Johnson, James H. *Listening in Paris: A Cultural History.* Berkeley: University of California Press, 1995.

Johnson, Paul E. *A Shopkeeper's Millennium: Society and Revivals in Rochester, New York, 1815–1837.* New York: Hill and Wang, 1978.

Jordan, Philip D. *The Evangelical Alliance for the United States of America, 1847–1900: Ecumenicism, Identity, and the Religion of the Republic.* New York: Mellen, 1982.

Jungmann, Joseph A. *The Mass of the Roman Rite: Its Origins and Development.* Translated by Francis A. Brunner. London: Burns and Oates, 1959.

Jursik, Peter. "Warren H. Hayes." 4 June 1980. Typescript in the Minneapolis History Collection, Minneapolis Public Library and Information Center, Minneapolis, Minn.

Kasson, John F. *Rudeness and Civility: Manners in Nineteenth-Century Urban America.* New York: Hill and Wang, 1990.

Kelly, J. Frederick. *Early Connecticut Meetinghouses: Being an Account of the Church Edifices Built before 1830 Based Chiefly on Town and Parish Records.* 2 vols. New York: Columbia University Press, 1948.

Kerber, Linda K. "Abolitionists and Amalgamators: The New York City Race Riots of 1834." *New York History* 48 (Jan. 1967): 28–39.

Kilde, Jeanne Halgren. "Spiritual Armories: A Social and Architectural History of Neo-Medieval Auditorium Churches in the U.S., 1869–1910." Ph.D. diss., University of Minnesota, 1991.

Kirby, Linda K. *Heritage of Heroes: Trinity United Methodist Church, 1859–1988.* Denver, Colo.: Trinity United Methodist Church, 1988.

Koch, Robert. *Louis C. Tiffany: Rebel in Glass.* 2d ed. New York: Crown, 1966.

Kreidberg, Marjorie. *Food on the Frontier: Minnesota Cooking from 1850 to 1900 with Selected Recipes.* St. Paul, Minn.: Minnesota Historical Society Press, 1975.

Kuke, Hans-Joachim. *Die Frauenkirche in Dresden: Ein Sankt Peter der wahren evangelischen Religion.* Worms: Wernersche Verlagsgesellschaft, 1996.

Lane, George A. *Chicago Churches and Synagogues.* Chicago: Loyola University Press, 1981.

Lane, Samuel A. *Fifty Years and Over of Akron and Summit County.* Np., nd.

Laqueur, Thomas Walter. *Religion and Respectability: Sunday Schools and Working-Class Culture, 1780–1850.* New Haven, Conn.: Yale University Press, 1976.

Larson, Paul Clifford, and Susan M. Brown, eds. *The Spirit of H. H. Richardson on the Midland Prairies: Regional Transformations of an Architecture Style.* Minneapolis, Minn.: University Art Museum and Ames: Iowa State University Press, 1988.

Lears, T. J. Jackson. *No Place of Grace: Antimodernism and the Transformation of American Culture, 1880–1920.* New York: Pantheon, 1981.

Lefebvre, Henri. *The Production of Space.* Translated by Donald Nicholson-Smith. Cambridge: Blackwell, 1991.

Lehmberg, Stanford E. *The Reformation of Cathedrals: Cathedrals in English Society, 1485–1603.* Princeton, N.J.: Princeton University Press, 1988.

Leonard, Delevan L. *The Story of Oberlin: The Institution, the Community, the Idea, the Movement.* Boston: Pilgrim Press, 1898.

Levine, Lawrence W. *Highbrow/Lowbrow: The Emergence of Cultural Hierarchy in America.* Cambridge, Mass.: Harvard University Press, 1988.

Lewis, Michael. "The Capitalist: God Is in the Packaging." *New York Times,* 21 July 1996, 94.

Lewis, Stanley T. "The New York Theatre: Its Background and Architectural Development, 1750–1853." Ph.D. diss., Ohio State University, 1953.

Lindman, Janet Moore. "Ritual Practice and the Creation of Baptist Orthodoxy in Eighteenth-Century America." Paper presented at the American Studies Association Annual Meeting. 11 Nov. 1998. Pittsburgh, Pa.

Lloyd, John Gilbert. *Stained Glass in America.* Jenkintown, Pa.: Foundation, 1963.

Loetscher, Lefferts A. "The Problem of Christian Unity in Early Nineteenth-Century America." *Church History* 32 (Mar. 1963): 3–16.

Loth, Calder, and Julius Trousdale Sadler, Jr. *The Only Proper Style: Gothic Architecture in America.* Boston: New York Graphic Society, 1975.

Luce, W. Ray. "Building the Kingdom of God: Mormon Architecture before 1847." *Brigham Young University Studies* 30 (Spring 1990): 33–45.

Lynes, Russell. *The Tastemakers.* New York: Harper and Bros., 1955.

Maass, John. *The Victorian Home in America.* New York: Hawthorn, 1972.

McClaugherty, Martha Crabill. "Household Art: Creating the Artistic Home, 1868–1893." *Winterthur Portfolio* 18 (Spring 1983): 1–26.

McConachie, Bruce A. *Melodramatic Formations: American Theatre and Society, 1820–1870.* Iowa City: University of Iowa Press, 1992.

——. "Museum Theatre and the Problem of Respectability for Mid-Century Urban Americans." In *The American Stage: Social and Economic Issues from the Colonial Period to the Present*. Edited by Ron Engle and Tice L. Miller. New York: Cambridge University Press, 1993. 65–80.

——. "Pacifying American Theatrical Audiences, 1820–1900." In *For Fun and Profit: The Transformation of Leisure into Consumption*. Edited by Richard Butsch. Philadelphia, Pa.: Temple University Press, 1990. 47–70.

McDannell, Colleen. *The Christian Home in Victorian America, 1840–1900*. Bloomington: Indiana University Press, 1986.

——. *Material Christianity: Religion and Popular Culture in America*. New Haven, Conn.: Yale University Press, 1995.

McFarland, John T., and Benjamin S. Winchester, eds. *The Encyclopedia of Sunday Schools and Religious Education*. New York: Nelson & Sons, 1915.

McLoughlin, William G., Jr. *Modern Revivalism: Charles Grandison Finney to Billy Graham*. New York: Ronald Press, 1959.

Marius, Richard. *Martin Luther: The Christian between God and Death*. Cambridge, Mass.: Harvard University Press, 1999.

Markus, Thomas A. *Buildings and Power: Freedom and Control in the Origin of Modern Building Types*. London: Routledge, 1993.

Marsden, George M. *The Evangelical Mind and the New School Presbyterian Experience: A Case Study of Thought and Theology in Nineteenth-Century America*. New Haven, Conn.: Yale University Press, 1970.

——. *Fundamentalism and American Culture: The Shaping of Twentieth-Century Evangelicalism, 1870–1925*. New York: Oxford University Press, 1980.

——. *Understanding Fundamentalism and Evangelicalism*. Grand Rapids, Mich.: Eerdmans, 1991.

Matthews, Glenna. *"Just a Housewife": The Rise & Fall of Domesticity in America*. New York: Oxford University Press, 1987.

Melton, Julius. *Presbyterian Worship in America: Changing Patterns since 1878*. Richmond, Va.: Knox, 1967.

Miller, Cyndee. "Churches Turn to Research for Help in Saving New Souls." *Marketing News*, 11 Apr. 1994, 1, 3.

Miller, Perry. *Errand into the Wilderness*. Cambridge, Mass.: Belknap, 1956.

Morgan, Edmund S. *The Puritan Family: Religion and Domestic Relations in Seventeenth-Century New England*. Rev. ed. New York: Harper & Row, 1966.

Muccigrosso, Robert. *American Gothic: The Mind and Art of Ralph Adams Cram*. Washington, D.C.: University Press of America, 1980.

Müller, Peter. *Die Frauenkirche in Dresden: Baugeschichte, Vergleiche, Restaurierungen, Zerstörung, Wiederaufbau*. Weimar: Böhlau Verlag, 1994.

Mullin, Donald C. *The Development of the Playhouse: A Survey of Theatre Architecture from the Renaissance to the Present*. Berkeley: University of California Press, 1970.

Mussulman, Joseph A. *Music in the Cultured Generation*. Evanston, Ill.: Northwestern University Press, 1971.

Naylor, Gillian. *The Arts and Crafts Movement: A Study of Its Sources, Ideals and Influence on Design Theory*. Cambridge, Mass.: MIT Press, 1971.

Nichols, L. Nelson. *The History of the Broadway Tabernacle of New York City*. New Haven, Conn.: Tuttle, Morehouse and Taylor, 1940.

Niebuhr, Gustav. "The Minister as Marketer: Learning from Business." *New York Times*, 18 Apr. 1995, 1.

——. "Where Religion Gets a Big Dose of Shopping-Mall Culture." *New York Times*, 16 Apr. 1995, 1.

Nylander, Jane C. "Toward Comfort and Uniformity in New England Meeting Houses, 1750–

1850." In *New England Meeting House and Church, 1630–1850*. Edited by Peter Benes and Philip D. Zimmerman. Boston: Boston University for the Dublin Seminar for New England Folklife, 1979. 86–100.

Ochse, Orpha. *The History of the Organ in the United States*. Bloomington: Indiana University Press, 1975.

Ochsner, Jeffrey Karl. *H. H. Richardson: Complete Architectural Works*. Cambridge, Mass.: MIT Press, 1982.

Odell, George C. D. *Annals of the New York Stage*. 15 vols. New York: Columbia University Press, 1928.

Olson, Sherry H. *Baltimore: The Building of an American City*. Baltimore, Md.: Johns Hopkins University Press, 1980.

Osteen, Mame. *Haven in The Heart of the City: The History of Lakewood Cemetery*. Minneapolis, Minn.: Lakewood Cemetery, 1992.

Otis, Philo Adams. *The First Presbyterian Church, 1833–1913: A History of the Oldest Organization in Chicago*. 2d rev. ed. Chicago: Revell, 1913.

Peck, George T. "Historical Account of the Fifth Avenue Presbyterian Church." In *A Noble Landmark of New York: The Fifth Avenue Presbyterian Church, 1808–1958*. New York: Fifth Avenue Presbyterian Church, 1960. 1–110.

Perciaccante, Marianne. "The Demographics of Diversity in the Burned-Over District." Paper presented at the American Society for Church History Annual Spring Meeting, 24–26 Mar. 1994, Oberlin, Ohio.

———. "Calling Down Fire: Charles Grandison Finney and Revivalism in Jefferson County, New York, 1800–1840." Ph.D. diss., University of Virginia, 1994.

Pessen, Edward. *Riches, Class, and Power before the Civil War*. Lexington, Mass.: Heath, 1973.

Pevsner, Nikolaus. *A History of Building Types*. Princeton, N.J.: Princeton University Press, 1976.

Pilgrim Congregational Church. *Our First One Hundred Years*. Cleveland, Ohio: Pilgrim Congregational Church, 1959.

Pollock, J. C. *Moody: A Biographical Portrait of the Pacesetter in Modern Mass Evangelism*. New York: Macmillan, 1963.

Rapoport, Amos. *The Meaning of the Built Environment: A Nonverbal Communication Approach*. Beverly Hills, Calif.: Sage, 1982.

Richards, Leonard L. *"Gentlemen of Property and Standing": Anti-Abolition Mobs in Jacksonian America*. New York: Oxford University Press, 1970.

Riess, Steven A. *City Games: The Evolution of American Urban Society and the Rise of Sports*. Urbana: University of Illinois Press, 1989.

Robertson, Darrel M. *The Chicago Revival, 1876: Society and Revivalism in a Nineteenth-Century City*. Metuchen, N.J.: Scarecrow, 1989.

Robinson, Willard B. *Texas Public Buildings of the Nineteenth Century*. Austin: University of Texas, 1974.

Rothschild, Nan A. *New York City Neighborhoods: The 18th Century*. New York: Academic, 1990.

Ryan, Mary P. *Cradle of the Middle Class: The Family in Oneida County, New York, 1790–1865*. Cambridge: Cambridge University Press, 1981.

———. "Gender and Public Access: Women's Politics in Nineteenth-Century America." In *Habermas and the Public Sphere*. Edited by Craig Calhoun. Cambridge, Mass.: MIT Press, 1992. 267–71.

Sandeen, Ernest R. *The Roots of Fundamentalism: British and American Millenarianism, 1800–1930*. Chicago: University of Chicago Press, 1970.

Schulz, Constance B. "Children and Childhood in the Eighteenth Century." In *American Childhood: A Research Guide and Historical Handbook*. Edited by Joseph M. Hawes and N. Ray Hiner. Westport, Conn.: Greenwood, 1985. 57–109.

Schuyler, David. *The New Urban Landscape: The Redefinition of City Form in Nineteenth-Century America*. Baltimore, Md.: Johns Hopkins University Press, 1986.

Schuyler, Montgomery. *American Architecture and Other Writings*. 2 vols. Cambridge, Mass.: Belknap, 1961.

Schwartz, H. W. *Bands of America*. Garden City, N.Y.: Doubleday, 1957.

Schwarzer, Michael. "The Social Genesis of the Public Theater in Germany." In *Karl Friedrich Schinkel: The Drama of Architecture*. Edited by John Zukowsky. Chicago: Art Institute of Chicago, 1994. 54-67.

Sellers, Charles. *The Market Revolution: Jacksonian America, 1815-1846*. New York: Oxford University Press, 1991.

Shand-Tucci, Douglass. *Ralph Adams Cram: Life and Architecture*. Amherst: University of Massachusetts, 1995.

Shiffler, Harrold C. "The Opposition of the Presbyterian Church in the United States of America to the Theatre in America, 1750-1891." Ph.D. diss., State University of Iowa, 1953.

Simon, John S. *John Wesley: The Master-Builder*. London: Epworth, 1927.

Sinnott, Edmund W. *Meetinghouse & Church in Early New England*. New York: McGraw-Hill Book, 1963.

Siry, Joseph. "Frank Lloyd Wright's Unity Temple and Architecture for Liberal Religion in Chicago, 1885-1909." *Art Bulletin* 73 (June 1991): 257-82.

Sklar, Katherine Kish. *Catherine Beecher: A Study in American Domesticity*. New Haven, Conn.: Yale University Press, 1973.

Smith, H. Shelton. "Editor's Introduction." In *Horace Bushnell*. Edited by H. Sheldon Smith. New York: Oxford University Press, 1965. 3-39.

Smith, Jonathan Z. *To Take Place: Toward Theory in Ritual*. Chicago: University of Chicago Press, 1987.

Stanton, Phoebe. *The Gothic Revival & American Church Architecture: An Episode in Taste, 1840-1856*. Baltimore, Md.: Johns Hopkins University Press, 1968.

Stell, Christopher. "Chapels and Meeting-Houses in Greater Manchester." *Archaeological Journal* 144 (1987): 7-11.

———. *An Inventory of Nonconformist Chapels and Meeting-Houses in Central England*. London: Her Majesty's Stationary Office, 1986.

———. *An Inventory of Nonconformist Chapels and Meeting-Houses in the North of England*. London: Her Majesty's Stationary Office, 1994.

———. "Puritan and Nonconformist Meetinghouses in England." In *Seeing beyond the Word: Visual Arts and the Calvinist Tradition*. Edited by Paul Corby Finney. Grand Rapids, Mich.: Eerdmans, 1999. 49-81.

Stevenson, Robert. *Protestant Church Music in America: A Short Survey of Men and Movements from 1564 to the Present*. New York: Norton, 1966.

Stewart, James Brewer. "The Emergence of Racial Modernity and the Rise of the White North, 1790-1840." *Journal of the Republic* 18 (Summer 1998): 181-217.

———. "Modernizing 'Difference': The Political Meanings of Color in the Free States, 1776-1840." *Journal of the Early Republic* 19 (Winter 1999): 691-712.

Szasz, Ferenc Morton. *The Divided Mind of Protestant America, 1880-1930*. University: University of Alabama Press, 1982.

Thompson, E. P. *The Making of the Working Class*. New York: Vintage, 1966.

Thumma, Scott. "Exploring the Megachurch Phenomenon: Their Characteristics and Cultural Contexts." Center for Social and Religious Research, Hartford Seminary. http://www.hartsem.edu/csrr/people/slt/megachurch.htm.

Tidworth, Simon. *Theatres: An Architectural and Cultural History*. New York: Praeger, 1973.

Tindall, George B., and David E. Shi. *America: A Narrative History.* 3d ed., brief. New York: Norton, 1993.

Torbert, Donald R. *Significant Architecture in the History of Minneapolis.* Minneapolis, Minn.: Minneapolis Planning Commission and Minneapolis Chapter, American Institute of Architects, 1969.

Trachtenberg, Alan. *The Incorporation of America: Culture and Society in the Gilded Age.* New York: Hill and Wang, 1982.

Trollinger, William Vance. *God's Empire: William Bell Riley and Midwestern Fundamentalism.* Madison: University of Wisconsin Press, 1990.

Turner, Victor W. *The Anthropology of Performance.* New York: PAJ, 1986.

——. *Dramas, Fields, and Metaphors: Symbolic Action in Human Society.* Ithaca, N.Y.: Cornell University Press, 1974.

——. *The Ritual Process: Structure and Anti-Structure.* New York: Aldine, 1969.

Upton, Dell. *Holy Things and Profane: Anglican Parish Churches in Colonial Virginia.* Cambridge, Mass.: MIT Press, 1986.

Van De Wetering, Maxine. "The Popular Concept of 'Home' in Nineteenth-Century America." *Journal of American Studies* 18 (1984): 5–28.

Von Rohr, John. *The Shaping of American Congregationalism, 1620–1957.* Cleveland, Ohio: Pilgrim Press, 1992.

Vyvyan, C. C. *Our Cornwall.* London: Westaway, 1948.

Walker, Randi Jones. *Emma Newman: A Frontier Woman Minister.* Syracuse, N.Y.: Syracuse University Press, 2000.

Ward, Susan Hayes. *The History of the Broadway Tabernacle Church: From Its Organization in 1840 to the Close of 1900, including Factors Influencing its Formation.* New York: Broadway Tabernacle Church, 1901.

Warner, Sam Bass. *Streetcar Suburbs: The Process of Growth in Boston, 1870–1900.* Cambridge, Mass.: Harvard University Press, 1962.

Weeks, Genevieve C. "Oscar C. McCulloch Transforms Plymouth Church, Indianapolis, into an 'Institution' Church." *Indiana Magazine of History* 64 (June 1968): 87–108.

Weisberger, Bernard A. *They Gathered at the River: The Story of the Great Revivalists and Their Impact upon Religion in America.* Boston: Little, Brown, 1958.

Weiss, Ellen. *City in the Woods: The Life and Design of an American Camp Meeting on Martha's Vineyard.* New York: Oxford University Press, 1987.

White, James F. *The Cambridge Movement: The Ecclesiologists and the Gothic Revival.* Cambridge: Cambridge University Press, 1962.

——. *Christian Worship in North America: A Retrospective, 1955–1995.* Collegeville, Minn.: Liturgical Press, 1997.

——. "From Protestant to Catholic Plain Style." In *Seeing beyond the Word: Visual Arts and the Calvinist Tradition.* Edited by Paul Corby Finney. Grand Rapids, Mich.: Eerdmans, 1999. 457–77.

——. *Protestant Worship and Church Architecture: Theological and Historical Concerns.* New York: Oxford University Press, 1964.

Wilentz, Sean. *Chants Democratic: New York City & the Rise of the American Working Class, 1788–1850.* New York: Oxford University Press, 1984.

——. *Houses of God: Region, Religion, and Architecture in the United States.* Urbana: University of Illinois Press, 1997.

Williams, Peter W. "Metamorphoses of the Meetinghouse: Three Case Studies." In *Seeing Beyond the Word: Visual Arts and the Calvinist Tradition.* Edited by Paul Corby Finney. Grand Rapids, Mich.: Eerdmans, 1999. 479–505.

Whiffen, Marcus, and Frederick Koeper. *American* Architecture. 2 vols. Cambridge, Mass.: MIT Press, 1983. 1–85.

Wright, David Gilmore. "Conception and Realization: An Historic Building Statement." In *The Restoration of the Lovely Lane Church, Baltimore City Station.* Baltimore, Md.: Trustees of the Methodist Episcopal Church, 1980.

Wright, Gwendolyn. *Building the Dream: A Social History of Housing in America.* New York: Pantheon, 1981.

——. *Moralism and the Model Home: Domestic Architecture and Cultural Conflict in Chicago, 1873–1913.* Chicago: University of Chicago Press, 1980.

Wyatt-Brown, Bertram. *Lewis Tappan and the Evangelical War against Slavery.* Cleveland, Ohio: Press of Case Western Reserve University, 1969.

Zaret, David. "Religion, Science, and Printing in the Public Spheres in Seventeenth-Century England." In *Habermas and the Public Sphere.* Edited by Craig Calhoun. Cambridge, Mass.: MIT Press, 1993. 212–35.

Index

Abbott, Lyman, 133
abolitionism, 87
  and the Broadway Tabernacle, 59-65
  and Chatham Street Chapel, 38-41
  Ultraism, 24, 60, 61, 63, 64
acoustics, 18, 34, 50, 115, 116, 222 n.7,
  250 n.15
Adix Bros., 153
Adler, Dankmar, 116, 117, 128, 224 n.27
Akron plan, 170, 191, 195
  benefits of, 177-79
  criticism of, 210
  description of original, 177-79
  and diagonal sanctuaries, 179-82
  origins of, 176, 268 n.29
  panopticon character of, 183-84
  rolling partitions in, 179, 182, 183-84,
  269 n.38
  separation from church building, 184-85
Albany Conference of 1852, 66, 72
Allegheny County Courthouse, Pittsburgh,
  Penn., 107
Allen, Moses, 225 n.4
All Souls' Unitarian Church, Chicago, Ill.,
  141
American Anti-Slavery Society, 38, 39
American Institute of Architects (AIA), 69, 70,
  72, 133, 234 n.92, 242 n.67
American Sunday School Union, 66, 176
American Tract Society, 38, 66
amphitheatre, 6, 20, 17, 51
  acoustics in, 18
  corporate body effect in, 43-44, 45, 143,
  223 n.22, 260 n.97
  and democracy, 143
  description of, 15-17

educational uses of, 50-53, 250 n.16
  in government buildings, 232 n.77
  history of, 119, 268 n.26
  relative power of participants in, 143, 199
  religious use of, 14-17, 23, 43, 51, 113-19,
  142
  See also acoustics; auditorium sanctuary
Andrew-Riverside Presbyterian Church,
  Minneapolis, Minn., 206
Angelus Temple, Los Angeles, Calif., 212
Anglican Church. See Church of England
Angus Long Room, New York, 225 n.16
anticolonization, 231 n.59
  and Chatham Street Chapel, 38-41
antiformalism. See Chatham Street Chapel,
  New York; Free Church movement;
  revivals; worship
antinomianism, 37, 47
Antioch Baptist Church, Cleveland, Ohio, 201
antislavery, 59-65. See also abolitionism;
  anticolonization
anxious bench, 22, 34
Apostle's Creed, 138
architectural style, 3, 6
  clerical analyses of, 101
  messages conveyed by, 104, 106-8
  See also Baroque architectural style; Carpenter
  Gothic architectural style; Classical Revival
  architectural style; Federalist architectural
  style; Gothic Revival architecture; Greek
  Revival architectural style; meetinghouse;
  Moderne architectural style; Queen Anne
  architectural style; Richardsonian
  Romanesque architectural style; Shingle style
  architecture; Stick style architecture
Arminianism, 25, 26, 64